# THE
# EAST GERMAN
# DICTATORSHIP

# THE
# EAST GERMAN
# DICTATORSHIP

## Problems and Perspectives in the Interpretation of the GDR

COREY ROSS

*Lecturer in Modern History, University of Birmingham, UK*

A member of the Hodder Headline Group
LONDON
Co-published in the United States of America by
Oxford University Press Inc., New York

First published in Great Britain in 2002 by
Arnold, a member of the Hodder Headline Group,
338 Euston Road, London NW1 3BH

http://www.arnoldpublishers.com

Co-published in United States of America by
Oxford University Press Inc.,
198 Madison Avenue, New York, NY10016

*British Library Cataloguing in Publication Data*
A catalogue record for this book is available from the British Library

*Library of Congress Cataloging-in-Publication Data*
A catalog record for this book is available from the Library of Congress

ISBN 0 340 76265 9 (hb)
ISBN 0 340 76266 7 (pb)

1 2 3 4 5 6 7 8 9 10

Production Editor: Anke Ueberberg
Production Controller: Bryan Eccleshall
Cover Design: Terry Griffiths

Typeset in 10/12 pt Sabon by Charon Tec Pvt. Ltd, Chennai, India
Printed and bound in Great Britain by MPG Books Ltd, Bodmin, Cornwall

What do you think about this book? Or any other Arnold title?
Please send your comments to feedback.arnold@hodder.co.uk

# Contents

# Preface

It was often said, half in jest, that the most difficult thing to predict under state socialism was the past. Though I rather doubt that many people would have regarded the future collapse of the communist system as any more predictable than the 'party line' on the past, the point about the malleability of history and about the connection between political power and the production of historical knowledge is nonetheless well taken. History played a key role in legitimating the communist regimes across Central and Eastern Europe, nowhere more so than in the 'half-nation-state' GDR. Of course, socialist regimes are far from unique in this regard, however overt and unsubtle their efforts to enlist the past in their service often were. As the pages that follow make clear, perceptions of GDR history in Western countries were, for a variety of reasons, anything but 'value-neutral'. Our understandings of the past are always conditioned by current concerns. They are constantly shifting with changes of perspective, evolving in line with current cultural trends and methodological innovations, and are not infrequently appropriated and instrumentalized for immediate political purposes. These are some of the factors that underlie historiographic debate and that make the study of the past relevant for the present.

These same issues also lie at the heart of this study, which is about the development of a particular field of historiography and the ways in which the debates that define it are related to the wider political, ideological and social framework in which they have taken place. In one sense this book represents a case study of the production of historical knowledge, of how a relatively new historiographical field begins to congeal. When I first began studying the GDR in the early 1990s, there existed only a fraction of the literature that is now available. Back then, the controversies often appeared inchoate, the contours of debate unclear, not least because of the difficulty of assimilating the huge amount of new empirical findings into a more general interpretive framework. Now, over a decade after the GDR's demise, the interpretive landscape has gradually become more visible. Yet it is still difficult to gain an overview of these debates, and many points of interpretation still seem more implicit than explicit in the scholarly literature. This book was written with precisely these problems in mind. Its aim is twofold: first, to provide readers with an overview and critical analysis of the key controversies and the literature on which they are based; and second, to help define or sharpen some of the contours of debate themselves, to offer an interpretive framework that makes some sense of the huge literature that has amassed over the years – especially the torrent of publications since 1990 – and that might hopefully encourage further discussion.

I have enjoyed considerable help while bringing this project to completion. I am very grateful to the Nuffield Foundation for its generous financial support towards research in Germany. Among the many colleagues with whom I have discussed the project, special thanks are due to Mary Fulbrook and Arnd Bauerkämper for their comments and encouragement. An immense debt of gratitude goes to Patrick Major and Judd Stitziel for their careful reading of the entire manuscript and for the many improvements I was able to make on the basis of their comments. For reasons of space, style and coherence, I was unable to translate all of their suggestions into the text. My guess is that any shortcomings in this book that readers might perceive were probably pointed out by them as well, so I bear sole responsibility. Thanks are also due to Christopher Wheeler of Arnold, who has made the production of this book more painless – indeed, more enjoyable – than I could have imagined. My greatest thanks go, as always, to my family: to Deborah, for listening and critiquing, as well as generally tolerating this project's presence in our house; and to Alex and Tessa, who not only ensured that I never spent too much time at my desk, but also constantly reminded me that thinking about the past, however interesting and rewarding it can be, is no match for enjoying the present.

Corey Ross<br>
Birmingham<br>
Autumn 2001

# Abbreviations

| | |
|---|---|
| *AfS* | *Archiv für Sozialgeschichte* |
| *APuZG* | *Aus Politik und Zeitgeschichte* |
| *BzG* | *Beiträge zur Geschichte der Arbeiterbewegung* |
| CDU | Christlich Demokratische Union Deutschlands (Christian Democratic Union of Germany) |
| *CEH* | *Central European History* |
| COMECON | Council for Mutual Economic Exchange |
| *DA* | *Deutschland Archiv* |
| *FAZ* | *Frankfurter Allgemeine Zeitung* |
| FDGB | Freier Deutscher Gewerkschaftsbund (League of Free German Trade Unions) |
| FDJ | Freie Deutsche Jugend (Free German Youth) |
| GDR | German Democratic Republic |
| *GG* | *Geschichte und Gesellschaft* |
| *GH* | *German History* |
| *GWU* | *Geschichte in Wissenschaft und Unterricht* |
| *HZ* | *Historische Zeitschrift* |
| *JHK* | *Jahrbuch für historische Kommunismusforschung* |
| *JMH* | *Journal of Modern History* |
| KPD | Kommunistische Partei Deutschlands (German Communist Party) |
| KVP | Kasernierte Volkspolizei (Garrisoned People's Police) |
| LDPD | Liberal Democratic Party of Germany |
| *ND* | *Neues Deutschland* |
| NES | New Economic System |
| NSDAP | Nationalsozialistische Deutsche Arbeiterpartei (National Socialist German Workers Party or Nazi Party) |
| NVA | Nationale Volksarmee (National People's Army) |
| PDS | Partei des demokratischen Sozialismus (Party of Democratic Socialism) |

| SAPMO-BA | Stiftung Archiv der Parteien und Massenorganisationen der DDR im Bundesarchiv |
| SBZ | Sowjetische Besatzungszone (Soviet Occupation Zone) |
| SED | Sozialistische Einheitspartei Deutschlands (Socialist Unity Party) |
| SMAD | Soviet Military Administration of Germany |
| SPD | Sozialdemokratische Partei Deutschlands (Social Democratic Party of Germany) |
| VEB | Volkseigener Betrieb (People's Own Enterprise) |
| VfZ | *Vierteljahrshefte für Zeitgeschichte* |
| ZfG | *Zeitschrift für Geschichtswissenschaft* |
| ZK | Zentralkomitee (SED Central Committee) |

# 1

# The changing picture of the GDR: Political, methodological and moral dimensions

## Introduction

Although the legacies of East German socialism will undoubtedly linger for many years in Germany, the German Democratic Republic (GDR) is, as they say, history. Of course in a strict sense it was 'history' from the moment it formally ceased to exist on 3 October 1990. But now, over a decade after its collapse, the GDR is gradually beginning to 'feel' like history as well. This has to do with more than just the fact that historians have become intensely interested in it, having finally lost any disciplinary inhibitions about the appropriateness of studying the GDR now that it no longer exists. For most of the second half of the twentieth century, the brutal and destructive Nazi past tended to overshadow perceptions of Germany and the Germans. But with the advent of the twenty-first century, the post-war successor states in Germany are now also rapidly beginning to appear strange and distant, relics of the Cold War that created and sustained them and that came to an end with the unexpected collapse of communism in 1989–90.

The GDR now seems particularly curious and foreign to many of us. The new unified Germany certainly bears much more resemblance to the old West German Federal Republic than to the GDR. In the annexation-like nature of German unification, relatively few East German[1] institutions survived the transition into the new Germany, whether from its economic, political or educational system. Many of the physical traces of the GDR have disappeared as well. The crumbling façades of its urban buildings have now by and large been renovated, the smell of brown coal and two-stroke

---

1 To prevent confusion, I should point out that 'East German', both as noun and adjective, is capitalized in the text when referring to the period before the demise of the state itself in 1990, and 'east German' or 'former East German' is used for the period afterwards.

engine exhaust has gradually dissipated, and the legendary Trabant car is nowadays more a collector's item than a widespread mode of transportation. It is increasingly difficult even for those who lived in the GDR to remember what life was like before the watershed events of 1989–90 which so strongly colour people's memories. Yet alongside the growing feeling of estrangement, the passage of time has in some ways improved our understanding of the GDR. The opening and exploration of the archives have obviously shed new light on the workings of the defunct state, and the turbulent political and social developments of the last decade have also offered a degree of hindsight (for better or worse) through which to view the GDR's history. Neither the access to internal sources nor the sheer passing of time has, however, made for greater consensus on scholarly interpretations of the GDR. While many of the debates before 1989 have been provisionally settled or have lost most of their heat, new controversies and points of argument have emerged with remarkable swiftness.

For a country of fewer than 20 million people that never seemed to stray very far out of Moscow's orbit, the GDR has long attracted a remarkable degree of scholarly interest. This is undoubtedly related to its central place – both geographically and symbolically – in the history of post-war Europe. Prior to the disintegration of the communist bloc, the two German states constituted the front line of the Cold War, a kind of 'national' microcosm of divided Europe at large. Both German states, moreover, represented models of their opposing political and economic systems: a stunningly efficient form of democratic capitalism in the West, a showcase for socialist productivity and political stability in the East. Confronting each other grimly across a strip of barbed wire and machine guns, the two Germanies were not only intrinsic products of the Cold War, but also quintessential symbols of the broader global conflict. After 1989 the two halves of Germany found themselves at the interface between the two halves of the previously bisected continent, again representing in miniature form the broader developments of a divided Europe trying to grow back together. As a model of Soviet-style socialism at the frontline of the Cold War (before 1989) and a forerunner of democratic transition at the seam between East and West (after 1989), interpretations of the GDR have, therefore, always been directly related to much wider political issues. Just as the Berlin Wall was the central symbol of the Cold War, the re-opened Brandenburg Gate has become a primary metaphor for Europe reunited.

Yet despite its symbolic character, some commentators have already deemed the GDR no more than a brief historic 'episode' or consigned it to a mere 'footnote of world history'.[2] Whereas the rise and fall of Soviet communism will undoubtedly form a substantial chapter of world history for future generations, the GDR will, in this view, constitute little more than a

---

2 Peter Bender, *Unsere Erbschaft. Was war die DDR – was bleibt von ihr?* (Hamburg, 1992), p. 155.

subplot of this story. So why should we expend so much effort researching it? Indeed, why are we studying the East German past? To counter the SED's myths and show how unjust the GDR was by 'enlightening' the public about various unpalatable facts so long hidden from public view? To aid the cause of 'inner unity' between the two former halves of Germany by building a new 'national' historical narrative through the lens of unification? To maintain a constant guard against the enemies of democracy by studying how they work and demonstrating the unjust nature of these regimes? To engage in an act of remembrance for the victims of the regime – to 'set the record straight' in at least a moral sense where judicial restitution is impossible?

In the context of unified Germany, faced by the twin challenges of wedding together its two rather different halves and finding a new place for itself within a rapidly changing world, these questions have had more than mere rhetorical significance. Although the GDR may eventually be regarded as little more than a footnote of world history, the East German past is still of great interest and promises to remain so for the foreseeable future. For millions of ordinary Germans it forms a crucial part of their own biographies and identities. For political elites, its legacies still strongly affect the German economy and inform the political culture of the unified state. For intellectuals, it represents the end of a particular utopia and a failed alternative to liberal-capitalist democracy. For historians in particular, it represents not only a remarkable historical experiment of building socialism in a highly industrialized region, but also a model of Soviet-style socialism that sheds light on the history of other Soviet bloc states whose archival deposits are still far less accessible.

For all of these reasons, the East German past continues to spark interest and debate well beyond Germany. Yet it is the changing political context within Germany itself that has most powerfully influenced and most closely reflected the shifting perceptions of the GDR over the years. Interpretations have always been divided and contested, just as much – perhaps even more – after 1989 as before. Prior to the GDR's collapse, the evolving relations between the two states crucially moulded the premises of interpretation on both sides of the Wall, as the academic reappraisals and the political thaws of the late 1960s and 1970s encouraged and mutually reinforced each other. Since 1990 debates about the GDR's history within a unified Germany have been likened to an 'ideological contest for the soul of the country',[3] with one side demanding a clear 'anti-totalitarian' consensus and the other calling for an anti-capitalist egalitarianism as the basis for a democratic future. The heated political and moral controversies about the East German past, the role of individuals and organizations in it, and its consequences for unified Germany have generated a complex 'mixture of current politics and contemporary history, of consternation (*Betroffenheit*) and the need for

---

3 Konrad Jarausch, 'Beyond Uniformity: The Challenge of Historicizing the GDR', in K. Jarausch (ed.), *Dictatorship as Experience: Towards a Socio-Cultural History of the GDR* (New York, 1999), p. 5.

reappraisal of the past'.[4] Of course all areas of historical enquiry – especially recent or contemporary history – are affected by changing political concerns, so East German history is by no means wholly exceptional in this regard. Yet the connection between scholarly research on the GDR and the shaping of current political consciousness in Germany has been quite explicit, and very much in line with the Federal Republic's tradition of contemporary historical research as 'political education' established after the débâcle of the Third Reich. In part because of the highly charged political atmosphere in post-war Germany, and in part because of the peculiar institutional landscape of scholarly research in Germany (especially the powerful role played by foundations in West Germany, some of them affiliated with political parties, not to mention the SED-dominated research institutes in the GDR), conflicting interpretations of the GDR have been a central point of debate about Germany's very political identity, its future development and its role in the wider world. To be sure, historical interpretations of the GDR have been much more than mere reflections of scholars' political inclinations or a weathervane for broader political winds. But it is nevertheless a basic contention of this book that the changing political framework in Germany has been of paramount importance to how scholars and the wider public have interpreted the GDR over the years.

Since the opening of the East German archives, GDR history has been the most booming field of historical research in Germany, resulting in a veritable avalanche of monographs, articles, personal memoirs and source editions. Even scholars researching in this field find it difficult to keep up with the huge amounts of information being generated. The torrent of research and publications has been so strong as to spawn a number of new journals to cope with the flow. The main pre-1989 organ of West German 'GDR research', *Deutschland Archiv*, found it necessary to double its issues to twelve per year throughout the 1990s. Several new research institutions focusing largely on East German history have also been founded, which broadly (though not neatly) reflect the differences of approach and interpretation: the *Zentrum für zeithistorische Forschung* in Potsdam (with an emphasis on social and cultural history), the Berlin branch of the *Institut für Zeitgeschichte*, as well as the more conservative *Hannah-Arendt-Institut für Totalitarismusforschung* in Dresden and *Forschungsverbund SED-Staat* at the Free University of Berlin. With so many questions unanswerable due to the lack of source material before 1990 and so much archival material to sift through afterwards, the mass of information swamping students of East German history sometimes seems more confusing than illuminating. My intention in writing this book is to help ameliorate this situation, to offer an overview of debates and interpretations that hopefully will be useful to anyone interested in the history of the GDR, whether undergraduates or scholars working in the field.

4 Jürgen Kocka, 'Chance und Herausforderung. Aufgaben der Zeitgeschichte beim Umgang mit der DDR-Geschichte', in Bernd Faulenbach *et al.* (eds), *Die Partei hatte immer recht – Aufarbeitung von Geschichte und Folgen der SED-Diktatur* (Essen, 1994), p. 241.

Besides the sheer volume of new publications on the GDR, the relative lack of clear lines of debate and interpretation such as characterize earlier periods of German history can often add to the confusion. The fuzzy contours of argument in some areas are, to be sure, not the result of a scholarly consensus on the interpretation of the GDR's history. Debates have been vigorous – downright acerbic at times – as the closeness of the subject under study makes for a multiplicity of quick impressions and almost invariably loads any scholarly interpretation with an unusually heavy moral and political weight. For a number of reasons, few broader syntheses have yet been attempted. The huge amounts of documentation produced by the East German regime, the constant uncovering of new archival material, and the current aversion among many historians towards 'metanarratives' and overarching structures of interpretation in principle have all gravitated against generalized accounts. Most of the consciously interpretive writing on the GDR has appeared in article form in various journals or edited anthologies which few non-experts are likely to encounter (quite apart from the fact that it has mostly appeared in German). The aim of this book is therefore not only to describe and evaluate the various arguments that have been put forward, but also to help discern, sharpen and define certain contours of interpretation that are often only implicit in the historical literature. It does not offer an overview of the development of historiography as such, but rather attempts to examine a number of central problems of interpretation, some more explicit in the literature than others, that have shaped the parameters of debate and that historians of the GDR currently face.

The structure of the book is thematic, revolving around the main issues that form the bulk of the study. The following chapter focuses on some of the broad, overarching categorizations of the GDR as a dictatorial political system, whether it is best understood as a form of 'totalitarian' dictatorship, as a 'Stalinist' regime or via less generic, more GDR-specific concepts. This issue leads directly to the question of how, if at all, we are to conceptualize East German 'society' as a realm more or less distinct from 'politics' and the total claims of the regime, which forms the subject of Chapter 3. Chapter 4 examines the East German economy, widely deemed the most productive in the entire socialist bloc, and the debates about its historical development and viability. The focus then shifts to the East German populace, first exploring the complex and politically loaded question of the character and significance of dissidence and opposition, and, second, assessing the events that led to the end of the regime from autumn 1989 into 1990 (Chapters 5 and 6, respectively). This is followed in Chapter 7 by an examination of how the GDR fits into the broader sweep of German history – whether particular traits or developments in the GDR were the result of 'German continuities' or what one might call 'communist commonalities'. Finally, in Chapter 8 I will attempt to consider the close relationship between debates about the East German past and current political controversies since 1990.

In each chapter I try briefly to summarize the conflicting interpretations and the current state of scholarly debates before offering an evaluation.[5] In so doing, I make no claims to provide an exhaustive literature overview. Because of the sheer volume of literature, the selection of topics and examples is intended to be illustrative, not definitive. The aim is to offer an analytical guide to key issues of debate and problems of interpretation, not a detailed description of the state of the field. Nor do I claim that these are the only debates or issues on which there has been or promises to be controversy. The themes addressed in this book are a reflection of both my own interests as well as the landscape of the literature and debates as they exist. Because of the uneven coverage of the literature and the spatial limits on the text, many important fields are covered rather briefly or subsumed under broader questions. There is, for instance, no separate chapter on foreign policy or cultural developments (I would have liked to give the latter more attention than I did). I try my best to offer a fair summary of others' views, but should state clearly at the outset that I do not intend to sit on the fence or try to adopt some spurious (and in any case unattainable) 'neutral' posture in my evaluations. The intention is not to mediate these debates but to participate in them, and if possible to help sharpen or clarify some of them.

## The political, methodological and moral framework of debate

Historical debates are never solely about the past. Yet probably more than most areas of historical enquiry, interpretations of the GDR have always been particularly closely connected to the present. Before 1990, the East–West divide ensured that no pronouncement about the GDR could be politically 'neutral'. In unified Germany, too, scholarly research on the GDR remains heavily laden with political and moral implications. Although the parameters of debate and the terms of reference have changed significantly over time, they have always been tightly bound to the changing political–ideological framework in Germany, from the anti-communist salvos of the early Cold War, through the revisionism of the détente era, to the present and supposedly 'post-historical' age of the market triumphant.

In the starkly polarized framework of the Cold War, interpretations of both German states and their historical background clearly served to uphold

---

5  This format consciously follows the example set by Ian Kershaw's superb *The Nazi Dictatorship: Problems and Perspectives of Interpretation*, 4th edn (London, 2000), whose explicit distinction between interpretations and evaluation has proven very helpful to many of my own students. Since the text is aimed at a broad readership, those familiar with many of the debates (or any reader of an impatient disposition) might find it most useful to forgo the summaries and proceed directly to the evaluation sections in each chapter. Some degree of repetition is unavoidable given this chapter structure, but I have tried to minimize it.

or undermine the respective political systems in divided Germany. Official self-definitions of the GDR were predictably legitimatory, and indeed changed relatively little over the years. As presented in the official *Concise History of the GDR*, the East German state was the product of the 'struggle of the working-class and all other democratic and progressive forces within our people for a Germany of peace, democracy and socialism'. 'Arisen out of the ruins and oriented towards the future' (in the opening words of the GDR's anthem) the East German state was legitimated historically as both the 'culmination of the antifascist-democratic liberation struggle' as well as 'the constitutional expression of the root-and-branch elimination of imperialism and militarism in the east of Germany and of the transfer of all power, political and economic, into the hands of the working people'.[6] In accordance with the communist understanding of fascism as 'the open terroristic dictatorship of the most reactionary, most chauvinist, and most imperialist elements of finance capital',[7] the founding of the GDR in 1949 and the preceding transformation of the Soviet Zone of occupation – including the expropriation of large landowners and the nationalization of most large-scale industrial enterprises – represented a clean break with the fascist past, a kind of socialist 'zero hour' after the bestiality of Nazism. In the mirror-image nature of Cold War relations, this humanitarian socialist transformation stood in stark contrast to the supposed historical development of the GDR's arch-enemy, the Federal Republic, where 'the imperialist grand bourgeoisie rules over the people, who are oppressed and have no share in the running or direction of the state and economy', thereby 'perpetuating in every regard the fateful and disastrous policies of the imperialist German Reich'.[8]

The official understanding of East German history was characterized by distinct periodizations that reflected Marxist views on different societal 'stages' on the path to socialism. The 'antifascist-democratic transformation' of 1945–49 was but 'the first stage of the people's democratic revolution,... the transition from capitalism to socialism and the advent of a new epoch in the history of the German people'. The next stage, usually conceived as 1949 to 1961, was officially regarded as the 'creation of the basis of socialism'. Like the 'antifascist-democratic transformation', this period was also marked by rapid social change: agricultural collectivization, the establishment of separate East German armed forces, far-reaching education reforms, the broad extension of the social welfare system. This decade of upheaval was then followed by the somewhat quieter 'path to developed socialist society' from 1961 to roughly the end of the 1960s, the era of Walter Ulbricht's economic experimentation and rising living standards in the shadow of the Wall. Under Erich Honecker, who took over the reins from Ulbricht in 1971, the GDR

---

6 Stefan Doernberg, *Kurze Geschichte der DDR* (Berlin, 1965), pp. 11–17, *passim*.
7 As formulated by Georgi Dimitroff and officially adopted by the Comintern in 1935. Georgi Dimitroff, *Gegen Faschismus und Krieg: Ausgewählte Reden und Schriften* (Leipzig, 1982), p. 50.
8 S. Doernberg, *Kurze Geschichte der DDR*, p. 11.

was officially presented as 'actually existing socialism', characterized by a stable and efficient economy and the 'unity of social and economic policy', or emphasis on consumer satisfaction today rather than utopia tomorrow.

Rather predictably, early West German and Anglo-American portrayals of the GDR present essentially a diametrically opposed picture. Although there was somewhat more diversity in approaches given the freer conditions of debate and publication in the West, the overwhelming view during the first two decades after the Second World War was an explicitly moralizing stance against the illiberal SED regime and a fundamental, unequivocal denial of its legitimacy. The commonly used term 'SBZ' (the German abbreviation for 'Soviet Occupation Zone'), the even more unadorned and dismissive 'zone', or the customary use of quotation marks for the 'so-called GDR' (a practice carried out by the low-brow *Bildzeitung* until 1989) denied the East German state any form of independence and legitimacy, and reduced it to a mere Soviet puppet regime. The GDR was essentially viewed as an unwanted and repressive dictatorship, a 'state that should not be'[9] encapsulated by the concept of 'totalitarianism', which was widely accepted in academic circles and which formed the basic counterfoil to the Federal Republic's own self-understanding. Not only did the concept of 'totalitarianism' conveniently bracket together dictatorships of the Left and Right, communism and Nazism, it also cast a favourable light on the 'democratic credentials' of the FRG.[10] It allowed the fledgling West German state to distinguish itself from both the Third Reich as well as the 'other Germany' across the Iron Curtain, whose anti-democratic and dictatorial nature represented an essential continuity with the Nazi past. The popular uprising of 17 June 1953, when the SED regime was nearly toppled by country-wide street demonstrations and was rescued only by the deployment of Soviet tanks, offered plenty of evidence to support this view. Indeed, 17 June became an official holiday in West Germany commemorating what was seen as the struggle for national unity in freedom and democracy.[11] Along with the 1953 uprising, the highly symbolic exodus of over three million East Germans to the FRG between 1949 and 1961 and the erection of the Berlin Wall in August 1961 (pitifully dubbed 'anti-fascist protective Wall' by East German authorities) formed the centrepiece of Western perceptions of the GDR as an illegitimate, 'totalitarian' regime.[12]

9  In the classic formulation of Ernst Richert, *Das zweite Deutschland – Ein Staat, der nicht sein darf* (Cologne, 1964).

10 For overviews, see Wolfgang Wippermann, *Totalitarismustheorien: die Entwicklung der Diskussion von den Anfängen bis heute* (Darmstadt, 1997); Alfons Söllner (ed.), *Totalitarismus: eine Ideengeschichte des 20. Jahrhunderts* (Berlin, 1997); Eckard Jesse (ed.), *Totalitarismus im 20. Jahrhundert: eine Bilanz der internationalen Forschung* (Baden-Baden, 1996), which also boasts an extensive bibliography. See also E. Jesse, 'Die Totalitarismusforschung und ihre Repräsentanten', in *APuZG*, B20/98, pp. 3–18.

11 Manfred Hettling, 'Umstritten, vergessen, erfolgreich. Der 17. Juni als bundesdeutscher National-feiertag', in *DA* 3/2000.

12 For the official West German view, see Bundesministerium für gesamtdeutsche Fragen, *Die Flucht aus der Sowjetzone und die Sperrmaßnahmen des kommunistischen Regimes vom 13 August 1961* (Bonn/Berlin, 1961); Bundesministerium für Vertriebene, Flüchtlinge und Kriegsgeschädigte, *Flucht aus der Sowjetzone* (Bonn/Berlin, 1964).

The lack of liberal democratic legitimation was, then, taken as the key normative criterion for approaching and understanding the GDR. This principle was not merely confined to the realm of public commemoration and 'political education', but also found concrete policy expression in West Germany's *Alleinvertretungsanspruch*, or claim to the sole representation of the German people, which was the foundation of the Federal Republic's foreign and 'German' policy over its first two decades. As Adenauer proclaimed to the West German parliament in October 1949:

> until the attainment of German unity, the Federal Republic is the only legitimate state organization of the German people. ... The Federal Republic of Germany considers itself responsible for the fate of the eighteen million Germans who live in the Soviet Zone. It assures them of its devotion and concern. The Federal Republic of Germany alone is authorized to speak for the German people. It recognizes the declarations of the Soviet Zone as non-binding for the German people.[13]

By the mid-1950s, as the division of Germany deepened with the integration of the two German states into their respective alliances, this claim to sole representation evolved into the so-called 'Hallstein Doctrine', according to which the West German government regarded the establishment of diplomatic relations with the 'so-called GDR' by third states as an unfriendly act amounting to an acceptance of the GDR's independent status and sovereignty, which the Federal Republic firmly denied in the interests of national unity. The claim to sole representation meant that the Federal Republic could not grant the GDR official recognition – a position which every West German government held until the unification process of 1989–90.

Although this fundamental principle was never breached, the changing nature of the GDR and the increasingly pluralistic political climate in West Germany contributed to both a diversification of views as well as a change in German–German relations in the later 1960s. The victory of a social–liberal coalition under the SPD Chancellor Willy Brandt in 1969 ushered in a new policy towards the GDR. Coinciding with a period of détente between the two superpowers, Brandt's initiative to achieve some sort of 'normalization' of relations – his so-called *'Ostpolitik'* – essentially entailed a trade-off of mutual recognition (keenly desired by the SED) in exchange for easing restrictions on travel and human contacts between the two states. The policy was dubbed *Annäherung* ('coming closer'): increasing contacts and concessions (personal, political and economic) in order to broaden the interaction between Germans of the GDR and FRG. At the time this policy was considered by its proponents to be more 'realistic' and consistent than the practice of constantly paying lip-service to the sacred cow of reunification in view of the continued existence of the GDR for the foreseeable future and the hardship caused by German division for millions of people with family and acquaintances on the other side of the Iron Curtain. Not everyone in West

13 The full text is reprinted in *Bundestag Stenographische Berichte*, 1. Wahlperiode 1949, p. 308.

Germany agreed, and the policy was quite fiercely criticized in conservative circles as an unconstitutional acceptance of the permanent division of Germany, a form of 'appeasement' of a communist dictatorship that would, in effect if not in intention, serve to prop up an illegitimate regime. Nonetheless, negotiations involving both German governments and the erstwhile Allies proceeded in 1970 and were eased with the replacement of the rather sceptical Ulbricht by the more obliging Honecker in 1971. The resulting Basic Treaty between the FRG and GDR officially recognized 'two German states in one German nation' and renounced the Hallstein Doctrine, though West Germany still refused to recognize the GDR as a completely foreign state, thus upholding a formal constitutional commitment to reunification while rejecting it as an immediate goal. In spite of the vastly improved relations after the Basic Treaty, the West German government still maintained a fairly consistent policy of non-recognition of the GDR in official publications and exhibits. It was symptomatic that the 'so-called GDR' was completely left out of the West German parliament's official exhibition of 'German' history.[14]

Meanwhile, *Ostpolitik* also significantly changed the GDR's understanding of itself. 'Coming closer' to West Germany was diplomatically and economically advantageous, but increasing contacts between GDR citizens and the wealthier, consumer-oriented West also entailed considerable political risks. Whereas SED policy prior to the Basic Treaty was to maintain strict separation from West Germany while continuing rhetorical support for unification, the reduction of political distance accompanying *Ostpolitik* prompted East German leaders to delimit more clearly the GDR's self-image, politics, social life, even history from that of the Federal Republic. Honecker's response to the policy of *Annäherung* was the complementary policy of *Abgrenzung*, or 'demarcation'. In concrete terms, *Abgrenzung* consisted of limiting contact with the West however possible under the terms of the Basic Treaty (for instance, raising transit fees and the minimum currency exchange requirement), replacing the word 'German' with GDR-specific slogans wherever possible, and emphasizing the cultural and societal separateness (and superiority) of the 'socialist Germany' in relation to its capitalist counterpart. Unification obviously remained out of the question, and any West German appeals to 'one German nation', whether sincere or rhetorical, were categorically attacked by the GDR leadership as a provocation upsetting European peace.

The goal of *Abgrenzung* was nothing less than to secure a new 'GDR identity'.[15] This required strenuous efforts given the numerous familial ties to

14 Deutscher Bundestag, Presse- und Informationsamt, *Fragen an die deutsche Geschichte. Ideen, Kräfte, Entscheidungen von 1800 bis zur Gegenwart* (Bonn, 1984).

15 On the SED attempt to construct a specific GDR identity and mythology, see generally Alan Nothnagle, *Building the East German Myth: Historical Mythology and Youth Propaganda in the German Democratic Republic, 1945–1989* (Ann Arbor, 1999); also Raina Zimmering, *Mythen in der Politik der DDR. Ein Beitrag zur Erforschung politischer Mythen* (Opladen, 2000).

West Germany, the memory and consciousness of a common 'German' past, and the continuing sense of 'Germany' as at least a social or cultural entity. The official line was that the development of socialism in the GDR and the existence of capitalism in the FRG caused the citizens of the two countries to grow apart, with different experiences and 'national consciousnesses'.[16] To underscore the point, a curious distinction was drawn between 'nation' (seen as entailing social, political, economic as well as cultural attributes) and 'nationality' (in the more narrow sense of ethnicity), which led to the rather ambiguous designation of East Germans as 'GDR citizens of German nationality'.[17] This policy of *'Entdeutschung'* (de-Germanization), as some Western commentators called it, was conspicuously displayed in the amendments to the GDR constitution in 1974, which no longer described the GDR as a 'socialist state of the German nation', but as a 'socialist state of workers and peasants'.[18] The titles of numerous institutions were also changed from 'German' to 'Workers and Peasants' (though, strangely enough, the *Deutsche Reichsbahn* survived). By the 1980s the policy of cultural *Abgrenzung* had led to a reassessment of the German past and a deliberate attempt to appropriate as much as possible into the 'progressive heritage' of the 'GDR nation'. In contrast to the FRG, which was portrayed as a cosmopolitan capitalist state with too many 'foreign' (read: American) influences, the GDR was the product of centuries of class struggle and embodied the best and most progressive aspects of German history.[19] Such controversial historical figures as Bismarck, Frederick the Great, and Luther were rehabilitated, their likenesses to be seen in the many new statues ordered by the chief supervisor for cultural matters, Kurt Hager. A national holiday was proclaimed in honour of Luther, Germany's first hero of class liberation, whose antipathy toward peasants was conveniently ignored. Although East German historians by and large obliged the party leadership with new historical interpretations that fitted the bill, there were a handful of more critical scholars who used the opportunity presented by these new political currents to carry out research in fields hitherto neglected for ideological reasons.[20]

16 At the time, some West German social scientists shared the idea that West German and East German 'national consciousnesses' were significantly diverging, and sought to study the phenomenon systematically. Cf. in particular Gebhard Schweigler, *National Consciousness in Divided Germany* (London, 1975).

17 Alfred Kosing and Walter Schmidt, 'Nation und Nationalität in der DDR', *Neues Deutschland*, 15 February 1975, reprinted in *DA* 8:11 (Nov. 1975), pp. 1221–8. See also Hermann Axen, *Zur Entwicklung der sozialistischen Nation in der DDR* (Berlin, 1973).

18 Reprinted in J.K.A. Thomaneck and J. Mellis (eds), *Politics, Society and Government in the German Democratic Republic: Basic Documents* (Oxford, 1989).

19 'From the Programme of the SED: on the development of a socialist national culture', May 1976, reprinted in J.K.A Thomaneck and James Mellis (eds), *Politics, Society and Government in the German Democratic Republic: Basic Documents* (Oxford, 1989), p. 320.

20 On the role of historians in the GDR, see esp. G. Iggers *et al.* (eds), *Die DDR-Geschichtswissenschaft als Forschungsproblem* (special issue no. 27 of *Historische Zeitschrift*) (Munich, 1998); Konrad Jarausch (ed.), *Zwischen Parteilichkeit und Professionalität. Bilanz der Geschichtswissenschaft in der DDR* (Berlin, 1991); Martin Sabrow (ed.), *Geschichte als Herrschaftsdiskurs. Der Umgang mit der Vergangenheit in der DDR* (Cologne, 1999); Ilko-Sascha Kowalczuk (ed.), *Paradigmen deutscher Geschichtswissenschaft* (Berlin, 1994); idem, 'Die DDR-Historiker und die deutsche Nation', *APuZG* B39/96, pp. 22–30.

Although scholarship in the West was far less constrained than in the GDR, there was nonetheless a close relationship between the political context and the conceptual framework in which scholarly work was carried out. The shifts in West German policy towards the GDR were in part derived from and in part provided further impetus for evolving views within the academic world. By the end of the 1960s, the GDR appeared a rather different animal from the early years. It was relatively productive given its unfavourable economic starting point, economic reforms were underway, it boasted a fine education system, a high percentage of women were in paid employment, the standard of living was fairly comfortable (Western care packages to relatives in the East were no longer so necessary), there was little evidence of popular dissent, and indeed there was seemingly less reason for it than before. To be sure, the GDR was not as wealthy as West Germany, but it had made real strides and its social security system was more generous and comprehensive. Book titles such as *The Calculated Emancipation, The GDR is no Longer Merely a Zone* and *The Planned Miracle*[21] signalled new ways of viewing the GDR. These journalistic accounts often painted a particularly rosy picture; as Hans Werner Schwarze argued, the SED was steering the East German state 'indeed very differently, but not less successfully than this occurs with the Federal Republic through the three democratic parties'. In the event that the Soviet Union should withdraw its guarantees to secure the GDR's existence, the outcome would 'certainly no longer be as simple to answer as many political optimists in the West like to think'.[22] Although such grotesquely positive assessments were by no means universally shared, they did reflect a broad desire to cease with the condemnatory tone towards the GDR and acknowledge both its shortcomings *and* its accomplishments.

These new views were related not only to the changing inter-German political framework, but also to concurrent methodological shifts, namely, the rise of social sciences in West German universities from the 1960s onwards. As communism reformed away from the terroristic excesses and crude mobilization practices of its early years, many Western scholars jettisoned what they saw as the 'politically and theoretically, methodologically and empirically outdated'[23] totalitarian model, with its myopic concern with political structures and implication of coercion and terror, and began to approach it in a more 'value free' and unprejudicial way, very much in the spirit of *Ostpolitik*. Normative moral categories were out; the point was no longer to apply Western terms and concepts to the East, but to adopt a 'system-immanent' approach, evaluating the GDR 'on its own terms'. Inspired

---

21  Hans Werner Schwarze, *Die DDR ist keine Zone mehr* (Cologne, 1969); Rüdiger Thomas, *Modell DDR: Die kalkulierte Emanzipation* (Munich, 1972); Joachim Nawrocki, *Das geplante Wunder. Leben und Wirtschaften im anderen Deutschland* (Hamburg, 1967).
22  H.W. Schwarze, *Die DDR ist keine Zone mehr*, p. 345.
23  G. Meyer, *Sozialistische Systeme. Theorie- und Strukturanalyse* (Opladen, 1979), p. 203.

by contemporary 'modernization' theories emanating from the United States, which attempt to embrace and link together various elements of political, cultural and socio-economic development in the industrial era, many scholars thought that the communists would, in their desire to industrialize and raise productivity, become more 'rational' and 'businesslike' in their behaviour. This approach suggested a kind of convergence over time between the two great systems of the day, liberal–capitalist democracy and communism, both of which faced similar pressures in their drives towards modernization and would presumably have to adopt similar strategies for coping with them. From this perspective, the GDR essentially represented an alternative to the Western model of capitalist modernization, and indeed what currently seemed the single most promising example given its high level of industrialization and apparent political stability.

The critical question was how, and to what extent, the drive for economic modernization would also entail a transformation of the internal political dynamics of the system. As Peter Ludz argued in his seminal 1968 book on the changing party elite[24] the running of an advanced industrial society necessitates the rise of technical experts who, by the latter 1960s, formed an 'institutionalized counter-elite' in the GDR, providing a counterweight to the powers of the party and *Politbüro*. At the same time he claimed to discern a new degree of political consensus as the increasingly pragmatic, career-oriented East German populace responded positively to the regime's appeals to economic rationality and modernization. In Ludz's view the GDR had developed from a 'totalitarian' one-party state into a functional form of 'consultative authoritarianism'. Although many scholars questioned his rather strong thesis about the rise of an institutionalized 'counter-elite', numerous subsequent studies supported the idea that the necessities of managing a modern industrial society limited and presumably would eventually end the 'arbitrary monocratic exercise of power'.[25] And although this entire approach to studying communist systems was in decline by the 1980s,[26] the GDR – generally considered the most modern and efficient socialist state – largely escaped this criticism. Scholarship on East German socialism tended

---

24 P.C. Ludz, *Parteielite im Wandel. Funktionsaufbau, Sozialstruktur und Ideologie der SED-Führung. Eine empirisch-systematische Untersuchung* (Opladen, 1968).

25 Especially noteworthy are Thomas Baylis, *The Technical Intelligentsia and the East German Elite: Legitimacy and Social Change in Mature Communism* (Berkeley, CA, 1974), quote here from p. 273; and Klaus v. Beyme, *Ökonomie und Politik im Sozialismus* (Munich, 1975); G.J. Glaeßner, *Herrschaft durch Kader* (Opladen, 1977); Gero Neugebauer, *Partei und Staatsapparat* (Opladen, 1978).

26 The failure of economic reforms and the widespread corruption of the Brezhnev years led many scholars to question the supposedly 'modernizing' function of the power-obsessed party apparatus and to emphasize instead the networks of patronage, privilege and palm-greasing under Soviet-style communism. See especially Ken Jowitt, 'Soviet Neotraditionalism: The Political Corruption of a Leninist Regime', *Soviet Studies* 35 (1983), pp. 275–97. For a recent and wide-ranging analysis along these lines, see Alena Ledeneva, *Russia's Economy of Favours: Blat, Networking and Informal Exchange* (Cambridge, 1998).

to abide by the older 'convergence' theory because the socialist system was simply seen to work better there than elsewhere.[27]

This general shift towards a 'system-immanent' approach does not mean that scholarship on the GDR was speaking in unison. The 1970s and especially the 1980s were characterized by a plurality of views. A number of conservative scholars explicitly clung to totalitarianism models and fundamentally questioned the legitimacy of the GDR by insisting on its dictatorial nature as an *Unrechtsstaat*, a state not governed by the rule of law. Siegfried Mampel, for instance, who fled from the GDR in 1978 and founded the *Gesellschaft für Deutschlandforschung* (Society for Research on Germany) in West Germany, unequivocally contended that there was no reason 'to depart from the totalitarianism concept, unless the point is to enhance the status of the political system of the GDR'.[28] Karl Wilhelm Fricke's pioneering work on opposition, the East German justice system and the secret police reminded readers of the central role of brute force and coercion in maintaining the SED regime.[29] Hermann Weber, arguably the leading Western historian of the GDR before its collapse, also painted a picture of the regime that placed its dictatorial character in the foreground, albeit rejecting the totalitarianism model for the GDR.[30] Although the parliamentary swing back to a conservative–liberal coalition in 1982 marked a change in the political climate in West Germany (following conservative trends elsewhere in the 1980s), neither the FRG's accommodationist policy towards the GDR nor patterns of scholarly interpretation altered dramatically. Despite the renewed emphasis on despotism and coercion in most other socialist regimes, well into the late 1980s the GDR was still widely perceived as an exception amidst the political and economic turbulence of the rest of Eastern Europe.[31] East Germany was still a place in which, as the joke went, Germans managed to make even socialism work.

The collapse of the GDR suddenly and quite dramatically changed the terrain of interpretation. Not only has the empirical basis expanded exponentially, but also the terms of debate, the categories of analysis and the political implications of scholarly argument have been radically transformed. One could roughly divide the post-1989 debate into several overlapping phases. Initially, in the early 1990s, debates about the GDR were highly politicized

---

27 Norman Naimark convincingly voiced early concerns about these relatively positive assessments of the GDR: 'Is it True What They're Saying about East Germany?', *Orbis* 23 (1979), p. 549–77.

28 Siegfried Mampel, in *Politische Systeme in Deutschland* (Berlin, 1980), p. 142.

29 Karl Wilhelm Fricke, *Opposition und Widerstand in der DDR* (Cologne, 1984); *Selbstbehauptung und Widerstand in der Sowjetischen Besatzungszone Deutschlands*, 2nd edition (Bonn/Berlin, 1966); *Warten auf Gerechtigkeit. Kommunistische Säuberungen und Rehabilitierungen. Bericht und Dokumentation* (Cologne, 1971); *Politik und Justiz in der DDR. Zur Geschichte der politischen Verfolgung 1945–1968* (Cologne, 1979); *Die DDR-Staatssicherheit. Entwicklung, Strukturen, Aktionsfelder* (Cologne, 1982); *Zur Menschen- und Grundrechtssituation politischer Gefangener in der DDR*, 2nd edition (Cologne, 1988).

30 Among his many works, see *Geschichte der DDR* (Munich, 1985); and *Die DDR 1945 bis 1990* (Munich, 2000). Weber's views on the value of totalitarianism theories will be discussed in Chapter 2.

31 See, for instance, the collection of articles 'The GDR at Forty', in *German Politics and Society* 17 (1989).

and characterized by the rapid publication of what has aptly been called a
'heroes, victims and villains literature':[32] a wave of '*Enthüllungsgeschichten*',
or sensationalist revelations about *Stasi* activity and links with prominent
literary and church figures; new documentation concerning the 'Stalinization'
of the SED and the high degree of Soviet influence; numerous memoirs of
dissidents, civic movement leaders, and party big-wigs. Gradually more
scholarly analyses appeared from both west German and east German
authors, though many of these were still quite polemical and politically contentious.[33] By the mid-1990s there were clear signs of a less condemnatory
and more open-ended approach, especially in the work associated with the
*Zentrum für zeithistorische Forschung* which broadened its focus beyond
the regime *per se* – the political system, party leaders and the *Stasi* – to
include more social and cultural themes as well. This period also witnessed
the work of the so-called 'Enquete Commission', a cross-party parliamentary enquiry into the history of the GDR that sought to attain a more sober
and non-partisan view of the East German past and its consequences for
unified Germany.[34] This non-partisan spirit only extended so far, of course,
since Marxist–Leninist approaches were largely consigned to the dustbin of
history, or at least the fringes of public discourse, along with many of the
historians who had practised them in the GDR. A more recent phase since
the mid-1990s has been characterized by a torrent of specialist monographs,
mostly emanating from German doctoral or *Habilitation* dissertations, as
well as the appearance of the first syntheses (of varying quality). On the
whole, the excitement about the East German archives had dampened somewhat by the latter 1990s. A more sober atmosphere gradually began to
surround scholarly interpretations of the GDR after public and journalistic interest finally started to wane.[35] Yet agreement on many of the basic
features of the regime and its place in German and European history is still
not in sight, and scholarly interpretations remain politically and morally
charged.

It is useful to think of the changing post-1989 interpretations of the
GDR as the product of interaction between three somewhat distinct, yet
closely interwoven, threads of debate: political, methodological, and moral.
Politically, the triumphalist sentiments about the victory of liberal-capitalist

32 Mary Fulbrook, *Interpretations of the Two Germanies, 1945–1990* (Basingstoke, 2000), p. 4.
33 Gerhard Besier, *Der SED-Staat und die Kirche* (Munich, 1993); G. Besier and S. Wolf, '*Pfarrer, Christen und Katholiken'. Das Ministerium für Staatssicherheit der ehemaligen DDR und die Kirchen* (Neukirchen, 1992); Klaus Schroeder (ed.), *Geschichte und Transformation des SED-Staates* (Berlin, 1994); Armin Mitter and Stefan Wolle, *Untergang auf Raten. Unbekannte Kapitel der DDR-Geschichte* (Munich, 1993).
34 The achievements and shortcomings of the commission's work are discussed in Chapter 8. The commis-sion's findings are published in a multi-volume series entitled *Materialien der Enquete-Kommission 'Aufarbeitung von Geschichte und Folgen der SED-Diktatur in Deutschland' des Deustchen Bundestags* (Bonn, 1994).
35 Not that media interest has waned continually, as the wave of events and commemorations in August 2001 surrounding the fortieth anniversary of the construction of the Wall clearly attests.

democracy over its arch-rival communist system have certainly percolated
into scholarly debate. Conservative political opinion, hardly enamoured
with the GDR in the first place, could shout the message from the rooftops:
socialism had failed, it was hopelessly inefficient, the masses did not want it.
The GDR was, after all, little more than a Soviet imposition and wholly
illegitimate '*Unrechtsstaat*'. The conservative historian Ernst Nolte, for
instance, has dismissed the GDR as a mere 'Soviet protectorate'; Hans-Peter
Schwarz has characterized it as a 'mega concentration camp'; various economists have explained why the hopelessly inefficient planned economy never
stood a chance.[36] In this condemnatory spirit, Klaus Schroeder and Jochen
Staadt have offered an overall assessment of the GDR as 'a dictatorship
wholly dependent on the Soviet Union, which kept itself going for forty
years through open and latent terror against its population'.[37] Some east
Germans, especially those who felt discriminated against for not toeing the
official line, have by and large agreed with this assessment. In a widely read
book based on previously inaccessible SED and *Stasi* reports, Armin Mitter
and Stefan Wolle, two such east German historians, have presented the
history of the GDR as an inexorable 'decline in stages' doomed to fail from
the start or at least from the June 1953 uprising, after which the relationship between regime and populace was essentially one of latent civil war.
This overall picture, which enjoys considerably wide currency outside of
the academy, is in many ways a mirror-image of Marxist–Leninist notions
about the ever-impending 'overall crisis' of capitalism, only applied to
communism instead.

Such interpretations amount to turning the older 'modernization' and
'convergence' theories on their head and clearly reflect the seismic shift that
has taken place. As the scale of the GDR's indebtedness, economic decline
and political–ideological stagnation was rapidly revealed in the early 1990s,
it seemed that it was precisely its modernization deficits that led to its collapse. In other words, this was a case of divergence from, not convergence
with, the Western 'norm' of democracy and capitalism. With amazing swiftness, social scientific theories of modernization that had so long been used
to explain the GDR's stability and apparent permanence now purported
to show why its unpredicted collapse was more or less inevitable. Sharp
critiques of 'our skewed picture of the GDR' began to appear in learned
journals.[38] The 'system-immanent' and detail-obsessed research before 1989
was likened to an ordnance survey map registering 'every farmstead and
undulation, but failing to show that the entire region was permanently

---

36 E. Nolte: 'Die fortwirkende Verblendung', *FAZ*, 22 February 1992; H.-P. Schwarz, 'Wenn der
    Namenspatron ein Massenmörder war', *Die Welt*, 17 January 1992.
37 K. Schroeder and Jochen Staadt, 'Der diskrete Charme des Status-quo: DDR-Forschung in der Ära der
    Entspannungspolitik', in K. Schroeder (ed.), *Geschichte und Transformation*, p. 309.
38 Hartmut Jäckel, 'Unser schiefes DDR-Bild. Anmerkungen zu einem noch nicht verjährten publizistischen
    Sündenfall', *DA* 23:10 (1990), pp. 1557–65; Wilfried von Bredow, 'Perzeptions-Probleme. Das schiefe
    DDR-Bild und warum es bis zum Schluß so blieb', *DA* 24:2 (1991), pp. 147–54.

under water'.[39] Why was this the case? A number of reasons have been suggested: the intrinsic shortcomings of the modernization theories on which so much pre-1989 GDR research was based, systematic statistical deception by the East German authorities, the 'political correctness' of détente and the pressure to discuss the GDR only in such a way that would serve the goal of decreasing tensions (*Entspannung*). As a methodological corrective, many scholars have advocated a return to 'totalitarianism' models with their clear focus on the repressive machinery and the imposed nature of the political system that had previously been woefully underemphasized. In addition, by bracketing the GDR together with the Third Reich, the concept of 'totalitarianism' also makes a clear moral statement about dictatorship that, for whatever reason, few scholars working on the GDR before 1989 seemed willing to take upon themselves.

Drawing this connection between methodology and morality has a number of implications for evaluating interpretations of the GDR both before and after 1989. By deliberately avoiding moral questions that were considered both 'unscientific' and politically unwise, the old GDR research has been seen to fail not only in scholarly terms, but also on moral grounds. Far from adopting a 'value-free' approach to the GDR, the more positive interpretations were, so the argument runs, in effect presenting a skewed and therefore partisan view that conformed to the spirit of détente and to the dominant social–liberal academic culture. In other words, political prejudices were hidden behind a veneer of value-neutrality. Such prejudices are, of course, a constant concern in historical interpretation and in this sense are not unique. What was distinctive about this line of criticism, however, was that it revolved not so much around accusations of 'taking sides' as around the *failure* to do so, the reluctance to adopt explicit normative criteria – in this case human rights and liberal democratic values – as the primary yardstick for evaluation. Echoing conservative criticisms of *Ostpolitik* in the early 1970s, the 'system-immanent' approach has been castigated as woolly-headed liberalism that effectively helped to sustain a dictatorial regime, trivialized communist crimes, and betrayed both the constitutional commitment to the unity of the German nation as well as the East Germans who were left in the lurch and consigned to their fate.[40] Many of these resentments were shared by east Germans who had refused to conform sufficiently to make an academic career in the GDR and felt doubly excluded after unification given the Western-dominated landscape of higher education in the East. As we will see, such resentments have certainly played a role in differing interpretations of the GDR, as well as in the heated controversies about who is 'fit'

---

39  H. Jäckel, 'Unser schiefes DDR-Bild', p. 1560.

40  The strongest criticisms to this effect are voiced by Klaus Schroeder and Jochen Staadt, 'Der diskrete Charme des Status-quo', and Klaus Schroeder and Jochen Staadt, 'Die Kunst des Aussitzens', in K. Schroeder (ed.), *Geschichte und Transformation*, pp. 347–54. More balanced, despite the inflammatory title, is Jens Hacker, *Deutsche Irrtümer. Schönfärber und Helfershelfer der SED-Diktatur im Westen* (Berlin, 1992).

to write GDR history, or more precisely who should be given a state-funded institutional basis for doing so.

All of this merely serves to underscore how interpretations of the East German past cannot be properly understood outside of the tight nexus of moral values, methodological concerns and the political–ideological context in which debates take place. With these factors in mind, we can now begin to investigate these debates in greater detail.

# 2

# The GDR as dictatorship: Totalitarian, Stalinist, modern, welfarist?

The GDR was, it has aptly been said, an 'artificial product of the Cold War'.[1] In both East and West, the political dictates of this contest between the two great societal systems of the twentieth century meant that there were ready-made labels to describe the nature and character of the East German regime from its very founding. The contraposed world-views were quickly and directly translated into polarized images of the GDR: on one side, an anti-fascist bulwark against capitalist imperialism, on the other, a repressive and illegitimate occupation regime – and in between, various denunciations of the 'Stalinist' perversion of communism that many left-wing intellectuals saw being perpetrated in the Soviet Union and implemented in East Germany. These opposing designations of the GDR were instrumental in shaping political consciousness in both German states and in legitimating the two opposing systems. As such, they not only tell us something about the self-understanding of those in power, but also offer an insight into the post-war experiences of many Germans who grew up and lived in one half of this 'divided nation' on the front line of the Cold War. Of course, these official self-portrayals were an integral part of the political confrontation between East and West, and are more suited for propagandistic than analytical ends. Yet as we have just seen, the institutional landscape of research in Germany, the changing political–ideological context and the nature of East–West relations also strongly influenced some of the basic premises and concepts of scholarly research and debate.

Given the crucial importance of the contemporary political framework to interpretations of the GDR while it existed, it can hardly be surprising that the unexpected collapse of the SED system over 1989–90 has triggered a search for new terms and concepts – and a revitalization of old ones – inspired by the overarching question of why East German socialism had

---

1 A description that is, it might be noted, just as applicable to the fledgling West German state. A. Mitter and S. Wolle, *Untergang auf Raten* (Munich, 1993), p. 161.

'failed'. Probably the most noteworthy change in the vocabulary has been the emergence of a broad consensus that the GDR was a 'dictatorship', despite the reluctance to use such condemnatory language before 1989. Although there are serious and well-founded doubts about the analytical usefulness of the term, the GDR is widely referred to as a 'dictatorship' in that it knew neither the separation of executive, legislative and judicial powers nor the rule of law, because it systematically infringed basic civil and human rights, and quite obviously because it was not democratically legitimated. To take this one step further, it is also commonly dubbed a 'party dictatorship' – that is, not a 'dictatorship of the proletariat' as the GDR presented itself – in that political power was concentrated in the hands of the party leadership which, although it may not have made all of the important decisions, certainly constituted the 'final instance' within the East German polity. Because this state of affairs was underpinned by Marxist–Leninist ideology, and because the ruling party described itself as 'socialist' and the system over which it governed as 'real existing socialism', it also seems relatively uncontroversial (apart from a few critics who dispute that the system had anything to do with 'true' socialism) to call the GDR a 'socialist party dictatorship'. But this term marks about the extent of agreement. Beyond this, there is vigorous dispute about the essential character of the GDR and where it should be located in the context of the various modern authoritarian systems that emerged in Europe during the twentieth century.

This chapter will begin by offering a brief summary of the basic contours of debate about the essence of the GDR, focusing first on what is undoubtedly the most influential concept, 'totalitarianism', and outlining the main stages of development and the principal variants within this approach as applied to the GDR. It will then consider the somewhat complementary notion of 'Stalinism', the relatively new but widely used idea of 'modern dictatorship', and several of the more well-known 'GDR-specific' concepts that have been suggested as analytical alternatives. Finally, it will attempt to offer an evaluation of the strengths and weaknesses of these various approaches when applied to the GDR.

# Interpretations

## *Totalitarianism*

Undoubtedly the most significant conceptual shift in approaches to the GDR after its collapse has been the renaissance of totalitarianism theories. Some of the reasons for this were adumbrated in the previous chapter, above all the blindness of much pre-1989 research towards the organs of repression and the desire for a clearer moral statement condemning dictatorial regimes in principle. This resurgence of totalitarian models is also related to processes of 'dealing with the past' in unified Germany. In confronting for a second time the legacies of a dictatorial regime on German soil, there has been a compelling temptation to couple this process with the experiences after the Nazi dictatorship. Probably most important, the startling revelations after 1990 about the truly Orwellian scale of *Stasi* surveillance strongly nourished the view that the GDR was a 'totalitarian' regime. Calling itself the 'sword and shield of the party', the *Stasi* at its zenith in the 1980s boasted around 100,000 paid employees as well as many thousands more 'informal collaborators'. Over the four decades of its existence it had managed to produce some 178 kilometres (!) of indexes and files. Not only had its informers thoroughly infiltrated most of the opposition groups, it also kept files on literally millions of ordinary East Germans; indeed, it even kept thousands of scent samples in glass jars for future use with police dogs should the need arise. It is little wonder that such an apparatus has been widely perceived as the 'main instrument of GDR totalitarianism' and an 'instrument of totalitarian rule'.[2]

In its classic formulations, 'totalitarianism' was in essence a generic, comparative concept used to bracket together fascist and communist states and to emphasize the similarities in their techniques of rule. This chapter will focus on 'totalitarian' models as applied to the GDR, thus leaving aside as far as possible the somewhat separate debates about comparisons between the Third Reich and Soviet Union or Third Reich and GDR, the latter of which we will revisit in Chapter 7.

The word 'totalitarian' originated in the early 1920s as an Italian antifascist epithet, and soon thereafter was appropriated by Mussolini, who spoke approvingly of the 'fierce totalitarian will' of his movement.[3] Over the course of the 1930s, the term came increasingly to be used in Western democracies to link fascism and Nazism with communism as merely different sides of the totalitarian coin – a view certainly encouraged by the Nazi–Soviet pact of 1939. Although such conflations were played down after the Nazi invasion of the Soviet Union in 1941, they re-emerged with a vengeance in the late 1940s with the onset of the Cold War. It is thus mistaken

2  These quotes from Clemens Vollnhals, 'Das Ministerium für Staatssicherheit. Ein Instrument totalitärer Herrschaftsausübung', in H. Kaelble *et al.*, *Sozialgeschichte der DDR*, pp. 498–518; and Uwe Thaysen, 'Rückzug, Verschleierung – und Rückkehr? Das Meisterstück der Regierung Modrow im Transformationsprozeß der DDR', *Recht und Politik* 30 (1994), p. 146. There is a truly massive literature on totalitarianism. For overviews, see Wolfgang Wippermann, *Totalitarismustheorien: die Entwicklung der Diskussion von den Anfängen bis heute* (Darmstadt, 1997); Alfons Söllner (ed.), *Totalitarismus: eine Ideengeschichte des 20. Jahrhunderts* (Berlin, 1997); Abbott Gleason, *Totalitarianism: The Inner History of the Cold War* (Oxford, 1995); Eckard Jesse (ed.), *Totalitarismus im 20. Jahrhundert: eine Bilanz der internationalen Forschung* (Baden-Baden, 1998). See also 'Die Totalitarismusforschung und ihre Repräsentanten', in *APuZG*, B20/98, pp. 3–18. On totalitarianism and *Diktaturenvergleich*, see especially Jürgen Kocka, *Vereinigungskrise. Zur Geschichte der Gegenwart* (Göttingen, 1995), pp. 91–101; also Hans Maier (ed.), *'Totalitarismus' und 'politische Religionen': Konzepte des Diktaturenvergleichs* (Paderborn, 1996).
3  See I. Kershaw, *The Nazi Dictatorship* (London, 2000), p. 23.

to regard the concept of 'totalitarianism' as a product of the Cold War, though without a doubt this was its heyday in terms of both popular and scholarly usage.

It was during the latter 1940s and early 1950s that the two 'classic' models of totalitarianism were developed and popularized by Hannah Arendt and Carl Friedrich. In her seminal treatise on totalitarianism,[4] Hannah Arendt stresses the revolutionary, radicalizing, structure-destroying aspects of totalitarian rule, which are based essentially on the terroristic execution of supposedly 'objective laws of history' derived from a single ideology claiming absolute, universal validity. In contrast to tyranny, which suffocates public life in a torpor of dissipated powerlessness, a central attribute of totalitarian authority is the constant mobilization of the masses for the great cause, whatever it may be. The result is a constant state of terror, a state of permanent movement and structurelessness that releases immense destructive energies directed both inwards and outwards. This excessive manifestation of force and terror triggers a spiral of aggressive dynamism that eventually culminates in self-destruction. In formulating this model, Arendt most certainly had Nazi Germany and Stalin's Soviet Union in mind. But while her analysis has been largely borne out in the case of the Third Reich, it is less satisfactory on Stalin's Soviet Union, and certainly bears little resemblance to the increasingly conservative and sclerotic communist systems after Stalin's death.

The even more influential model of totalitarianism advanced by Carl Friedrich and Zbigniew Brzezinski possesses little of the 'dynamic' character emphasized by Arendt.[5] Instead, it emphasizes the efforts to control and plan all areas of life through modern technical and organizational means according to the dictates of a single binding ideology. Friedrich's famous 'six-points' outlined what he saw as the principal features of totalitarianism: an official ideology, a single mass party, terroristic police control, monopoly over the media, monopoly over arms, and central control of the economy. Because the millenarian ideology and its claims to universal validity are not as central to this model, Friedrich and Brzezinski allow for the continued existence of 'islands of separateness' such as the Church or family within such systems. This also implies that a ritualization and routinization of the system are not only possible, but indeed contribute to the regime's stability and capability to reproduce itself. Although clearly more appropriate for the GDR than Arendt's model, the main shortcomings of this approach have often been pointed out. Above all, it is a static model that does not account for internal changes within the governing system, let alone explain why change might happen in the first place. It also paints an unconvincingly monolithic picture of 'totalitarian regimes' which generally does not stand up to close scrutiny.

4  Hannah Arendt, *The Origins of Totalitarianism* (London, 1951).
5  Carl Friedrich and Zbigniew Brzezinski, *Totalitarian Dictatorship and Autocracy* (Cambridge, MA, 1956).

As the communist regimes in Europe stabilized after Stalin's death, 'totalitarian' theorists increasingly turned their attention away from the Third Reich and Stalinist Soviet Union towards the current Eastern-bloc states. As terror waned in these regimes and ideological dynamism gave way to a systematization and increasing ritualization of politics, totalitarian theorists adapted by either limiting their usage of the term to National Socialism and the Stalinist period of communism or by reformulating the concept to accommodate the changes taking place. Martin Drath, for instance, considered the classic totalitarian concepts only partially applicable to the GDR or post-Stalin Soviet Union.[6] It was more useful in his view to distinguish between what he called 'primary' and 'secondary' aspects of the totalitarian phenomenon. Drath saw the 'primary' characteristics as twofold: first, the attempt to impose a new world-view and value system different to that previously dominant in society; and second, the striving towards social homogenization and political indoctrination that extended into the private sphere. The means and methods of realizing this aim were 'secondary' phenomena which could change in both their nature and their intensity.[7] In a somewhat similar vein, Peter Graf Kielmannsegg's reformulation of the totalitarian concept focused on the decisive role played by ideology and the party apparatus as instruments of monopolistic social control.[8] In this scheme the single ideology is crucial for offering a binding set of official values and norms (a world-view) and the party becomes indispensable – as well as increasingly omnipresent in state and society – by virtue of its role as executor of this monopolizing process. Although these basic structural features remain, they are not as static as in Friedrich and Brzezinski's model, but rather set in train a process of institutionalization and bureaucratization of totalitarian rule as the post-revolutionary party/state bureaucracy essentially functions to preserve a vestige of its revolutionary dynamic and the ideological character of its rule in the face of the increasingly mundane and technical systematization of government. Karl Dietrich Bracher, too, viewed the core of totalitarian rule – characterized in his view by the total claim to rule, the leadership principle, the exclusive ideology and the mobilization of the masses – as preserved in most communist regimes despite the relativization of terror and the increasingly conspicuous signs of dissolution during the Brezhnev era.[9]

---

6  M. Drath, 'Totalitarismus in der Volksdemokratie', introduction to Ernst Richert, *Macht ohne Mandat. Der Staatsapparat in der Sowjetischen Besatzungszone Deutschlands* (Cologne/Opladen, 1958).

7  Siegfried Mampel makes a similar point in distinguishing between 'essential' elements and constants within the system (the monopoly of power and exclusive ideology) and 'variable' elements (the means of control, the precise content of ideology and theory). See S. Mampel, *Totalitäres Herrschaftssystem. Normativer Charakter – Definition – Konstante und variable Essenzialien – Instrumentarium* (Berlin, 2001); S. Mampel, 'Versuch eines Ansatzes für eine Theorie des Totalitarismus', in Konrad Löw (ed.), *Totalitarismus*, 2nd edn (Berlin, 1993), pp. 13ff.

8  P. Graf Kielmannsegg, 'Krise der Totalitarismustheorie?', in M. Funke (ed.), *Totalitarismus. Ein Studien-Reader zur Herrschaftsanalyse moderner Diktaturen* (Düsseldorf, 1978), pp. 61ff.

9  K. D. Bracher, 'Aufarbeitung der Geschichte und Bestand der Demokratie', *DA* 27:9 (1994), pp. 1004–7. See also his previous assertions in *Totalitarismus und Faschismus. Eine wissenschaftliche und politische Begriffskontroverse* (Munich/Vienna, 1980), pp. 10–17.

After 1989, one of the most vociferous advocates of this general definition of totalitarianism has been Klaus Schroeder, who has argued that the GDR was a 'totalitarian' system that was characterized by 'a monistic centre of power with unlimited and exclusive claim to authority as well as an ideology with exclusive character'.[10]

In the meantime, Anglo-American reformulations of the 'totalitarian' concept were moving in a somewhat different direction. It suffices for our purposes here to sketch out the seminal model of Yale political scientist Juan Linz, who for decades has been at the forefront of research on dictatorial political systems. For him, authoritarianism should be viewed as a distinct type of regime alongside – not between – democracy and totalitarianism.[11] The primary difference between authoritarian and totalitarian regimes – both of which are seen as dictatorial – is not so much a matter of wholly distinctive features as of the degree to which certain features are manifested: namely, the degree of political pluralism, the intensity of ideological orientation and the extent of mass political mobilization. Whereas totalitarian regimes are characterized by a single centre of power, authoritarian regimes show limited political pluralism. A totalitarian regime possesses a single, exclusive and often anti-traditional ideology; an authoritarian regime rests on a more traditional, less clearly demarcated set of ideas and values. Whereas a crucial element of any totalitarian regime is its staged plebiscitary nature and attempted mobilization of the masses, an authoritarian regime contents itself with political apathy (an example of an authoritarian regime might be Franco's Spain or any number of right-wing Latin American dictatorships). The basic idea is that a 'totalitarian' regime can turn into an 'authoritarian' one as the degree of political monism, ideological orientation and mass mobilization decreases, as was clearly the case to varying degrees in different Eastern-bloc states during the Brezhnev era (and to some extent under Kruschev).

By the 1970s scholars were seriously questioning whether the GDR was better characterized as an 'authoritarian' regime given the greater leniency it showed towards dissidents than in the 1950s and 1960s, the pact between State and Church in 1978 formally granting the latter a degree of institutional autonomy, as well as the more general acceptance of mere outward conformity as sufficient for leading a quiet life and pursuing a promising career without serious hindrance.[12] As we have already seen, Peter Christian Ludz's notion of 'consultative authoritarianism' coined in the late 1960s was an important first step along this path. Borrowing directly from Juan

---

10 K. Schroeder, 'Einleitung: Die DDR als politische Gesellschaft', in K. Schroeder (ed.), *Geschichte und Transformation des SED-Staates* (Berlin, 1994), pp. 11–26, here p. 13.

11 Cf. his seminal entry in Fred Greenstein and Nelson Polsby (eds), *Handbook of Political Science*, vol. 3: *Macropolitical Theory* (Reading, MA, 1975), pp. 175–411. For a more recent and up-to-date statement of his views, see Juan Linz and Alfred Stepan, *Problems of Democratic Transition and Consolidation: Southern Europe, South-America and Post-Communist Europe* (Baltimore, 1996).

12 See, for instance, Bernhard Marquardt, *DDR – Totalität oder autoritär?* (Bern, 1986).

Linz's terminology, Eckard Jesse has recently suggested the neologism 'autalitarian' (a mixture of 'authoritarian' and 'totalitarian') as a description of the curious mixture of 'hard' and 'soft' aspects of SED rule, especially during the latter 1980s.[13] Others arguing in a similar vein have dubbed the GDR, at least after the mid-1950s, a 'post-totalitarian' regime in the sense that it maintained its older structures of authority but had lost its conviction and utopian attraction.[14] In the mid-1990s Linz himself altered his position somewhat, suggesting that the GDR (alongside Hungary, Czechoslovakia and Bulgaria) is better understood as 'post-totalitarian' – a whole new regime type added to his old tripartite model – rather than 'authoritarian' since both the nature as well as the degree of pluralism, mobilization and ideological orientation were all significantly different from that of an 'authoritarian' regime.[15] Differentiating still further, Linz cites the GDR (along with Czechoslovakia) as an instance of 'frozen' post-totalitarianism in which – for various reasons and despite the tolerance of some critics of the regime – most of the control mechanisms of the party-state stayed in place for a long period and did not evolve as in Hungary or to a lesser extent in Poland. Of all the variants of 'totalitarianism' that have been offered over the years, this is arguably the most useful.

## Stalinism

After the SED regime collapsed, the term 'Stalinism' also experienced something of a revival in both scholarly and wider public debate, though it continued to play a secondary role in relation to totalitarianism. The term of course refers in a narrow sense to the particular political system erected in the Soviet Union under Stalin from about 1925 until his death in 1953. After the Second World War, the various Central and East European countries in which the Soviet-style system was introduced were usually included under the rubric of Stalinism. We will return to the issue of the extent to which political and social life in the GDR derived from patterns established in the Soviet Union or from more specifically 'German' traditions in Chapter 7. For the time being, we will limit ourselves to the concept of 'Stalinism' and its application to the GDR.

The term was originally popularized in the 1930s by Leo Trotsky, Stalin's arch-rival within the ruling elite of the Soviet communist party, as an epithet criticizing the despotic and extremely brutal nature of Stalin's rule at that time. Stalin's Soviet Union was characterized by a strictly centralized and hyper-disciplined party, murderous purges of political rivals or even potential

13 E. Jesse, 'War die DDR totalitär?', in *APuZG*, B40/94, pp. 12–23.
14 These characteristics were most clearly shared with Czechoslovakia, which Vaclav Havel himself has emphasized in his book *Versuch, in der Wahrheit zu leben* (Reinbek, 1989), p. 16.
15 J. Linz and A. Stepan, *Problems of Democratic Transition*, pp. 47, 254.

rivals carried out by a ruthless secret police, the corresponding establishment of a highly privileged and slavishly obedient bureaucratic stratum of
loyal cadre, an extensive system of forced labour camps, and a campaign of
class genocide and enslavement against supposedly 'parasitical' social strata
such as the entrepreneurial middle classes and wealthy peasants who were
seen as political enemies.[16] The concept 'Stalinism' developed simultaneously with 'totalitarianism', and the Soviet Union under Stalin was seen
from the beginning as one of the two great prototypes of 'totalitarianism'
alongside Hitler's Germany. Without using the term, Trotsky himself drew
this connection in 1936: 'Stalinism and fascism are, despite the great differences in terms of their social basis, symmetrical phenomena. In many
regards they are terrifyingly similar.'[17] The term does not, therefore, necessarily imply a rejection of 'totalitarianism' theories, but can be used either in
accordance with it or as a partially competing concept that sets different
accents. 'Stalinism' is, then, not a singular, clearly defined concept. Quite the
contrary, the term has been employed over time by different individuals and
groups in a multitude of ways for a variety of reasons. As applied to the
GDR, one might conceive of it as having three quite distinct usages: denunciatory, apologetic and analytical.

At the height of the Cold War, the term was used above all in a pejora-
tive manner essentially synonymous with 'communist totalitarianism' for
denouncing communist regimes and communist ideology itself from a liberal–
democratic standpoint.[18] The term also highlighted the Soviet roots of the SED
regime as a foreign imposition on German society, very much in line with the
continued employment of the term 'SBZ' long after the formal founding of the
East German state.[19] After submerging somewhat under the softer political
language of the détente years, the adjective 'Stalinist' has been redeployed in a
similar condemnatory fashion in some quarters since the GDR's collapse. Its
denunciatory usage has been twofold: first, to tar the East German regime with
the same brush as the horrifically brutal years of 'high Stalinism' in the Soviet
Union; and second, to suggest that the roots of communist terror could be
traced as far back as the writings of Marx himself, especially in his ideas about
the preferability of monocratic over pluralistic structures of political rule.[20]

---

16  The literature on Stalinism is extraordinarily rich. Useful inroads are Sheila Fitzpatrick (ed.), *Stalinism:
New Directions* (London, 2000); S. Fitzpatrick, *Everyday Stalinism: Ordinary Life in Extraordinary
Times* (Oxford, 1999); Moshe Lewin, *The Making of the Soviet System: Essays in the Social History of
Interwar Russia* (New York, 1994); Ronald Grigor Suny, *The Soviet Experiment* (Oxford, 1998), part 3.
Also useful from a comparative perspective is Ian Kershaw and Moshe Lewin (eds), *Stalinism and
Nazism: Dictatorships in Comparison* (Cambridge, 1997).

17  L. Trotsky, *Verratene Revolution* (orig. 1936), p. 9.

18  For example, Horst Duhnke, *Stalinismus in Deutschland. Die Geschichte der Sowjetischen Besatzungszone*
(Berlin, 1955).

19  Bundesministerium für gesamtdeutsche Fragen, *SBZ von A-Z. Ein Taschen- und Nachschlagebuch über
die Sowjetische Besatzungszone Deutschlands*, 4th edn (Bonn, 1958); Bundesministerium für gesamtdeutsche Fragen, *SBZ von 1945 bis 1954* (Bonn, 1956).

20  Christoph Kleßmann has roundly – and quite rightly, in my view – criticized the highly undifferentiated use of the term in the early 1990s: 'Historical differentiations threaten to submerge under the political

At the same time, the concept has also been instrumentalized from the opposite end of the political spectrum by many communists and humanist Marxists keen to dissociate socialism or communism *per se* from its grotesque 'perversion' under Stalin. Ever since the 1930s, Trotskyites have considered Stalinism nothing less than a 'betrayal of socialism'. After the collapse of the GDR it has been argued that forty years of East German Stalinism represented 'not a "flawed attempt", not a "false model" of socialism, but rather its grave-digger'.[21] This apologetic usage of the term has echoed among more mainstream Marxist–Leninists as well, who tend to see Stalinism as 'a system of dictatorial – including terroristic – practices of rule in state and society in contradiction to the ideals of socialism'.[22] Indeed, some have even surmised that the collapse of 'Stalinist' socialism might finally allow the reignition of the pure flame of unperverted socialism.[23]

'Stalinism' is, therefore, every bit as politically loaded as 'totalitarianism'. But the concept nonetheless has been used analytically by scholars working on the GDR to delineate a specific phenomenon or certain hangovers of a particular phase in the development of communist regimes with a greater degree of specificity than broader theories of 'totalitarianism' allow. Arguably the foremost scholar to adopt a clearly defined concept of 'Stalinism' as a fundamental prop to his interpretation of the GDR is Hermann Weber. Because Weber's definition can by and large be regarded as the standard among most scholars working on the GDR,[24] it suffices to confine ourselves to it here. In his pioneering overviews of East German history, Weber uses the term 'Stalinism' in both a specific and general sense: on the one hand, to denote the *specific* phenomena of arbitrary rule and the personality cult; and on the other, to refer to the more *general* 'societal-political system' that developed under Stalin.[25] Weber argues that after 1945, both the general and specific phenomena of 'Stalinism' were transferred to Eastern Europe under Soviet control, including the SBZ/GDR. First with Stalin's death in 1953, and especially after Kruschev's denunciation of Stalin's excesses at the Soviet party's twentieth congress in 1956, efforts were made

---

(*Contd*)

    indignation over the mismanagement and irresponsibility of the "gerontocracy" around Honecker. Stalinism is degenerating into a label for GDR history.' C. Kleßmann, 'Das Problem der doppelten Vergangenheitsbewältigung', in *Neue Gesellschaft/Frankfurter Hefte* 12/91, pp. 1102ff.

21  Wolfgang Weber, *DDR – 40 Jahre Stalinismus* (Essen, 1993), p. 148.
22  Gerhard Lozek, 'Stalinismus – Ideologie, Gesellschaftskonzept – oder was?', in Manfred Behrend *et al.*, *Beiträge zur Stalinismus-Diskussion* (Berlin, 1997), p. 76.
23  See, for instance, Jürgen Kuczynski, *Asche für Phönix. Aufstieg, Untergang und Wiederkehr neuer Gesellschaftsordnungen* (Cologne, 1992).
24  For example, in Harold Hurwitz, *Die Stalinisierung der SED. Zum Verlust von Freiräumen und sozialdemokratischer Identität in den Vorständen 1946–1949* (Opladen, 1997); Andreas Malycha, *Die SED. Geschichte ihrer Stalinisierung 1946–1953* (Paderborn, 2000); Klaus von Beyme, 'Stalinismus und Post-Stalinismus im osteuropäischen Vergleich', in *Potsdamer Bulletin* no. 13 (July 1998), pp. 8–22.
25  I.e. characterized by communist one-party rule, abrogation of intra-party democracy, centralized control of the state and all spheres of public and political life, lack of intellectual freedom or pluralism,

to overcome the specific attributes of Stalinism (the personality cult, the arbitrariness of violence and punishment). However:

> the basis of the terror regime, the concentration of power in the hands of the hegemonic party, survived by and large unscathed. ... In spite of visible signs of modernization in many areas, the socio-political system of Stalinism (or of neo-Stalinism) remained untouched in the GDR.[26]

Clearly, this definition resonates with many of the 'totalitarian' conceptions outlined above, especially with those which distinguish between enduring 'primary' versus mutable 'secondary' attributes, and is not intended as an outright rejection of totalitarianism theories by most scholars who employ it. The two concepts are not irreconcilable. The issue of whether to approach the GDR as an instance of 'Stalinism' versus 'totalitarianism' is not like the question of employing general theories of fascism or totalitarianism to the Third Reich, where proponents of the former by and large reject the latter as a useful heuristic device, and vice versa. Nonetheless, the very use of this term instead of 'totalitarianism' does imply that the GDR is better approached as a specifically communist dictatorship and that it is more fruitfully compared to and categorized with other communist regimes than with the broader category of 'totalitarian' dictatorships of both Left and Right. Weber himself is rather sceptical about the heuristic value of 'totalitarian' theories. Although he considers the GDR 'absolutely a totalitarian dictatorship', he contends that 'the concept or theory of totalitarianism is of little use to the historian for understanding this dictatorship', above all for capturing the dynamics of stabilization and internal political change over time, as well as the grounds and forms of opposition and dissidence.[27] In this view, 'totalitarianism' is simply too broad and vague to grasp some fundamental aspects of the system which are better captured by 'Stalinism' or, after the great dictator's death, 'neo-' or 'post-Stalinism'.

## The GDR as 'modern dictatorship'?

Not everyone, however, has been advocating more specific frames of reference for the GDR. Among some scholars the solution to the problems of applying the concept of totalitarianism to the history of the GDR has run in

(*Contd*)

the militarization and regimentation of all spheres of life, the lack of basic human rights, a dogmatic ideology (Marxism–Leninism), strict central economic planning, stark social differences including the establishment of a new privileged bureaucracy, and the total subordination of the unions and other 'mass organizations' to the ruling party.

26 Hermann Weber, 'SED und Stalinismus', in *Die DDR im vierzigsten Jahr. Geschichte, Situation, Perspektiven* (Cologne, 1989), pp. 4ff. His definition of Stalinism can also be found in H. Weber, *DDR: Grundriß der Geschichte* (Hannover, 1991), pp. 13–15. Even in the 1976 version of this work, Weber uses the concept 'Stalinism' as the 'central term for the characterization of the SED dictatorship'.

27 See the comments in *Materialien der Enquete-Kommission*, vol. IX, pp. 622–3.

quite the opposite direction. If the advantage of 'Stalinism' as an analytical tool lies in its greater specificity when referring to communist regimes, the disadvantage of course lies in its preclusion of other axes of comparison. If, however, the problem of the 'totalitarian' concept lies in its inability to capture significant changes in the nature of the regime over the forty years of its history – especially if applied to the 1970s and 1980s – and in the associations it has with the far more brutal Third Reich and Soviet Union under Stalin, then perhaps a better solution than retreating into ever greater specificity would be to use an even more general, but less politically loaded term.

This is certainly the rationale behind the notion of 'modern dictatorship', which has enjoyed considerable popularity after 1989, especially among social historians interested in comparative history. Suggested by Jürgen Kocka as an alternative shorthand description of the East German regime, it represents a more 'neutral' and broadly applicable concept than totalitarian theory. The term is intended to refer only to certain kinds of dictatorships of the twentieth century characterized by bureaucratic administration, modern means of control and mobilization (propaganda, surveillance by a state security system), a mass party with claims to absolute political power as both ruler and means of rule, and a binding, all-encompassing ideology. At the heart of the concept is the 'modern' form of dictatorial authority in the age of the 'masses', above all its pseudo-plebiscitary nature which distinguishes it from both previous forms of 'dictatorial' rule as well as other twentieth-century military dictatorships or more traditional monarchical systems. Under this definition, the GDR was clearly a 'modern dictatorship' along with all the other Soviet-style communist regimes as well as the Third Reich and fascist Italy.[28] According to Kocka, the advantage of the term 'modern dictatorship' lies above all in the avoidance of confusion and questionable associations of unbridled terror and violence that plague the term 'totalitarianism'. Moreover, unlike totalitarianism, with its association of brutality and radicalism, 'modern dictatorship' can be more or less appropriately used for the GDR over the whole of its history, including its rather stagnant final decade.[29]

Yet the notion of 'modern dictatorship' is itself not wholly free from problematic associations. Regardless of the original intentions behind the term, it does raise the question of the GDR's 'modernity' more generally and has been used as a springboard for analysing the issues involved.[30] Although

---

28 J. Kocka (ed.), *Historische DDR-Forschung*, introduction (Berlin, 1992), pp. 25ff; J. Kocka, 'Ein deutscher Sonderweg. Überlegungen zur Sozialgeschichte der DDR', *APuZG* 40/94, pp. 34–45.

29 J. Kocka, 'The GDR: A Special Kind of Modern Dictatorship', in K. Jarausch (ed.), *Dictatorship as Experience*, pp. 17–26.

30 See above all the collection of essays in H. Kaelble *et al.*, *Sozialgeschichte der DDR*, especially Martin Kohli, 'Die DDR als Arbeitsgesellschaft? Arbeit, Lebenslauf und soziale Differenzierung', pp. 31–61; also K. Jarausch (ed.), *Dictatorship as Experience*. Cf. also Ilja Srubar, 'War der reale Sozialismus modern? Versuch einer strukturellen Bestimmung', *Kölner Zeitschrift für Soziologie und Sozialpsychologie* 43 (1991), pp. 415–32; Wolfgang Zapf, 'Der Untergang der DDR und die soziologische Theorie der Modernisierung', in Bernd Giesen and Claus Leggewie (eds), *Experiment Vereinigung* (Berlin, 1991), pp. 45f.

the GDR's collapse has led to an emphasis on its supposed modernization 'deficits' in relation to Western societies, answers to the question of its relative modernity are highly ambiguous and vary radically with the point of reference. Compared to the Third Reich or other Soviet satellite states, the GDR's oft-cited level of gender equality, high degree of industrialization, emphasis on technology and science and high degree of secularization seem relatively modern. But when considered alongside the Federal Republic and other 'Western' societies the GDR appears relatively unmodern, even anti-modern, in view of the weak tertiary sector of employment, the low degree of mass consumption and technical innovation, and most importantly the 'primacy of politics' over all basic economic, political and social institutions. When viewed through the lens of 'modernization', the picture of the GDR that emerges is therefore contradictory and ambivalent – hardly surprising given the excessively normative character of the modernization theory underlying the concept of 'modern dictatorship'. As Kocka himself has put it, 'a comparison of historical modernity seldom leads to simple results, but rather more often to conclusions along the lines of "on the one hand ... but on the other hand"'.[31]

This emphasis on the many contradictions of East German society – between ideology and practice, intentions and outcomes, rhetoric and reality – has characterized a broad swathe of historical research since 1990. As Peter Bender has put it:

> The GDR was not just a *'Stasi'*-state, it was also a country in which – in many areas at least – people simply tried to lead normal lives. ... It was not just a gigantic education- and stultification-machine, but also a country in which culture thrived. The GDR destroyed many people and drove almost five million (*sic*!) out of the country, but it also, for a time at least, aroused people's enthusiasm.[32]

In trying to conceptualize the relationship between dictatorial authority and everyday life, Stefan Wolle has similarly suggested that 'the problem lies in perceiving the phenomenon GDR as contradictory, or at least ambivalent, in and of itself'.[33]

A number of commentators from sociology and history have responded to the many apparent contradictions of East German society with various GDR-specific terms that attempt to capture these paradoxes. The term 'education dictatorship' (*Erziehungsdiktatur*), for instance, has been suggested to highlight the paternalistic nature of the regime's attempts to educate its citizens, especially young people, to identify with socialist ideals and the East German state.[34] Stefan Wolle's term 'loving dictatorship' (*Diktatur der*

31  J. Kocka, 'Ein deutscher Sonderweg. Überlegungen zur Sozialgeschichte der DDR', *APuZG* 40/94 (7 October 1994), p. 44, cited in K. Jarausch, 'Care and Coercion', p. 55.

32  Peter Bender, *Unsere Erbschaft. Was war die DDR – was bleibt von ihr?* (Hamburg, 1992), p. 11.

33  Stefan Wolle, 'Herrschaft und Alltag. Die Zeitgeschichtsforschung auf der Suche nach der wahren DDR', *APuZG* 26/97, pp. 30–8.

34  Particularly stimulating has been Dorothee Wierling's work on youth and generation in the GDR. See D. Wierling, 'Die Jugend als innerer Feind. Konflikte in der Erziehungsdiktatur der sechziger Jahre',

*Liebe,* referring to *Stasi* chief Erich Mielke's infamous pronouncement 'But I love you all!') points in a similar direction by conceptualizing SED authority as a caring and disciplining father looking out for the best interests of East German subjects who found themselves in the position of immature children, of legal minors. The party leaders knew what was best, taught East Germans how to think, and treated opposition as *'Unerzogenheit'*, or bad upbringing, that needed to be remedied.[35] Certainly one of the more popular concepts has been Rolf Henrich's critique of GDR socialism as a 'tutelary state', which points to the central contradiction between the regime's emancipatory rhetoric and repressive practices. An East German lawyer and founder member of the civil rights organization 'Neues Forum', Henrich sought to renew what he called the 'enterprise of Enlightenment': people's 'self-realization through our own actions' which the SED's denial of individual rights for East German 'citizens' had stymied.[36] A number of other commentators have emphasized the curious *quid pro quo* of generous cradle-to-grave welfare provisions in exchange for uncontested party predominance. Günter Grass, for instance, has spoken of the GDR as a 'commodious dictatorship' and Konrad Jarausch has offered the very useful notion of a 'welfare dictatorship' that suggests not only a trade-off, but a more profound conceptual link between the dynamics of state support and civic impotence in the GDR.[37]

What all of these more modest and GDR-specific labels share is a concern to capture the central contradiction between the emancipatory (or at least well-intentioned) and repressive aspects of East German socialism, a contradiction which is often lost in the broader generic categorizations outlined above. But this recourse to a more specific terminology – which I broadly support in view of the rather abstract level of debate so far – certainly does not mean that overarching categorization is impossible or undesirable. Indeed, the degree of uniqueness of the specific features of the GDR which these labels highlight can ultimately only be established by implicit or explicit comparison with other regimes, for which more generally applicable concepts are necessary. We therefore need to assess the strengths and weaknesses of the various concepts as vehicles for explaining and contextualizing the dictatorial system in the GDR.

(Contd)
  in H. Kaelble *et al.* (eds), *Sozialgeschichte der DDR*, pp. 404–25; D. Wierling, 'The Hitler Youth Generation in the GDR: Insecurities, Ambitions and Dilemmas', in K. Jarausch (ed.), *Dictatorship as Experience*, pp. 307–24.
35 Stefan Wolle, *Die heile Welt der Diktatur. Alltag und Herrschaft in der DDR 1971–1989* (Berlin, 1998), pp. 126–8.
36 Rolf Henrich, *Der vormundschaftliche Staat. Vom Versagen des real existierenden Sozialismus* (Frankfurt, 1989).
37 Günter Grass, *Ein weites Feld* (Göttingen, 1995); Konrad Jarausch, 'Care and Coercion: The GDR as Welfare Dictatorship', in K. Jarausch (ed.), *Dictatorship as Experience*, pp. 47–69; K. Jarausch, 'Realer Sozialismus als Fürsorgediktatur. Zur begrifflichen Einordnung der DDR', *APuZG* B20/98, pp. 33–46.

# Evaluation
## The GDR as 'totalitarian' regime?

In spite of the continued deployment of the concept by some scholars and
the revival of its popularity after 1989, a variety of criticisms have been
advanced against the designation of the GDR as an instance of 'totalitarianism'. These range from arguments that it is a fundamentally flawed concept
with little heuristic value in and of itself to doubts about its applicability to
the particular case of the GDR regardless of its usefulness – and however
limited this might be – for understanding other dictatorial regimes. Of these
two general categories, I find the latter argument more convincing.[38]

To begin with the first position, categorical rejections of the totalitarianism concept have frequently been based on the perception that it is little
more than a Cold War anti-communist propaganda tool. Certainly this was
the official position of East German scholarship before 1989, which dismissed the totalitarianism 'doctrine' as nothing other than a 'basic compo-
nent of bourgeois ideology'.[39] Similar critiques of the political function of
totalitarianism theories as an anti-communist instrument of political integration could also be heard in the West during the 1970s and 1980s.[40] After
1989, a number of academics and politicians associated with the PDS
(*Partei des demokratischen Sozialismus*, the SED's successor party) have
maintained this uncompromising rejection of the concept, occasionally with
laconic reference to Marx's famous dictum that 'the ruling ideas of the age
are the ideas of the ruling class'.[41] Such summary dismissals are in my view
both inconsistent and dogmatic: inconsistent because the employment of
'totalitarianism' as an anti-communist term of abuse during the Cold War
(which the concept pre-dates, as we have seen) in many ways mirrors
the simultaneous and equally crude instrumentalization of Marx's ideas,
which (as most such critics would agree) nonetheless constitute a venerable
intellectual tradition; and dogmatic because they amount to a peremptory
denigration of an idea without any attempt to engage with it.

---

38  Ian Kershaw takes a similar position for the case of the Third Reich, *The Nazi Dictatorship*, pp. 36–7.
39  Autorenkollektiv unter Leitung von Gerhard Lozek, *Die Totalitarismus-Doktrin im Antikommunismus.*
    *Kritik einer Grundkomponente bürgerlicher Ideologie* (Berlin, 1985). It is worth noting that Lozek, along
    with a few other 'critical Marxist' scholars, has quite radically revised his views on this in the 1990s. Cf.
    G. Lozek, 'Zum Diktaturvergleich von NS-Regime und SED-Staat. Zum Wesen der DDR im Spannungsfeld
    von autoritären, aber auch demokratischen Strukturen und Praktiken', in Dietmar Keller, Hans Modrow
    and Herbert Wolf (eds), *Ansichten zur Geschichte der DDR*, vol. 4, pp. 109–21.
40  See, for instance, the rather polemical statement by Reinhard Kühnl, arguably the leading voice in the
    FRG, 'Zur politischen Funktion der Totalitarismustheorien in der BRD', in Martin Greiffenhagen,
    Reinhard Kühnl and Johann Baptist Müller (eds), *Totalitarismus. Zur Problematik eines politischen
    Begriffs* (Munich, 1972), pp. 7–21.
41  Cf. esp. the views of leading PDS politician Uwe-Jens Heuer, 'Totalitarismus – Karriere eines Begriffs',
    in *Marxistische Blätter* (1995) 3, pp. 65f.

A more substantial objection is that the totalitarianism concept conflates the form or structure of ruling systems with their content. As a result, the specific ideology and aims of these regimes (ultimately humanitarian in the case of communism and wholly inhumane in the case of Nazism) and the consequences of these differences are obscured.[42] This is closely related to the issue of whether the concept might actually imply a certain 'playing down' (*Verharmlosung*) of Nazi crimes, an issue we will deal with in more detail in Chapter 7. There are, in my view, both unconvincing and credible aspects to this objection. Rather unconvincing is the notion that communism and Nazism can be considered fundamentally different because of their different aims and intentions. Form and content cannot be hermetically separated from each other; the former certainly says something about the latter and the techniques of rule show some striking similarities. In addition, comparing the brutal *reality* of one regime with the humane *intentions* of another is obviously methodologically flawed. However, the objection that ideological differences did play a significant role in the development of these systems is quite justified. It is simply not the case that 'the ideological differences that undoubtedly existed ... were of no practical consequence' or that the focus on ideology as a significant difference between supposedly 'totalitarian' regimes is 'a mere assertion, an intellectual construct'.[43] As Sigrid Meuschel has rightly pointed out, real and significant differences grew out of the different ideologies. Whereas National Socialism was a quintessentially charismatic and 'emotional' movement, East German communism was relatively 'rational' and 'pseudo-scientific', indeed overly so insofar as it believed that the Party could control everything centrally. This meant that it had very different effects on East German society, ranging from patterns of social and economic change to the direct instrumentalization of the state apparatus.[44] Furthermore, communist ideology, and in particular the crass difference between its utopian claims and rather grim social reality, played an important role in shaping the nature of opposition in these regimes right up to and beyond the far-reaching reform efforts in Czechoslovakia under Dubcek.[45] Finally, the old assertion that it hardly matters for what ideological reasons the Nazis or communists persecuted their victims – that such differences are a mere 'intellectual theoretization' – may well be true with regard to the perceptions of the victims themselves (would one really care whether one was jailed or murdered by a Nazi or communist?), but it is an abnegation of the historian's task to ignore the role of ideology in the origin, motivation, and nature of different instances of persecution as merely 'theoretical'.[46]

---

42 One of the classic statements along these lines is Helga Grebing, *Linksradikalismus gleich Rechtsradikalismus. Eine falsche Gleichung* (Stuttgart, 1971).

43 Quoted from Horst Möller, *Materialien der Enquete-Kommission*, vol. IX, pp. 578–9, 584.

44 Sigrid Meuschel, 'Nationalsozialismus und SED-Diktatur in vergleichender Perspektive', *DA* 27:9 (1994), pp. 1001–3.

45 Hermann Weber, *Materialien der Enquete-Kommission*, vol. IX, p. 622.

46 See the exchange between Horst Möller and Sigrid Meuschel in *Materialien der Enquete-Kommission*, vol. IX, pp. 601–10, *passim*.

Probably the most compelling criticism is that totalitarianism concepts do not adequately describe the actual structures or sources of rule in specific regimes but rather tend to reflect the regimes' own aims, taking them, as it were, at their word. As numerous commentators have pointed out, totalitarian theories base their analytical tools on the very constructs which they seek to examine, thus reproducing the totalitarian ideology instead of analysing it.[47] The would-be 'totalitarian' party's ideological claims serve as the primary measure of reality rather than the actual social conditions and mechanisms of rule. As a result, the concept, however defined, cannot adequately grasp the peculiarities of the systems it proposes to classify. Even when applied to the apparatus of power itself, the 'home territory' of totalitarianism theory, it can paint a misleading picture. Neither the body of regime functionaries nor the mass organizations, especially at the grass-roots level, were as sleekly efficient or controllable as such models suggest.[48] More importantly, totalitarian concepts are clearly inadequate when analysing developments outside of this realm such as the social and cultural developments which help to shape and sustain dictatorial rule. Although sheer coercion was obviously crucial in maintaining the East German regime, its stability was based on more than just repression, as scholars have repeatedly emphasized.[49] The same basic shortcomings also explain why dissent and opposition are not well catered for by totalitarianism models and why it has relatively little to say about the regime's collapse.[50]

In response to these objections, supporters of totalitarian theories frequently contend that these issues are of secondary importance, that the totalitarian 'claims' or intentions of the ruling party are paramount.[51] But this leads to a fourth criticism, namely that the totalitarianism concept makes a fuzzy distinction between intentions and reality, or in other words between actual systems of domination as opposed to a 'tendency' towards total authority and control which opens up the possibility of extending it so widely that its analytical value is irretrievably diluted.[52] No one would

---

47  See especially W. Wippermann, *Totalitarismustheorien*; also Arnold Sywottek, '"Stalinismus" und "Totalitarismus" in der DDR-Geschichte', in *Deutsche Studien*, vol. 30 (1993), no. 117/118, pp. 25–38; Mario Keßler and Thomas Klein, 'Repression and Tolerance as Methods of Rule in Communist Societies', in K. Jarausch (ed.), *Dictatorship as Experience*, pp. 109–21.

48  I have attempted to argue this point in *Constructing Socialism at the Grass-Roots: The Transformation of East Germany 1945–65* (Basingstoke, 2000).

49  Cf. Mary Fulbrook, *Anatomy*, pp. 8–17; Ralph Jessen, 'DDR-Geschichte und Totalitarismustheorie', in *Berliner Debatte Initial*, vol. 5 (1995), no. 4, pp. 17–24; M. Keßler and T. Klein, 'Repression and Tolerance'.

50  Mary Fulbrook, 'The Limits of Totalitarianism: God, State and Society in the GDR', *Transactions of the Royal Historical Society*, series 6:7, pp. 25–52; Hermann Weber, *Materialien der Enquete-Kommission*, vol. IX, p. 622; Detlef Pollack, 'Die konstitutive Widersprüchlichkeit der DDR. Oder: War die DDR-Gesellschaft homogen?', *GG* 24 (1998), pp. 110–31.

51  Horst Möller, for instance, speaks of 'the goal – that is, not always the reality – of political co-ordination'. In his view, the failure to describe actual structures 'does not detract from the totalitarian claims'. *Materialien der Enquete-Kommission*, vol. IX, pp. 579, 581.

52  Cf. Gert-Joachim Glaeßner, 'Das Ende des Kommunismus und die Sozialwissenschaften. Anmerkungen zum Totalitarismusproblem', in *DA* 28:9 (1995), pp. 920–36. Kershaw again makes a similar point about the Third Reich, *The Nazi Dictatorship*, p. 38.

argue that the project of rulers is unimportant. Clearly, intentions to arrogate total power to a single party lie at the heart of any notion of a 'totalitarian' regime. But the projects of charismatic rulers such as Hitler or Stalin arguably show more differences than similarities to the systematized and increasingly stagnant post-Stalin regimes of Eastern Europe. Moreover, this focus on totalitarian 'claims' is itself rather vague insofar as it is not always clear what claims are being referred to: claims to exclusive authority and power, or claims on citizens' 'bodies and souls'? SED leaders maintained their total claims to authority from start to finish, allowing no political alternatives and legitimating their rule by the possession of an exclusive and putatively 'true' ideology. But far-reaching demands on bodies and souls were less characteristic of the regime by the 1970s when all that was asked from the general populace was outward conformity in exchange for social security and rising living standards.

This points to a final and most common criticism: that totalitarianism concepts, however defined, are fundamentally static.[53] Eckard Jesse's description of the GDR as 'autalitarian' clearly recognizes this problem, but still offers no explanation for why this change came about. Likewise, although Juan Linz and Alfred Stepan's designation of the GDR as 'post-totalitarianism' seems in many respects a useful re-formulation of the concept, it is much better at explaining the nature of the transition to democracy after 1989 than the developments that led up to the events of that year. Their very fitting concept of 'frozen' post-totalitarianism neatly captures the advancing political sclerosis at the 'top' of the regime, but nonetheless says little about the changing societal and generational currents underneath the surface ice of the regime's gerontocracy.[54]

The basic problem, it would seem, is that 'totalitarianism' is not really a theory. It is not a systematic set of related ideas which together add up to a coherent explanatory model. Rather, it is better understood and deployed as a loose concept or shorthand descriptive device, a 'list of different characteristics which does not designate any systematic internal cohesion' and which 'cannot indicate any social or political dynamic, any direction in which the uncontested coexistence of these characteristics in National Socialism, Stalinism and in part in the SED-dictatorship developed'.[55]

Understood in these terms, I see no reason for 'totalitarianism' as a concept to be wholly discarded in view of the remarkable similarities in the techniques of rule among a wide variety of twentieth-century dictatorial regimes that were shared by the GDR. It can indeed be quite useful as a shorthand linguistic label for describing a particular type of modern

---

53 Christoph Boyer, 'Totalitäre Elemente in staatssozialistischen Gesellschaften', in Klaus-Dietmar Henke (ed.), *Totalitarismus* (Dresden, 1999), pp. 79–91; Mary Fulbrook, 'The Limits of Totalitarianism'; W. Wippermann, *Totalitarismustheorien*; A. Sywottek, '"Stalinismus" und "Totalitarismus" in der DDR-Geschichte'; Ralph Jessen, 'DDR-Geschichte und Totalitarismustheorie'.
54 E. Jesse, 'War die DDR totalitär?'; J. Linz and A. Stepan, *Problems of Democratic Transition*.
55 Sigrid Meuschel in *Materialien der Enquete-Kommission*, vol. IX, p. 599.

dictatorial project with far-reaching mobilizing and plebiscitary intentions and for denouncing that project from a liberal–democratic standpoint. Along these same lines, it seems perfectly appropriate as a designation of any regime's 'total claims' to authority and unwillingness to recognize the autonomy of any sphere of social and political life in principle, however this might have worked out in practice. The term 'totalitarian' is clearly applicable to the GDR in all of these regards for most, if not all, of its history.

However, its usage beyond this seems largely fruitless. In analytical terms, it arguably obscures more than it reveals since it focuses on what are essentially superficial (if undeniable) similarities between very different regimes while simultaneously bracketing out serious consideration of social and cultural developments. Moreover, because of the multitude of different definitions of the term, its usage in any specific context is often confusing and misleading. On balance, the advantages the term presents for analysing the GDR are heavily outweighed by its disadvantages, which lie not only in its inherent conceptual shortcomings but also in the inevitable political colouring attached to it.

If the notion of 'totalitarianism' is to have any meaning beyond the very broad and generalized one outlined above, then it seems best to view it not as a system in itself, but as a radical phase in the development of certain modern authoritarian systems of rule that gives way to either collapse or systematization.[56] Defined in these terms, it is clearly applicable to both the Third Reich and Stalin's Soviet Union, where the 'state' in many ways was replaced by personality and where '"politics" – as a rationally expedient pursuit of limited goals – [was replaced] by ideological vision and unprecedented levels of state-sanctioned violence' towards the societies they ruled.[57] While this concept could be seen to cover certain aspects of the early years of the post-war Soviet satellite states including the GDR (above all the 'witch-hunt' atmosphere surrounding the political purges of the late 1940s and early 1950s), it most certainly is not applicable to the post-Stalin East European states, where the term becomes little more than a superficial epithet. Overall it would seem that the GDR can be considered a 'totalitarian' regime, but only at crippling expense to the concept itself.

## *The GDR as Stalinism?*

Does the concept 'Stalinism' present a more satisfactory designation of the dictatorial system in East Germany? It does boast a number of clear

---

56 An argument put forward by, among others, Ian Kershaw, 'Totalitarianism Revisited: Nazism and Stalinism in Comparative Perspective', *Tel Aviver Jahrbuch für deutsche Geschichte*, vol. 23 (1994), pp. 23–40.

57 Ibid., p. 33. This tends to support the view that terror is crucial for establishing and consolidating 'totalitarian' regimes in their early stages. Cf. Claude Lefort, *The Political Forms of Modern Society. Bureaucracy, Democracy, Totalitarianism* (Cambridge, 1986), who disagrees with Friedrich's consideration of terror as an 'aberration' and Linz's relegation of terror to a relatively unimportant criterion for 'totalitarian' status.

advantages. For one thing, it is more inclusive of social and economic phenomena than 'totalitarianism'. At the heart of most scholars' notions of 'Stalinism' is not only the centralization of political power, but also the state-directed social transformations such as forced collectivization, industrialization and expropriation of property, the creation of a new bureaucratic stratum of privileged 'cadre' loyal to the regime and the establishment of a particular kind of centrally planned economy. 'Stalinism' denotes, in other words, more than just a system of rule; it also refers to a particular socio-economic system, an 'organization of social mobility which created the upper stratum of Soviet society that helped support the political leadership'.[58] A second advantage when applied to the GDR is the emphasis it lays on Soviet influence in Germany, from its effects on the German Left in the inter-war years (the internecine struggles between communists and socialists which reverberated in the SBZ and early GDR) to particular Soviet institutions and practices imported into East Germany. Indeed, the notion of 'Stalinization' captures many of the crucial political and social developments of the 1940s and early 1950s, which saw the end of any specifically 'German' road to socialism with the onset of the party purges.[59]

Most importantly, the concept 'Stalinism' pays much closer attention to ideology, where the ideas that underpinned the state socialist system came from and the effects they had. 'Stalinism' lends itself especially well to distinguishing the particular brand of communism that prevailed in the Soviet bloc, including the GDR, from 'communism' in the broader sense as a set of political and social ideas largely pre-dating Stalin's rule and some capable of functioning within democratic and parliamentary states (such as France and Italy). Though usage of the term in this sense can, as we have already seen, harbour apologetic tendencies, this distinction is undoubtedly important in view of the quite vitriolic debate about the nature and extent of the 'crimes of communism' that has flared up after its collapse. The publication of Stéphane Courtois' 'black-book of communism' in 1997 has sparked a broad discussion somewhat similar to that following the publication of Solzhenitzyn's *Gulag Archipelago* in 1974.[60] Although much of the material presented in the book is uncontroversial, many of its conclusions are simplistic or lack a sense of proportion,[61] unequivocally condemning

58 Hans-Henning Schröder, 'Der Stalinismus – ein totalitäres System? Zur Erklärungskraft eines politischen Begriffes', in *Osteuropa* 2/1996, pp. 150–63, here p. 160.

59 It should be pointed out, however, that recent research into the 'Stalinization' of the SED has shown that the impetus behind this process came as much from within the German party as from the Soviet Union. Cf. Harold Hurwitz, *Die Stalinisierung der SED. Zum Verlust von Freiräumen und sozialdemokratischer Identität in den Vorständen 1946–1949* (Opladen, 1997); Andreas Malycha, *Die SED. Geschichte ihrer Stalinisierung 1946–1953* (Paderborn, 2000). On the party purges more specifically, see the exhaustive study by Thomas Klein, *'Für die Einheit und Reinheit der Partei'. Die innerparteilichen Kontrollorgane der SED in der Ära Ulbricht* (Cologne, 2002).

60 Stéphane Courtois (ed.), *Le livre noir du communisme: crimes, terreur, répression* (Paris, 1997).

61 See the sharp criticism by Eric Weitz, *Potsdamer Bulletin* 13 (July 1998), pp. 67–72. More polemical critiques are Jens Mecklenburg and Wolfgang Wippermann (eds), *'Roter Holocaust'? Kritik des Schwarzbuchs*

'communism' – treated here in far too monolithic fashion – as a criminal system and tracing this back to its very ideology. There can, of course, be little doubt that many horrific crimes were perpetrated under, and in the name of, communism. But surely Hermann Weber is correct to reject the idea that 'the' ideology of an undifferentiated notion of 'communism' was criminal.[62] This argument in no way suggests that Stalin alone was responsible for 'perverting' what was otherwise a basically sound idea. The point is rather that any evaluation of these issues must make some distinction between communism as radical social *movement* on the one hand (which itself comprised different traditions and practices) and repressive *regime* on the other. True, the movement itself displayed a certain tendency towards physical violence. But this was only one reason for the violence and terror of the communist regimes.

Despite these advantages, there are a number of problems associated with the term 'Stalinism' and its application to the GDR. At the most basic level, doubts must be raised about a concept that refers to a single individual and that suggests an intrinsic connection between a wide array of phenomena and the actions of one man. Does the very term 'Stalinism' perhaps obscure the real origins and nature of the system to which the term refers? It suffices for our purposes here to point out that the relationship between 'Stalin and his Stalinism' – the relative importance of the person and intentions of the great dictator as opposed to structural factors within Soviet society – has been hotly debated.[63] To relate this point more directly to the GDR, if Stalin himself is central to the system that bears his name, is there much point in using the term after his death in 1953? After all, the notion of 'de-Stalinization' is widely used to describe developments in communist societies after the mid-1950s (the end of arbitrary terror and the personality cult as well as the somewhat 'softer' pursuit of socio-economic goals after 1956). Characterizing the GDR after this period as 'Stalinism' can therefore be rather confusing. Even if one distinguishes as Weber does between *specific* traits that ceased and *general* ones that continued, there are nonetheless clear disadvantages associated with employing a concept or terminology so broad and flexible that it remains applicable even after certain of its central attributes no longer pertain.

Like totalitarianism, the concept of 'Stalinism' thus presents significant problems when applied to the whole of the GDR's history. Measured against Weber's criteria of 'Stalinism', the turbulent 1950s and the relatively quiet

(Contd)
    *des Kommunismus* (Hamburg, 1998); Johannes Klotz (ed.), *Schlimmer als die Nazis? Das 'Schwarzbuch des Kommunismus' und die neue Totalitarismusdebatte* (Cologne, 1999).

62  Hermann Weber and Ulrich Mählert (eds), *Terror. Stalinistische Parteisäuberungen 1936–1953* (Paderborn, 1998); also useful is Gerd Koenen, *Utopie der Säuberung. Was war der Kommunismus?* (Berlin, 1998).
63  Cf. J. Arch Getty and Roberta Manning (eds), *Stalinist Terror: New Perspectives* (New York, 1993); Ronald Grigor Suny, 'Stalin and his Stalinism: power and authority in the Soviet Union, 1930–1953', pp. 26–52; also, Mark von Hagen, 'Stalinism and the politics of post-Soviet history', in I. Kershaw and M. Lewin (eds), *Stalinism and Nazism*, pp. 285–310 offers a useful overview of debates, as does Chris Ward, *Stalin's Russia* (London, 1993).

1970s bear little resemblance to each other apart from the very basic structure of the GDR's political institutions. Moreover, it is exceedingly problematic to bring any period of the GDR's history, even the late 1940s and early 1950s, under the same heading as the Soviet Union of the 1930s. The Soviet Union under Stalin differed from the GDR *significantly* in its structure of political authority (i.e. the immense power of Stalin himself). Furthermore, it differed *fundamentally* in its degree of brutality and terror and *markedly* in the staggeringly mobile, unsettled nature of what has aptly been called the 'quicksand society' of the Soviet Union in the 1930s.[64] In response to these criticisms some scholars would maintain that the system always retained its *potential* for terror and that this was a crucial source of stability. Yet in my view this rationale for retaining the term 'Stalinism' after the 1950s only presents more problems. Not only does it tend to relativize the horrors of 'high Stalinism' in the Soviet Union (or, conversely, magnify those of the post-Stalin era), it also obscures the development of other important sources of stability in such systems.

These considerations have led many scholars to prefer the term 'post-Stalinism' for the East European state socialist regimes after the mid-1950s. This concept, which to my mind represents a clear improvement over 'Stalinism' when applied to the GDR, basically emphasizes Weber's distinction between 'specific' and 'general' features by viewing the changes that took place after Stalin's death as constituting a more fundamental break in regime typology. In its common usage 'post-Stalinism' designates, in other words, a system that had passed through the radical phase of Stalin's rule but still bore the stamp of this experience and retained many of the basic societal features that arose during this dynamic transitional period. The system in many ways resembles a shell of its former self: armed with oppressive political and security structures, but without the utopian self-belief and millenarian zeal to use them. Characterized by increasing systematization and ritualization, it is no longer as interested in competing with and defeating the West as in securing what achievements it has already made. The emphasis is no longer on change, but preservation, even via concessions if necessary – a notion which obviously fits very well with the Honecker era in particular, albeit in a merely descriptive, not explanatory, manner.

In summary, I would contend that the concept of 'Stalinism' is best limited to the 'specific' elements which Weber outlines (arbitrary terror, personality cult) and the period during which they flourished. Otherwise it is too broad and misleading in its connotations. It brackets together very different styles of governance and greatly underemphasizes the fundamental difference between the radicalizing dynamic of the Soviet Union under Stalin and the sclerotic stagnation of state socialism's later decades. For precisely the same reasons, the term's applicability – if at all – to the GDR is certainly

---

64 For these reasons, Martin McCauley, for instance, suggests that the GDR was never a truly 'Stalinist' regime even in the 1940s or 1950s. *The German Democratic Republic since 1945* (Basingstoke, 1983), p. 103.

best limited to the period before 1956, however half-hearted Ulbricht's 'de-Stalinization' was. Although 'Stalinism' does possess certain merits as a shorthand concept, it is difficult in the final analysis to escape Eckard Jesse's conclusion that its application to the GDR (especially if not qualified by 'neo' or 'post' for the period after the mid-1950s) tends towards both demonization and apologia: demonization in that the GDR was hardly like 'high Stalinism' in the Soviet Union, and apologia in that it suggests the basic health of the communist idea that had been perverted by 'Stalinism'.[65]

## *'Modern', 'educational' and 'welfarist'?*

Is the GDR, then, better conceived of by more the neutral, less politically loaded concept of 'modern dictatorship'? The answer depends entirely on what one means by the term. As I have already mentioned, its usage by historians since the early 1990s has sometimes proceeded in ways not intended by Kocka, who originally suggested it as no more than a generalized alternative to 'totalitarianism' designating certain 'modern' plebiscitary forms of dictatorial authority distinct from older or more traditional authoritarian regimes. Some of the criticisms of the term have therefore been off the mark, especially those positing a positive association with the word 'modern' and thereby completely missing the point of the concept.[66]

To be fair, the term does invite the question of the modernity of the East German system in a broader sense than merely its authoritarian techniques of rule. How much can the concept offer in this sense? As we have seen above, a number of aspects of the GDR were unambiguously 'modern' by any definition of the term: its ideology, its attempts at social engineering, its emphasis on technology, its deliberate break with many older traditions. The GDR was also well endowed with the macabre side of modernity: the secret police, the authoritarian nature of its welfare state, its overexploitation of the natural environment. However, it is equally clear that the GDR was not especially 'modern' in many ways. For one thing, Soviet-style socialism did not represent the 'modernizing' force in the highly developed industrial area of East Germany that it did in many other regions of Central and Eastern Europe, and certainly in Russia.[67] Moreover, even its own seemingly 'modern' emancipatory pretensions were ambivalent at best. A high proportion of women were in paid employment but there was no women's movement as such and the political sphere was heavily male-dominated. The deliberate conservation of a blue-collar workers' milieu was directly related to the weak service sector and general economic stagnation in the latter

---

65  E. Jesse, 'War die DDR totalitär?', p. 14.
66  For example, Wolfgang Schuller, 'Modern und fürsorglich?', *FAZ*, 13 May 1998, p. 10.
67  A point highlighted by Ivan Berend, *Central and Eastern Europe 1944–1993: Detour from the Periphery to the Periphery* (Cambridge, 1996).

decades.[68] In terms of methodology, the application of western-oriented concepts to communist systems raises a number of concerns quite apart from the normative problems associated with ideas of 'modernity' and 'modernization' in the first place. Conceived in this way, the concept of 'modern dictatorship' offers more questions than answers, more problems than solutions.

Employed as a more 'neutral' alternative to totalitarianism, the concept is of very limited analytical use. The reason for this is that it represents less an alternative to totalitarianism than a mere dilution of it, offering nothing significantly new. As Kocka describes it, the primary criteria of a 'modern dictatorship' are essentially synonymous with the basic features of 'totalitarianism': bureaucratic administration, modern means of control and mobilization, the mass party with its claims to absolute control, and the legitimation of these claims via a single, binding ideology.[69] To its credit, the concept is less politically loaded and avoids the terroristic associations with the Third Reich and Stalin's Soviet Union that are rather problematic for the GDR. But on balance it indeed seems little more than an 'anodyne substitution' for totalitarian models.[70]

A more promising approach in my view is to concentrate more on what was specific to the GDR in terms of its internal character and broader context. This is certainly not meant to suggest that it was a wholly unique regime beyond comparison with others; Soviet influence was a crucial part of the equation, and the GDR obviously showed a number of fundamental similarities with the other socialist regimes under Soviet hegemony. But much of the 'labelling' debate and 'model mania' that has pervaded the discussion since 1990 has seemed overly abstract and unconnected to actual historical developments, perhaps because much of it has been carried out by people who have done little or no empirical research on East Germany. Any understanding of the GDR needs to recognize a number of relatively unique features: above all its heavy reliance on the Soviet Union, its attempts to overcome the catastrophic first half of the twentieth century in Germany (i.e. its relation to the Nazi past), and its unique relationship to its 'other half' in the West. As I mentioned above, it is also crucial to recognize the fundamental contradiction at the heart of the state socialist project, the tension between its emancipatory goals and repressive practice. Some of the more modest GDR-specific concepts are quite good at this, in particular Konrad Jarausch's notion of 'welfare dictatorship'.[71] This concept captures the aims of the regime and especially the content of its policies (welfare, or *Fürsorge*, which connotes both individual care and collective assistance) better than ideas such as 'tutelary state' or 'educational dictatorship', which

---

68 Cf. Peter Hübner, 'Arbeiterklasse als Inszenierung? Arbeiter und Gesellschaftspolitik in der SBZ/DDR', in R. Bessel and R. Jessen (eds), *Grenzen*, pp. 199–223.
69 J. Kocka, 'The GDR: A Special Kind of Modern Dictatorship', pp. 21–2.
70 I. Kershaw, 'Totalitarianism Revisited', p. 25.
71 K. Jarausch, 'Care and Coercion'.

say little about what the regime was actually trying to 'teach'. It is also capable of going beyond merely *reflecting* the tension between care and coercion to positively *connecting* them by highlighting how the GDR's welfarist social provision was inextricably linked to its illiberal paternalistic practices; it was a 'nanny state' without the liberal ideological premises that could limit the extent of its intervention and control. The concept meshes particularly well with the development of a kind of 'post-utopian' materialist form of legitimation under Honecker, which itself is directly related to the GDR's financial indebtedness and eventual inability to 'deliver the goods' that helped undermine the regime's authority and ultimately contributed to its collapse. A final advantage worth mentioning is that it reflects East Germans' own ambivalent experiences and memories of the GDR as a caring and simultaneously coercive state, something that has certainly not always been the case in GDR historiography (discussed more fully in Chapter 8).

These controversies about which labels best describe the GDR are not just a part of historiography, but are also part of the broader process of 'coming to terms' with the East German past. Wrangling over terminology and abstract concepts often seems pointless. As should be amply clear from the above discussion, some concepts fit certain aspects more neatly, highlight certain themes more clearly, explain or describe certain developments more convincingly than others. One term or concept cannot possibly capture the complexities of the East German past or cover developments evenly over all four decades. I see no reason to try to do so. Torsten Diedrich and Hans Ehlert have summed up the problem neatly: 'Even if one were to combine the various models of interpretation and speak of a "modern socialist welfare-dictatorship of Stalinist-Soviet character", one would still hardly achieve conceptual mastery over the multitude of different phenomena and processes.'[72] Such scepticism is by no means intended to deny the undoubted importance of theory to historical understanding or to recommend a naïve empiricism, but rather to point out the limits of particular concepts against historical evidence. Surely the task of historians is to paint a more complex and nuanced picture of the East German past than the adherence to one concept or another would allow.[73]

Yet discussion about concepts and terminology is both necessary and important because words strongly influence contemporary perceptions and condition the questions we ask in the future. Since every concept has explanatory limits and ideological overtones, various terms will doubtless

---

72 Torsten Diedrich and Hans Ehlert, '"Moderne Diktatur" – "Erziehungsdiktatur" – "Fürsorgediktatur" oder was sonst? Das Herrschaftssystem der DDR und der Versuch seiner Definition', *Potsdamer Bulletin für Zeithistorische Studien* 12 (1998), p. 25.

73 It is with these concerns in mind that Hermann Weber has enjoined fellow historians 'to re-focus scholarly debates on content'. H. Weber, '"Assymetrie" bei der Erforschung des Kommunismus und der DDR-Geschichte? Probleme mit Archivalien, dem Forschungsstand und bei den Wertungen', *APuZG* 47/26 (1997), p. 8.

continue to compete as definitions of the GDR. That our views on the GDR have radically changed as the reluctance before 1989 to call it a 'dictatorship' has given way to a broad consensus that it was one – whether 'totalitarian', 'Stalinist', 'modern' or whatever – is a more than ample demonstration of the connection between the dominant conceptual vocabulary and interpretations derived from scholarly research. Indeed, one of the crucial issues since the collapse of the regime has been whether this conceptual shift has swung too far in the other direction, whether the focus on the 'GDR as dictatorship' has resulted in a too narrowly politics-oriented historiography and 'top-down' perspective on East German society that neglects the social and cultural realm and treats it as little more than an object of dictatorial manipulation. Can the history of state socialism in East Germany be sufficiently understood in terms of its system of rule? It is to this question that we now turn.

# 3

# *State and society in East Germany*

Assessing the social impact of the SED's 'socialist experiment' and evaluating the relationship between state and society in the GDR is one of the most important and challenging tasks facing historians of post-war Germany. Besides being a central question of interpretation in its own right, processes of social change are also crucial in explaining the root causes of the revolutionary events of 1989 and the collapse of the regime. Moreover, the relationship between political and social developments in the GDR has not been merely a historical question in post-unification Germany; the nature, extent and consequences of the regime's efforts at social control and homogenization provide indispensable background for understanding the social transformation in the 'new federal states' after 1989 as well. Finally, empirical enquiry into these issues has implications for our understanding of state–society relations well beyond the former GDR's borders, and indeed throughout the rest of the former Soviet bloc where access to archival sources is far more limited. For all these reasons, this has been an area of considerable interest and debate since 1990.

For many years, however, this was not a central focus of research. Although significant advances were made after the pathbreaking analyses of Ludz and others in the 1960s, the inaccessibility of internal sources and the questionable reliability of official data presented researchers with certain insurmountable barriers. This was not just a problem for Western researchers; there was also a great reluctance within the GDR to undertake serious societal self-examination. There were, for example, no sophisticated quantitative surveys of social structure carried out in East Germany, and the situation was little better with regard to qualitative surveys of social trends and popular opinion.[1] Perhaps more important than the scarcity of reliable information

---

1 To clarify this point, I should add that although social scientists as well as government authorities compiled an array of statistics on social structure, the categories with which they organized the data rendered them of little practical use.

was the fact that scholarly research on the GDR was widely geared towards serving political interests. In both East and West, portrayals of East German history performed a legitimatory function for the two competing states. In the GDR in particular, where the parameters of academic discourse were far narrower, history was an integral part of official attempts at legitimation and 'demarcation'. This legitimatory function was best served by a narrow political history of party resolutions, policy enactments and public figures who transformed the eastern part of the Reich into either the 'better Germany' or a Soviet puppet regime, depending on one's perspective. The instruments and techniques of social history, which often point more towards the contradictions and ambiguities of historical developments, were far less suitable towards this end. The purpose of historical research and the methodologies employed thus corresponded and, in conjunction with the perennial source problem, by and large encouraged a more traditional political historiography instead of social–historical research on East Germany.

With the downfall of the regime and the massive extension of the source base, a much more differentiated understanding of East German society has become possible. A huge amount of archival material and a rapidly growing scholarly literature are now available. Of course the nature and thematic coverage of the sources produced by such a political system invite a variety of different interpretations. The lack of independent societal institutions on whose sources social historians often rely means that one is forced to use material produced by and for the regime, which had very different intentions for the use of this information than historians and which tended in any event to focus on its own activities. Yet it already seems clear that the major issues of interpretation have more to do with different theoretical assumptions and ideological divides among scholars than with the problems presented by the sources. The debate is characterized by fundamental disagreements about the relationship between political and social developments under state socialism as well as about the boundaries and definition of what a 'social history' of the GDR might look like.

Much of the problem lies in the nature of the object under study. The GDR was first and foremost a product of international (dis)agreements and interventions and was only secondarily a 'social' entity. The social history of the GDR thus refers to an object that, all pre-1945 and post-1989 continuities of course notwithstanding, has an unusually distinct beginning and end point, both of which were determined in large measure by *political* interests, and indeed primarily those of the Soviet Union. A social history of the GDR is therefore not dealing, as is usually the case, with a social formation that broadly transcends a particular political order, as, for example, Poland or Hungary or for that matter 'Germany', all of which have witnessed a succession of different political regimes over the past century or so.[2] As a state,

---

2 Of course all social formations present definitional problems over time, and indeed immense ones in the case of the three examples cited, but the point about the GDR still arguably stands in relative terms.

the GDR is easy enough to define as a web of organizations and institutions that are now gone. When they collapsed, much of what constituted 'East German society' disappeared with them. Put rather pointedly, East German society owed many of its basic characteristics to the establishment of a particular political regime, and indeed one which in principle was not willing to grant autonomy to any area of society and which deliberately embarked on a programme of radical social reform.

This raises a number of difficult questions. Is there any point in talking about East German 'society' as a realm more or less distinct from 'politics'? Indeed, is it sensible or even possible to write a 'social history' of the GDR? If so, what would be the focus and how would it relate to the political structures of this most pervasive and interventionist regime? The different answers to these questions form one of the main theoretical debates since 1989 within scholarship on the GDR.

## Interpretations

Official self-descriptions of East German society before 1989 were, quite predictably, never concerned with these questions. Rather, they were based exclusively on a Marxist understanding of 'society' as the 'totality of social relations among people' which, determined by the means of production, developed through different historical 'formations' eventually to be subjected to rational planning and steering in the era of socialism through the knowledge and application of immutable laws of the social world.[3] According to these laws, the 'repressed classes' under capitalism had to abolish the remnants of the feudal elite – the large landowners, the industrial bourgeoisie as well as the traditional educated bourgeoisie – in order to gain and exert political power in the 'workers' and peasants' state' through their representative vanguard, the socialist party. The abolition of the private ownership of the means of production, the expropriation and redistribution of land, and the termination of bourgeois educational privileges were to usher in an egalitarian society in which class and status differences would be a thing of the past and social equality and justice would replace centuries of exploitation and repression. In official portrayals, this is precisely what happened in East Germany. The 'people's ownership' of industry, the land reform and agricultural collectivization, the transformation of the educational system and the introduction of an expansive system of welfare and subsidies together constituted a fundamental social revolution which left in its wake a more just and homogenous society composed of 'two classes and one stratum' – workers, farmers and a progressive, humanistic 'intelligentsia'.

---

3 See the entry for 'society' (*Gesellschaft*) and related terms in *Kleines Politisches Wörterbuch* (Berlin, 1988), pp. 324–39, *passim*.

Though few would doubt the far-reaching, even revolutionary nature of social change in the GDR, it was always plain to see that such an ideologically pious and hopelessly undifferentiated description of East German society was as fictitious as it was self-serving for the SED.[4]

The recent debate about the nature of East German 'society' was sparked by the sociologist Sigrid Meuschel in a highly influential study on the relationship between 'legitimation and party rule' which in many ways serves as a central reference point for much of the subsequent discussion.[5] Published in 1992 and grounded in the language of modernization theory, this study essentially represents a reversal of many of the earlier portrayals of East German societal development derived from this approach. Based on a systematic examination of SED ideology as manifested in published works, party programmes and resolutions – all available before the opening of the East German archives – Meuschel argues that 'the execution of the total claims of the party to steer the overall process of societal transformation fundamentally altered the character of society'. The realization of these claims demanded:

> [the] centralization of the economic, political and other societal resources, the destruction of the relative independence of class- and interest-groups, parties and associations, and in addition the dismantling of autonomous institutions and regulatory mechanisms such as the market and law, the public sphere and democracy.

Instead of a trend towards increasing societal differentiation which many scholars either claimed (or at least expected) to discern, and despite the SED's constant talk of a new East German 'society' as its ultimate goal, Meuschel contends that 'a power-politically inspired process of social non-differentiation took place, which robbed the economic, scholarly, judicial and cultural subsystems of their autonomy'. Somewhat ironically, in the final analysis it was not the state that 'withered away' in the course of the party's rule, 'it was rather a process of the withering away of society'. The end result of the claims of the total state was, in other words, a far-reaching 'shut-down' (*Stillegung*) of social institutions and a *de facto* fusion of politics, economics, law, art, even leisure as the state extended and consolidated its control over these various spheres of what is commonly called 'society' in Western liberal polities.[6]

In some respects this argument echoes the revived totalitarian approaches in its emphasis on the ever-expanding and all-pervading character of the state. Klaus Schroeder, for instance, has portrayed the GDR as a 'political

---

4 Cf. P. Hübner, 'Arbeiterklasse als Inszenierung?'. Internally, some East German authorities did make far more complex distinctions about social structure, as some of the recent work on consumption and market research has demonstrated. See Chapter 4, footnote 60.

5 Sigrid Meuschel, *Legitimation und Parteiherrschaft. Zum Paradox von Stabilität und Revolution in der DDR* (Frankfurt a. M., 1992).

6 Ibid., p. 10. Cf. also S. Meuschel, 'Überlegungen zu einer Herrschafts- und Gesellschaftsgeschichte der DDR', in *GG*, vol. 19 (1993), pp. 5–14. Comparable arguments based on a similar institutional approach have also been advanced by M. Rainer Lepsius, 'Die Institutionenordnung als Rahmenbedingung der Sozialgeschichte der DDR', in Kaelble *et al.*, *Sozialgeschichte*, pp. 17–30.

society' in which there was a 'far-reaching identity of private and public spheres, and in which there was to be almost no sphere free of state control'.[7] The totalitarian rule of the 'SED state' left effectively no autonomy in the economy, social institutions, the law, even everyday life. What the party decided was essentially put into practice by the state through a mixture of supervision and seduction, indoctrination and repression. The advantage of Meuschel's account over this rather one-dimensional portrayal is that it focuses not exclusively on the 'SED state', but also on the needs of and developments within the realms of the economy, law, and culture. Yet common to both views is the tendency to deal only with the formal system of power and thus the adoption of a decidedly 'top-down' perspective. This not only reduces historical reality to what is essentially a narrow political history, but also leaves the party and state apparatus as the only, or at least the only important, historical actors.

For these reasons, the thesis of the 'shut-down' society has been received with some scepticism among social historians. While there is little disagreement that the basic thrust of SED policy was aimed at the abolition of societal and institutional autonomy, doubts have been raised as to how far this actually succeeded and what the effects really were. Clearly, any attempt to answer this question cannot focus solely on the party and state but needs to consider seriously the role of ordinary East Germans as well as the ways in which social structures and processes impeded, shaped and adapted political incursions 'from above'. This recognition of the need to broaden the focus of historical research to include other actors and entities has prompted a search for guiding concepts that allow more room for the social dimension. Social historians are broadly in agreement about the necessity of approaching East Germany's social history as more than a series of party resolutions and political interventions. Yet within the parameters of this basic consensus, which should not be obscured by the following discussion concentrating on the differences of interpretation, the question of the relative emphasis placed on political and social factors has generated considerable discussion.

At one end of the spectrum are calls for a fundamental break with the idea of a 'shut-down' society. In an influential article in direct response to Meuschel's thesis, the historian Ralph Jessen has argued against the assumption of a 'one-sided relationship of dependence between state and society', suggesting instead the 'relative autonomy of the social dimension' in the GDR's history.[8] As he points out, SED policy was hardly reducible to the realization of a stringent plan or 'script', but was characterized by a mixture of ideologically based goals as well as significant improvisation

7 K. Schroeder (ed.), *Geschichte und Transformation*, introduction, p. 13. For an application of this approach see his synthesis, *Der SED-Staat*, pp. 512–46.
8 R. Jessen, 'Die Gesellschaft im Sozialismus. Probleme einer Sozialgeschichte der DDR', in *GG*, vol. 21 (1995), pp. 96–110.

to accommodate existing conditions. There was no socialist 'zero hour'; East Germany was not a *tabula rasa* upon which the party could build a new society. Industrial and confessional structures, city–countryside relations, the huge population shifts resulting from the expulsion of ethnic Germans from much of Eastern Europe, traditional professional and occupational structures as well as class-specific socio-cultural milieux were all part of the terrain on which East German socialism was to be built. Moreover, the SED's attempts to mould society often produced unintended results due to both the societal structure it inherited as well as the contradictions of its own policies, a prime example being the nearly ubiquitous networks of bartering for scarce goods and services that emerged as a result of the shortcomings of the planned economy. East German 'society' should, according to Jessen, be approached as an 'autonomous, not a derivative entity', a 'highly complex mixture of the ideologically-derived dictatorial attempts on the one hand and the remaining and newly emerging net weight of social structures and processes on the other'. In this view there was, simply put, 'no shut-down society'.[9]

At the other end of the spectrum is the widely employed notion of a '*durchherrschte Gesellschaft*', or society 'ruled through and through', which in its most common usage (as distinct from its originally intended meaning)[10] essentially represents a dilution of Meuschel's argument. As Jürgen Kocka, one of Germany's leading social historians, has argued in a much-cited article, social-historical research on the GDR must proceed less from the conventional question of the social basis of political processes and more from the political basis of social processes.[11] In his view, the 'ubiquitous political power' of the party had 'deep and far-reaching societal consequences' and 'moulded society all the way into its finest branches'. East German society was, therefore, 'to a large degree an artificial product of political power, dependent on, formed and made possible by it' – a point which is scarcely different from Meuschel's own argument. However, Kocka simultaneously insists that East German society and everyday life cannot be reduced to political steering and control: 'It would be false to assume that party and state rule totally moulded and determined society.'[12]

The questions that arise from these partially compatible and partially opposing positions are, first, the extent to which the regime succeeded in transforming social structures and regulating social life, and second, where

---

9 Ibid., pp. 99, 100.
10 Alf Lüdtke originally coined the term in '"Helden der Arbeit" – Mühe beim Arbeiten. Zur mißmutigen Loyalität von Industriearbeitern in der DDR', in Kaelble *et al.* (eds), *Sozialgeschichte*, p. 188, and has subsequently clarified it as meaning not a society completely ruled by political interests, but rather that, relative to more open societies, authority was more a feature of everyday life in the GDR. 'For the GDR, it is not the success of authority strategies that are conspicuous, but rather the extent to which they served as a reference point.' Alf Lüdtke, 'Die DDR als Geschichte. Zur Geschichtsschreibung über die DDR', *APuZG* B36/98, p. 12.
11 J. Kocka, 'Eine durchherrschte Gesellschaft', in Kaelble *et al.* (eds), *Sozialgeschichte*, pp. 547–53, here p. 547.
12 Ibid., pp. 548–50.

the limits to this process lay – the 'limits of dictatorship', to borrow from the title of an anthology of essays co-edited by Ralph Jessen and Richard Bessel.[13] What acted as social brakes to dictatorial control, how can these limits be defined and where were they located? A number of factors can be readily discerned. In their introduction, Bessel and Jessen point to the structural and mental continuities from the pre-socialist past; the organizational chaos of the immediate post-war years which hardly gravitated in favour of strict central control; the existence of a wealthier and more attractive Western alter-ego which placed constraints on various policy areas (especially before the border around West Berlin was closed) and precluded easy appeals to patriotism; the obviously heavy dependence on the Soviet Union; and perhaps most importantly, what one might call the self-induced limits, the overburdening of the regime inevitably resulting from the very attempt to control and steer everything. Despite the unlimited nature of the SED's power in principle, in practice there was a wide variety of limits to what could be surveyed and controlled by the regime. The relationship between political authority and social change was therefore more fluid and far less uni-directional than notions such as a 'political society' or 'shut-down' society would suggest.

Two further discussions of state–society relations in the GDR have advanced the debate in slightly different directions. In a stimulating introduction to a collection of essays on authority and '*Eigen-Sinn*' (which one might loosely translate as 'a sense of one's interests'), Thomas Lindenberger has argued forcefully against any neat conceptual division between 'active' rulers and 'passive' ruled, and has criticized the polar oppositions of 'state' and 'society' as fundamentally flawed.[14] Borrowing from Alf Lüdtke's earlier work on shopfloor politics and the history of everyday life,[15] he contends that dictatorial rule must not be conceived as something wholly separate from society and social practices, but rather needs to be approached as a social process in and of itself. At base, authority is a product of social interaction between rulers and ruled, and dictatorial control must be understood as existing in an interdependent relationship with ordinary people's own meaning and agency. As Lüdtke has put it, authority (*Herrschaft*) and society (*Gesellschaft*) 'should not be conceived as opposites or as elements of a hierarchy ... Authority is socially produced – society and individuals are shaped by authority.'[16] Although the SED regime managed to abolish the autonomy of social organizations, its representatives at the

13  R. Bessel and R. Jessen (eds), *Die Grenzen der Diktatur: Staat und Gesellschaft in der SBZ/DDR* (Göttingen, 1996).
14  T. Lindenberger, 'Die Diktatur der Grenzen. Zur Einleitung', in T. Lindenberger (ed.), *Herrschaft und Eigen-Sinn in der Diktatur. Studien zur Gesellschaftsgeschichte der DDR* (Cologne, 1999), pp. 13–44.
15  Alf Lüdtke, *Eigen-Sinn. Fabrikalltag, Arbeitererfahrungen und Politik vom Kaiserreich bis in den Faschismus. Ergebnisse* (Hamburg, 1993); A. Lüdtke (ed.), *Herrschaft als sozialer Praxis. Historische und sozio-anthropologische Studien* (Göttingen, 1991).
16  Alf Lüdtke, 'Die DDR als Geschichte. Zur Geschichtsschreibung über die DDR', *APuZG* B36/98, p. 3.

grass-roots – the factory secretaries, the local police plenipotentiaries (*Abschnittsbevollmächtigte*, or ABVs), the FDJ functionaries, etc. – nonetheless depended on a degree of popular cooperation in order to carry out orders from above, whether to adopt new farming techniques, to fulfil plan quotas or to make a good crowd showing for May Day parades. Coercion and indoctrination alone were hardly suitable for encouraging people to become an honorary union representative, a member of an arbitration committee, a police assistant or a National Front local representative. Indeed, there was a certain interest in ensuring that not all such matters were left to party zealots. Thus ordinary people played a part in the construction of East German socialism, and indeed one that was more than merely reactive. To be sure, adopting a defensive posture in response to incursions 'from above' was common enough, and one clearly should not lose sight of the gross assymetry of this power relationship. But ordinary people could frequently use the structures at hand in their own interests, adapting and changing them in the process.

This micro-historical 'bottom-up' perspective on state–society relations has implications for our understanding of politics and society in the GDR more generally. In Lindenberger's view, 'East German society' (in the sense of a social realm not wholly controlled by the regime) clearly existed, but only at the lowest proximal level of social organization where some small degree of autonomous interest articulation was possible – the small worlds of the factory floor, the village, the office. Although this echoes in some ways both the 'totalitarian' notion of residual 'islands of separateness' emphasized by Friedrich and Brzezinski as well as Günter Gaus' famous description of the East German 'niche society' of family, friends, and garden allotments that existed outside of the 'official' system,[17] what is crucially different about Lindenberger's conceptualization is the emphasis on *overlap* – not separateness – between the formal/public and informal/'private' world. These small worlds were not so much 'islands of separateness' as limited fields of interaction and negotiation between regime and society. Moreover, these remnants of societal autonomy were not just a residual hangover from the pre-socialist past, but in many ways acted as an 'informal' substitute for the lack of formal independent interest representation that the party dictatorship brutally repressed. In Lindenberger's view, East German society was, therefore, 'neither dead nor shut-down, but above all limited' to the local level and relatively small groups of people.[18]

The sociologist Detlef Pollack has similarly argued for the need to break down the oppositions of 'politics' and 'society', though from the more 'top-down' perspective of structural sociology than the 'history from below' approach. Despite employing the same modernization–theoretical principles as Meuschel, Pollack reaches the very different conclusion that the result of the SED's attempt to control and manipulate all elements of society was not

---

17  Günter Gaus, *Wo Deutschland liegt* (Munich, 1983).
18  T. Lindenberger, 'Die Diktatur der Grenzen', p. 36.

its absorption by the state, but rather a number of insoluble societal tensions. In his words, the GDR was a 'constitutively contradictory' society, torn between a variety of opposing societal forces such as the requirements of the formal economic system versus informal networks, the impetus of political homogenization versus the need for differentiation in modern industrial society, the mantra of egalitarianism versus the harnessing of self-interest, to name just a few.[19] These contradictions were, according to Pollack, as unavoidable as they were destabilizing – unavoidable insofar as the SED was unwilling to cede social power to any other institutions, associations or individuals that could represent and potentially resolve these alternatives; and destabilizing insofar as the state socialist system had little chance of surviving once these fundamental and irreconcilable contradictions came into the open. The GDR therefore gave the *impression* of stability as long as these contradictions were kept 'invisible' by the closed society and lack of an independent public sphere, but rapidly fell apart at the seams once they were exposed. To avoid any confusion, it should be stressed that the SED's far-reaching stranglehold on societal institutions is not at issue here. Pollack's point is rather that enforced societal *uniformity* under strict party control must not be confused with greater societal *coherence*. In his view, the result of the SED's attempts to homogenize society was actually quite the opposite – social fragmentation and disintegration – due to its underestimation of the strength and persistence of inherited social structures and its refusal to give free rein to any social forces, consequently failing to activate them, resolve them, or bind them effectively into the system.[20]

Although the approaches we have briefly summarized here do not lend themselves to neat categorization, they can, broadly speaking, be understood as falling into two fairly distinct categories. One influential interpretation, echoing totalitarianism theory, contends that East German society was essentially a product and object of dictatorial intervention which left little significant scope for societal autonomy. Thus the 'social history' of the GDR (both in the sense of a sectoral history concerned specifically with social structures and processes as well as the more synthetic notion of a 'history of society') can by and large be treated as a 'political history' of the SED's efforts to transform and control society which were essentially – though of course not perfectly – realized by the power of the one-party state. By contrast, the dominant position among social historians rejects the notion of a one-sided relationship of dependence or 'primacy of politics'. It is necessary, however, to distinguish between two different approaches within this category of

---

19  Detlef Pollack, 'Die konstitutive Widersprüchlichkeit der DDR. Oder: War die DDR-Gesellschaft homogen?', in *GG* 24 (1998), pp. 110–31. A very similar version of this article appeared in English as 'Modernization and Modernization Blockages in GDR Society', in K. Jarausch (ed.), *Dictatorship as Experience*, pp. 27–45.

20  See also the quite pointed exchange between Pollack and Sigrid Meuschel in *GG* 26 (2000), 'Machtmonopol und homogenisierte Gesellschaft. Anmerkungen zu Detlef Pollack', pp. 171–83; 'Die offene Gesellschaft und ihre Freunde', pp. 184–96.

interpretation. First, it is widely accepted that there were various limits to the dictatorial control of East German society, though there is some debate as to the degree of societal autonomy or dependence that actually existed. Second, it has been argued that the opposing categories of state and society must be transcended and replaced by an emphasis on the interaction between political and social processes as well as between the regime and ordinary people.

We can now assess the merits and shortcomings of these different approaches on the basis of recent social-historical research on the GDR.

# Evaluation

An evaluation of the relationship between politics (the intentions and policies of the governing authorities) and social developments (the changing structures and practices of interaction between individuals and groups) in the GDR must begin by recognizing that there are two issues at stake: first, the question of the nature and degree of independent or semi-independent interest articulation that existed beyond the web of party-controlled social organizations; and second, how effectively the regime was able to steer processes of social change and development more broadly speaking in the direction it wanted. Although somewhat distinct, these two different perspectives on the 'social realm' in the GDR are of course closely interrelated in that the SED's intention to create a society according to Marxist–Leninist design plans incorporated both of these elements. Interest-representation was to become the sole preserve of the leading party which supposedly governed in the 'objective' interests of the working masses, and the SED was also to act as both instigator and principal executor of a programme of radical social revolution in East Germany. The underlying question that links these two issues is how far the actual results of this intended social revolution – that is, the real face of East German socialist society – corresponded to the rationale behind it, and what factors served to augment, hinder or re-shape it.

As the preceding survey of interpretations makes clear, this question can be approached both at different levels (the aggregate or the particular) as well as from different perspectives ('top-down' or 'bottom-up'). The aggregate level is the obvious place to start. There can be little doubt, and, indeed, there is little disagreement, that the socialist regime brought about major, fundamental social change in East Germany. Structures of class, patterns of ownership and wealth distribution, access to education, gender relations, contours of work, family life and religiosity – all these witnessed far-reaching transformation over the forty years of East German socialism. Of course there were changes in many of these spheres in Western societies over the same period. But overall they went significantly further in the GDR than in the West, including its Western counterpart, the FRG. The fact that both the nature and degree of these changes were more than a reflection of 'secular' societal trends common to the entire industrialized world testifies to the power of the socialist party/state in deliberately bringing about social transformation. The abolition of private ownership of land and industry, the installation of a centralized economic planning system, the politically and socially selective control of education and career advancement (whereby 'working-class' background and/or political reliability were paramount), the repression of nearly all forms of autonomous, independent organizations (clubs, unions, citizens' leagues, etc.) and opposing political parties representing diverse social interests – no sphere was excluded in principle from the SED's claims to complete monopoly over society. There is, then, plenty of reason to stress the immense power of the dictatorial regime in effecting social change and controlling social processes. Many, though by no means all, historians would agree with Kocka that political domination and dictatorial intervention must serve as the basis for the examination of the GDR's social history.[21]

But clearly the matter cannot be left there. Political domination may be the starting point for a social history of the GDR, but it is not necessarily the end point. The notion that 'the cause of all societal transformations was exclusively political'[22] cannot convincingly be maintained on methodological or empirical grounds. Methodologically, this one-dimensional 'totalitarian' interpretation unacceptably reduces history to little more than a narrow definition of politics in which the regime *per se*, its structures, its organs of repression and its leaders (and of course the Soviets) appear as the only important actors. The role of ordinary East Germans, the weight of older social structures, milieux and mentalities is by and large left out of the analysis. Even worse, it does not even raise the question of how the regime's social vision was carried out on the ground or to what degree the outcomes corresponded to the intentions. The picture that consequently emerges is of a broad correspondence between intentions and outcomes, between rhetoric and reality, thus by and large taking the communist societal project for granted and thereby reproducing, albeit in a mirror-image reversal, the very picture of East German society that the SED purveyed in its propaganda. Needless to say, such an approach that emphasizes the omnipotence of the communist regime can offer few explanations for its eventual disintegration and collapse apart from various 'design flaws' (economic rigidity and lack of democratic legitimacy) in the very plans that it implemented.[23] A final problem with this approach is that it posits a clarity of purpose and design on the part of the SED leadership that obscures both the constraints within which its plans could be carried out as well as the often pragmatic, improvised response to the societal conditions confronting them, whether in the form of material concessions to key professional groups, toleration of informal

---

21  J. Kocka, 'Eine durchherrschte Gesellschaft', p. 547.
22  Wolfgang Schuller in *Berliner Zeitung*, 28/29 March 1998.
23  A point emphasized particularly by Detlef Pollack, 'Die konstitutive Widersprüchlichkeit der DDR'; 'Die offene Gesellschaft und ihre Freunde'.

networks of trading and procurement, or the rather inegalitarian introduction of individual incentives in order to enhance labour performance.

Indeed, a plethora of empirical studies published since the early 1990s has
highlighted the inadequacies of such an exclusively politics-centred approach.
The findings of recent social-historical research (especially on the formative
years of the GDR, the period from the latter 1940s to the early 1960s) point
clearly to a much more complex relationship between the revolutionary designs
of SED policy and actual social developments in East Germany. The emerging
picture of the 'socialist transformation' is a mixture of ideologically derived
intervention on the one hand and the unpredictable, unplanned actions of
ordinary people on the other. In practice, the transformation of East German
society could not merely be a process of dictation but also entailed a degree of
negotiation, however implicit, informal and asymmetrical it may have been.
Although the end result must undoubtedly be regarded by any standard as
fundamental social change, it now appears that the SED's various political
interventions into society and its efforts to control all social developments were
often neither immediately *nor completely* realized on the ground, and in many
cases only a more 'workable' version could ultimately be implemented.[24]

This is certainly becoming clear with regard to many professional groups.
Although the denazification of the professions – which had been, to varying
degrees, quite successfully Nazified in the Third Reich – was widely deemed
a crucial prerequisite for the creation of a 'new Germany', reconstruction
was the order of the day, for which professional expertise was sorely needed.
Policy regarding these groups was thus determined by two not fully compatible sets of interests: on the one hand, securing an adequate supply of appropriately skilled and experienced experts necessary for economic recovery,
educating the younger generation and maintaining public health; and on the
other, replacing the 'reactionary' and 'bourgeois' professionals with a new
elite drawn from the previously underprivileged and supposedly 'progressive'
classes of workers and farmers.

The scale of the transformation and the degree of political control varied
considerably between different groups. At one end of the scale, the teaching
profession underwent particularly rapid and thorough change because of its
perceived importance in securing the 'democratic order' in East Germany as
well as the fact that roughly 85 per cent of teachers at all levels had been
members of the Nazi party. After the war roughly half of all teachers in the
SBZ were immediately purged and replaced by thousands of inexperienced
and ill-prepared 'new teachers'.[25] In stark contrast to the situation in the

---

24 Cf. the important collection of essays in *AfS* 39 (1999), whose thematic focus was the social history of
the GDR.
25 Brigitte Hohlfeld, *Die Neulehrer in der SBZ/DDR 1945–1953: Ihre Rolle bei der Umgestaltung von
Gesellschaft und Staat* (Weinheim, 1992). It should be noted that roughly one-half of those dismissed in
1945 had been reinstated by the 1950s in order to alleviate the dire shortage of teachers that resulted
from the purges. For an overview in English, see John Rodden, *Repainting the Little Red Schoolhouse:
A History of Eastern German Education, 1945–1995* (Oxford, 2001).

schools, the medical profession offers probably the clearest example of social and occupational continuity. Because of concerns about public health, few were removed from their positions despite the fact that in some areas up to 80 per cent had been members of the NSDAP. Even the traditional 'bourgeois' pattern of self-recruitment into the medical profession remained by and large intact into the 1960s due to the maintenance of stringent Latin requirements and the necessity of steering a softer course *vis-à-vis* doctors in order to keep them from leaving for the West. The huge demand for doctors and their ability to emigrate westwards before 1961 undermined a thoroughgoing reform of the medical profession for at least two decades.[26] Ralph Jessen has found similar, though somewhat less pronounced, personnel continuity and 'milieu persistence' among the university professoriate, especially in the scientific and technical fields that were less politically sensitive and of greater immediate economic benefit than the humanities.[27] The transformation and political control of the engineering profession were also hindered well into the 1960s by both the failure to recruit significant candidates from among the industrial working class as well as the need to retain older 'bourgeois' experts through lucrative special contracts and perks.[28] Eventually there was far-reaching change in all professions. However, it is now becoming clear that the transformation took much longer and was more contradictory, the older continuities lasted longer and were more persistent, than has often been assumed.[29]

At the other end of the social spectrum, the SED's attempts to mobilize workers and gain control over production in the 'People's Own' factories suffered from arguably more serious problems. This was especially disappointing for party officials given the high hopes initially placed on the historic role

---

26  Cf. Anna-Sabine Ernst, *'Die beste Prophylaxe ist der Sozialismus': Ärzte und medizinische Hochschullehrer in der SBZ/DDR 1945–1961* (Münster, 1997); Anna-Sabine Ernst, 'Von der bürgerlichen zur sozialistischen Profession? Ärzte in der DDR 1945–1961', in Bessel and Jessen (eds), *Die Grenzen*, pp. 25–48; Christoph Kleßmann, 'Relikte des Bildungsbürgertums in der DDR', in Kaelble *et al.* (eds), *Sozialgeschichte*, pp. 254–70, especially p. 258. At the Humboldt University, the percentage of children from professional families studying medicine during the 1950s and early 1960s remained around 10 per cent higher than the average for all faculties, reaching 30 per cent by 1963, by which time the percentage of workers' children studying medicine was only slightly higher at around 35 per cent.

27  Ralph Jessen, *Akademische Elite und kommunistische Diktatur. Die ostdeutsche Hochschullehrerschaft in der Ulbricht-Ära* (Göttingen, 1999). However, it should be noted that the SED was relatively successful in transforming East German universities in comparison to neighbouring regimes. John Connelly, *Captive University: The Sovietization of East German, Czech, and Polish Higher Education, 1945–1956* (Chapel Hill, 2000).

28  Dolores Augustine, 'Frustrierte Technokraten. Zur Sozialgeschichte des Ingenieurberufs in der Ulbricht Ära', in Bessel and Jessen (eds), *Die Grenzen*, pp. 49–75.

29  This point can be extended to include the persistence of 'bourgeois' values and norms (aided by the SED itself), specific confessional milieux and notions of occupational prestige. Cf. Anna-Sabine Ernst, 'The Politics of Culture and the Culture of Everyday Life in the DDR in the 1950s', in David Barclay and Eric Weitz (eds), *Between Reform and Revolution: German Socialism and Communism from 1840 to 1990* (New York, 1998), pp. 489–506; C. Kleßmann, 'Relikte des Bildungsbürgertums in der DDR', C. Kleßmann, 'Zur Sozialgeschichte des protestantischen Milieus in der DDR', *GG*, vol. 19 (1993), pp. 29–53; Helmut Steiner, 'Berufsprestige im DDR-Alltagsbewußtsein der 60er Jahre', in Ludwig Elm, Dietmar Keller and Reinhard Mocek (eds), *Ansichten zur Geschichte der DDR*, vol. 8 (Bonn/Berlin, 1997), pp. 100–23.

of the industrial workforce. Although the communist regime indeed managed to refashion the structures and culture of work in the factories in a number of ways, for the most part these were contrary to intentions. The initial hopes among broad sections of the industrial workforce for a socialist-inspired transformation of Germany after the horrors of Nazism quite rapidly turned into disillusionment and disinterest once the party began taking over the initially elected interest-representing bodies in the factories, the shop councils and union organizations.[30] Moreover, because of the lack of a clear wage incentive and the constant shortage of skilled labour, the regime continually had to wrestle with the problem of substandard productivity, poor industrial discipline and wage inflation. Attempts to raise productivity showed little effect, not least because many factory managers were anxious to keep shopfloor discontent beneath the threshold of conflict even if this came at the expense of the planned economy. Shopfloor disputes over the introduction of 'harder' work norms or performance-related pay, the reduction of bonuses, crackdowns on extended lunch breaks, etc. were often settled *en locale* via informal mechanisms of conflict regulation that ultimately had to be tolerated to maintain the social peace, and thus also to uphold the appearance of a healthy and ideologically sound relationship between the workers and 'their' state.[31]

Sometimes these attempts at control in the factories had the opposite effect to what was initially intended. The most obvious example was the introduction of the 'socialist brigades' in the latter 1950s, modelled on the Soviet 'shock brigades' of the 1920s and 1930s. Though intended as a means of increasing productivity and 'educating' workers into 'socialist citizens', the brigades served rather as a forum for the collective articulation of workers' own interests *vis-à-vis* factory managers. They were widely instrumentalized by workers as a means of gaining greater autonomy and decision-making power within the factories, including demands for establishing their own norms, calculating their own bonuses, procuring supplies, even deciding on such matters as vacation leave, hiring and firing.[32] Although the

---

30 Many workers soon began to draw comparisons between their lack of rights under the Nazis and under the new communist regime. Cf. P. Hübner, '"Wir wollen keine Diktatur mehr..." Aspekte des Diktaturenvergleichs am Beispiel einer Sozialgeschichte der Niederlausitzer Industriearbeiterschaft 1936 bis 1965', in J. Kocka (ed.), *Historische DDR-Forschung*, pp. 215–32; P. Hübner, 'Die Zukunft war gestern: Soziale und mentale Trends in der DDR-Industriearbeiterschaft', in Kaelble *et al.* (eds), *Sozialgeschichte*, pp. 171–87. For an interesting emphasis on rupture, not continuity, in workers' experiences, see Helmut Smith, 'The Demography of Discontinuity in Bitterfeld, 1930–1953', in Peter Hübner and Klaus Tenfelde (eds), *Arbeiter in der SBZ-DDR* (Essen, 1999), pp. 811–22.

31 Peter Hübner, *Konsens, Konflikt, Kompromiß. Soziale Arbeiterinteressen und Sozialpolitik in der SBZ/DDR 1945–1970* (Berlin, 1995); P. Hübner, 'Balance des Ungleichgewichtes. Zum Verhältnis von Arbeiterinteressen und SED-Herrschaft', in *GG*, vol. 19 (1993), pp. 15–28; P. Hübner, 'Arbeitskonflikte in Industriebetrieben der DDR nach 1953. Annäherungen an eine Struktur- und Prozeßanalyse', in Poppe *et al.* (eds), *Zwischen Selbstbehauptung und Anpassung*, pp. 178–91; Jeffrey Kopstein, *The Politics of Economic Decline in East Germany, 1945–1989* (Chapel Hill, 1997); C. Ross, *Constructing Socialism at the Grass-Roots*.

32 On the brigades, see especially Jörg Roesler, 'Die Produktionsbrigaden in der Industrie der DDR. Zentrum der Arbeitswelt?', in Kaelble *et al.* (eds), *Sozialgeschichte*, pp. 144–70; Jörg Roesler, 'Gewerkschaften und Brigadebewegung in der DDR, Ende der 40er bis Anfang der 60er Jahre', *BzG*, vol. 38 (1996),

SED cracked down on these brigades in 1960, the practice of informal negotiation at the factory level and the attendant problems of wage drift and
insufficient productivity gains remained a central feature of the socialist
shopfloor right up to the collapse of the regime. 'Real existing socialism' in
the factories of the GDR bore little resemblance to the SED's initial vision.[33]

The socialist transformation of the countryside, though in the end more
successful from the SED's point of view, faced similar problems at the grass-
roots. Recent research into the reception and realization of the SED's campaigns for land reform and agricultural collectivization in the villages shows
a much more gradual and contested process than the statistics on land redistribution or the growth of collective farming suggest. Although the land
reform of the 1940s clearly constituted a deep structural caesura in terms of
land ownership and distribution, its social effects were also shaped by existing village milieux. In many local communities older habits of social defer-
ence proved a persistent obstacle to the drive to dispossess the large
landlords, as did the deep-rooted orientation towards large estate farming
prevalent in some areas. Old networks of social relations in the villages
readily lent themselves to corruption in the distribution of land and inven-
tory, often benefiting the established and relatively well-off farmers instead
of the landless 'new farmers' as intended. The subsequent collectivization
campaigns were similarly dogged by older village continuities, habits of
individual work and notions of private property. Indeed, the tight thicket of
social contacts in the countryside meant that village functionaries were
often unreliable representatives of the regime. Their divided loyalties often
hindered as much as supported collectivization efforts. Although the corpus
of rural functionaries was far more reliable and professionalized by the
1960s, even the 'fully collectivized countryside' after the all-out collectivization campaign of spring 1960 was in many ways a hybrid of the SED's aims,
farmers' interests and the older village milieu. For one thing, it took several
years to get many collective farms that existed on paper actually to farm
collectively. Moreover, the divide between the haves and have-nots frequently passed into the new collective structure all but unscathed. Wealthier
farmers often acted in supervisory roles, and it was fairly common for them
to form collectives that excluded any weaker farms. Yet by the mid-1960s
most farmers became resigned to their fate and the collectivized system was

(Contd)
no. 3, pp. 3–26; Jörg Roesler, 'Probleme des Brigadealltags: Arbeitsverhältnisse und Arbeitsklima in volkseigenen Betrieben', *APuZG*, 47/38 (1997), pp. 3–17; 'Zur Rolle der Arbeitsbrigaden in der betrieblichen
Hierarchie der VEB: eine politik- und sozialgeschichtliche Betrachtung', *DA*, vol. 30 (1997), pp. 737–50.
See also P. Hübner, '"Sozialistischer Fordismus?" Oder: Unerwartete Ergebnisse eines Kopiervorganges.
Eine Geschichte der Produktionsbrigaden in der DDR', in Alf Lüdtke *et al.* (eds), *Amerikanisierung*,
pp. 96–115; P. Hübner, 'Syndikalistische Versündigungen? Versuche unabhängiger Interessenvertretung
für die Industriearbeiter der DDR um 1960', *JHK* (Berlin, 1995), pp. 100–17; Rüdiger Soldt, 'Zum
Beispiel Schwarze Pumpe: Arbeiterbrigaden in der DDR', *GG*, vol. 24 (1998), pp. 88–109.
33 On industrial workers generally, see the exhaustive anthology edited by Peter Hübner and Klaus
Tenfelde, *Arbeiter in der SBZ-DDR* (Essen, 1999). On the long-term political effects of the productivity
problems in the factories, see esp. J. Kopstein, *The Politics of Economic Decline*.

firmly established. Besides having no alternative parties or organizations to represent their interests, farmers also had no *informal* village equivalent to the established practice of 'wage deals' in industry (instances of petty corruption notwithstanding). Perhaps most important, in many areas the 'village milieu' that had so long hindered and refracted the regime's attempts to transform and control the countryside was itself gradually eroding under the force of migration to the cities and conglomeration of individual farms.[34]

Gender equality and women's emancipation counted as 'one of the greatest accomplishments' of the GDR and were continually presented as 'proof' of the 'superiority of socialism over capitalism'. Based on the socialist definition of women's emancipation as freedom from social dependence on men and equality in relation to the means of production, SED policy in this sphere followed two interrelated goals: to mobilize women's labour for the economy and, more generally, to establish equal rights, pay and opportunities for men and women. With the help of a broad array of social policies geared towards enabling women to combine work and family (crèches, maternity leave), by the 1980s the GDR had one of the highest rates of female employment in the world at around 90 per cent, compared to approximately 50 per cent in West Germany. Yet questions have nevertheless been raised about the actual extent of 'emancipatory' change. It has frequently been pointed out that the bulk of social support was less for 'women' than for 'mothers' and that the lack of corresponding measures supporting paternity leave – even in comparison to some West European countries – meant that men were not better integrated into family activities. Thus easing the combination of work and family for women – the classic 'double burden' – actually conserved rather than undermined traditional gender roles and unequal life chances. Most East German women underwent a career setback with the birth of children. As was also the case in the West, women were greatly underrepresented in the professions and were more poorly paid even with equal qualifications despite all the advancement measures.[35] In addition, traditional notions of 'men's' and

---

34 On the land reform and collectivization, see esp. Arnd Bauerkämper, *Ländliche Gesellschaft in der kommunistischen Diktatur: Zwangsmodernisierung und Traditionen in Brandenburg von 1945 bis zu den frühen sechziger Jahren* (Cologne, 2002); A. Bauerkämper (ed.), *'Junkerland in Bauernhand'? Durchführung, Auswirkungen und Stellenwert der Bodenreform in der Sowjetischen Besatzungszone,* (Stuttgart, 1996); A. Bauerkämper, 'Von der Bodenreform zur Kollektivierung. Zum Wandel der ländlichen Gesellschaft in der Sowjetischen Besatzungszone Deutschlands und DDR 1945–1952', in H. Kaelble *et al.* (eds), *Sozialgeschichte*, pp. 119–43; A. Bauerkämper, 'Die Neubauern in der SBZ/DDR 1945–1952. Bodenreform und politisch induzierter Wandel der ländlichen Gesellschaft', in R. Bessel and R. Jessen (eds), *Die Grenzen*, pp. 108–36; N. Naimark, *The Russians*, pp. 150–66; C. Ross, *Constructing Socialism at the Grass-Roots.*
35 Cf. Heike Trappe, *Emanzipation oder Zwang? Frauen in der DDR zwischen Beruf, Familie und Sozialpolitik* (Berlin, 1995); Grit Bühler, *Mythos der Gleichberechtigung in der DDR* (Frankfurt a. M., 1997). See also Gisela Helwig, 'Frauen im SED-Staat', in *Materialien der Enquete-Kommission*, vol. III: 2, pp. 1223–74; A. Sorensen and H. Trappe, 'Frauen und Männer: Gleichberechtigung – Gleichstellung – Gleichheit?', in Johannes Huinink *et al.* (eds), *Kollektiv und Eigensinn. Lebensläufe in der DDR und danach* (Berlin, 1995), pp. 189–222. Also J. Huinink and M. Wagner, 'Partnerschaft, Ehe und Familie in der DDR', in J. Huinink *et al.*, pp. 145–88; L. Ansorg and Renate Hürtgen, 'The Myth of Female Emancipation: Contradictions in Women's Lives', in K. Jarausch (ed.), *Dictatorship as Experience*, pp. 163–76; Dagmar Langenhahn and Sabine Roß, 'The Socialist Glass Ceiling: Limits to Female Careers', in K. Jarausch, pp. 177–91.

'women's' work proved remarkably persistent in the GDR. Although by the 1970s East German women were relatively independent both financially and in terms of family planning, the GDR nonetheless remained a 'patriarchal' society that, in the words of one observer:

> reproduced anew the social inequality of women and men ... beginning with the education system, through occupational qualification, the structuring of career and work, and via its one-sided social policy geared towards the compatibility of employment and motherhood instead of parenthood.[36]

As these examples demonstrate, the socialist transformation of East Germany was both more gradual and contradictory than either the SED's revolutionary rhetoric or notions of 'totalitarianism' would suggest. Older social networks, structures and orientations significantly slowed and refracted the changes. But they could not hinder them altogether. By around the mid-1960s the main thrust of the SED's social programme was complete. The face of East German society as it appeared until the late 1980s was becoming recognizable. As numerous observers have commented, in the shadow of the Wall there emerged a tacit, pragmatic arrangement between rulers and ruled that by and large held sway until the latter 1980s. In contrast to the increasingly differentiated society in West Germany, characterized by a more open and liberal political culture with the growth to maturity of a new generation in the 1960s, the basic structure of East German society was increasingly 'undifferentiated', at least insofar as its many organizations and institutions were controlled by the SED and interspersed with party cadre. From this comparative perspective, the most conspicuous characteristic of 'real socialist' society was undoubtedly the degree of interpenetration with the SED, which was not prepared to declare any realm of society beyond its sphere of influence. Yet it is inadequate to leave the matter there, for society and everyday life in the GDR clearly amounted to more than dictatorial tutelage.

For one thing, certain realms of social life retained a degree of autonomy from the politically controlled organizations. Networks of family and acquaintances, neighbourhoods, villages, even work collectives served as nodes of semi-independent social interaction that were simultaneously part of the broader social fabric, and thus ultimately influenced by the official parameters of social life. Although family life in the GDR was strongly influenced by state policies encouraging high levels of female employment (and making childcare in crèches the norm rather than the exception), the family still served as a primary fixture of a private sphere in which a largely 'unpolitical' personal life could be pursued. Much the same could be said more generally of the famous 'datcha' or 'garden allotment' culture in East Germany which Western observers have emphasized since the 1960s. These relatively autonomous realms were a central feature of social life in the

36 Marina Beyer, preface to G. Winkler (ed.), *Frauenreport '90* (Berlin, 1990), p. 8.

GDR and served as a kind of 'ideal world' (*'heile Welt'*)[37] at one remove from the everyday frustrations and pressures of conformity.

Besides these residual pockets of autonomy, there also developed a range of informal social relations and processes that effectively compensated for the lack of any formal representation of group interests under the one-party state. Because unions and other organizations served essentially as mouthpieces for the SED, social concerns and interests were by and large articulated through informal networks of friends and acquaintances that could pursue common interests out of 'public' view. As a substitute for a functioning market, for instance, there developed personal bartering circles where goods and services could be traded, often without the exchange of money. These rudimentary market structures were particularly useful for trading luxury or scarce goods such as used automobiles.[38] Likewise, as a substitute for genuine civil or consumer rights, letters to satirical magazines or especially petitions to state authorities frequently served as a means of short-circuiting the system and having one's views or complaints heard.[39] The delicate balance of interests informally maintained in the factories in lieu of unions is yet another example. The effect of these informal networks was in many ways ambiguous since they served both to support as well as undermine the official system. While they mitigated many of the worst shortcomings of the planned economy and political system, they also made economic and social processes far less controllable for the central authorities.[40]

The existence of a wealthy and attractive Western counterpart just across the border also exerted a powerful influence on East German society, conspicuously giving the lie to communist rhetoric about the demise of capitalism and the superiority of socialism. The 'virtual emigration' in front of the television that took place daily in most East German households continually reinforced perceptions of West Germany's wealthy consumer society. The widespread dreams of the 'golden West' and the function of the Deutschmark as an unofficial second currency nurtured and represented an alternative value system in direct competition with 'real existing socialism' in the GDR. Western clothing styles, music and leisure activities were particularly prominent among the younger generation, and were tolerated by the authorities after the SED abandoned its hopeless crusade against 'Western decadence'

---

37  S. Wolle, *Die heile Welt der Diktatur. Alltag und Herrschaft in der DDR 1971–1989* (Berlin, 1998).

38  Before the introduction of used car advertisements in the 1980s, cars were informally advertised for sale by leaving a window slightly open for written offers to be posted through. Cf. Jonathan Zatlin, 'The Vehicle of Desire: The Trabant, the Wartburg, and the End of the GDR', *GH*, vol. 15 (1997), pp. 358–80.

39  On petitioning during the final years of the regime, see J. Zatlin, 'Ausgaben und Eingaben: Das Petitionsrecht und der Untergang der DDR', *ZfG*, vol. 45 (1997), pp. 902–17. See also the more general but somewhat problematic overviews by Felix Mühlberg, 'Konformismus oder Eigensinn? Eingaben als Quelle zur Erforschung der Alltagsgeschichte der DDR', *Mitteilungen aus der kulturwissenschaftlichen Forschung*, vol. 19 (1996), pp. 331–45; also I. Merkel and F. Mühlberg, 'Eingaben und Öffentlichkeit', in I. Merkel (ed.), *'Wir sind doch nicht die Mecker-Ecke der Nation'. Briefe an das DDR-Fernsehen* (Cologne, 1998), pp. 9–32.

40  On the function and effects of such informal networks in Russia, see Alena Ledeneva, *Russia's Economy of Favours: Blat, Networking and Informal Exchange* (Cambridge, 1998).

in the 1960s. Although the East German media did its best to counter the positive image of the West by emphasizing the less salubrious aspects of capitalist society such as unemployment and criminality, such efforts were largely in vain due to popular scepticism towards the official media as well as the fact that such social problems remained abstract to the vast majority of East Germans not permitted to travel west.

As a means of conceptualizing this mixture of political intervention 'from above' and the various forces that hindered it on the ground, the idea of the 'limits of dictatorship' seems in many ways to recommend itself. While not denying the immense power of the regime to effect social change and control societal developments, it nonetheless pays attention to the many brakes to dictatorial control – whether deriving from pre-socialist legacies or the SED's own policies – that so often hindered and deflected the SED's social programme. As useful as this concept has been, it nonetheless harbours certain drawbacks. Superficially at least, it does put people and processes excluded by the 'totalitarian' paradigm back into the historical picture. Policy-makers and enforcers are not the only *dramatis personae*; 'ordinary' people, their ideas, agendas and actions are included as well. Yet it also reproduces the basic conceptual framework of this paradigm in two interrelated ways. First, by taking the intentions of the regime as the starting point for examination, both approaches measure the actual results of the SED's social policies – successful or otherwise – in its own terms. Common to both views is a weighing-up of plans versus outcomes, of social developments 'on paper' versus what happened 'in practice'. The measuring stick remains the intentions of the regime. Second, both concepts suffer from the same notion of dictatorial power as something vaguely locatable at the 'centre' of the regime and emanating outwards towards its own periphery over the society which it governed. The difference lies in whether one sees this power as essentially limitless or encountering certain formidable limits, beyond which it does not reach. Although I am not suggesting that this was the intention behind the term, the usage of the phrase 'limits of dictatorship' does invite this conceptualization of power as divided into 'politics-dominated' and 'politics-free' areas of society. If one explicitly jettisons this idea of power as definable by limits and instead views it as a more diffuse and ubiquitous field of social influence,[41] it is far easier to overcome the conventional dichotomy between 'regime' and 'society' and reach a more subtle understanding of their relationship as areas of overlap, or better still as fields of negotiation and articulation of different values and interests.

This is precisely the point of 'authority as social praxis' advanced by Lüdtke and Lindenberger.[42] 'Authority' in this view is more than an assymetrical

41 As do Lüdtke and Lindenberger, employing a conceptualization of power based on the work of Michel Foucault, though comprising both 'discourse' as well as an apparatus.
42 A. Lüdtke (ed.), *Herrschaft als soziale Praxis. Historische und sozial-anthropologische Studien* (Göttingen, 1991), pp. 9–63; T. Lindenberger, 'Die Diktatur der Grenzen'; A. Lüdtke, 'Alltagsgeschichte und ihr möglicher Beitrag zu einer Gesellschaftsgeschichte der DDR', in Bessel and Jessen (eds), *Die Grenzen*, pp. 298–325.

power relationship based on social institutions, coercion and a legitimating ideology (the classic Weberian concept of power); it is also a process of interaction and mutual dependence between rulers and ruled that can rest on informal structures and practices as well as formal ones. Seen in this light, political authority is a process of give and take, of compensation in exchange for subjugation. Of course, one must not overlook the huge imbalance of power, the mechanisms of control and repression that differed markedly from liberal democratic polities. As proponents of the 'totalitarianism' paradigm are keen to point out, any approach that diverts attention away from the concentration of power in the hands of political leaders, the lack of democratic accountability and the organs of repression or that posits any meaningful popular input into political decision-making processes, runs the risk of playing down the negative aspects of the regime and ultimately blurs the distinction between democracy and dictatorship.[43] As real as these risks are, I see little evidence that scholars adopting this approach are obscuring these distinctions or beautifying the regime; if anything they are merely balancing out the hitherto heavily regime-centred debate. In the meantime a substantial amount of recent research on the interactions between the East German populace at large and the representatives of the regime at the grass-roots has significantly enhanced our understanding of how these processes of asymmetrical negotiation, of give-and-take, worked.

Obvious though it seems, it is worth stating explicitly how unhelpful it is to pit state versus society in East Germany (or anywhere else, for that matter). One of the distinguishing characteristics of the GDR was that the state did not so much rule *over* society as *through* it.[44] Probably the clearest expression of this was the huge participation rates in mass organizations such as the FDJ or especially the FDGB (which boasted some ten million members, or around 60 per cent of the entire population). Although these statistics can, on the one hand, be interpreted as an indication of a 'totalitarian' attempt at mass mobilization, on the other, they also indirectly suggest that everyday practices in the mass organizations hardly resembled the vaunted 'transmission' function allotted to them. At the local level, the FDJ was far more effective as a dance organizer than as a crucible for creating new 'socialist personalities', and even the central party authorities had to recognize and eventually make concessions to the predominance of Western youth culture. According to a youth survey carried out in 1969, only one-fifth of FDJ members based their membership on political conviction, only one-half found FDJ-life interesting and one-fourth reported that there had been no more than one local member assembly in the previous six months.[45]

43 Cf. S. Mampel, in *Politische Systeme in Deutschland* (Berlin, 1980), p. 142.
44 A point made emphatically by Mary Fulbrook, 'Methodologische Überlegungen zu einer Gesellschaftsgeschichte der DDR', in Bessel and Jessen (eds), *Die Grenzen*, pp. 274–97.
45 SAPMO-BA DY30/IVA2/2021/370, 'Kurzfassung über Probleme und Folgerungen zur Bewußtseinsentwicklung Jugendlicher in der DDR, die vom Zentralinstitut für Jugendforschung anläßlich der "Umfrage 69" vorgelegt wurden', pp. 11–12.

The FDGB, despite encompassing almost everyone in paid employment, was all but invisible to its masses of members and arguably served more to waste the energies of thousands of honorary functionaries than to motivate the workforce.[46] Structures such as the work brigades and collective farms were also characterized by a certain give-and-take at the local level and could, as we have already seen, be instrumentalized by ordinary people. Even the tightly controlled process of censorship was based on a degree of negotiation between different groups (publishers, ministers, artists, scientists, educationalists) with different interests (financial, political, aesthetic, pedagogical) and as such was influenced by social forces.[47] It seems almost needless to say by this point that it is a great impoverishment of our understanding of the GDR's history to reduce East German 'society' merely to formal intermediary structures that were repressed by the one-party state, thus obscuring these localized networks of interaction.

To flip the perspective around, the 'state' also comprised more than just the central authorities and cannot be clinically separated from 'society'. Local officials, factory managers and low-level functionaries were by no means always reliable representatives of the central authorities. They were as much a part of GDR society as they were cogs in the machinery of the state. Often there was precious little to distinguish them from 'ordinary' East Germans in terms of their political opinions and loyalties, especially in the early years. Although enormous personnel problems had to be expected in the 1940s and 1950s, many rank-and-file functionaries continued to play a rather dubious role well after the regime was established, sometimes 'going native' when facing their local clientele over farming practices, working conditions, wages and bonuses, housing complaints, etc.[48] It was often exceedingly difficult or impossible for many functionaries on the ground to apply 'official' rules or principles to their everyday decisions and activities. The common practice of settling issues over payment and conditions in the factories informally and without interference from higher levels of the state or party apparatus unfamiliar with local conditions and the everyday concerns of production (paramount among them the retention of a sufficient labour supply) was not the only, merely the most conspicuous, example of this.

For all of these reasons, it would seem that the cleavages in East German society are more usefully conceived as running between the centre and the periphery – in other words between the programme of the political leadership and social realities at the grass-roots – than between 'regime' and 'populace' or 'politics' and 'society'. But does this mean that 'society' in the GDR

---

46  Cf. the excellent study by Sebastian Simsch, *Blinde Ohnmacht. Der Freie Deutsche Gewerkschaftsbund zwischen Diktatur und Gesellschaft in der DDR 1945 bis 1963* (Göttingen, 2002).

47  Cf. Sylvia Klötzer and Siegfried Lokatis, 'Criticism and Censorship: Negotiating Cabaret Performance and Book Production', in K. Jarausch (ed.), *Dictatorship as Experience*, pp. 241–63.

48  I have attempted to argue this at length in my *Constructing Socialism at the Grass-Roots: The Transformation of East Germany, 1945–1965* (Basingstoke, 2000). See also J. Kopstein, *The Politics of Economic Decline*; T. Lindenberger, 'Creating State Socialist Governance. The Case of the Deutsche Volkspolizei', in K. Jarausch (ed.), *Dictatorship as Experience*, pp. 125–41.

is best understood as a localized, proximal phenomenon, as a very real part of 'real existing socialism' albeit 'limited' to a small scale and small units as Lindenberger suggests? There is certainly much to recommend this view. Apart from the churches, which were the only formally autonomous institutions in the GDR after the landmark 1978 Church–State agreement, it is only at this level that we find significant collective interest articulation. It is primarily here that we encounter the informal functional substitutes for those intermediary structures and institutions that we normally call 'society' in Western liberal parlance. In addition, this focus on the local negotiation of power between rulers and ruled has the salutary effect of expanding our view of the social dimension beyond mere residual 'islands of separateness' (such as the half-legal and illegal opposition groups of the 1980s, the West-oriented youth subculture and the tolerated 'niches' of the private world) that lay by and large outside the influence of the 'official', formal sphere. Yet in spite of the great advantages of this approach, the notion of a 'limited society' still invites a rather narrow view of the social dimension by confining it to small-scale structures and local processes above which the dictatorially controlled 'political realm' presumably held sway. This conceptualization, too, circuitously reproduces the very distinction between the social and political realms that the focus on the interaction between rulers and ruled seeks to break down. Can we really separate a broader 'political' realm above the local level from the influences of older social structures, new social trends and processes? Did the existence and effects of this 'limited society' not have far-reaching political implications for the regime? Is it possible to employ this more 'interactive' conception of social and political processes in the GDR for understanding East German society in the broadest sense?

I would suggest that we can, and indeed that we must if we are to offer an adequate explanation of the great paradox of the 1980s: namely, the uneasy coexistence on the one hand of continued conformity and stagnation and on the other of new currents of disintegration and dissent which eventually fed into the mass exodus, the mass demonstrations and the revolutionary events of 1989. We will return to debates surrounding the fall of the regime in Chapter 6. Nonetheless, for our purposes here the question of how an 'undifferentiated' or even a 'limited' and localized society, indeed, one that showed relatively few signs of a nascent 'civil society' such as in Poland or Hungary during the course of the 1980s, could slip so quickly out of party control and become mobilized so strongly against the regime has to be considered.

Although there are no clear-cut answers to this question, Detlef Pollack's notion of the 'constitutive contradictoriness' of East German society (awkward though it is in English translation) seems to offer a plausible approach.[49] Instead of reconciling or resolving the conflicting societal pressures in the GDR – political homogenization versus the need for functional

---

49 D. Pollack, 'Die konstitutive Widersprüchlichkeit'; D. Pollack, 'Modernization and Modernization Blockages'.

differentiation, central economic planning versus individual initiative, demarcation from versus orientation towards the West, formal organization versus informal networks, breaking with or celebrating and maintaining national traditions – the basic characteristic of East German society was constant and systemic tension between them. In each of these cases, the socialist experiment in the GDR drastically underestimated the persistence and inherent strength of these societal pressures and as a result was constantly faced with unintended consequences. Whether it was the need for more devolved economic decision-making, the motivating power of individual self-interest, the attractiveness and partial emulation of the Western model or the development of informal trading networks, state actions produced different effects than were intended *to which the state itself then had to adjust*. In other words, social structures and processes had far-reaching (not just localized and proximal) political consequences. Just as there were no completely 'politics-free' zones in East German society, so too were there no areas of politics completely immune from social forces.

The leadership responded to these unintended effects by attempting to integrate them into the formal system itself: introducing performance incentives and widening pay differences, paying attention to consumer desires, increasing economic exchange with the West, tolerating informal trading networks, reviving older national symbols and traditions as a means of political integration, etc. As Pollack paradoxically puts it, 'the extensive reduction of social reality, which was connected with the socialist construction of society, was, in other words, compensated for by a strange recognition of social complexity, which had been ignored initially'.[50] This closely echoes Ralph Jessen's earlier argument that

> The unique feature about this political-social system was not that society was 'shut down'. Rather, it seems much more as if the ever-expanding, undifferentiated, unlimited state, precisely because it had lost its limits, in a certain sense became increasingly *vergesellschaftet* (which one might translate as 'shaped by society').[51]

Of course the goal of these adjustments was not to devolve decision-making or strike a balance with other interests, but rather the securing of party power in the face of these challenges. This meant that the fundamental problem – the centralization of authority – remained in place, thus blocking the necessary reform of the system. As long as these societal tensions were kept under the surface through the control of public debate, the GDR appeared to be a stable state. But with the emergence of an independent public sphere in autumn 1989, facilitated by the disintegration of the outer barriers of the system, the regime rapidly fell apart under the strain.

The homogenizing pressures of the SED's social programme were, then, ultimately counterproductive, and indirectly encouraged the formation of

50 D. Pollack, 'Modernization and Modernization Blockages', p. 40.
51 R. Jessen, 'Die Gesellschaft im Staatssozialismus', p. 106.

subcultures and alternative value systems that some political scientists were recognizing before 1989.[52] Indeed, by the 1980s these pressures were also producing some rather heterogenous and inegalitarian results which appear to have contributed to the eventual societal mobilization against the regime.

Empirical research on social class and mobility has clearly shown that generation is a key factor for understanding East German social structure and how processes of political integration and stabilization changed over time.[53] Due to both the purges of older elites as well as the westward population drain before 1961, the 1950s and early 1960s witnessed unprecedented opportunities for upward mobility for those with the 'correct' political sensibilities or nominally 'working-class' backgrounds. A large portion of this *'Aufbaugeneration'* owed its social position to the socialist state and many understandably developed a certain identification with it. Already by the mid-1960s, however, opportunities for upward mobility were drying up. The class structure became less fluid since many positions were already filled by relatively young cadre nowhere near retirement age. To make matters worse, the new service class increasingly began to recruit from among its own ranks, thus reproducing and reinforcing the new social stratification. The overall outcome by the 1970s was, in contrast to the utopian rhetoric, an increasingly stagnant society that was particularly frustrating for the younger generation, 'blocked from without by the Wall, and blocked from within by a frozen, rigid social structure'.[54] It was no coincidence that the bulk of demonstrators in 1989 were under 45 years of age. Besides the generational divide, there were of course other forms of inequality within socialist society that were hardly new in the 1980s: special privileges, payment differentials, regional prioritization of consumer provision (i.e. favouring Berlin).[55] And of course the spectrum of social inequality was not as wide as in the West; the absolute differences between groups were smaller and the relative lack of consumer goods made displays of status

52  For instance, Antonia Grunenberg, *Aufbruch der inneren Mauer. Politik und Kultur in der DDR 1971–1990* (Bremen, 1990); Christiane Lemke, *Die Ursachen des Umbruchs 1989. Politische Sozialisation in der ehemaligen DDR* (Opladen, 1991). See also Winfried Thaa *et al.*, *Gesellschaftliche Differenzierung und Legitimitätsverfall des DDR-Sozialismus* (Tübingen, 1992).

53  Among the first studies to suggest a strong connection between social mobility and political stability was the path-breaking oral history project of L. Niethammer, D. Wierling and A. von Plato, *Die Volkseigene Erfahrung. Eine Ärchaeologie des Lebens in der Industrieprovinz der DDR* (Berlin, 1991). Cf. also L. Niethammer, 'Erfahrungen und Strukturen. Prolegomena zu einer Geschichte der Gesellschaft der DDR', in Kaelble *et al.*, *Sozialgeschichte*, pp. 99–105. On social structure and mobility generally, see Heike Solga, *Auf dem Weg in eine klassenlose Gesellschaft? Klassenlagen und Mobilität zwischen Generationen in der DDR* (Berlin, 1995); Johannes Huinink *et al.* (eds), *Kollektiv und Eigensinn*; Karl Ulrich Mayer and Martin Diewald, 'Kollektiv und Eigensinn: Die Geschichte der DDR und die Lebensverläufe ihrer Bürger', *APuZG* B46/96, pp. 8–17; Heike Solga, 'Klassenlagen und soziale Ungleichheit in der DDR', *APuZG* B 46/96, pp. 18–27.

54  R. Jessen, 'Mobility and Blockage during the 1970s', in K. Jarausch (ed.), *Dictatorship as Experience*, pp. 341–60, here p. 346.

55  Scholarly work on social inequality and privilege in state socialism goes all the way back to the 1950s, and in particular the pathbreaking work of Milovan Djilas, *The New Class: An Analysis of the Communist System* (New York, 1957).

more difficult. But such 'objective' differences were arguably less important than the gaping chasm between official rhetoric and social realities. Moreover, it was widely perceived that social inequalities were growing. A key example was the expansion of the so-called 'Intershops' (shops selling luxury items in exchange for Western currency) since the 1970s, which made access to Western currency (predominately through relations in the West) a key factor in individuals' living standards. The new social stratifications that arose from such developments were a source of widespread popular anger and flatly contradicted the SED's stated goal of creating an egalitarian society in which everyone should be rewarded according to their accomplishments instead of 'according to the residence of their aunt', as the communist dissident Wolfgang Harich bitterly put it.[56]

Irreconcilable societal tensions, a widespread feeling of stagnation and a consequent pressure for alternatives all combined to undermine the SED's political hegemony and mobilize East German society 'from below'. In many ways it appears that the 'socialist experiment' in East Germany created its own problems, ultimately becoming a victim of its own over-ambitious societal programme. Based on the communist vision of a more egalitarian society and nourished by the technocratic idea that the social order could be engineered according to abstract ideological principles, the 'socialist transformation' of East Germany conspicuously failed to account adequately for the complexities of modern industrial society.[57] As a result the SED was continually confronted by an array of unintended consequences: the 'hidden bargaining' in the factories, a West-oriented youth broadly averse to being 'organized', a grumbling and politically apathetic country-side, widespread complacency among the party and mass organizations at the grass-roots, widespread minor corruption and collusion, the 'shadow economy' as partial compensation for the contradictions and inefficiencies of the planned economy, the list goes on. These were not just residual elements in an otherwise 'totalitarian' or 'political' society, nor were they simply 'hangovers' from the pre-socialist past or reflections of 'design flaws' inherent in communist plans. These features were themselves 'East German society', which was a product of interaction between Soviet imports and German legacies, between societal construction and societal autonomy, between dictatorial intervention and human actions, between central authorities and grass-roots.

---

56 *Kölner Stadtanzeiger*, 13 May 1978, cited in J. Zatlin, 'Consuming Ideology. Socialist Consumerism and the Intershops', in Hübner and Tenfelde (eds), *Arbeiter in der SBZ-DDR*, p. 570.
57 Cf. the discussion in K. Jarausch, 'Die gescheiterte Gegengesellschaft. Überlegungen zu einer Sozialgeschichte der DDR', *AfS* 39 (1999), pp. 1–17.

# 4

# The East German economy: 'Planned miracle', victim of circumstance or fundamentally flawed?

The performance and inner workings of the East German economy have always been of considerable interest to scholars. The SBZ/GDR was, apart from the western parts of Czechoslovakia, the first (and so far only) advanced industrial region to attempt to build a Soviet-style socialist economy. In addition, throughout the post-war period the East German economy was the brightest star in the Soviet economic galaxy. It not only supported the highest living standard in the entire Eastern bloc, but was also the most productive economy and boasted relatively advanced optical, machine-building and chemical industries. The GDR was widely deemed the best chance for a socialist planned economy to work given its advanced industrial infrastructure, its first-rate education system as well as a highly trained and disciplined workforce – more what Marx had in mind for constructing a new socialist order than backward, largely rural 1920s Russia. Moreover, because of its inherent economic competition with West Germany, where a capitalist market economy was (re)established after the war, the East German economy was symbolic of the broader competition between the two great socio-economic systems of the world. Like its Western counterpart, the GDR was widely seen as a model of its economic system: disciplined, well organized, efficient and businesslike, if indeed never achieving the same levels of material wealth as the FRG.

The collapse of the GDR in 1989–90, not just politically, but also economically, radically altered perceptions of what many had deemed the second German success story, the 'planned miracle'.[1] The opening of the account books and thorough examination of the physical state of the East German economy have revealed a degree of dilapidation, indebtedness and

1 Joachim Nawrocki, *Das geplante Wunder: Leben und Wirtschaften im anderen Deutschland* (Hamburg, 1967).

environmental damage that few would previously have guessed. Whereas the question before 1989 was by and large 'How does the East German economy work?', after 1989 it has changed to 'Why did it not work?' Now that we can view the East German economy through the lens of its decline and disintegration, there has been a certain fixation on the reasons for its 'failure' – if indeed the word 'failure' is an appropriate term for an economy which managed to offer people a reasonably comfortable living standard, creditable recreational, cultural and educational facilities and, apart from some of the poorest pensioners, effective guarantees against poverty.

Of course, the East German economy did not 'fail' in any absolute sense against some universal, objective criterion, but against the performance of Western economies, and in particular its main economic referent, the FRG. Under Ulbricht, competition with and eventual overtaking of the West German economy were the primary overarching goals; under Honecker economic performance was still compared, if implicitly, to that of the FRG both by functionaries as well as the East German populace at large. The economic gap between the two Germanies was clearly a major hindrance to the stabilization of the regime and a key factor in its demise. One of the pivotal issues in the literature is why East Germany lagged so far behind the West. Was the planned economic system essentially doomed to a relatively poor performance because of structural deficits, or was it capable of functioning in principle but crucially weakened by inauspicious conditions, poor decisions on the part of the communist leadership, or the very nature of the relationship between party, ideology and economy? At the heart of the issue is the degree to which the GDR's economic decline was a product of design, accident or circumstance.

Any evaluation of this exceedingly broad question must address a whole raft of issues, only some of which we can focus on here. This chapter will pay particular attention to the starting point of the East German economy, its performance in terms of growth and productivity over time (much of which is discussed in relation to the FRG, as this 'system-comparative' approach was long prevalent in the scholarly literature), and the key question of what one might call its periodization of economic decline, determining the crucial decisions and turning points that, with hindsight, appear to have sealed the fate of the East German economy. Integrally related to this latter question are the attempts at economic reform in the 1960s that are central to any analysis of the GDR's economic history.

Before addressing the main contours of scholarly interpretation, it seems necessary at first to offer a thumbnail sketch of the historical development of the East German economy for the sake of orientation. Ever since the division of Germany in the late 1940s, it was clear that the SBZ/GDR confronted an array of economic hurdles. Unlike the western occupation zones, whose economic recovery was strongly supported by American aid in the form of the European Recovery Plan, the SBZ was stripped of many of its economic resources by Soviet authorities desperate for reparations to revive their own severely war-torn economy. Until the early 1950s the SBZ/GDR witnessed the dismantling of entire industrial plants, reparations from running production (the confiscation of goods produced instead of productive capacity itself), the mass extraction of uranium deposits (which continued over the following decades) as well as general occupation costs. Even apart from the effects of Soviet reparations, the East German economy was also strongly affected by German division. Not only was it isolated from most of its previous markets in the larger Western economic bloc, it was also crucially cut off from its traditional raw material supplies in the Ruhr, the centre of Germany's coal and steel industry.

The first steps towards economic reform – *not* with the goal of immediately establishing a Soviet-style system – were the land reform of 1945 and the expropriation of large enterprises from 1946. The socialization of industry and agriculture gathered pace during the 1950s with agricultural collectivization and further expansion of the 'people's own' sector to include many smaller and medium-sized enterprises. During the 1950s the regime embarked on a number of huge heavy industry projects to ameliorate the shortage of raw materials, funnelling all available resources into the expansion of the GDR's own energy and steel industries at the expense of consumption and living standards. After the uprising of June 1953 the supply of consumer goods was increased, facilitated by the end of reparations and an increase in Soviet credits. Overall, the 1950s were a period of high growth, and by the latter years of the decade the official target was to catch up with and overtake the FRG in per capita consumption of basic consumer goods by the end of 1961. This utterly unrealistic target was predictably not achieved, and in fact productivity and living standards slumped as a result of the final collectivization of agriculture in 1960 and increasing numbers of refugees to the West during the international political crisis over the future of West Berlin.

In 1962, the SED leadership reassessed its system of central planning that had organized post-war reconstruction. Economic functionaries had long recognized that the rigid system of prices and central steering resulted in the much bemoaned 'tonnage ideology' and offered too little incentive for technical progress or innovation. Influenced by the so-called Liberman debate in the Soviet Union, the East German leadership unveiled plans for a 'New Economic System' (NES) in 1963, whose basic idea was to increase efficiency and productivity through greater flexibility and a new system of 'economic levers': prices, profits, credit, wages and bonuses. The binding principle was that of 'material interest': profits and bonuses were to serve as an incentive for greater performance. Economic performance in the mid-1960s suggested that the reforms were having a positive effect, which moreover was beginning to have a tangible effect on living standards. But because of both the economic imbalances associated with the introduction of the reforms as well as conflicting political interests in Berlin and Moscow, the NES was quietly dismantled in the late 1960s and a more traditional centrally administered system reinstated.

Under Honecker, whose assumption of the party leadership in 1971 was directly related to this policy shift, the East German economy was set in a different direction. The idea was no longer to demand sacrifices in the present for the goal of socialism in the future, but to consume what the system could deliver in the here and now – the so-called 'unity of social and economic policy'. Social spending and living standards increased significantly after *Ostpolitik* as the East German economy benefited from its trade with the FRG, which the West German government insisted be considered 'domestic trade', thus free from tariffs and duties. Through trading and financial links with West Germany, the GDR was in effect a 'secret member of the European Community', which goes some way towards explaining its relatively strong economic performance within the Soviet bloc.[2] By the later 1970s, however, Honecker's brand of consumer socialism was seriously undermined by the explosion of raw material prices, above all the after-effects of the 'oil shock' of the early 1970s, which led to substantial trading deficits with both the West and the Soviet Union. Guaranteed bank loans from West Germany helped the GDR weather the economic storms of the early 1980s, but did little to improve the basic competitiveness of East German industry.

East German leaders pinned their hopes on the new technologies of microelectronics – especially robotics, data processing and the expansion of CAD/CAM in the GDR's traditionally strong machine-building sector – by wagering huge investments on the eventual pay-offs of computerization. But East German microelectronic technology already lagged too far behind that of the USA and Japan to be internationally competitive. The technology needed for the GDR's modernization programme, as well as the consumer products that its population desired, came from the West, which meant more borrowing from the 'non-socialist world'. Growth and productivity stagnated, and by the end of the 1980s the GDR's debts were spiralling out of control. After the Wall fell, the planned economy was unable to withstand the haemorrhage of labour to the West (which was, after all, the main reason for its construction in 1961) or to compete on equal terms with technologically superior and culturally more desirable Western products. After the currency union at a 1:1 exchange rate in July 1990, East German enterprises were no longer shielded by an inconvertible currency, but were fully exposed to market competition. The result was massive de-industrialization, unemployment and rising social tensions throughout East Germany. The union of the two economies was largely an act of West German annexation, though this was arguably hard to avoid given the state of the East German economy by 1990. Although partly a result of the terms of economic and political union agreed after 1989, the economic trauma of the early 1990s

2 The beneficial effects of these trade links with the West have been questioned by Michael Geyer, 'Industriepolitik in der DDR', in J. Kocka and M. Sabrow (eds), *Die DDR als Geschichte* (Berlin, 1993), pp. 122–34.

was ultimately the culmination of a long history of relative decline.[3] The degree to which this decline resulted from difficult circumstances, systemic flaws or poor decision-making is open to different interpretations, to which we can now turn.

# Interpretations

Ever since the GDR's founding, the starting point of its economy and the issue of its 'footing the bill' for the war on behalf of all of Germany have been a point of controversy. Debate about the scale of Soviet reparations is indeed as old as the phenomenon itself. In the early years, the almost universal view in both Germanies was of a systematic and thorough 'plundering of the Zone by the Soviets'. Stories abounded of factories being dismantled, workforces laid off, valuable capital equipment being hauled off to the Soviet Union where it sometimes rusted on railway carriages after failing to be reassembled. Few Germans were aware of the scale of destruction in the Soviet Union, and the general reluctance to recognize other countries as victims in the midst of post-war privations in Germany generated little understanding for the reparations and especially the practice of dismantling. Early discussion in the West was mixed since the political implications of blaming the Soviets were rather ambivalent. While some played down the scale of reparations in order to highlight the deficiencies of the socialist planned economy, many voices in the West German political and media establishment continued to draw attention to reparations as a means of showing how vindictive and exploitative the Soviets were.[4] In East Germany the issue of reparations was a no-man's land. The files of the Office for Reparations remained under lock and key with no chance of being opened for scholarly research. Party officials were obviously concerned about Soviet sensibilities; bringing up reparations hardly served to deepen 'German–Soviet friendship' or to portray the GDR's great benefactor in glowing terms. The emphasis in official rhetoric and propaganda was instead on the alleged Western 'disruption' of the East German economy, the Western allies' reneging on prior agreements about Soviet reparations from the western zones (thus increasing the burden on the SBZ) and on the tacit

---

3 This is, however, a point of some debate. Many former East German officials contend that the 'collapse' of the economy after summer 1990 was more a consequence of the West German federal government's decisions than the difficulties of the East German economy itself. Cf. for example, Gerhard Schürer, 'Die Wirtschafts- und Sozialpolitik der DDR', in Dietmar Keller, Hans Modrow and Herbert Wolf (eds), *Ansichten zur Geschichte der DDR*, vol. 3 (Bonn/Berlin, 1994), p. 169.

4 For instance, the *FAZ* reported on 25 August 1953 that reparations up to the end of 1951 reached some 60 billion dollars; *Der Telegraf* reported on 28 November 1953 that the figure was 240 billion DM – both several times the actual amount. Cited in Rainer Karlsch, *Allein bezahlt? Die Reparationsleistungen der SBZ/DDR 1945–53* (Berlin, 1993), p. 11.

'economic war' waged by Western imperialists to undermine the socialist project.[5]

As the gap between the West and East German economies widened over the years, East German writers commonly pointed to a bad start as the primary culprit.[6] In this view, the GDR suffered more than the FRG from a supposedly higher level of destruction during the war, the higher level of reparations as well as the detrimental effects of German division. The predominance of light industry in East German manufacturing – or more to the point, the lack of basic heavy industries – hampered growth by creating supply bottlenecks that rendered much of the GDR's existing capital stock useless, or at the very least forced it to operate well under capacity. In addition, the severance of some traditional Western trade links with the onset of the Cold War not only forced the East German economy to reorient itself towards its less developed eastern neighbours, but also forced it to build up its own heavy industries – for instance, the massive expansion of mining for its own rather mediocre coal deposits, the huge steel mills of Eisenhüttenstadt – that were extremely capital-intensive, thus draining investment away from other industries and seriously curtailing consumer living standards. This is the basic argument of the standard East German economic history of the early years, which strongly emphasizes the hurdles confronting the GDR:

> the consequences of the period of rearmament, the degree of destruction during the war, the necessary reparations, the uneven locational factors of productive forces which developed into real disproportions in the process of German division, and finally the first effects of the Cold War, especially the economic war against the GDR.[7]

According to this view, the economic gap between the two systems was by and large due to secular or 'system-indifferent' factors not endemic to the planned economy itself. Since this emphasis on factors 'external' to the East German economic system also tends to expunge the blame from those who managed it, it is hardly surprising that it has survived in many of the personal memoirs of former East German political leaders.[8] Yet this view is not just confined to East German apologia or the self-exculpatory efforts of its leaders, but is also shared by some Western scholars after the collapse of the regime. As Wilma Merkel and Stefanie Wahl have argued in a seminal post-*Wende* study, despite all the inbuilt inefficiencies of the centrally planned

5 At the ninth plenum of the SED Central Committee in April 1965, Ulbricht demanded from the FRG 120 billion DM as compensation for reparations and 'Wirtschaftskrieg'.

6 Cf. Horst Barthel, *Die wirtschaftlichen Ausgangsbedingungen der DDR* (Berlin, 1979); G. Neumann, *Die ökonomischen Entwicklungsbedingungen des RGW, Bd. 1: 1945–1958* (Berlin, 1980); J. Roesler, V. Siedt and M. Elle, *Wirtschaftswachstum in der Industrie der DDR 1945–1970* (Berlin, 1986).

7 H. Barthel, *Die wirtschaftlichen Ausgangsbedingungen*, p. 170.

8 For instance Gerhard Schürer, chairman of the State Planning Commission, who insists that the SED 'did not in reality inherit anything that they could have run down'. *Gewagt und verloren. Eine deutsche Biographie* (Frankfurt/O., 1996), p. 32. A far more self-exculpatory account is Günter Mittag, *Um jeden Preis. Im Spannungsfeld der Systeme* (Berlin, 1991).

economy, 'the main reason for the declining material living standard in the GDR in relation to the FRG was, however, the adverse economic starting conditions in the late 1940s and early 1950s that already established early on the sizeable economic lag of the GDR behind the FRG'.[9]

The bulk of Western writing, and indeed most scholarly writing in general since 1989, refutes this view. Although the disadvantages associated with Soviet reparations and the effects of German division are widely recognized as important factors in the equation, most Western scholars have argued that the gap between the two economies resulted at least as much from the inherent inefficiencies of the planned economy itself as from the unfavourable start. As Wolfgang Stolper concluded in a meticulous study of the 1950s: 'The East German economy has performed more poorly than the West German economy by whatever tests one wishes to apply.'[10] Although Soviet extractions and the continuous loss of trained people to the West bore a major part of the blame, 'this cannot be the whole story'. According to his calculations, per capita GNP in East Germany rose no more than in West Germany in spite of the increases in relative amounts spent on investments. This suggested, then, 'a relative inefficiency of investments in East Germany compared to West Germany'. Numerous studies of the East German economy over the following decades reached similar conclusions about the relative inefficiences of the socialist planned economy in comparison to liberal market economies, especially to the particularly dynamic form of social market economy in West Germany. By the time the regime collapsed, a sizeable literature had emerged on the 'distorted world of Soviet-type economies'.[11]

Since the demise of the system and the much improved availability of economic data, the notion that the economic starting conditions were the main reason for the lag behind the West has been subjected to more far-reaching criticism. The strongest objection has been registered by Christoph Buchheim, who attributes the GDR's economic problems, even during its first decade, primarily to the planned economic order itself. Indeed, Buchheim advances the unorthodox argument that in many ways the starting conditions were reasonably good.[12] Although dismantling certainly created supply bottlenecks, these were often relatively easily mitigated through investment and had only a modest impact on living standards since consumer industries were largely untouched. As for reparations out of running production,

---

9 W. Merkel and S. Wahl, *Das geplünderte Deutschland. Die wirtschaftliche Entwicklung im östlichen Teil Deutschlands von 1949 bis 1989* (Bonn, 1991), p. 64.

10 Wolfgang Stolper, *The Structure of the East German Economy* (Cambridge, MA, 1960), p. 441.

11 Cf. Jan Winiecki, *The Distorted World of Soviet-Type Economies* (Pittsburgh, 1988); Peter Rutland, *The Myth of the Plan* (London, 1985); see also the classic study by János Kornai, *The Socialist System. The Political Economy of Communism* (Oxford, 1992).

12 Which helps to explain why early growth rates in the SBZ were actually above those in the western zones. Cf. Christoph Buchheim (ed.), *Wirtschaftliche Folgelasten des Krieges in der SBZ/DDR* (Baden-Baden, 1995); C. Buchheim, 'Kriegsfolgen und Wirtschaftswachstum in der SBZ/DDR', *GG* 25 (1999), pp. 515–29; C. Buchheim, 'Die Wirtschaftsordnung als Barriere des gesamtwirtschaftlichen Wachstums in der DDR', in *Vierteljahrshefte für Sozial- und Wirtschaftsgeschichte* 82 (1995), pp. 194ff.

Buchheim argues that they were, on balance, a stimulus to growth insofar as they created employment and constituted a form of demand. The reparations in the early years were therefore not the serious impediment to growth as so often portrayed, but 'rather had a positive overall effect on the economy of the SBZ in comparison to the situation in western Germany'.[13] Although this may sound surprising, it was a consideration of Allied politicians at the time; the punitive Morgenthau Plan stipulated that there should be no reparations out of running production for precisely this reason. In Buchheim's view, even the problems commonly attributed to German division were more a product of the Soviet-style system. Instead of securing the necessary raw materials by exporting as much as possible from the GDR's existing modern industries (chemicals, electrical goods, machine-building) as market incentives would have dictated, investment was cut off from these sectors, leaving them to fall behind world standards, and funnelled into the expansion of heavy industry, which was over-emphasized for largely ideological reasons (the expansion of heavy industry was central to the 'Soviet path' to socialism). As Buchheim concludes

> The disadvantageous effects of dismantling and German division on the economic development of the GDR did not arise of themselves, but rather because of the existence of a planned economy that was further organized according to the Soviet model. In actuality these effects are therefore rather attributable to the economic order.[14]

Because the GDR's economic starting point serves as a reference baseline for subsequent economic performance, these debates are inseparable from questions about economic growth and productivity over the course of its history. Unfortunately, performance indicators are notoriously difficult to calculate for Soviet-style planned economies. Official East German statistical data – whether intended for public consumption or not – is at best only an indirect reflection of actual economic performance since it rests on 'artificial' prices not determined directly by supply and demand. Moreover, any data must be calculated according to a realistic exchange rate (not the official one!), also taking into consideration price distortions between different groups of goods (some subsidized and others not), structural differences of the East German economy compared to Western economies (above all the relatively small service sector), and most problematic of all, differences in the relationship between the price and quality of goods.

Against this background it is easy to understand why the actual state of the East German economy could remain hidden for so long.[15] It also helps explain why Western estimates of East German growth and productivity have varied

---

13  C. Buchheim, 'Kriegsfolgen und Wirtschaftswachstum', p. 524.
14  Ibid., p. 526.
15  Cf. Peter von der Lippe, 'Die gesamtwirtschaftlichen Leistungen der DDR-Wirtschaft in den offiziellen Darstellungen. Die amtliche Statistik der DDR als Instrument der Agitation und Propaganda der SED', in *Materialien der Enquete-Kommission*, vol. II: 3, pp. 1973–2193.

widely over the years. Many of the studies conducted by the German Institute for Economic Research (DIW) during the 1970s and 1980s estimated GDR productivity at around 70 per cent that of West Germany.[16] Rosier estimates by the World Bank actually posited that the East German economy was the tenth strongest in the world and more productive than that of the UK.[17] The most crass overestimation of East German economic performance posited a per capita income of US$10,440, above that of West Germany.[18] Such inflated evaluations were based on what Merkel and Wahl have aptly called a 'huge deception-strategy aimed both inwards and outwards' on the part of the SED leadership.[19] Since 1990 it is generally accepted that by the end of the 1980s the East German economy hardly managed one-third the level of West German productivity. Estimates of comparative rates of growth have also been dramatically revised. In contrast to the old DIW calculations based on an exchange rate of 0.81 DM to 1 GDR-Mark, Merkel and Wahl (whose growth calculations are now more or less accepted) have based their study on the assumption that the value of goods and services in GDR-Marks decreased from 96 per cent to 56 per cent relative to the DM from 1950 to 1989. Official East German growth statistics were obviously unrealistic in suggesting higher overall growth rates than the FRG since the founding of the two states (i.e. blaming the gap on the adverse conditions before 1949). According to Merkel and Wahl, over the period 1950 to 1989 GNP per capita rose by 276 per cent in the GDR, as compared to 415 per cent in the FRG.[20]

It is generally agreed, then, that East Germany's economic performance was well below what most estimates suggested before its collapse. More controversial is how growth and productivity developed over time, which has direct implications for understanding the *reasons* for its decline. Estimates vary considerably. Whereas Merkel and Wahl suggest that the GDR achieved only 50 per cent of West German productivity levels as early as 1950, Bart van Ark argues that the figure was only 40 per cent and Albrecht Ritschl a significantly higher 68 per cent.[21] Since it is reasonably clear that the productivity ratio was around 30 per cent by the late 1980s,

16 H. Wilkens, *Das Sozialprodukt der Deutschen Demokratischen Republik im Vergleich mit der Bundesrepublik Deutschland* (Berlin, 1976); Manfred Melzer, *Anlagevermögen, Produktion und Beschäftigung der Industrie im Gebiet der DDR von 1936 bis 1978 sowie Schätzung des künftigen Angebotspotentials* (Berlin, 1980). For an overview, see Albrecht Ritschl, 'An Exercise in Futility: East German economic growth and decline, 1945–89', in Nicholas Crafts and Gianni Toniolo (eds), *Economic Growth in Europe since 1945* (Cambridge, 1996), pp. 498–540.

17 Cf. *1980 World Bank Atlas* (Washington, DC, 1980), p. 16. According to Gerhard Schürer, this tenth place ranking was never believed internally in either general or per capita terms. G. Schürer, 'Die Wirtschafts- und Sozialpolitik der DDR', in *Ansichten zur Geschichte der DDR*, vol. 3, p. 154.

18 *Handbook of Economic Statistics* (Washington, DC, 1986), pp. 24–5

19 W. Merkel and S. Wahl, *Das geplünderte Deutschland*, p. 11.

20 Ibid., pp. 46–55.

21 Ibid.; B. van Ark, 'The Manufacturing Sector in East Germany: A Reassessment of Comparative Productivity Performance, 1950–1988', in *Jahrbuch für Wirtschaftsgeschichte* (1995) no. 2, pp. 75–100; A. Ritschl, 'Aufstieg und Niedergang der Wirtschaft der DDR: Ein Zahlenbild 1945–1989, in *Jahrbuch für Wirtschaftsgeschichte* (1995), no. 2, pp. 11–46.

the lower figures for 1950 suggest that the East German economy lost less ground over the period 1950–89 than the higher figures do. Although the performance of the planned economy is not particularly impressive in any of these calculations, the lower figures emphasize the inherent circumstances in which the East German economy started over the shortcomings of the planned economy itself, the higher figures vice versa.

These differing views on the development of growth and productivity over time are inextricably linked to the overarching issue of the periodization of East German economic decline. Was the GDR ever economically capable, even in principle, of achieving a performance comparable to that in the West, or indeed of avoiding falling prey to the inherent deficiencies of the planned economic system? The caesura of 1989–90 has certainly produced a more unfavourable interpretation of the centrally planned economy's chances of survival. There was genuine surprise, even among many experts, at the scale of indebtedness and infrastructural deterioration by the end of the 1980s. Even in the latter half of the decade some commentators were still contending that the GDR's economic performance demonstrated that the centrally planned economy could produce impressive results. Armed now with hindsight and better data, it is difficult to see how the GDR economy could have survived much longer without radically reducing borrowing, curtailing popular living standards and revolutionizing its entire economic system. We know that the East German economy 'collapsed' with exposure to world competition, and it would seem that politically practicable solutions to the GDR's economic problems were hardly in sight by the end of the 1980s.[22] But when did this terminal decline begin? Was the planned economy 'doomed' to fail, and if so, from what point onwards? Again, these questions about the timing of economic decline cannot be separated from the question of its causes. Were systemic defects paramount, thus affording little chance of more than substandard performance from the very beginning? Or was the East German economy crucially weakened through poor decision-making by a rigid and narrow-minded political leadership who should shoulder much of the responsibility?

Broadly speaking, answers to these questions have tended to run in two directions. The dominant view in the West, which has come to prevail more generally after 1989, is that the GDR economy never had much chance of long-term survival, that the crucial watershed came with the introduction of a rigid system of central planning.[23] This interpretation closely echoes the vast body of economic and social scientific research on the 'socialist system'

---

22 For a brief but informative overview, see André Steiner, 'Zwischen Konsumversprechen und Innovationszwang. Zum wirtschaftlichen Niedergang der DDR', in Konrad Jarausch and Martin Sabrow (eds), *Weg in den Untergang. Der innere Zerfall der DDR* (Göttingen, 1999), pp. 153–92.

23 Cf. Oskar Schwarzer, *Sozialistische Zentralplanwirtschaft in der SBZ/DDR. Ergebnisse eines ordnungspolitischen Experiments (1945–1989)* (Stuttgart, 1999); Gernot Gutmann and Werner Klein, 'Herausbildungs- und Entwicklungsphasen der Planungs-, Lenkungs- und Kontrollmechanismen im Wirtschaftssystem', in *Materialien der Enquete-Kommission*, vol. II: 3, pp. 1579–647.

which has repeatedly pointed to the defiencies of the centrally planned economy, ranging from controlled prices that do not adequately reflect cost or value (the 'price problem') to the lack of performance and innovation incentives caused by the abolition of private ownership of industry (the 'property problem'). The 'property problem' may be summarized as follows. Unlike property rights in capitalist economies, where owners have both the right to decide how their business is run as well as the right to dispose of the profits thereby generated, property rights in socialist planned economies are 'divided'. In other words, responsibility for decision-making is decoupled from the right to dispose of any profits. Whereas there is a direct connection between risk and reward under capitalism, management decisions in socialist planned economies tend not to entail such performance incentives, whether negative (financial loss because of poor decisions) or positive (reward for good decisions). Indeed, in many ways the incentive structure had counterproductive effects since it was in managers' interests not to perform too well. In terms of positive incentives, the lure of bonuses, etc. for plan fulfilment only superficially acted as performance stimulants. In actuality they had the opposite effect since they simultaneously created an inbuilt incentive for factories not to give accurate information about their performance capabilities to the higher authorities in order to receive 'weak plans' that could easily be fulfilled. The same problem also existed at the factory level, where the incentive structure on the shopfloor often encouraged workers to underperform and resist 'stiff' norms.[24] As for negative incentives, failing enterprises were usually thrown a lifeline, which hardly gravitated in favour of enhancing performance or innovation. The state's guaranteeing the life of an enterprise meant that managers did not face the discipline of the 'bottom line', but rather operated within what Kornai has called 'soft budget constraints'.[25] The resulting inefficiencies and lack of accurate information about demand produced the chronic shortages and surpluses of goods that so characterized the socialist economies.

Arguably more important than the 'property problem' was the 'price problem'. Unlike prices in market economies, which reflect supply and demand and therefore serve as a crucial system of feedback for producers – a basis for 'rational' investment and management decisions – centrally determined prices in socialist economies are of little informational value for producers, which made profitable management and investment decisions well nigh impossible. GDR planners and enterprises have been likened to ancient mariners who had to negotiate treacherous waters in a fog, with no compass, coordinates or map (i.e. little view of world prices), and only occasional glimpses of this solid 'land'.[26] Their only hope was for the fog to lift

24  Cf. generally J. Kopstein, *The Politics of Economic Decline*; P. Hübner, *Konsens, Konflikt, Kompromiß*; C. Ross, *Constructing Socialism at the Grass-Roots*, Chapters 3 and 8.
25  J. Kornai, *The Socialist System*, pp. 489–97.
26  Christian Heimann, *Systembedingte Ursachen des Niedergangs der DDR-Wirtschaft. Das Beispiel der Textil- und Bekleidungsindustrie 1945–1989* (Frankfurt a. M., 1997), p. 36.

(i.e. the introduction of market-oriented prices). But as numerous commentators have argued, the communist system was fundamentally incapable of undertaking such reforms. Any profound, lasting, and effective economic transformation would require a radical change in both the political structure and the nature of property relations. Indeed, it would even require an ideological re-think since effective economic reform – which would have to include more free-floating prices determined by market forces instead of political prerogatives – flatly contradicted the communist party's claim to authority over the economy. Liberalization in the economic realm cannot happen without liberalization in the political realm. Because of this affinity between the political and economic elements of the system, the ruling communist party was not willing to cede control over economic affairs to the market. As Kornai puts it:

> Stalinist classical socialism is repressive and inefficient, but it constitutes a coherent system. When it starts reforming itself, that coherence slackens and its internal contradictions strengthen. In spite of generating a whole series of favorable changes, reform is doomed to fail: the socialist system is unable to renew itself internally so as to prove viable in the long run.[27]

The system is not capable of a renewal that could free it of its dysfunctional features while retaining the sole rule of the communist party and the dominance of the state sector in the economy, since these are, in this view, the root causes of its dysfunctional features in the first place.

This understanding of the workings of the socialist system has obvious implications for interpreting the nature and timing of East Germany's economic decline. Reform attempts in the GDR never, in this view, presented a genuine opportunity to achieve fundamental reform since party authority over the economy was never part of the equation – an argument largely supported by the most thorough and detailed study to date.[28] While no one disputes that reform attempts and other decisions were important chapters in the GDR's economic history, the systemic nature of its inefficiencies and its incapability of internal reform means that, as Johannes Bähr has put it, 'the decisive caesura was without question the course settings of 1948–1950' (when this fatally flawed system was introduced in the GDR) 'whose long-term effects stretch across the decades of division'.[29]

Although the system itself was clearly a large part of the problem, not everyone shares such an emphatically 'system-determined' interpretation. A smaller number of scholars have emphasized several key decisions and turning-points later on. The decision to develop the GDR's own heavy industry (even

---

27 J. Kornai, *The Socialist System*, p. xxv.
28 Cf. A. Steiner, *Die DDR-Wirtschaftsreform der sechziger Jahre. Konflikt zwischen Effizienz- und Machtkalkül* (Berlin, 1999), pp. 557ff.
29 Johannes Bähr, 'Institutionenordnung und Wirtschaftsentwicklung. Die Wirtschaftsgeschichte der DDR aus der Sicht des zwischendeutschen Vergleichs', *GG* 25 (1999), p. 555.

after the early 1950s, when it arguably 'had to'[30]) is often viewed as a fateful policy with far-reaching consequences. Not only did this drain investment away from the GDR's traditionally strong machine-building and chemicals industries, but the relatively high cost of energy and raw materials dragged down productivity and competitiveness across the whole economy.[31] The SED leadership's gamble on developing its own microelectronics industry in the 1980s is also widely considered a fateful decision. Without yielding significant dividends, it swallowed up vast sums of investment to the detriment of other sectors and added substantially to the mounting debt crisis of the 1980s.[32]

Yet it is the period around the late 1960s and early 1970s – from the failed economic reform attempts to the introduction of Honecker's new brand of 'consumer socialism' – that stands out most clearly as an alternative watershed in the history of the East German economy. This is certainly the view of some former East German officials. According to Gerhard Schürer, the problems originated at the Eighth Party Congress in 1971, when it was decided that the GDR must support a generous consumer society and welfare state: 'It was hardly visible then, but that was when the switches were set. From then on the train traveled millimeter by millimeter in the wrong direction. It traveled away from the realities of the GDR.'[33] Harvard historian Charles Maier largely agrees with this assessment, qualifying the common view that long-term problems and contradictions ultimately brought down communism: 'Long term liabilities ... need not be fatal. All economies have bottlenecks and stagnant sectors.'[34] Marxism–Leninism is certainly 'not the only way to produce industrial ruins',[35] as the various rust-belts of western Europe and North America testify. After all, Western economies have had their own problems and planned economies did manage to achieve creditable growth rates from the 1950s into the 1970s, even if their lower developmental baselines presented more opportunity for rapid growth. According to Maier, 'the disabling failures ... came later. Schürer was right when he looked to the early 1970s as the watershed for the Communist economy. ... Socialist policy makers might have evolved toward more flexible production in the 1960s, but then put off reforms for a fateful

30 Gerhard Schürer – along with most former East German leaders – still insists on the necessity of expanding domestic heavy industry, 'Die Wirtschafts- und Sozialpolitik der DDR', *Ansichten zur Geschichte der DDR*, vol. 3, pp. 131–71.

31 Cf. A. Steiner, 'Wirtschaftliche Lenkungsverfahren in der Industrie der DDR Mitte der fünfziger Jahre. Resultate und Alternativen', in C. Buchheim (ed.), *Wirtschaftliche Folgelasten des Krieges*, pp. 271f; J. Roesler, 'The Rise and Fall of the Planned Economy in the GDR, 1945–1989', *GH*, vol. 9 (1991), pp. 46–61.

32 Cf. C. Maier, *Dissolution: The Crisis of Communism and the End of East Germany* (Princeton, NJ, 1997), pp. 73–8; Harry Maier, 'Die Innovationsfähigkeit der Planwirtschaft in der DDR – Ursachen und Folgen', *DA* 26: 7 (1993), pp. 807–18; J. Roesler, 'The Rise and Fall of the Planned Economy'; Gerhard Schürer, 'Die Wirtschafts- und Sozialpolitik der DDR', p. 161.

33 Taken from Schürer's confession to the Central Committee in November 1989, quoted from C. Maier, *Dissolution*, p. 60.

34 C. Maier, *Dissolution*, p. 79.

35 M. Geyer, 'Industriepolitik in der DDR', p. 123.

decade or more.'[36] Errors occurred then that resurfaced with a vengeance in the 1980s. In the wake of the world slow-down of the early 1970s, West and East faced similar problems, but the East reacted very differently by recentralizing, avoiding the kind of painful restructuring that occurred in many Western economies, and returning to tried methods.[37]

The reform attempts of the 1960s play a crucial role in this interpretation. Both before and after 1989 it has been argued that the abrogation of the reforms was not inevitable, but rather the result of flaws in its design, changing winds blowing from Moscow and a domestic political struggle leading to a specific decision on the part of the party leadership. In other words, the end of the reforms was not 'pre-programmed' into the system itself; they rather fell victim to a combination of political machinations (both domestic and in relation to Moscow) and poor management.[38] As Jörg Roesler has argued, the piecemeal introduction of the reforms revealed a number of unforeseeable disadvantages which repelled functionaries at various levels. They not only benefited some enterprises more than others, but also led to problems of supply by the end of the 1960s.[39] Yet the main reason for their abrogation was political power. In Roesler's view, the end of the reforms was certainly not the only alternative for solving the problems of disproportions and shortages associated with the reforms, which would merely have required a lowering of the unrealistic plan goals and growth targets. 'However, the new majority in the *Politbüro* was not concerned with economics, but with politics.'[40] As the new leadership around Honecker saw itself confronted with a loss of power to the market, they sacrificed the long-term prospects of the GDR's economy in favour of their own political interests by nipping the reform mechanisms in the bud. Whereas Ulbricht had seized the opportunity to create a form of 'mixed economy' in the shadow of the Wall, this opportunity was wilfully 'gambled away' by Honecker and his cronies. Had the leadership reached a less self-interested decision, the situation would have been quite different. According to Roesler, 'It is by no means erroneous to conclude that there was a chance in the history of the GDR to achieve a dynamic and competitive economy and thereby to secure the GDR's economic existence as a socialist German state'.[41]

---

36  C. Maier, *Dissolution*, pp. 79, 81.

37  This view is shared by J. Roesler, 'The Rise and Fall of the Planned Economy', pp. 56–8.

38  Cf. for instance, Gert Leptin and Manfred Melzer, *Economic Reform in East German Industry* (Oxford, 1978); Michael Keren, 'The New Economic System in the GDR: An Obituary', *Soviet Studies* 24 (1973), pp. 554–87; A. Steiner, 'Abkehr vom NÖS. Die wirtschaftspolitischen Entscheidungen 1967/68 – Ausgangspunkt der Krisenprozesse 1969/70?', in J. Cerny (ed.), *Brüche, Krisen, Wendepunkte: Neubefragung von DDR-Geschichte* (Leipzig, 1990), pp. 247–8; Monika Kaiser, *Machtwechsel von Ulbricht zu Honecker. Funktionsmechanismen der SED-Diktatur in Konfliktsituationen 1962 bis 1972* (Berlin, 1997), Chapters 2 and 5.

39  Jörg Roesler, *Zwischen Plan und Markt. Die Wirtschaftsreform 1963–1970 in der DDR* (Berlin, 1991), pp. 156–7.

40  Ibid., p. 157.

41  Ibid., p. 162; see also J. Roesler, 'Das NÖS als Wirtschaftskonzept. Sichten, Tatsachen, Interpretationen', *DA* 31 (1998), p. 398. Walter Halbritter, one of the leading proponents of the NES at the time, makes a

Despite this insistence on historical 'contingency' within the constraints of the socialist system, there is broad agreement that the planned economy had serious intrinsic problems and that these weaknesses became increasingly visible over time. The difference, then, is essentially one of emphasis: how important were systemic defects in relation to poor decisions on the part of the communist leadership? Any attempt to address this question must consider a number of issues. Do the 'system-determined' explanations neglect or downplay the importance of the actions of political leaders? Do they underestimate the potential of the reform attempts? Did the political leadership in effect sacrifice the needs of the economy in order to shore up – at least for the time being – their own power? Was this a case of self-serving mismanagement of a problematic but not utterly doomed economic system which actually performed reasonably well given the circumstances? Or, conversely, were such political decisions themselves built into the system? Does the alternative emphasis on contingency adequately take into account the structural constraints on political actors resulting from the very functioning of the planned economy? Were the SED leaders perhaps less *unwilling* than they were *unable*, in the context of the socialist system, to embark on meaningful reforms? The evaluation that follows attempts briefly to take account of these and other questions raised by the debates we have just encountered.

# Evaluation

It seems sensible to begin with the GDR's economic starting point. It appears clear that, in terms of capital stock, the SBZ/GDR was no worse off than the western zones at the end of the war. Although the area that was to become the SBZ/GDR was traditionally less industrialized than the western parts of Germany, during the rearmament push of the 1930s and especially during the war it benefited more than other regions in terms of investment in war-relevant industries, so capital stock was actually more modern by 1945. Overall, the productivity gap at the end of the war was negligible. Recent research also shows that the GDR's area suffered less, not more, destruction from bombardment and fighting than the western zones, in contrast to the view put forward in most East German accounts.[42]

Nonetheless, it is also clear that East Germany lost a large portion of its economic potential to reparations of various kinds whereas capital stock in

---

(*Contd*)
similar argument in 'Was geschah wirklich in und mit der Reform des "NÖS" in der DDR und wohin zielte ihre objektive Tendenz?', in Ludwig Elm, Dietmar Keller and Reinhard Morek (eds), *Ansichten zur Geschichte der DDR*, vol. 6 (Bonn/Berlin, 1996), pp. 299–336.

42 See, generally, C. Buchheim (ed.), *Wirtschaftliche Folgelasten des Krieges*.

the western zones was left relatively unscathed by the occupation forces. Precisely how much the SBZ/GDR lost is difficult to calculate; official Soviet statistics are not very useful and estimates are still not entirely agreed. Recent work on the actual scale of Soviet reparations and dismantling has on the whole corrected the earlier estimates downwards.[43] The most thorough examination to date concludes that the scale of reparations was at the very least around US$14 billion (1938 prices), which was actually more than the Soviet Union had demanded (US$10.4 billion).[44] According to these figures, the GDR lost around 30 per cent of its 1944 industrial capacity to dismantling, whereas the corresponding figure for West Germany was only 3 per cent.[45] The GDR therefore lost approximately ten times as much industrial capacity to dismantling as the FRG, and if one includes reparations from running production this ratio becomes considerably higher.[46] Moreover, because transport and communications were also partially dismantled, there occurred a certain 'derationalization of the production apparatus'[47] that resulted in numerous shortages and bottlenecks as well as a lack of investment and consumer goods. While the West German economy was being subsidized by Marshall Aid, the SBZ/GDR was being systematically stripped. Economically (as well as politically, one might add), it is hard to escape the conclusion that East Germany by and large 'footed the bill' for the war. Indeed, between 1945 and 1953 it was subjected to the highest known level of reparations in the twentieth century.[48]

The effects of dismantling and national division were not just limited to the early years, but only fully manifested themselves over the longer term. The dismantling of certain sectors of industry and infrastructure led to serious structural problems in the East German economy. Transport in particular became a long-term bottleneck with repercussions across the entire economy. Huge amounts of investment were funnelled into these problem areas, which had disadvantageous consequences for investment and competitiveness in other branches of industry. The effects of reparations from running production, which, as Buchheim shows, indeed helped stimulate growth during the early years, also harboured many long-term disadvantages. Not only was the East German economy obviously deprived of much of its output, but Soviet economic needs also dictated that the GDR produce particular *kinds* of goods for reparations. This required significant structural changes such as the expansion of heavy machine building and even the

---

43  L. Baar, R. Karlsch and W. Matschke, *Kriegsfolgen und Kriegslasten Deutschlands. Zerstörungen, Demontagen und Reparationen* (Berlin, 1993); Baar *et al.*, 'Kriegsschäden, Demontagen und Reparationen', in *Materialien der Enquete-Kommission*, vol. II: 2, pp. 868–988.
44  R. Karlsch, *Allein bezahlt?*, p. 230. This is not far from the calculation of US$16.3 billion by Jörg Fisch, *Reparationen nach dem zweiten Weltkrieg* (Munich, 1992), pp. 50ff, but is well below that of Merkel and Wahl (100 billion RM), *Das geplünderte Deutschland*.
45  Ibid., p. 233.
46  Ibid., pp. 99–105.
47  J. Bähr, 'Institutionenordnung und Wirtschaftsentwicklung', p. 540.
48  R. Karlsch, *Allein bezahlt?*, p. 228.

establishment of whole new industrial branches such as shipbuilding. These new branches were not only very costly in terms of investment and subsidization, but also numbered among the least innovative areas of industry.[49] National division only exacerbated the negative effects of reparations, which according to Karlsch could have been overcome much more easily in a unified Germany. Hence the long-term effects of reparations grew in the course of the 1950s into real obstacles to growth, which ultimately resulted in an 'investment gap of several years'.[50]

Detrimental though the scale of reparations was, the idea that this was the *main* cause for the GDR's lag behind the FRG is over-stretched for a variety of reasons.[51] By way of comparison, neighbouring Czechoslovakia was a net receiver of reparations after the war but still showed the same gap to the West as the GDR. It has also been pointed out that although the economy of West Berlin was hit just as hard as East Berlin by the first wave of reparations before the Western allies arrived in July 1945, a gap soon emerged between the two halves of the city that was similar to the overall German gap.[52] In addition, recent research on individual branches of East German industry has shown that some branches hardest hit by reparations (e.g. tool- and machine-building) became exemplary, whereas the little affected consumer goods industries lagged far behind.[53] It might of course be objected that reparations in West Berlin say little since they took place for only a very short period of time compared to the SBZ/GDR as a whole, where they remained harsh throughout 1945–46 and continued until 1953. Furthermore, the fact that machine-building recovered from the particularly harsh regime of dismantling to become one of the most productive sectors of the East German economy does not, of course, disprove the detrimental effect of reparations to the economy as a whole since the remaining resources were concentrated on particular branches of industry at the expense of others. But at the very least these points of comparison demonstrate that a variety of factors were at work (national division, the drain of skills and know-how to the West, the lack of individual incentives and missing market mechanisms) of which reparations were only one, albeit probably the single most important during the early years.[54]

As we have seen, there is quite substantial disagreement over the extent to which the long-term East German lag behind West Germany can be attributed to these unfavourable starting conditions. One thing that seems clear is that the East–West gap did not result solely from inauspicious

49 L. Baar, R. Karlsch and W. Matschke, 'Kriegsschäden, Demontagen und Reparationen', p. 932; R. Karlsch, 'Umfang und Struktur der Reparationsentnahmen aus der SBZ/DDR 1945–1953. Stand und Probleme der Forschung', in C. Buchheim (ed.), *Wirtschaftliche Folgelasten des Krieges*, p. 69.

50 R. Karlsch, *Allein bezahlt?*, p. 238.

51 Merkel and Wahl argue that the economic gap was 'in the main caused by the reparations to the Soviet Union'. *Das geplünderte Deutschland*, p. 26.

52 J. Bähr, *Industrie im geteilten Berlin (1945–1990)* (Munich, 2001).

53 C. Heimann, *Systembedingte Ursachen des Niedergangs der DDR-Wirtschaft.*

54 R. Karlsch, *Allein bezahlt?*, p. 240.

circumstances as East German accounts generally contended. The GDR certainly suffered from a poor start, but this does not explain why it continued to fall further and further behind. Even Merkel and Wahl, who stress the adverse starting conditions more than most other scholars, lay considerable emphasis on the 'inherent structural weaknesses' of the planned economy.[55]

Yet the converse view that the system itself is primarily to blame from the very beginning is not entirely convincing. Some aspects of this argument are more compelling than others. The idea that the oft-cited 'disproportions' resulting from national division were largely the product of central planning – or at least were greatly exacerbated by it – seems largely plausible. As Buchheim contends, a market economy would indeed have reacted very differently to the challenges the GDR faced, and would have tended to concentrate on its existing strengths in order to compensate for its weaknesses through trade. As others have pointed out, in West Germany the 'disproportions' deriving from national division (though there were far fewer) were quickly overcome through new trading links.[56] Although some expansion of heavy industry was probably necessary in the early years, the extent of the GDR's programme in this area was certainly due as much to ideological predilections – the communist romance of coal and steel – as to 'objective' economic needs.[57] Yet one should not underestimate the strain of reorienting trade towards the less developed industrial economies in the East. This not only meant significant structural changes, but also removed innovation and performance incentives since these economies could always be used to 'dump' goods unsaleable in the West or even in the GDR. Even less compelling is the idea that the oft-cited starvation of investment during the 1950s was due primarily to the planned economy itself rather than high reparations of investment goods to the Soviet Union.[58] While one can see the point that such bottlenecks are far less frequent in market economies because increased demand creates higher prices, thus funnelling investment into the affected area and allowing it to expand, this argument seems both to underplay the huge scale of reparations from the GDR and to perceive such investment decisions in too narrowly economic terms, thus losing sight of what was politically practicable. A market economy may well have overcome these bottlenecks more quickly, but after the extraction of reparations there were not as many resources left over for investment as in the West.

---

55 W. Merkel and S. Wahl, *Das geplünderte Deutschland*, p. 64. If per capita GNP in East Germany sank from 50 per cent of West Germany's level in 1950 to 30 per cent by 1989, this means that the starting point was crucial (most of the productivity gap was already discernible before the planned economic system was established firmly enough to make a significant long-term difference) but that the shortcomings of the planned economy served to widen significantly the gap that already existed.

56 J. Bähr, 'Institutionenordnung und Wirtschaftsentwicklung', p. 541.

57 A. Steiner, 'Wirtschaftliche Lendungsverfahren in der Industrie der DDR', pp. 291–2. The build-up of domestic heavy industry was also encouraged by the lack of rational prices under the socialist economy that obscures the advantages of international trade. Cf. C. Buchheim, 'Kriegsfolgen und Wirtschaftswachstum in der SBZ/DDR', pp. 525–6.

58 C. Buchheim, 'Kriegsfolgen und Wirtschaftswachstum in der SBZ/DDR', p. 527.

Moreover, there were political constraints to how far consumption and living standards could be neglected in the interests of ameliorating these bottlenecks. The SED leadership had to strike some kind of balance between production and consumption, and was particularly attuned to this problem after the upheavals of June 1953.[59] In very simple terms, consumption represented the interface between ordinary people and the economy, so it was politically imperative to make whatever improvements were possible.[60] Equally important (and closely related to this point), during the 1950s the leadership also had to do its best to keep the already short supply of labour from leaving for West Germany, which – thanks in large part to its more generous treatment by its occupiers – was already achieving a far higher living standard than the GDR.[61]

Because of the uncertainties of the quantitative data and because it is generally agreed that a significant East–West gap existed by 1950, it has been suggested that developments during 1948–50, the period immediately following the introduction of two opposing economic systems in East and West Germany, are crucial for determining the reasons for the divergence in economic performance.[62] Did it begin to open before 1948, thus pointing the finger at reparations? Or did it rest more on systemic factors and therefore open up by and large after 1948? It seems clear that industrial

59 On the role of consumption in the 1953 crisis, see Katherine Pence, '"You as a Woman Will Understand": Consumption, Gender and the Relationship between State and Citizenry in the GDR's Crisis of 17 June 1953', *GH* 19 (2001), pp. 218–52.

60 There is a growing literature on consumption and consumer culture in the GDR. For studies focusing on the regime and consumer policy, see Mark Landsmann, 'Dictatorship and Demand: East Germany Between Productivism and Consumerism, 1948–1961', PhD dissertation, Columbia University, 2000; J. Zatlin, 'Consuming Ideology'; J. Zatlin, 'The Vehicle of Desire'; A. Steiner, 'Dissolution of the Dictatorship over Needs? Consumer Behavior and Economic Reform in East Germany in the 1960s', in S. Strasser *et al.* (eds), *Getting and Spending* (Cambridge, 1998), pp. 167–85; B. Ciesla and P. Poutrus, 'Food Supply in a Planned Economy: SED Nutrition Policy between Crisis Response and Popular Needs', in K. Jarausch (ed.), *Dictatorship as Experience*, pp. 143–62; P. Heldmann, 'Konsumpolitik in der DDR. Jugendmode in den sechziger Jahren', in H. Berghoff (ed.), *Konsumpolitik. Die Regulierung des privaten Verbrauchs im 20. Jahrhundert* (Göttingen, 1999), pp. 135–58; S. Merl, 'Sowjetisierung im Welt des Konsums', in K. Jarausch and H. Siegrist (eds), *Amerikanisierung und Sowjetisierung in Deutschland 1945–1970* (Frankfurt a. M., 1997), pp. 167–94. For works adopting a more cultural historical and anthropological approach, see Ina Merkel, *Utopie und Bedürfnis. Die Geschichte der Konsumkultur in der DDR* (Cologne, 1999); Katherine Pence, 'From Rations to Fashions: The Gendered Politics of East and West German Consumption, 1945–1961', PhD dissertation, University of Michigan, 1999; Elizabeth Ten Dyke, 'Tulips in December: Space, Time and Consumption before and after the End of German Socialism', *GH* 19 (2001), pp. 253–76. For an excellent example of how to combine both of these approaches, see Judd Stitziel, 'Fashioning Socialism: Clothing, Politics, and Consumer Culture in East Germany, 1948–1971', PhD dissertation, Johns Hopkins University, 2001. On consumption in the Eastern bloc generally, see Susan Reid and David Crowley (eds), *Style and Socialism: Modernity and Material Culture in Post-War Eastern Europe* (Oxford, 2000).

61 On efforts to curb emigration and the social and political effects of the mass exodus before summer 1961, see C. Ross, 'Before the Wall: East Germans, Communist Authority and the Mass Exodus to the West', *Historical Journal* vol. 45 (2002), no. 4; C. Ross, '"Sonst sehe ich mich veranlasst, auch nach dem Westen zu ziehen": Zum Zusammenhang von Republikflucht, SED-Herrschaft und DDR-Bevölkerung vor dem Mauerbau', in *DA* 34:4 (2001), pp. 613–27; Patrick Major, 'Vor und nach dem 13. August 1961', *AfS*, vol. 39 (1999), pp. 371–400.

62 J. Bähr, 'Institutionenordnung und Wirtschaftsentwicklung', p. 548.

production actually grew more quickly in the SBZ than in the western zones until 1948. After 1948 the East–West gap emerged that would characterize the entire economic development of the two German states until 1989. As Bähr argues:

> This course of development is conclusive proof that the weak growth of the GDR rested on institutional factors. With the transition to a centrally planned economy, East German growth fell behind that of West Germany. The gap could not be closed over the following decades.[63]

Buchheim, too, contends that the gap opens in 1948 once the western zones coordinated their economic system and the centrally planned economy took hold in the East.[64] This argument is not, in my view, entirely convincing. For one thing, higher growth in the SBZ before 1948 rested in large part on the fact that western growth was so low. Reparations in the SBZ not only represented demand but also required that some form of command economy be in place. By contrast, in the western zones there was far less demand and little economic system at all before 1948. Thus the SBZ could show higher growth rates but still be heavily burdened by dismantling and reparations. With the introduction of the DM – and with it a more coherent economic system – in the western zones in 1948, the West German economy quickly (and not surprisingly) surpassed the SBZ. Moreover, this entire approach seems to posit too simple a relationship between 'systemic'/'system-indifferent' factors and pre-/post-1948 developments. One cannot assume that a gap opening after 1948 must be due to systemic weaknesses and one opening before 1948 to 'system-indifferent' circumstances because reparations and dismantling could be 'system-indifferent' but still generate their worst effects well after 1948. Indeed, as Karlsch argues, the effects of reparations were by no means limited to the 1940s, but grew in the 1950s into significant obstacles.[65]

In terms of periodization, it seems hard to escape the tentative conclusion that reparations and dismantling were the central factors behind the GDR's economic problems during the early years. This is in any event the conclusion reached by Rainer Karlsch, who contends that 'the dismantling and reparations from running production did not alone lead to the clear lag of the SBZ behind the western zones before the founding of the two states. However, among the various factors they were the most important at least until 1950.'[66] The FRG had it far easier in terms of aid, reparations, and the influx of motivated skilled workers that the GDR had lost. In the long term the migration of firms and people was probably more important than dismantling and reparations in that there was a direct relationship between the

---

63 Ibid., p. 543.
64 C. Buchheim, 'Die Wirtschaftsordnung als Barriere des gesamtwirtschaftlichen Wachstums', p. 200.
65 R. Karlsch, *Allein bezahlt?*, p. 234.
66 R. Karlsch, *Allein bezahlt?*, pp. 228, 239; the same argument is made in L. Baar, R. Karlsch and W. Matschke, *Kriegsfolgen und Kriegslasten Deutschlands*; Baar *et al.*, 'Kriegsschäden, Demontagen und Reparationen'.

GDR's loss and the FRG's benefit.[67] As regards the 1950s, 'the reconstruction of the economy in East Germany could only be completed seven to ten years later than in the Federal Republic, above all because of reparations'.[68]

The importance of reparations was only clearly overtaken, so to speak, by systemic factors later on, and especially under Honecker. In other words, the primary reasons for East Germany falling behind the West changed over time. However one rates the importance of systemic deficiencies during the 1940s and 1950s, by around the mid-1960s they clearly became critical. This period witnessed the first major technological leap since the end of the war, above all in microelectronics and computing technology, and the Eastern economies by and large failed to leap with the West. The socialist economies were hardly helped by the technology embargo – the so-called Cocom list of goods banned from East–West trade – but this was not the root of the problem. The planned economy had proved reasonably adept at organizing extensive production (producing more by pouring in more resources), but was ill-equipped for encouraging intensive production (producing more through the application of new techniques). This requires innovation, which clearly is not the strong suit of the centrally planned economies.[69] The new microelectronic and computing technologies in particular called for flexibility and rapid innovation in order to keep pace. It is not going too far to say that by the mid-1960s the centrally planned economy, which had proved its usefulness for organizing economic recovery during the two decades after the war, was becoming increasingly obsolete.

It was precisely this lack of flexibility and innovation that motivated the economic reform attempts of the 1960s. Communist leaders across the Soviet bloc recognized that the system of central planning needed to change, and quite significantly at that, if it were to maintain its momentum, let alone keep pace with the West. The dismantling of the reforms and subsequent recentralization of the economy in the early 1970s not only left these problems unaddressed, but actually cemented them back in. This failure to adjust its economic system and undergo painful structural reforms was undoubtedly a crucial watershed in the GDR's economic history, marking what many scholars see as

---

67 Cf. J. Bähr, 'Die Firmenabwanderung aus der SBZ/DDR 1945–1950', in W. Fischer *et al.* (eds), *Wirtschaft im Umbruch. Strukturveränderungen und Wirtschaftspolitik im 19. und 20. Jahrhundert* (St. Katharinen, 1997), pp. 229–49. The idea that this could be compensated by increasing women's employment is unconvincing because it fails to take account of the difference in terms of qualification. A. Ritschl, 'Aufstieg und Niedergang der Wirtschaft der DDR'.

68 R. Karlsch, *Allein bezahlt?*, p. 240.

69 Cf. esp. Hans-Jürgen Wagener, 'Anlage oder Umwelt? Überlegungen zur Innovationsschwäche der DDR-Wirtschaft', in *Berliner Debatte Initial* 1/1995, pp. 67–82; also J. Bähr and D. Petzina (eds), *Innovationsverhalten und Entscheidungsstrukturen. Vergleichende Studien zur wirtschaftlichen Entwicklung im geteilten Deutschland 1945–1990* (Berlin, 1996); A. Bauerkämper, B. Ciesla and J. Roesler, 'Wirklich wollen und nicht richtig können. Das Verhältnis von Innovation und Beharrung in der DDR-Wirtschaft', in J. Kocka and M. Sabrow (eds), *Die DDR als Geschichte*, pp. 116–21; also revealing are the remarks of Claus Krömke, personal consultant to Günter Mittag, 'Innovationen – nur gegen den Plan', in Theo Pirker *et al.*, *Der Plan als Befehl und Fiktion. Wirtschaftsführung in der DDR* (Opladen, 1995), pp. 33–66; Hans Joas and Martin Kohli (eds), *Der Zusammenbruch der DDR* (Frankfurt a. M., 1993), p. 21.

the beginning of the long, terminal downhill slide. Whether the 'retreat from reform'[70] was *the* critical watershed in East Germany's economic history or whether it was largely 'pre-programmed' into the socialist system itself is a point of some debate, as we have seen. The NES patently did not transform the GDR's economy in any fundamental sense. But could it have? Might socialist policy-makers realistically have evolved towards market-based production in the 1960s? Was far-reaching reform ever really a viable prospect, or was this effectively impossible within the context of the socialist system? These are speculative questions geared more for social scientists or economists than for historians. For our purposes here it is more helpful to rephrase the question: were the reforms ever very far-reaching in intent, if not effect?

The bulk of evidence strongly suggests that they were never about fundamental reform. Indeed, the NES was arguably geared more towards maintaining the political and economic system than reforming it. From the very beginning, the entire reform effort was more a political than economic programme; its aim was not a partial liberalization of the economy for its own sake, but rather in order to secure SED power and stabilize the GDR by improving its economic performance. It is hardly surprising, then, that the reforms were hamstrung from the outset by political expediency. For instance, the 1:1 Valuta/DM exchange rate, which greatly overestimated the value of the East German currency, was a face-saving political decision that hindered exports and encouraged imports. In addition, fears of the potential for unrest in the factories meant that the issue of productivity was never pushed through on the shopfloor.[71] Most importantly, the main problem with central planning was signally not overcome: the lack of accurate information about scarcity, demand or labour productivity – in other words, market-oriented prices. Any economic system needs some kind of 'real' indicators to give producers feedback on how effective their actions and decisions are (whether there is a demand for their products, whether they should make certain investments, etc.) regardless of whether these decisions are made 'centrally' or not. Internally, the GDR operated almost completely within a system of 'artificial' indicators which had serious ramifications for investment and innovation. Price policy underlay the entire system, so it stands to reason that economic reforms had to include price reforms, if not begin with them. In the event, the SED never even fully reformed prices for raw materials, let alone industrial and consumer prices. Some decision-making powers were decentralized, but central control over prices was made only slightly more flexible. Indeed, it now seems quite clear that the problem was never really on the agenda for reform. As Steiner has convincingly argued in his massive study of the NES:

> To cross the boundary towards the market would ultimately have placed in question the control of the central authorities and with it the prerogative of the

70  C. Maier, *Dissolution*, p. 78.
71  A point elaborated at length by J. Kopstein, *The Politics of Economic Decline*.

party and its right to formulate overall economic goals. The revocation of this systemic premise was, however, never in mind, so it therefore remained necessary to secure the coherence of the steering- and coordination mechanism through further planning.[72]

Instead of letting prices float more freely as a means of feedback, the basic structures of central control were maintained. Indeed, the number of people working in the economic administration during the reforms actually increased instead of decreased. This increase was not, as has sometimes been argued, merely a reflection of 'teething problems' associated with the introduction of the reforms, but rather part of the overall design – the same measures were foreseen for further reforms after 1971 which in the event never took place.[73]

The reforms were, then, essentially confined to the margins of the system. Because planning remained dominant, it is mistaken to view this as a form of mixed economy, a 'mixture of state intervention and market regulation'[74] or a 'consistent coupling of general economic goals with market-oriented activities on the part of individual enterprises'.[75] Any market orientation was arrested in its embryonic stages and restrained by the strictures of the plan since even the reformers did not wish to cross certain boundaries (especially regarding cost-oriented prices). The central problem was that it is impossible to simulate market mechanisms effectively without introducing the basic institutions – at the very least 'real' prices – on which they rest. The NES rather seems like an instance of what Kornai has called 'indirect bureaucratic control' – bureaucratic steering via the use of 'levers' instead of simple directives, decentralizing planning but retaining central control over key resources.[76] Because this fundamental price problem remained, the idea that the NES represented a possibility 'to achieve a dynamic and competitive economy and thereby to secure the GDR's economic existence as a socialist German state'[77] is not very convincing. Nor, for that matter, is the idea that the reforms in the GDR were 'potentially explosive'. While it is surely correct that 'the logic of decentralization, incentives, and free prices was inherently expansive',[78] this logic did not, as we have just seen, go very far in the GDR.

---

72 A. Steiner, *Die DDR-Wirtschaftsreform*, p. 557. Gerhard Schürer also contends that 'nothing was ever fundamentally changed' concerning the centralized pricing system. A. Steiner, 'Die Wirtschafts- und Sozialpolitik der DDR', p. 143.
73 A. Steiner, *Die DDR-Wirtschaftsreform*, p. 552.
74 J. Roesler, 'Das NÖS als Wirtschaftskonzept', p. 398; cf. also W. Halbritter, 'Was geschah wirklich in und mit der Reform des "NÖS"?'.
75 Herbert Wolf in *Neues Deutschland*, 2/3 March 1991.
76 J. Kornai, *The Socialist System*, pp. 488, 507–8.
77 J. Roesler, 'Das NÖS als Wirtschaftskonzept. Sichten, Tatsachen, Interpretationen', *DA* 31 (1998), p. 398. Walter Halbritter, 'Was geschah wirklich in und mit der Reform des "NÖS"?'.
78 C. Maier, *Dissolution*, pp. 88–9. Herbert Wolf, one of the main proponents of the NES in the 1960s, has recently argued that the success of the reforms would inevitably have required fundamental political changes. H. Wolf, 'Verhältnis von Ökonomie und Politik in der DDR – Möglichkeiten und Realitäten ihrer Entwicklung', in *Ansichten zur Geschichte der DDR*, vol. 6, p. 75.

In many ways the scenario just presented echoes the classic argument that the threat posed by marketization to the position of bureaucrats predisposes them to preserve their own power at the expense of economic efficiency. But it is not enough to leave matters there. The reforms also fell victim to the logic of imperial control, which dictated that Soviet interests were best served by maintaining leaders loyal to Moscow in the various states in its orbit. The brutal and symbolic repression of the reforms in Czechoslovakia in August 1968 was motivated by the fear that reformers would break the party monopoly and eventually withdraw from the Soviet bloc altogether. Yet perhaps even more important than Soviet interests for the specific case of the GDR was its rather unique political situation. It is crucial to distinguish between the question of 'could socialism reform itself' and 'could socialism in East Germany reform itself?' Several factors are important here. First, the GDR formed the front line in the Cold War and was of great strategic importance to the socialist bloc; there was no desire for even a chance of political instability. Second, the special economic interconnectedness of the GDR and Soviet Union – tightly bound to each other by the exchange of crucial raw materials and finished products – also gravitated against reform. Most importantly, the GDR's 'semi-national' status presented it with unique problems. With neither democratic nor 'national' legitimacy, its whole *raison d'être* was to offer a competing socio-economic system from that pertaining in West Germany. Far-reaching economic reforms thus directly impinged on the basis for the GDR's very existence. As Ulrich Beck put it, 'Poland minus communism is still Poland; but the German Democratic Republic minus communism is – the Federal Republic'.[79] Since reformist experimentation was hampered by a whole array of such 'non-systemic' factors, it seems overstretched to say that the East German reforms were doomed to fail because of the system itself. Although it is hard to see how far-reaching economic reform might take place within the classic 'socialist system', some form of mixed economy and limited political pluralism (as the Czechs were pursuing in 1968) is not wholly unimaginable. In any event, the idea that reform was impossible is not provable. Yet it is extremely difficult to imagine how reforms might have succeeded *in the GDR*.[80] The particularly acute – indeed existential – risks presented by the reforms go some way towards explaining why the SED was so lukewarm about them at home and so keen to help stamp them out elsewhere.

---

79  U. Beck, 'Opposition in Deutschland', in Bernd Giesen and Claus Leggewie (eds), *Experiment Vereinigung: Ein sozialer Grossversuch* (Berlin, 1991), p. 24.

80  The otherwise stimulating and wide-ranging account in C. Maier, *Dissolution*, does not clearly make this distinction. By contrast, Stefan Bollinger lays particular emphasis on the fact that 'the reform approaches in Berlin and Prague were fundamentally different'. Bollinger, 'Die halbe Reform – Neues Ökonomisches System: für eine effektivere Wirtschaft, aber nicht für einen demokratischen Sozialismus', in *Ansichten zur Geschichte der DDR*, vol. 4, p. 243. It should be pointed out that this tends to undermine the common argument that the NES represented a 'missed opportunity' for reforming East German socialism, which Bollinger himself asserts.

Given both the GDR's economic position at the end of the 1960s as well as the internal workings of its political system, the outcome of this 'conflict between efficiency and power'[81] was, if not pre-programmed, then certainly heavily weighted towards the latter. Economically, the failure of the East to open up to world markets during the era of reform was largely due to the fact that it could no longer compete with the West, especially in terms of quality. Hence the GDR and other socialist states tended to seek sanctuary from the competitive pressures of the world market in COMECON, which in turn merely cemented their economic backwardness.[82] It was easiest for communist leaders to take the path of least resistance, understandably avoiding the potential for mass unrest if they underwent the kind of reforms the West went through. Of course all political systems present a certain temptation to base economic decisions on political criteria. But in centrally planned economies this temptation is magnified for the simple reason that politics and ideology play a key role in economic decision-making in the one-party state. The dismantling of the reforms in the early 1970s is ultimately a story of political expediency over the needs of the economy.

However probable or inevitable one deems this outcome to be, it is important to recognize that the subsequent situation did not revert to the *status quo ante*. At one level, the recentralization of economic planning did represent a return to tried and (dis)proven methods which left the root problems unaddressed. But the conversion to Honecker's 'consumer socialism' was a new departure and, indeed, one that positively exacerbated the problems. This new brand of socialist economy was *not* the only possible outcome to the failure of the reforms. The 'unity of social and economic policy' was by no means inevitable, but rather a conscious choice between what by the end of the 1960s were two competing visions for the future of East German socialism. Whereas Ulbricht remained fixated on his goal of overtaking the West economically – even if this meant lowering living standards in the interests of higher capital investment – Honecker saw the GDR's long-term interests best served by abandoning the goal of national unification, ceasing to compete with the West on its own narrow economic terms, and introducing a socialist form of consumer society within the GDR's abilities. This ultimately rested on a different understanding of the fundamental aims and purpose of state socialism, which in Honecker's view should not be measured solely by Western criteria.[83] With hindsight we know this was a fateful decision. The introduction of this vision without

---

81 So the fitting subtitle of A. Steiner's detailed study, *Die DDR-Wirtschaftsreform*.

82 For an overview of the effects of COMECON membership, see C. Buchheim, 'Wirtschaftliche Folgen der Integration der DDR in den RGW', in C. Buchheim (ed.), *Wirtschaftliche Folgelasten des Krieges in der SBZ/DDR*, pp. 341–61; also Ludolf Herbst, 'Die DDR und die wirtschaftliche Integration des Ostblocks in den sechziger Jahren', in ibid, pp. 363–80.

83 Cf. the discussion in A. Steiner, *Die DDR-Wirtschaftsreform*, pp. 550f; J. Kopstein, *The Politics of Economic Decline*, pp. 73–4; W. Halbritter, 'Was geschah wirklich in und mit der Reform des "NÖS"?', pp. 334.

corresponding improvements in productivity amounted to buying the short- and mid-term stability of the GDR at the price of its long-term economic viability.[84]

The decisions of the early 1970s were, then, without doubt a crucial watershed in the history of the East German economy. From this point on the GDR was living beyond its means. The decision to subsidize consumption at the expense of investment greatly increased the rate of the downward spiral that had begun to rotate at the birth of the GDR's planned economy in the late 1940s. This change of direction should not, however, be misconstrued as *the* crucial turning-point, since the primary causes of the GDR's economic woes – the fundamental systemic problems – had been present since the decisions of the late 1940s and were left essentially unaddressed throughout its history. The reform attempts of the 1960s represented an attempt to slow the rate of rotation of the downward spiral, not to tackle the underlying problems. Without the acceleration of the 1970s, the spiral might have continued to spin relatively slowly as it did over the previous decades, with the East German economy never achieving the performance levels of the West but nonetheless displaying some positive growth in spite of the fundamental shortcomings at its centre, or at the very least deteriorating at a slower rate than it did.[85]

In the event, however, the conservative socialism that Honecker introduced proved prohibitively costly with the global recession of the 1970s and early 1980s. By this time the 'unity of social and economic policy' was in many ways functioning as a mask to hide the GDR's fundamental economic problems as far as possible behind a veneer of consumerism. Attempts were made to improve some aspects of production, above all in the fields of microelectronics and aeronautics, but overall the GDR never successfully made the transition to a 'post-industrial' economy. As Steiner has put it: 'The severely limited capability of the state socialist economic system to sustain economic and technical-innovational change was ultimately the decisive cause of the GDR's economic weakness during its last decade.'[86] The oft-cited foreign trade deficits were a symptom, not a cause of the problem. Estimates of the level of debt vary, yet it is clear that by the end of the 1980s the GDR was headed for insolvency.[87] The problems were compounded by the deterioration of the GDR's capital stock, all of which required

---

84 Christoph Boyer and Peter Skyba, 'Sozial- und Komsumpolitik als Stabilisierungsstrategie. Zur Genese der "Einheit von Wirtschafts- und Sozialpolitik" in der DDR', *DA* 32: 4 (1999), pp. 577–90.

85 My thinking on these issues, as well as many others in this chapter, has benefited greatly from discussions with Judd Stitziel, who originally suggested the spiral imagery. This is, broadly speaking, also the argument advanced in Günter Kusch *et al.*, *Schlußbilanz – DDR. Fazit einer verfehlten Wirtschafts- und Sozialpolitik* (Berlin, 1991).

86 A. Steiner, 'Zwischen Konsumversprechen und Innovationszwang', p. 183.

87 Armin Volze argues that the original Western estimates of $13–14 billion were approximately correct, 'Ein großer Bluff? Die Westverschuldung der DDR', *DA* 29:5 (1996), pp. 701–13. Gerhard Schürer has revised his earlier estimate of 49 billion Valutamarks down to 20.3 billion, 'Das Ende der DDR-Wirtschaft', in *Ansichten zur Geschichte der DDR*, vol. 6, pp. 375–407.

immediate and massive economic changes if it were to survive for long.[88] Again, the problem was that such a change would essentially have removed the GDR's reason to exist alongside the FRG, as Otto Reinhold, Chief of the SED Academy for Social Sciences, repeatedly emphasized over the summer and autumn of 1989.[89]

In the light of this saga of mismanagement, the question of 'who knew what' rather posed itself after 1989.[90] Honecker was certainly not willing to accept responsibility, but instead blamed his successors for wrecking the 'blossoming economy' that they supposedly inherited from him.[91] Günter Mittag, the *Politbüro* member with special responsibility for the economy, likewise denied all responsibility for the disaster, mendaciously presenting himself as a reformer whose ambitions were always thwarted by the 'dogmatists' within the leadership who refused to change course.[92] Both claims are the stuff of legend. The entire *Politbüro* knew how dire the situation was by 1988 at the latest. Why, then, did it 'lead the GDR with open eyes into economic and political bankruptcy'?[93] It seems insufficient to blame the leaders in a personal sense; Honecker himself hardly seems to have displayed much grasp of the economic situation. The decisions and behaviour of the top functionaries were a major factor not so much because these people were stupid or stubborn (though one might well make such a case regarding certain individuals), but rather because of the structures in which they operated, the culture and dynamics of the decision-making process among the SED leadership. As M. Rainer Lepsius has argued, the activities of the economic functionaries were severely limited by the political control over the economy. Typical of their behaviour was

a fragmentation of the perception of reality, a shunting of decisions and action to a higher level of the hierarchy (ultimately Günter Mittag), a consequential laming of all activity and a retreat into the continuation of the daily routine and proven techniques of crisis management within one's own sphere of competence.

In Lepsius' view, the economic functionaries were 'engaged, experienced, and loyal to the regime, but limited in their abilities as a collective'.[94] This

---

88 For a detailed overview of the GDR's economic situation in its closing years, see Eberhard Kuhrt *et al.* (eds), *Die Endzeit der DDR-Wirtschaft* (Opladen, 1999); E. Kuhrt *et al.* (eds), *Die wirtschaftliche und ökologische Situation der DDR in den achtziger Jahren* (Opladen, 1996).

89 Hans-Hermann Hertle and Gerd-Rüdiger Stephan (eds), *Das Ende der SED. Die letzten Tage des Zentralkomitees* (Berlin, 1997), p. 332.

90 Maria Haendcke-Hoppe-Arndt, 'Wer wußte was? Der ökonomische Niedergang der DDR', *DA* 28:6 (1995), pp. 588–602.

91 Quoted in Reinhold Andert and Wolfgang Herzberg, *Der Sturz. Erich Honecker im Kreuzverhör* (Berlin, 1990), p. 431.

92 G. Mittag, *Um jeden Preis.*

93 Hans-Hermann Hertle, 'Der Weg in den Bankrott der DDR-Wirtschaft. Das Scheitern der "Einheit von Wirtschafts- und Sozialpolitik" am Beispiel der Schürer/Mittag Kontroverse im Politbüro 1988', *DA* 25:2 (1992), p. 127.

94 M. Rainer Lepsius, 'Handlungsräume und Rationalitätskriterien der Wirtschaftsfunktionäre in der Ära Honecker', in Theo Pirker *et al.*, *Der Plan als Befehl und Fiktion*, p. 362.

assessment tallies with the insider observations of Siegfried Burmeister, who (somewhat apologetically) blames the system above all else:

> What radius of action did the system give them? To what extent were they even in a position to perceive alternative points of view? In my thirty-five years of experience from the low levels to the ministries and the Central Committee, the room for maneouvre in thought and action was extremely limited.[95]

Again, the close relationship between economics, ideology and political decisions was a crucial factor throughout the GDR's history, including its demise.

In the end, no one within the SED leadership wanted to take the necessary steps, no one thought it was possible to make the about-face to consumer austerity that would be necessary to stop the rot.[96] Honecker's consumer socialism had made living standards and social spending the fundamental basis of the regime's claim to legitimacy. The ideological utopia of the early years was lost; indeed the zeal had even evaporated among the leadership. Nowhere was this clearer than in Egon Krenz's remarks upon hearing the extent of the debt in May 1989: 'We now need to look forward. For me there is no question whether the unity of economic and social policy should be continued. It must be continued because it *is* socialism in the GDR!'[97]

The GDR's economic troubles undermined any 'materialist legitimation' that the regime might have claimed. Indeed, they directly discredited the regime because it had consistently refused to let economic activities develop independent of political control. Yet economic failures did not inevitably lead to regime collapse and unification with the Federal Republic. Other social and political factors were arguably more important during the crucial events of autumn 1989. Long-term economic decline was a crucial backdrop that fed the swelling popular dissatisfactions of the 1980s and weakened the will of the regime from within. The general populace was becoming less and less prepared to acquiesce in the SED tutelage that for so long had formed the basis of governance in East Germany, and lower-level functionaries were growing increasingly perplexed and despondent about the leadership's refusal to tune into the reforms emanating from Moscow. It is to the role of opposition and dissent in the GDR's history and the revolutionary events of 1989 that we now turn in the next two chapters.

---

95  S. Burmeister, 'Kooperation, kalter Krieg und Konkurrenz im Handel zwischen den beiden deutschen Staaten', in *Ansichten zur Geschichte der DDR*, vol. 6, p. 242.

96  Which, according to Schürer, was a monthly debt of 500 million Valutamark, a rate that would make the GDR insolvent by 1991.

97  From Hans-Hermann Hertle, 'Die Diskussion der ökonomischen Krisen in der Führungsspitze der SED', in Theo Pirker *et al.*, *Der Plan*, pp. 343–4.

# |5|

# Opposition and dissent: Fundamental feature or fringe phenomenon?

Questions concerning the nature and extent of opposition towards the SED regime touch on one of the fundamental problems of understanding the GDR's history, namely, its inherent stability or instability. Quite obviously, the foundation, forty-year existence and downfall of the East German regime were in large part the consequence of international political constellations after the Second World War. But what role did domestic patterns of opposition and conformity play in sustaining and undermining the regime? Does the long-standing German reputation for political obedience (whether deserved or undeserved) offer any explanations? Was the bulk of the populace in some sense complicit in sustaining the regime through apathy or an unwillingness to risk punishment? Did the relative economic success of the GDR keep the level of popular discontent below boiling point and deprive would-be dissident movements of popular backing? Or was sheer coercion the key? Was the employment or mere threat of force enough to preclude most forms of dissent and opposition from emerging in the first place? What, in short, was the role of East Germans themselves in allowing the regime to reproduce itself, and how important is this for explaining the GDR's oft-cited stability and unexpected collapse?

These questions have always been, and will no doubt remain, strongly coloured by moral and political overtones. The issue of who undermined the regime and who sustained it – by actions if not intentions – has direct implications not only for the credibility of individual public figures, but also for the self-understanding of the millions of 'ordinary' east Germans in the 'new *Bundesländer*'. It is thus hardly surprising that dissent and opposition have been interpreted in radically different ways in both popular and scholarly discourse. On the one hand, popular opposition to the SED regime, however latent it remained and however forcefully repressed by the coercive apparatus of the state, has been viewed as a constant and fundamental feature of East German society, as the events of autumn 1989 supposedly 'proved'. On the other hand, the GDR has also widely been viewed not only as the most stable, but indeed the most tranquil state in the Soviet bloc. Before 1989, the uprising of 17 June 1953 was the sole manifestation of mass protest. Moreover, in comparison to Poland, Hungary and Czechoslovakia, there was relatively little intra-party dissent within the SED. The handful of intellectual dissidents were by and large cut off from the broad masses of East Germans, who for their part had supposedly retreated into the sanctuary of private life. In this view, dissent and opposition were, for most of the GDR's history, a fringe phenomenon of little fundamental importance. These contradictory images of a politically disaffected population kept in submission only by force and a broadly conformist populace unenthusiastically complying with the realities of life in the GDR have not been reconciled since 1989.

As one might expect, debates about dissent and opposition in the GDR have built on the sophisticated conceptual vocabulary of the resistance historiography on the Third Reich.[1] For all the differences between these two regimes and the forms of dissenting behaviour under them, the central issue is in some respects the same: is the nature of conflict and consensus in the GDR better captured by notions of broad societal 'resistance' or 'immunity' to dictatorial rule, or by more narrow concepts of consciously articulated political and/or moral 'opposition'? Before 1989 the terms 'dissent' and 'opposition' usually referred to only a handful of critical intellectuals or political heretics voicing alternative views. Popular disaffection and dissent were seen as largely irrelevant, insofar as they existed at all. Since 1989 this tendency has partially reversed. Dissidents have increasingly been seen as less important – swept away, as they were, by the tide of political plurality in 1990 – than the fact that 'the people' wanted to get rid of the regime. Images of pervasive societal '*Resistenz*' (a term coined by Martin Broszat for the Third Reich, denoting the functional effects of social structures, mentalities and small-scale actions limiting the societal penetration of dictatorial authority and the achievement of total control)[2] have become widespread, especially in the new *Bundesländer*, where there is an understandable desire to downplay compliance and to posit a broad if implicit conflict between 'regime' and 'society' which ultimately felled the regime.

---

1 See the superb overview in I. Kershaw, *The Nazi Dictatorship* (London, 2000), Chapter 8. For an explicit comparison between dissent in the Third Reich and GDR, see C. Kleßmann, 'Opposition und Resistenz in zwei Diktaturen in Deutschland', *HZ*, vol. 262 (1996), pp. 453–79. See also M. Rainer Lepsius, 'Sozialhistorische Probleme der Diktaturforschung', in J. Kocka and M. Sabrow (eds), *Die DDR als Geschichte*, pp. 97–100; Peter Steinbach, 'Diktaturerfahrung und Widerstand', in Klaus-Dietmar Henke, Peter Steinbach and Johannes Tuchel (eds), *Widerstand und Opposition in der DDR* (Cologne, 1999), pp. 57–84; Werner Bramke, 'Widerstand und Dissens. Gedanken über die Vergleichbarkeit von Widersetzlichkeit im Faschismus und im "realen Sozialismus"', in Konrad Jarausch and Matthias Middell (eds), *Nach dem Erdbeben: (Re)Konstruktion ostdeutscher Geschichte und Geschichtswissenschaft* (Leipzig, 1994), pp. 219–43; Bernd Stöver, 'Leben in Deutschen Diktaturen. Historiographische und methodologische Aspekte der Erforschung von Widerstand und Opposition im Dritten Reich und in der DDR', in Detlef Pollack and Dieter Rink (eds), *Zwischen Verweigerung und Opposition: Politischer Protest in der DDR 1970–1989* (Frankfurt a. M., 1997), pp. 30–53.

2 Cf. M. Broszat, *Nach Hitler* (Munich, 1986), pp. 68–91, originally published as 'Resistenz und Widerstand', in M. Broszat et al. (eds), *Bayern in der NS-Zeit*, vol. 4, pp. 691–709.

Debates about opposition and dissent are, as this last point makes abundantly clear, inseparable from wider questions about the relationship of the SED regime and East German society. Indeed, a better historical understanding of opposition can only be achieved by placing such actions within their social and political context and approaching them as an intrinsic part of this broader issue. This means that any examination of opposition is simultaneously an examination of conformity. Not only did the former take place in the midst of the latter, but the boundaries between the two were fluid and ever-changing, and more often than not ran through individual people as they were continually confronted by the moral choices and pressures of life under the constraints of dictatorship.

This chapter will begin by offering an overview of how scholars have defined and used the concepts of dissent and opposition over the years before moving on to evaluate the nature and significance of 'opposition' (in the narrower political sense) and '*Resistenz*' (in the broader societal sense) in the history of the GDR.

# Interpretations

For a regime that made such far-reaching claims on the hearts and souls of its citizens, the SED's own views on opposition and dissent were remarkably vague and contradictory. Publicly, at least, there were no interpretations of opposition at all. In accordance with its self-understanding as the representative of the objective interests of the people, the SED officially denied not only the existence, but even the very possibility of opposition to its rule. As the entry for the term 'opposition' in the GDR's *Concise Political Dictionary* explains:

> In socialist states there exists no objective political or social basis for opposition against the prevailing societal and political circumstances. Because the socialist state serves as both the embodiment of the people's interests and the executor of its will, because the power of the state in fact derives from the people, because it serves the maintenance of peace, the construction of socialism and thereby the constant development of both a comprehensive form of democracy as well as the continually improving fulfilment of the material and spiritual needs of all working people – because of this, all opposition against the socialist order would be directed against the working people themselves.[3]

Simply put, it made no sense to oppose one's own interests. For the sake of ideological consistency, manifestations of political dissent could only be regarded as the result of 'imperialist subversion' or as 'hangovers' from the

---

3 Autorenkollektiv, *Kleines Politisches Wörterbuch* (Berlin, 1967), p. 471. The entry remained essentially unchanged in all subsequent editions.

past, which of course became increasingly unconvincing the longer the GDR existed.[4]

Yet at the same time as denying the very existence of opposition, the party and state were also continually producing it. As Karl Wilhelm Fricke pointed out long ago, political opposition in the GDR was largely 'determined by the system' in the sense that anyone not seen to be agreeing was *de facto* a political opponent and criminalized for being one.[5] In other words, because of the SED's claims to total control and authority, it often created its own 'enemies' by designating deviant actions and forms of behaviour (for example, taking part in a church service or having long hair) as 'dissent' or 'opposition' that were not necessarily intended as such and that under less 'totalizing' regimes would be of no consequence whatsoever. In this sense the far-reaching claims of the regime thus created, not eradicated, deviant behaviour. As Eckard Jesse has put it: 'The history of the GDR is the history of continual repression, but simultaneously also the history of permanent opposition.'[6] Only in such an interventionist system as the GDR was a gargantuan police force like the *Stasi* necessary to keep track of such widespread potential for 'opposition', for which, ideologically speaking, there was no 'objective' basis. The SED was in the untenable position of denying the very thing that it was persecuting.

In the early Federal Republic, public attention was constantly drawn to acts of opposition against the 'occupation socialism' imposed on East Germany by the Soviets. In the late 1940s there was a constant stream of non-socialist politicians who were forced to leave for the West.[7] By the middle of the 1950s, several thousand members of the Christian Democratic and Liberal Democratic parties had been arrested, jailed or forced to resign, and around 5,000 former Social Democrats were also jailed for resisting the blatant communist dominance of the so-called 'Socialist Unity Party' after its founding in 1946.[8] Oppositional activities in universities and schools, for which many young people were given draconian sentences, were also a particular focus of attention.[9]

---

4  So strong was the myth of subversion that it has survived the events of 1989. According to former *Stasi* chief Markus Wolf, 'not by a long stretch did every oppositional voice in the GDR have its origins in this country; the West German organizations, behind which the Western secret services attempted to hide, increasingly accelerated their activities in the GDR.' Idem, *Spionagechef im geheimen Krieg. Erinnerungen* (Munich, 1997), p. 109.

5  K. W. Fricke, *Opposition und Widerstand in der DDR* (Cologne, 1984), p. 18.

6  E. Jesse, 'Artikulationsformen und Zielsetzungen von widerständigen Verhalten in der Deutschen Demokratischen Republik', in *Materialien der Enquete-Kommission*, vol. VII: 1, p. 1028.

7  As early as 1945, high-profile political leaders such as Waldemar Koch (LDPD), Andreas Hermes and Walter Schreiber (CDU) were lauded for speaking out against the expropriation of property without compensation, for which all three were forced to resign their positions. In 1947, CDU leaders Jakob Kaiser and Ernst Lemmer were removed from their positions for refusing to participate in the SED-controlled 'People's Congress Movement'.

8  Beatrix Bouvier has calculated that from 1946 to 1956 between 5,000 and 6,000 former Social Democrats were either imprisoned or interned in forced labour camps. B. Bouvier, *Ausgeschaltet! Sozialdemokraten in der Sowjetischen Besatzungszone und in der DDR 1945–1953* (Bonn, 1996), p. 258.

9  Particularly noteworthy are Marianne Müller and Egon Erwin, '... stürmt die Festung Wissenschaft!' Die Sowjetisierung der mitteldeutschen Universitäten seit 1945 (Berlin, 1953); and Thomas Ammer, *Universität*

The escalation of the 'class struggle' after the SED's second party conference in July 1952 provoked a broad wave of discontent across many segments of East German society. The attempted collectivization of agriculture led to protests in the villages and increased the flow of migration westwards. The attacks on the church and the criminalization of its youth organizations alienated many religious people. Most importantly, the increases in work norms and basic prices in spring 1953 led to a wave of strikes in the factories, and eventually provided the spark for the uprising of 17 June 1953. Over 16 and 17 June some 560 cities and towns witnessed strikes and disturbances; 32 people were shot and killed; around 1,600 participants received jail sentences. The 17 June was for many years a national holiday in West Germany, celebrated as the day on which freedom-loving East Germans rose in a heroic but unsuccessful attempt to throw off the yoke of communist oppression and to unite Germany in freedom and democracy.[10] For the Federal Republic, June 1953 went down in post-war history as the first in a series of uprisings against Soviet hegemony: 1953 was followed by Hungary and Poland in 1956, by Czechoslovakia in 1968, by Poland in 1980–81, and eventually most of Eastern Europe in 1989. It served as a powerful symbol of popular opposition to the regime, which the continuing stream of refugees to the West and the erection of the Berlin Wall in August 1961 – both well documented in publications by the Federal government[11] – only confirmed. A series of autobiographical accounts of life in the 'Zone' and documentary publications on individual court cases against regime opponents helped to concretize the continuing persecution of dissent and to give it a human face.[12]

Whereas early Western views on dissent in the SBZ/GDR generally followed the notion of 'anti-totalitarian' resistance that had developed with reference to the Third Reich, the phenomenon of communist-inspired opposition to the GDR's leadership and the apparent quieting of popular dissent after the erection of the Wall began to change the perspective by the mid-1960s. New terms such as 'anti-Stalinist', 'inner-communist' or 'democratic communist opposition' referred to the alternative views emanating from intellectual circles and from within the upper echelons of the SED, all of which attracted increasing scholarly attention. The shift of perspective was clearly manifested with the publication of Martin Jänicke's detailed study of

(Contd)
   *zwischen Demokratie und Diktatur. Ein Beitrag zur Nachkriegsgeschichte der Universität Rostock* (Cologne, 1969).

10 M. Hettling, 'Umstritten, vergessen, erfolgreich. Der 17. Juni als bundesdeutscher Nationalfeiertag', *DA* 3/2000.

11 Bundesministerium für gesamtdeutsche Fragen, *Die Flucht aus der Sowjetzone und die Sperrmaßnahmen des kommunistischen Regimes vom 13 August 1961* (Bonn/Berlin, 1961); Bundesministerium für Vertriebene, Flüchtlinge und Kriegsgeschädigte, *Flucht aus der Sowjetzone* (Bonn/Berlin, 1964).

12 See, for instance, Erika Hornstein, *Die deutsche Not. Flüchtlinge berichten* (Cologne, 1960); E. Hornstein, *Staatsfeinde. Sieben Prozesse in der 'DDR'* (Cologne, 1963).

the 'anti-Stalinist opposition against Ulbricht' in 1964,[13] which traced the development of a 'Third Way' vision within intellectual and political circles as well as its eventual elimination from the party leadership during the course of the 1950s.[14] Other scholarly works followed, and by the end of the 1960s a substantial literature on 'inner-communist' opposition had emerged.[15] In the 1970s, the expulsion of dissident artists and intellectuals such as Wolf Biermann and Rudolf Bahro, as well as the house arrest of Robert Havemann, further boosted interest in the 'inner-communist' opposition, which increasingly came to be regarded as synonymous with 'opposition' in the GDR more generally. Rather curiously, research on the GDR was in one important respect moving in the opposite direction from contemporary research on the Third Reich. Instead of broadening the focus beyond elites to German society more generally, research on opposition in the GDR was increasingly concentrated on a handful of critical intellectuals with unorthodox political views.

By the 1970s, the overall picture of opposition and dissent had therefore evolved significantly. This was due not only to the changing political climate of détente, but more importantly to the fact that most manifestations of dissent and opposition had transformed significantly in the meantime. There had been a pronounced shift from the fundamental rejection of the regime in the early years to a more partial and moderate form of criticism that sought to reform East German socialism 'from within' rather than discard it altogether. For this very reason the term 'dissidence' gradually eclipsed 'opposition', which seemed to posit a more fundamental form of antagonism than actually prevailed. Moreover, popular opposition to the regime, however discontented the masses were with various aspects of life in the GDR, was increasingly hard to spot under the tranquil surface of East German society, and quite understandably was ascribed little immediate political relevance compared to the 'numerically small but nonetheless dangerous'[16] inner-communist oppositional groups. Günter Gaus' famous notion of the East German 'niche society' of family, friends and garden allotments gained widespread currency in the early 1980s and rather summarized the dominant Western view of political stability and conformity.[17]

---

13  M. Jänicke, *Der dritte Weg. Die antistalinistische Opposition gegen Ulbricht seit 1953* (Cologne, 1964).

14  There were a number of internal SED purges in the 1950s, including Ulbricht's rivals Rudolf Herrnstadt and Wilhelm Zaisser in the aftermath of June 1953 and the ousting of Karl Schirdewan, Fred Oelßner, and the dissident group around Wolfgang Harich and Walter Janka in 1956–58.

15  Among the most notable works are Alfred Kantorowicz, *Der geistige Widerstand in der DDR* (Troisdorf, 1968); Dieter Knötzsch, *Innerkommunistische Opposition. Das Beispiel Robert Havemann* (Opladen, 1968); and H. Weber, *Demokratischer Kommunismus? Zur Theorie, Geschichte und Politik der kommunistischen Bewegung* (Hannover, 1969).

16  H. Weber and Manfred Koch, 'Opposition in der DDR', in Hans-Georg Wehling (ed.), *DDR* (Stuttgart, 1983), p. 137.

17  G. Gaus, *Wo Deutschland liegt*.

Although oppositional tendencies were clearly no longer a primary focus of scholarly research on the GDR,[18] there was nonetheless a continuing trickle of publications that kept dissent and coercion in view.[19] Karl Wilhelm Fricke's 1984 study of 'opposition and resistance in the GDR' was a milestone in a number of respects.[20] Not only did it represent the first synthesis covering both elite and popular forms of dissent, it was also the first study to analyse non-conformist behaviour within a clear conceptual framework (no doubt influenced by the concurrent debates on opposition and dissent in the Third Reich). In the early 1980s, West German interest in dissenting groups was beginning to increase in any event with the emergence of parallel peace movements against superpower missile deployment in the two Germanies and with the rising visibility of 'autonomous movements' throughout the Soviet bloc.[21] A certain breakthrough was finally achieved at the annual conference of GDR studies in 1989 when issues of opposition were given more attention than before. But such 'opposition' as was discussed was still limited to small groups under the aegis of the church.[22] The unexpected eruption of popular anger towards the regime later that year still caught everyone by surprise. The events and experiences of 1989

18 Since 1989 this has been a focus of criticism against the mainstream 'GDR research' institutions in West Germany. As Dietrich Staritz suggested in 1987, the lack of research in this area resulted less from an alleged desire to play down conflict within the GDR in the spirit of détente than from the widespread view that opposition against the SED was 'such an obvious characteristic of the GDR's past and present that closer analysis actually seems unnecessary'. D. Staritz, 'Die SED und die Opposition', in I. Spittmann (ed.), *Die SED in Geschichte und Gegenwart* (Cologne, 1987), pp. 78–97, here p. 78.

19 Especially noteworthy is Karl Wilhelm Fricke's series of works on dissent and political persecution: K. W. Fricke, *Selbstbehauptung und Widerstand in der Sowjetischen Besatzungszone Deutschlands*, 2nd edition (Bonn/Berlin, 1966); *Warten auf Gerechtigkeit. Kommunistische Säuberungen und Rehabilitierungen. Bericht und Dokumentation* (Cologne, 1971); *Politik und Justiz in der DDR. Zur Geschichte der politischen Verfolgung 1945–1968* (Cologne, 1979); *Die DDR-Staatssicherheit. Entwicklung, Strukturen, Aktionsfelder* (Cologne, 1982); *Zur Menschen- und Grundrechtssituation politischer Gefangener in der DDR*, 2nd edition (Cologne, 1988). See also I. Spittmann and K. W. Fricke (eds), *17. Juni 1953. Arbeiteraufstand in der DDR* (Cologne, 1982); J. Rühle, G. Holzweissig and I. Spittmann (eds), *13. August 1961: Die Mauer von Berlin* (Cologne, 1981).

20 See footnote 5.

21 W. Büscher *et al.* (eds), *Friedensbewegung in der DDR. Texte 1978–1982* (Hattingen, 1982); K. Ehring and M. Dallwitz, *Schwerter zu Pflugscharen. Friedensbewegung in der DDR* (Reinbek bei Hamburg, 1982); P. Wensierski, 'Friedensbewegung in der DDR', *APuZG* B17 (1983), pp. 3–15; Roger Woods, *Opposition in the GDR under Honecker* (London, 1986); G. Minnerup, 'Systemopposition und nationaler Frage in beiden deutschen Staaten', in *Die beiden deutschen Staaten im Ost-West Verhältnis. 15. Tagung zum Stand der DDR-Forschung* (Cologne, 1982), pp. 51–62; H. Weber and M. Koch, 'Opposition in der DDR'; W. Büscher, 'Die evangelischen Kirchen in der DDR – Raum für alternatives Denken und Handeln?', in *Die DDR vor den Herausforderungen der achtziger Jahre. 16. Tagung zum Stand der DDR-Forschung* (Cologne, 1983), pp. 158–66; H. Knabe, 'Neue Soziale Bewegungen als Problem der sozialistischen Gesellschaft', in *Das Profil der DDR in der sozialistischen Staatengemeinschaft. 20. Tagung zum Stand der DDR-Forschung* (Cologne, 1987), pp. 106–19; D. Staritz, 'Die SED und die Opposition'.

22 For the first time, two East German civil rights activists, Ehrhart Neubert and Wolfgang Templin, gave presentations at the conference. E. Neubert, 'Gesellschaftliche Kommunikation im sozialen Wandel', in *Die DDR im vierzigsten Jahr. 22. Tagung zum Stand der DDR-Forschung* (Cologne, 1989), pp. 38–57; W. Templin, 'Zivile Gesellschaft – Osteuropäische Emanzipationsbewegung und unabhängiges Denken in der DDR seit Beginn der achtziger Jahre', in ibid., pp. 58–65; see also G. Minnerup, 'Politische Opposition in der DDR vor dem Hintergrund der Reformdiskussion in Osteuropa', in ibid., pp. 66–74.

strongly suggested that popular 'opposition' was a more widespread and fundamental feature of the GDR than most commentators had previously thought. Over the course of 1990 this view was confirmed by the cascade of revelations about the scope of *Stasi* surveillance and its immense archive of reports compiled on internal 'enemy activities'.

Since the collapse of the regime the previous dearth of research on dissent and opposition has turned into a body of literature numbering hundreds of works. We can only highlight the main contours of this literature here, focusing on a handful of contributions marking the outer parameters of interpretation so as to make the different positions and issues of debate as visible as possible.

Much of the literature from the early 1990s was devoted to the dissidents and autonomous groups that rose to prominence during autumn 1989. The very term 'opposition' was at first associated primarily with these civic movements, many of whose members published documentary editions of *Stasi* material or autobiographical works about the dissident groups of the 1970s and 1980s.[23] Yet from the beginning there were conflicting views even among former dissidents as to whether their actions before autumn 1989 could reasonably be considered 'opposition', not least because many of the groups emphatically disavowed this description before then. Whereas Ehrhart Neubert and Wolfgang Rüddenklau, for instance, unambiguously described their activities as 'opposition', Martin Gutzeit, one of the co-founders of the SDP, concluded that the oppositional self-understanding of the groups developed only patchily and gradually over the final months of the regime's existence.[24] The issue soon became a point of contention since the conferring of the label 'GDR opposition' carried with it a certain moral cachet in unified Germany.

The question of the extent of 'opposition' to the regime among the wider populace has been equally contentious. The debate was enlivened in 1993

23  There is a sizeable literature of this sort. Among the most noteworthy works are A. Mitter and S. Wolle (eds), *Ich liebe euch doch alle! Befehle und Lageberichte des MfS. Januar–November 1989* (Berlin, 1990); M. Beleites, *Untergrund: Ein Konflikt mit der Stasi in der Uran-Provinz* (Berlin, 1991); R. Eppelmann, *Fremd im eigenen Haus. Mein Leben im anderen Deutschland* (Cologne, 1993); E. Loest, *Die Stasi war mein Ackermann. Oder: mein Leben mit der Wanze* (Göttingen, 1991); H. J. Schädlich, *Aktenkundig* (Berlin, 1992); W. Rüddenklau, *Störenfried. DDR-Opposition 1986–1989* (Berlin, 1992); V. Wollenberger, *Virus der Heuchler. Innenansicht aus Stasi-Akten* (Berlin, 1992); Gerhard Rein (ed.), *Die Opposition in der DDR. Entwürfe für einen anderen Sozialismus* (Berlin, 1989).

24  M. Gutzeit, 'Der Weg in die Opposition. Über das Selbstverständnis und die Rolle der "Opposition" im Herbst 1989 in der ehemaligen DDR', in W. Euchner (ed.), *Politische Opposition in Deutschland und im internationalen Vergleich* (Göttingen, 1993), pp. 84–114. W. Rüddenklau, *Störenfried*; Ehrhart Neubert, *Geschichte der Opposition in der DDR 1949–1989* (Bonn, 1997). The sizeable anthology edited by Eberhard Kuhrt *et al.* similarly treats 'opposition' as essentially synonymous with the independent dissident groups, from whose ranks most of the volume's contributors are drawn. See E. Kuhrt *et al.* (eds), *Opposition in der DDR von den 70er Jahren bis zum Zusammenbruch der SED-Herrschaft* (Opladen, 1999). Some interesting recent case studies of the independent groups use the term 'opposition' in similar fashion: Michael Richter and Erich Sobeslavsky (eds), *Die Gruppe der 20. Gesellschaftlicher Aufbruch und politische Opposition in Dresden 1989–90* (Cologne, 1999); Udo Scheer, *Vision und Wirklichkeit. Die Opposition in Jena in den siebziger und achtziger Jahren* (Berlin, 1999).

by Armin Mitter and Stefan Wolle, two former East German historians who had been held back in their careers for voicing unorthodox opinions, with the publication of their book *Untergang auf Raten*, or 'downfall in stages'. This study represented the first attempt to analyse patterns of popular opinion and dissent over a substantial stretch of time on the basis of a wide selection of previously classified *Stasi*, police and party reports. Their findings paint a picture of broad, almost universal, popular loathing of the regime, which was based on little more than 'Russian bayonets'.[25] Focusing on four political flashpoints – summer 1953, the 'thaw' and Hungarian uprising of 1956, the erection of the Wall in 1961 and the Prague Spring of 1968 – they portray the history of the GDR essentially as a 'countdown at whose end could only be its downfall'.[26] From 1953 onwards it was clear that the GDR was little more than 'an artificial product of the Cold War without inner legitimation. ... In spite of all appearances to the contrary, at no point over the following 36 years did it possess greater internal consistency'.[27] The GDR's oft-cited stability was based on coercion; the popular notion of a 'niche society' of unpolitical East Germans was profoundly misleading. When the chance to topple the regime finally presented itself in 1989, the populace readily seized upon it. In this view, the history of the GDR was essentially that of a latent civil war between regime and populace which burst into the open after the Soviet Union pulled the props from under the SED.[28]

This could hardly stand in more stark contrast to the conclusions of Heinz Niemann and Walter Friedrich, two former East German sociologists who have analysed popular opinion in the GDR on the basis of surveys carried out during the 1960s and 1970s. According to Niemann, the survey reports

> prove that a clear majority of the populace, at least for the period from 1965 to 1978, 'accepted' the GDR and recognized the SED's claim to the leadership of state and society. The system could therefore consider itself as 'legitimated' by the majority *qua* mass loyalty.[29]

Popular opposition, however one might define it, was marginal and was in any event far surpassed by popular support. Using the same material, Walter Friedrich has argued directly against the 'latent civil war' thesis in favour of

25 A. Mitter and S. Wolle, *Untergang auf Raten: Unbekannte Kapitel der DDR-Geschichte* (Munich, 1993), p. 161.
26 Ibid., p. 8.
27 Ibid., pp. 161–2.
28 It is worth noting that Stefan Wolle's subsequent work has offered a far more differentiated view of popular opinion and political behaviour. Cf. S. Wolle, *Die heile Welt der Diktatur. Alltag und Herrschaft in der DDR 1971–1989* (Berlin, 1998).
29 H. Niemann, *Hinterm Zaun. Politische Kultur und Meinungsforschung in der DDR – die geheimen Berichte an das Politbüro der SED* (Berlin, 1995), p. 8. The same argument is made in his earlier work *Meinungsforschung in der DDR. Die geheimen Berichte des Instituts für Meinungsforschung an das Politbüro der SED* (Cologne, 1993), pp. 61–3.

what he calls a more 'complex' view.[30] As he points out, the majority of East Germans rated the GDR highly in terms of job security, peace policy, educational opportunities, cultural opportunities and various other aspects of everyday life, but rated it poorly with regard to the economic lag behind West Germany, travel restrictions, the lack of reliable information and the lack of democratic influence on policy-making. Without sufficiently considering the fact that East Germans were given no alternative but to 'accept' or 'identify with' the socialist system in the GDR, Friedrich goes so far as to contend that:

> The thesis of the democratic illegitimacy of the authoritarian form of government over the four decades of the GDR cannot be verified by the results of social scientific research. On the contrary, this shows that large majorities of the various strata of the population by and large identified themselves with the values, goals and institutions of the socialist system.[31]

In spite of the obvious apologist overtones of this argument, Niemann and Friedrich find themselves in some respects in the strange company of many former East German dissidents who wholeheartedly agree that the bulk of the East German populace was *not* in opposition to the regime. As Ehrhart Neubert, a former civil rights activist, has argued in the first post-*Wende* synthesis of opposition in the GDR:

> The rapid downfall of the GDR should not conceal the fact that the long-lived domestic political stability derived from SED policies which induced people into active cooperation and passive toleration. The images of the mass uprising of 1989 should not obscure the loyalty of the majority of the populace towards the simultaneously unloved SED state.[32]

In his view, the hallmark of popular political behaviour in the GDR was not 'opposition' or even passive '*Resistenz*', but rather conformity, and indeed a brand of conformity that was 'not merely a shrinking back from the repressive force of the SED, but an expression of a lack of mental freedom, a bond of "conviction"'. This 'conviction' was born not out of a positive identification with the regime as Niemann and Friedrich suggest, but rather out of powerlessness and the lack of an easy alternative. It was a 'reflex against the external suppression that became internalized for the sake of one's own exoneration'.[33] The same basic argument has been made by Friedrich Schorlemmer, another former civil rights activist, albeit in sharper terms: 'Many people sold themselves in the GDR. Whoever condemns the former leadership should remember that they were covered by the grovelling of ninety-eight percent of the people.'[34]

---

30  W. Friedrich, 'Regierte die SED ständig gegen die Mehrheit des Volkes?', in Jochen Cerny, Dietmar Keller and Manfred Neuhaus (eds), *Ansichten zur Geschichte der DDR*, vol. 5 (Bonn/Berlin, 1994), pp. 123–47, here p. 123.
31  Ibid., p. 133.
32  Ehrhart Neubert, *Geschichte der Opposition*, p. 17.
33  Ibid., p. 18.
34  Friedrich Schorlemmer, interview in *FAZ-Magazin*, 8 Oct. 1993, pp. 70f.

In this view, the pressures to conform and the many bonds that tied people to the system – like social mobility and job security – resulted in an inability to engage in political conflict or, put somewhat differently, a keen ability to avoid it. This 'mass flight away from conflict'[35] could hardly be more different from notions of broad societal 'resistance' against the regime. Indeed, Neubert argues that even instances of refusal were ultimately an element of overall conformity, a kind of pressure valve of discontent that made it easier for people to conform when and where it mattered. The symbiosis of refusal and conformity thus 'stabilized the political system much more than it placed it in question'.[36] Because of the exonerating function of conformity, the minority of people who chose not to conform were 'not only exposed to political pressure, but also experienced a complete lack of understanding from those around them, who felt provoked or even threatened by the civic courage of others'.[37] In the view of many former dissidents, the only real 'opponents' of the SED regime were those who stood up for their beliefs and consciously engaged in conflict with the authorities with the aim of limiting the regime's power.[38] This perspective essentially limits 'opposition' to the dissident groups who sought to claim public space from the regime, and clearly delineates them from the conformist masses who by and large did what they were told and supported the regime in their actions, if not intentions.

These largely irreconcilable interpretations we have just encountered are based on different sources, different sets of questions and on differing conceptions about the fundamental relationship between state and society in the GDR, none of which are wholly separable from the political views and interests of those involved in the debates. The disagreements over whether opposition and dissent were central features or marginal phenomena in the history of the GDR raise a number of questions that we will now explore in more detail. What can reasonably be taken as constituting 'opposition' and 'resistance' in the GDR? Who was engaged in it? What was the extent of oppositional behaviour in East German society more broadly speaking? And what, if anything, was the effect?

# Evaluation

One could, of course, simply argue that answers to these questions depend entirely on how one defines the terms. At one level this is certainly true; designating certain specific actions or forms of behaviour as 'dissent' or 'opposition' is clearly a matter of definition. There are no set meanings

35 E. Neubert, *Geschichte der Opposition*, p. 22.
36 Ibid., p. 24.
37 Ibid., p. 17.
38 Ibid., pp. 27, 29.

of these terms, no objective 'outside' perspective that could adjudicate the different conceptualizations and determine a singular, universally applicable set of criteria. In other words, answers to these questions leave much to one's own point of view and to the vagaries of political debates. Yet these definitions are nonetheless – or rather precisely because of this fluidity – quite important, for they structure not only our current understanding of the GDR and those who lived in it, but also the questions we ask about it in the future. If one widens the scope to include the many forms of political discontent and everyday passive '*Resistenz*' it is difficult to escape the conclusion that the vast majority of East Germans – even many within the SED rank-and-file – stood in opposition to the regime at various times. If one employs instead a narrower definition that includes only active, conscious and organized attempts to undermine the regime, then the result will be that there was almost no, or at least very little, genuine opposition in the GDR. Thus the typology of dissenting behaviour that we select has direct implications for our overall picture of the GDR.

The complexity of the definitional problems already becomes apparent when one considers how the regime itself defined non-conformist and oppositional behaviour. As we have seen, official views were remarkably ambiguous. Even in the realm of criminal law, where one would most expect a distinct definition of punishable actions, the regulations were extraordinarily vague. Whether one looks at the 1950 Law for the Protection of Peace, Article Six of the constitution (on 'boycott- and war-mongering'), or Paragraph 106 of the GDR's Criminal Code (on 'rabble-rousing hostile to the state'), the spectrum of actions that might fall under each of these was vast and incongruous. Not even the internal regulations of the *Stasi* – which, unlike the Criminal Code, were top secret – offer many concrete pointers as to what precisely might constitute 'hostile-negative actions' or 'underground political activities'.[39]

If the party and state offered no clear categorizations of dissenting behaviour in principle, did they nonetheless do so in practice? Whether a particular form of behaviour was punished and how severe the sanctions were are undoubtedly useful indicators of official views on dissent. The SED had a wide range of sanctions at its disposal, including the organs of 'political justice' and the *Stasi*, internal party punishments, limitations placed on one's career opportunities and the denial of privileges for wayward officials. As Karl Wilhelm Fricke and Falco Werkentin have shown, there were in practice a number of types of behaviour that, if detected, invariably incurred significant sanctions through the criminal justice system. These included any efforts at political organization outside of the official SED-dominated

39 Cf. generally *Materialien der Enquete-Kommission*, vol. VIII; Klaus-Dietmar Henke *et al.* (eds), *Anatomie der Staatssicherheit. Geschichte, Struktur und Methoden. MfS Handbuch* (Berlin, 1995); K. W. Fricke, *MfS Intern* (Cologne, 1991); J. Gauck, *Die Stasi-Akten. Das unheimliche Erbe der DDR* (Hamburg, 1991); D. Gill and U. Schroeter, *Das Ministerium für Staatssicherheit. Anatomie des Mielke-Imperiums* (Berlin, 1991).

institutional landscape, any Western contacts that might be considered dangerous to the state (i.e. having the potential for espionage), and any attempts to leave the GDR illegally. In the early years this also included measures against certain social groups such as large-scale owners of land or industry, against semi-independent milieux such as the churches, and against potential political opponents both inside and outside of the SED.[40]

Yet for a number of reasons the repressive practices of the party and state do not offer a satisfactory typology of dissent and opposition. For one thing, punishments for particular acts were not uniform but sometimes rather arbitrary in their severity. Due to the SED's 'instrumental' understanding of the role of law, designations of concrete actions as 'opposition' and appropriate sanctions against them were frequently decided not in accordance with a guiding set of legal principles, but with regard to the particular situation (whether a case might go 'public' in the West and jeopardize trade negotiations, whether it might have negative repercussions at home, etc.). Hence they do not offer a clear indicator of the degree of oppositional behaviour. Moreover, the spectrum of acts that were punished in practice changed considerably over time. Whereas membership in one of the Protestant *Junge Gemeinden* or the reception of Western radio and television were initially punishable, they subsequently became tolerated. Perhaps most importantly, the groups and individuals that attracted so much of the regime's attention (communist dissidents, the 'autonomous' peace, civil rights and environmental groups) often did not view their own actions as a form of political opposition and did not intend them as a direct threat to the regime. Whether as a result of a paranoid view of East German society or a cynical attempt to maximize its own budget (or both), the *Stasi* created many of its own 'resistance phantoms'[41] out of actions that were neither 'hostile to the state' nor intended as such. As the former dissident Markus Meckel has pointed out, 'One did not even need to be politically active to get caught in the mill of the repressive apparatus'.[42]

Clearly, then, the motivations that underlay dissenting behaviour must be taken into account. The problem, however, is that this approach is hardly more reliable than the regime's own vague and inconsistent definitions. Probably the greatest obstacle is that genuine intentions can hardly be deduced. *Stasi* sketches of individuals' intentions, though numerous, are fraught with the kinds of methodological dangers just outlined. Autobiographical recollections of previous actions likewise harbour pitfalls, especially the blurring of memory through subsequent experiences and the temptation

---

40 Cf. generally K. W. Fricke, *Politik und Justiz in der DDR*; F. Werkentin, *Politische Strafjustiz in der Ära Ulbricht* (Berlin, 1995).

41 The apt description from Lutz Niethammer, 'Erfahrungen und Strukturen. Prolegomena zu einer Geschichte der Gesellschaft in der DDR', in H. Kaelble *et al.* (eds), *Sozialgeschichte der DDR*, pp. 95–115, here p. 96.

42 M. Meckel and M. Gutzeit, *Opposition in der DDR. Zehn Jahre kirchliche Friedensarbeit – kommentierte Quellentexte* (Cologne, 1994), p. 26.

to paint one's own ambitions as more oppositional than was the case at the time. In addition, because of the risks involved, genuine intentions were by no means directly reflected in public statements. Because the threat of punishment was significantly reduced if an action could not clearly be identified as oppositional, many expressions of dissent (petitions, declarations) were deliberately couched in a conciliatory tone and often employed the regime's own vocabulary in order to minimize the risk of sanctions.

It is therefore plainly necessary to establish some set of external criteria in order to categorize and analyse different forms of dissenting behaviour. The difficulties involved in this task are painfully apparent when one considers the discussion about resistance under the Third Reich. In spite of a literature running into thousands of works, there is still no prospect of a generally accepted typology of dissenting behaviour.[43] Although the discussion about the GDR is still embryonic by comparison, a number of conceptual schemes have been put forward.[44]

In a first attempt at a more systematic categorization, Ilko-Sascha Kowalczuk has proposed a model of 'oppositional behaviour' (*widerständiges Verhalten*) which includes any action that 'limits, hinders or places in question the all-embracing claims to authority', whether 'organized or not organized, in groups, individually or institutionally'.[45] 'Resistance and

---

43  Cf. I. Kershaw, *The Nazi Dictatorship*, Chapter 8. Some commentators have questioned the entire enterprise on the grounds that a precise definition of terms is hardly possible. See, for instance, the comments of Karl Wilhelm Fricke in *Materialien der Enquete-Kommission*, vol. VII: 1, p. 15.

44  The discussion was given a significant boost with the initiation of the *Enquete* commission's deliberations over the question of who and what constituted 'opposition' – not that the result was anything like a consensus. Whereas Rainer Eckert argued that the autonomous groups in the GDR should be referred to as 'opposition', Martin Jander found it 'difficult to apply this concept to the groups crystallizing during the 1970s and 1980s'. Whereas Christoph Kleßmann defined 'opposition' specifically as an 'at least rudimentarily organized form of divergence from the dominant political line with recognizable ideological and political alternatives', Eckhard Jesse employed it as a broad umbrella concept encompassing an array of other terms such as resistance (*Widerstand*), *Resistenz* and dissidence. Cf. R. Eckert, 'Die revolutionäre Krise am Ende der achtziger Jahre und die Formierung der Opposition', in *Materialien der Enquete-Kommission*, vol. VII: 1, pp. 684ff; M. Jander (unter Mitarbeit von Thomas Voß), 'Die besondere Rolle des politischen Selbstverständnisses bei der Herausbildung einer politischen Opposition in der DDR außerhalb der SED und ihrer Massenorganisationen seit den siebziger Jahren', *Materialien der Enquete-Kommission*, vol. VII: 1, p. 932; C. Kleßmann, 'Opposition und Dissidenz in der Geschichte der DDR', in *APuZG*, B5/91, pp. 52–62, which contrasts this definition of 'opposition' with a more diffuse notion of 'dissidence' as 'conscious, albeit partial refusal and deviance'; E. Jesse, 'Artikulationsformen und Zielsetzungen von widerständigen Verhalten in der Deutschen Demokratischen Republik', in *Materialien der Enquete-Kommission*, vol. VII: 1, pp. 987–1030, here pp. 997, 1000. There was, it might be noted, a limited discussion of these issues in the 1980s as well. Whereas Karl Wilhelm Fricke suggested a spectrum of behaviour ranging between the two poles of 'opposition' (defined as 'relatively open and relatively legal' political dissent) and 'resistance' (*Widerstand*, defined as political dissent 'deprived of any possibility of open and legal expression'), thus prioritizing the form of behaviour over the content or motivations, Dietrich Staritz warned against making legality a primary criterion and insisted instead on the necessity of distinguishing 'between partial and fundamental opposition' and on the importance of focusing on the grey zone 'between conscious oppositional actions and individual or collective refusal'. K. W. Fricke, *Opposition und Widerstand*, p. 13. D. Staritz, 'Die SED und die Opposition', pp. 78, 95.

45  Ilko-Sascha Kowalczuk, 'Von der Freiheit, Ich zu sagen. Widerständiges Verhalten in der DDR', in R. Eckart et al. (eds), *Zwischen Selbstbehauptung und Anpassung. Formen des Widerstandes und der Opposition in der DDR* (Berlin, 1995), pp. 85–115, here p. 90.

opposition', used here synonymously, serve as a general, overarching concept that is divided into four sub-categories: (1) societal refusal (akin to
'*Resistenz*', generally passive and reactive); (2) social protest (petitions,
complaints, limited strikes, concerned mostly with immediate material
issues); (3) political dissent (a small minority who took sanctions into
account); and (4) mass protest, the rarest form of oppositional behaviour
occurring only in June 1953 and autumn 1989.[46] Both the actions themselves and their effects serve as the criteria for categorization. The overall
image is of a pyramid of behaviour, with each step up representing both a
'higher' form of opposition and a more infrequent one.[47]

It is often difficult, however, to distinguish between the different levels of
this scheme. The distinction between societal refusal and social protest in
particular is extremely fuzzy since most of the common forms of complaint
could fall under either category. An additional problem is that these actions
do not necessarily form a clear hierarchy. The bottom three levels (societal
refusal, social protest, political dissent) are fluid and run into each other,
and all are qualitatively different from open protest, especially if this
involved rejecting the regime in its entirety.[48] More importantly, the sub-
sumption of the entire spectrum of critical attitudes and actions in the GDR
under the terms 'opposition' and 'resistance' seems to me both inappropriate and unhelpful for discerning between qualitatively different kinds of
behaviour. Can organized protest with the aim of toppling the regime really
be brought under the same heading as complaining to the authorities about
one's flat? Of course Kowalczuk is not suggesting that these actions should
be equated, but the use of such emotive terms as 'resistance' and 'opposition' as overarching concepts spanning such a broad range of behaviour
does raise this problem.

Kowalczuk's model is typical of most in its focus on what might be called
the 'energy' or vigour of protest against the regime, how universal the rejection of SED dominance is and how far one is prepared to take it. In this
sense Ehrhart Neubert's tripartite model of 'opposition, resistance and dissent' is unique in its near exclusive concentration on the strategies and
means of dissent. In his view, the crucial distinction was whether deviant
behaviour manifested itself through legal or illegal means, whether one tried
to use and expand the legal opportunities for dissent within the GDR or
rejected the regime's norms wholesale. This allows, in his words, for 'a
fundamental distinction between opponents who insisted on legal activities
and created the preconditions for this in the first place, and those who

---

46 Ibid., p. 97.
47 Ibid., p. 114. By way of comparison, this model is not unlike the one advanced by Detlev Peukert for
   categorizing oppositional behaviour in the Third Reich. See Detlev Peukert, *Inside Nazi Germany:
   Conformity and Opposition in Everyday Life* (London, 1987).
48 This problem is exacerbated by the incongruity of some of the individual levels, for instance the inclu-
   sion of petitioning (which was legal) and limited strikes (which were illegal and potentially dangerous)
   under the single heading of social protest.

renounced legal means and drew their legitimacy solely from their rejection of the SED-state'.[49] The former he calls 'opposition', the latter 'resistance' (*Widerstand*). 'Dissent' (*Widerspruch*) refers simply to a more dilute form of conscious political deviance. Examples of 'opposition' were the 'bourgeois' parliamentary parties during the early years, the various autonomous groups of the 1980s, and the groups that abandoned the sanctuary of the church in autumn 1989 to found their own political platforms.[50] Instances of 'resistance' were the mass revolts of 1953 and 1989, the efforts of repressed milieux to represent their interests where no legal means were possible (e.g. elements of the SPD and bourgeois parties, farmers against collectivization), individual acts such as painting anti-SED slogans or distributing leaflets, and flight or emigration to the West.[51] 'Dissent', by far the most common, might encompass the encoded protests of artists and intellectuals, the '*Resistenz*' of various subcultures (such as religious or youth milieux) short of political engagement with the regime, and everyday criticisms, jokes, etc. that acted as a kind of political pressure valve.[52]

The shortcomings of this approach are, in my view, substantial. Not only is the 'political energy' of dissent marginalized, which itself leads to incongruous categorizations such as mass revolt and mere emigration to the West falling under the same heading of 'resistance', but more importantly, the aims and motivations are obscured. In Neubert's scheme, 'opposition' is largely limited to the autonomous groups of the 1970s and 1980s and those segments of the church that supported them. But this inevitably raises the question of what these groups were opposing. The principle of one-party rule or its repressive practices? East German communism *per se* or its failure to reform? The very idea of a separate East German state or merely the rigid leadership that governed it? The partiality or generality of criticism seems crucially important to any evaluation of 'opposition'. Nor should the motivation and self-understanding of would-be dissenters be wholly ignored. Although self-understanding is, as we have seen above, a problematic criterion, doubts must be raised about the granting of a near monopoly on the label 'opposition' to groups which by and large neither viewed nor described themselves as such before 1990.

A more convincing model is Hubertus Knabe's ten-point scale ranging from *Resistenz* to partial criticism, social protest, passive resistance, new social movements, political protest, dissidence, political opposition, active resistance, and finally to open revolt.[53] The different points on the scale are

---

49 E. Neubert, *Geschichte der Opposition*, p. 29.
50 Ibid., pp. 29–31.
51 Karl Wilhelm Fricke and Bernd Eisenfeld have likewise treated illegal emigration as a form of 'resist-ance': K. W. Fricke, 'Fluchthilfe als Widerstand im Kalten Krieg', *APuZG* B38/99, pp. 3–10; B. Eisenfeld, 'Die Ausreisebewegung – eine Erscheinungsform widerständigen Verhaltens', in R. Eckart *et al.* (eds), *Zwischen Selbstbehauptung und Anpassung*, pp. 192–223.
52 E. Neubert, *Geschichte der Opposition*, pp. 32–3.
53 H. Knabe, 'Was war die "DDR-Opposition"? Zur Typologie des politischen Widerspruchs in Ostdeutschland', *DA* 29:2 (1996), pp. 184–98.

distinguished on the basis of the level of risk incurred, the scope of criticism (partial or general), the public or private mode of expression and the level of activity or passivity involved in any concrete action. As Knabe quite rightly points out, the notion of a continuum not only suggests a fluidity of movement between the various categories, but also lends itself more readily to understanding dissent not as a static 'type' of behaviour but as a *process*; that is, as a form of behaviour whose expression and continuation were dependent on circumstances, on the social position of the individual or group concerned, and on the response it elicited from the authorities (which, as we have already noted, was not always consistent). 'Partial criticism' could quite quickly turn into social protest or even passive resistance; indeed, under some circumstances (such as June 1953 and autumn 1989) these could turn into revolt, the most extreme form of behaviour on Knabe's scale. At the same time as allowing for fluidity, Knabe's usage of the more neutral term 'dissent' as the overarching concept and his limited definitions of the more loaded terms 'opposition' and 'resistance' avoids some of the pitfalls of employing these emotive concepts too indiscriminately. There is a clear distinction between, say, the risky, organized, politically motivated and fundamentally hostile actions of the 'Eisenberger Circle' (smuggling forbidden literature, isolated acts of sabotage);[54] the quasi-legal and partial criticism of the autonomous groups of the 1980s; a principled but nonetheless reactive and defensive refusal to perform military service; a small-scale strike over working conditions without wider moral or political motivations; and having long hair and blue jeans.

While these forms of behaviour cannot be hermetically sealed off from each other, it seems useful to me, at least for the sake of simplicity, to emphasize two distinctions along Knabe's rather elaborate scale: first, between fundamental 'resistance' and the broad band of partial 'protest'; and second, between active 'opposition' and passive forms of *'Resistenz'*.[55] In practice, the difference between passive non-conformity and active protest was quite stark. Unlike most forms of passive non-conformity, engaging in organized acts of 'dissidence' or 'opposition', even within the parameters established by the regime, entailed considerable sacrifices and reflected a willingness to act in order to bring about change. There was an even broader gulf between these forms of behaviour and 'resistance' proper, which entailed both great risks – long prison sentences or, in extreme cases, the death penalty – and a fundamental moral stance of antipathy towards

---

54 See Patrick von zur Mühlen, *Der 'Eisenberger Kreis'. Jugendwiderstand und Verfolgung in der DDR 1953–1958* (Bonn, 1995).

55 This scheme is similar to that advocated by Rainer Eckart, who divides 'dissenting behaviour' into three categories: (1) 'resistance' (*Widerstand*), which comprised illegal and fundamental struggle against the communist regime with the aim of eliminating it; (2) 'opposition/dissidence', which designates relatively open and at least partially legal rejection of the regime in certain areas with the aim of reforming it; and (3) *'Resistenz'* and refusal, encompassing various forms of passive refusal and non-conformity in everyday life. R. Eckart, 'Widerstand und Opposition in der DDR. Siebzehn Thesen', *ZfG* vol. 44 (1996), pp. 49–67.

the regime as such. We might therefore alter Knabe's scale by conceiving of it as more compact towards the '*Resistenz*' pole and 'stretching out' towards the pole of mass revolt. Whereas the more low-level forms of dissent over-lapped considerably, this overlap shrank as the level of risk and activity increased, eventually to reveal a broad gulf between most forms of dissent and 'resistance' proper.

If this conceptualization might help us to clarify what we mean by 'dissent', 'opposition' and 'resistance', there remains the important issue of their extent within the GDR. How continuous and widespread were they? Was dissent, to return to the opening question, a central and abiding characteristic of the regime or merely a marginal feature?

In approaching this question, it is crucial to recognize the relationship between the evolving nature of dissent and the changing context in which it took place. A basic distinction must be made between the 'fundamental opposition of Social Democratic, Christian and other groups and individu-als in the late 1940s and 1950s and the groups of the 1970s and 1980s whose predominant aim was the reform of the socialist system'.[56] There were a number of reasons for this overall shift. First, many fundamental opponents of the regime left for the West during the 1950s. For those who remained, the lack of an 'exit' option understandably tended to moderate oppositional behaviour. Second, as the political system stabilized and the economy began to improve noticeably in the 1960s, oppositional efforts also seemed less likely to gain broad popular support from material discon-tent. At the same time, the advent of *Ostpolitik* and mutual recognition seemed to guarantee the GDR's continued existence for the foreseeable future, so fundamental opposition seemed largely pointless in any case. The best many critics could hope for was reform within the existing system. Third, the GDR's signing of the Helsinki Declaration in 1975 (includ-ing Basket Three concerning human rights) and the Church–State agreement of March 1978 guaranteeing a degree of institutional autonomy for the 'Church in Socialism' (in the oft-quoted phrase of Bishop Albrecht Schönherr) gave critics both additional political leverage against the regime as well as a semi-independent sanctuary in which to voice and organize their criticism. The Protestant Churches played an important role in shaping internal dissent during the 1980s. Finally, the hole in the Iron Curtain from May 1989 onwards and the Soviet renunciation of the Brezhnev Doctrine radically changed both the scope and the tone of opposition, which became increasingly widespread and fundamental as concession after concession was wrung out of the regime.

It is therefore clear that dissenting behaviour changed greatly over time in both its scope and essential character. In this sense it is wrong to speak of

---

56 U. Poppe, R. Eckert and I.-S. Kowalczuk, 'Opposition, Widerstand und widerständiges Verhalten in der DDR. Forschungsstand – Grundlinien – Probleme', in R. Eckart *et al.* (eds), *Zwischen Selbstbehauptung und Anpassung*, p. 16.

'the opposition' in the GDR. Before autumn 1989, the various strands of organized and semi-organized dissent were not closely interrelated and did not form any coherent coalition of opposition. The views and activities of the 'bourgeois' parties and SPD during the early years were quite different from those of the communist critics. Likewise, the reformist intellectual opposition within the SED differed markedly – apart from certain 'Third Way' notions – from the dissident groups of the 1980s in terms of both their social composition and the extent of criticism.[57] How extensive were these relatively organized and visible forms of dissent, and how appropriate is it to call them 'opposition'?

We have already seen that the 'oppositional' credentials of the autonomous movements that came into the spotlight during autumn 1989 is the subject of some controversy. In my view, the label seems rather inappropriate. This is not in any way meant to downplay the dissident activities of these small groups or the sacrifices they made. They represented a small percentage of the East German populace with the courage of their convictions and a willingness to make sacrifices for them. For these reasons they deserve admiration and respect. For analytical purposes, however, the crucial question is not their moral authority, but rather what, precisely, they were opposing before 1990: the GDR *per se* or merely the SED regime? As several commentators have pointed out, the bulk of East German dissidents failed to see that opposition to one effectively meant opposition to both.[58] The dissidents by and large sought to reform communism, not to topple it, which set them apart from the oppositional groups in most of the Soviet bloc who had given up on reforming communism and instead anticipated its demise. Because of their socialist views and their unique inability to invoke the concept of the nation, East German dissidents faced an intractable 'dilemma of opposition'.[59] The taboo of a national discourse was based not only on the nationalist excesses of the Nazi past, from which everyone clearly had to distance themselves, but also on the problem of German division, which meant

---

57 Cf. Dieter Rink, 'Ausreiser, Kirchengruppen, Kulturopposition und Reformer. Zu Differenzen und Gemeinsamkeiten in Opposition und Widerstand in der DDR in den 70er und 80er Jahren', in D. Pollack and D. Rink (eds), *Zwischen Verweigerung und Opposition*, pp. 54–77. By contrast, Christoph Kleßmann stresses the threads of continuity between the various forms of 'opposition' throughout the history of the GDR, including the intellectual opposition of the 1950s–60s and the dissident groups of the 1980s. Although I agree with his refutation of the idea that the events of 1989 were wholly without intellectual precedent in the GDR's history, positing this degree of continuity errs in the opposite direction, in my view. See C. Kleßmann, 'Opposition und Dissidenz in der Geschichte der DDR', *APuZG*, B5/91, pp. 52–62.

58 This case is argued most strongly by Christian Joppke, *East German Dissidents and the Revolution of 1989: Social Movement in a Leninist Regime* (Basingstoke, 1995). See also John Torpey, *Intellectuals, Socialism and Dissent: The East German Opposition and its Legacy* (Minneapolis, 1995); Hubertus Knabe, 'Sprachrohr oder Außenseiter? Zur gesellschaftlichen Relevanz der unabhängigen Gruppen in der DDR – Aus Analysen des Staatssicherheitsdienstes', *APuZG* B20/96, pp. 23–36; Detlef Pollack, 'Außenseiter oder Repräsentanten? Zur Rolle der politisch alternativen Gruppen in der DDR', in D. Pollack (ed.), *Die Legitimität der Freiheit. Politisch alternative Gruppen in der DDR unter dem Dach der Kirche* (Frankfurt a. M., 1990), pp. 227ff.

59 C. Joppke, *East German Dissidents*, p. 200.

that the extinction of the GDR would amount to the victory of West German capitalism. The problem with this inability to invoke the concept of national self-determination was that, as Joppke puts it, 'no genuine opposition to communism was possible' without it.[60] Whom was one otherwise claiming to represent? The *East German* people? Accepting this category itself amounted to adopting the regime's definition of membership. Because of their rejection of both a national discourse and Western capitalism, most of these dissidents did not revoke their basic loyalty to the GDR and consequently remained caught within its socialist self-definition. As we will see in the next chapter, this partial and incomplete rejection of the regime meant that the groups tended to lag behind events as they unfolded throughout autumn 1989.

The extent of opposition represented by the autonomous groups was, therefore, rather more limited than is often assumed. Can the same be said of the degree of opposition from within the party itself? Clearly this is an important question since those already in positions of power – Zaisser, Herrnstadt, Wollweber, Schirdewan – were uniquely situated to initiate far-reaching changes from the top. All the research shows that opposition within the leading ranks of the party represented a huge threat to Ulbricht, who nearly lost his job after June 1953 and was on thin ice throughout much of 1956.[61] As Manfred Wilke has pointed out, the risks involved in attempting to oust the current leader were great; as far as the authorities were concerned, these efforts were nothing short of 'counter-revolutionary'.[62] But the crucial question once again is: what precisely were these people opposing? Certainly not the GDR *per se*, and for the most part not even the anti-pluralist and undemocratic nature of the SED regime. This so-called 'intra-party opposition' was by and large directed against Ulbricht and his style of rule. Neubert and Kowalczuk are quite right to deny 'oppositional' status to the struggles over power and privileges within the SED on the grounds that they were fought not against, but within the prevailing system.[63] Indeed, many of the SED critics such as Zaisser, Herrnstadt, Wollweber and Schirdewan were themselves representatives of the repressive apparatus. They were wholly uninterested in notions of a more 'democratic socialism' and merely wanted to steer a slightly different course in order to enhance the regime's authority. Not only were the *actual* effects of such criticism rather minimal, but from this point of view even the *potential* effects seem less than dramatic. One merely has to pose the counter-factual

---

60  Ibid., p. 202.
61  A good recent account in English is Peter Grieder, *The East German Leadership 1946–73* (Manchester, 1999).
62  Manfred Wilke and Tobias Voigt, 'Opposition gegen Ulbricht – Konflikte in der SED-Führung in den fünfziger Jahren', in Klaus-Dietmar Henke *et al.* (eds), *Widerstand und Opposition in der DDR*, pp. 211–40, here p. 240.
63  Neubert, *Geschichte der Opposition*, p. 33; Kowalczuk, 'Von der Freiheit, Ich zu sagen', p. 97. For a competing viewpoint rather typical of the PDS milieu, see Wilfriede Otto, 'Opposition und Widerstand zwischen Hoffnung und Enttäuschung', in *Ansichten zur Geschichte der DDR*, vol. 3, pp. 227–56.

question: had this intra-party 'opposition' succeeded in its aims, would the political system have changed substantially? The simple answer is no, at least not as long as one was determined to maintain the existence of a strictly separate GDR alongside the Federal Republic. Indeed, if one grants 'oppositional' status to such critics, it seems difficult to deny it to Honecker himself, who was, after all, an 'opponent' of the 'Ulbricht system' during the late 1960s until his ascent to the party chairmanship in 1971.

Unlike the party, the Protestant Churches clearly had been a centre of far-reaching opposition. In the early years they provided one of the major social and institutional bases of 'immunity' to the regime and its teachings. In the 1940s and early 1950s, church leaders and many Christian communities were willing to enter major ideological struggles with the state over a range of issues affecting the churches. They bitterly opposed the abolition of religious instruction in schools (whose curriculum from 1951 onwards was to be steeped in the materialist world-view of Marxism–Leninism), the systematic discrimination against members of the '*Junge Gemeinden*' (criminalized in 1952 as an alternative to the FDJ), and the introduction of a secular youth confirmation service called the *Jugendweihe* in 1954, ultimately to no avail.[64] Apart from opposition towards specific measures affecting the churches, they were also a centre of protest against the remilitarization of the mid-1950s and the campaign of forced agricultural collectivization in 1959–60.[65] Some individual pastors remained resolutely opposed to cooperation with the communist authorities, or sought to appear to cooperate with them only in order to create or maintain leeway for pursuing dissident activities.

But for a number of reasons the churches as institutions became less and less antagonistic towards the regime. Popular religiosity and church attendance figures declined rapidly from the late 1950s onwards in the face of systematic discrimination against anyone with strong religious ties.[66] The continuation of head-on confrontation with the state authorities seemed inappropriate by the 1960s if the church wanted to retain any influence among the population. By the 1970s fundamental opposition appeared downright impracticable. If the Federal Republic was pursuing a policy of

64 Cf. Hermann Wentker, '"Kirchenkampf" in der DDR. Der Konflikt um die Junge Gemeinde 1950–1953', *VfZ*, vol. 42 (1994), pp. 95–127; H. Wentker, 'Die Einführung der Jugendweihe in der DDR: Hintergründe, Motive und Probleme', in H. Mehringer (ed.), *Von der SBZ zur DDR. Studien zum Herrschaftssystem in der Sowjetischen Besatzungszone und in der Deutschen Demokratischen Republik* (Munich, 1995), pp. 139–65; R. Goeckel, *The Lutheran Church and the East German State* (Ithaca, 1995); older, but still good is Horst Dähn, *Konfrontation oder Kooperation? Das Verhältnis von Staat und Kirche in der SBZ/DDR 1945–1980* (Opladen, 1982).

65 H. Dähn, *Konfrontation oder Kooperation?*; D. Pollack, *Kirche in der Organisationsgesellschaft. Zum Wandel der gesellschaftlichen Lage der evangelischen Kirchen in der DDR* (Stuttgart, 1994); C. Ross, '"What about peace and bread?" East Germans and the Remilitarization of the GDR, 1952–1962', *Militärgeschichtliche Mitteilungen*, vol. 58 (1999), pp. 111–35.

66 An excellent discussion of these developments is D. Pollack, 'Von der Volkskirche zur Minderheitskirche. Zur Entwicklung von Religiosität und Kirchlichkeit in der DDR', in Kaelble *et al.* (eds), *Sozialgeschichte*, pp. 271–94.

'change through coming closer', then why not the churches within the GDR? In this context there were only two realistic alternatives: either to renounce contacts with the state and thereby retreat behind the walls of the church, or to make certain concessions in order not to relinquish a role in society. Simply put, the Catholic Church chose the former option and the much larger Protestant Church chose the latter. Only by coming to terms with political realities and embarking on a 'balancing act between conformity and refusal'[67] could the Protestant Church remain a meaningful actor in East German society.

After 1989, the increasingly harmonious relations between church and state – or more precisely the links between church leaders and the *Stasi* – came under withering attack. In a series of books based on *Stasi* records, Gerhard Besier has essentially accused church leaders of tacking too close to the wind and of developing a 'chummy relationship' ('*Kumpanei*') with the regime.[68] Although perhaps an appropriate indictment of a few particularly acquiescent individuals – most notably the famous Thuringian Bishop Moritz Mitzenheim, and more controversially in the case of Manfred Stolpe, which we will discuss in Chapter 8 – the argument is not very convincing in general terms. Even apart from its questionable moral and political undertones, the fixation on church leaders and *Stasi* files to the exclusion of other sources and levels of analysis fatally obscures the political and social context in which the church found itself, caught as it was between the political realities of the GDR and the desire to maintain its influence in an increasingly secular society. While it is clear that the churches were interested first and foremost in self-preservation instead of actively undermining the regime, the '*Kumpanei* thesis' seems completely inadequate for understanding their ambivalent role in the GDR.[69] That they adapted with the times and should not be stylized as a 'bastion of resistance' is obvious. The extent of church opposition shrank dramatically after the battles of the 1950s. By the 1980s, it served both to destabilize the regime in its capacity as a relatively independent social realm – a collector and haven of nonconformity – and simultaneously had stabilizing effects by 'ghettoizing' dissidence and functioning as a kind of 'buffer' between the regime and its most vocal domestic critics.

67  D. Pollack, *Kirche in der Organisationsgesellschaft.* See also Rudolf Mau, *Eingebunden in den Realsozialismus? Die Evangelische Kirch als Problem der SED* (Göttingen, 1994); and Thomas Raabe, *SED-Staat und katholische Kirche. Politische Beziehungen 1949–1961* (Paderborn, 1995). For the Catholic Church, see Ute Haese, *Katholische Kirche in der DDR. Geschichte einer politischen Abstinenz* (Düsseldorf, 1998).

68  G. Besier and S. Wolf (eds), *'Pfarrer, Christen und Katholiken'. Das Ministerium für Staatssicherheit der ehemaligen DDR und die Kirchen* (Neukirchen, 1992); G. Besier, *Der SED-Staat und die Kirche. Der Weg in die Anpassung* (Munich, 1993); G. Besier, *Der SED-Staat und die Kirche 1969–1990. Die Vision vom 'Dritten Weg'* (Berlin, 1995).

69  This argument is put strongly by Christoph Kleßmann, 'Zur Sozialgeschichte des protestantischen Milieus in der DDR', *GG* 19 (1993), pp. 29–53, esp. pp. 51–2. See also M. Fulbrook, *Anatomy of a Dictatorship*, pp. 87–125; and, very generally, D. Pollack, *Kirche in der Organisationsgesellschaft.*

Although the extent of popular dissent in East German society at large has received less media attention than the controversies surrounding the church, it is in many ways a more important question. It is also far more difficult to answer. For one thing, the sources available paint conflicting pictures and leave considerable scope for interpretation. Moreover, the very questions we ask of the sources are directly related to underlying assumptions about the relationship between the SED regime and society. But despite these problems, recent studies have made it clear that 'dissent' was not limited to a handful of dissidents and intellectuals. Even if one disagrees with the overall conclusions of Mitter and Wolle, their work leaves little room for doubt on that score. The problem with their notion of a latent civil war between regime and populace is that it overestimates both the extent and the continuity of popular dissent. One reason for this is the focus of this and other works on major political flashpoints – 1953, 1956, 1961 and 1968 – whereby the emphasis inevitably, and somewhat one-sidedly, is on discontent and conflict. Not only were these periods of unusually high tension among the populace, but the authorities were themselves especially attuned to 'enemy activities' when they felt vulnerable and were more likely to find trouble when they were looking for it. In addition, general doubts must be raised about relying so heavily on the 'Kafkaesque records' of a bureaucracy as ideologically blinkered and divorced from reality as the *Stasi* for ascertaining the extent of dissent within the populace at large. As Lutz Niethammer and others have suggested, the techniques of oral history can provide a salutary corrective.[70] Another problem with this 'coercion thesis' is the failure to recognize that the nature of the regime's stability and the factors upon which it was based changed significantly over time. There were shifting social bases of consent and discontent – for instance, the key differences in generational experiences that we have already seen. Although popular discontent was widespread and constant, and although 'Soviet bayonets' obviously formed the outer parameters of the regime's stability, it is too simplistic – or glosses over too much – to read 1989 directly out of 1953.[71]

It is equally easy, however, to underestimate the scale of popular discontent and criticism. Neubert and other former dissidents are undoubtedly correct to emphasize the widespread conformity of the bulk of the populace. Any careful reading of the sources or the bulk of relevant literature points to the conclusion that apathy and political indifference were far more

---

70 L. Niethammer, 'Erfahrungen und Strukturen', pp. 95–7, from which I also take the term 'Kafkaesque'. See also Uta Stolle, 'Traumhafte Quellen. Vom Nutzen der Stasi-Akten für die Geschichtsschreibung', *DA* 30 (1997), pp. 209–21.

71 Mary Fulbrook has repeatedly made this point: 'Methodologische Überlegungen zu einer Gesellschaftsgeschichte der DDR', p. 282; *Anatomy of a Dictatorship*, pp. 15–16. For an explicit analytical comparison between 1953 and 1989, see Detlef Pollack, 'Bedingungen der Möglichkeit politischen Protestes in der DDR. Der Volksaufstand von 1953 und die Massendemonstrationen 1989 im Vergleich', in D. Pollack and D. Rink (eds), *Zwischen Verweigerung und Opposition*, pp. 303–31.

prevalent than dissent. Yet the notion that popular conformity was based on 'conviction' or that most ordinary people were 'bound' to the regime pays insufficient attention to the fact that there was, for most of the GDR's history, little alternative to the prevailing situation. When a viable choice finally seemed to emerge in 1989, mass action was the result. After all, as Kowalczuk has pointed out on this very issue, the fact that the SED never would have won an open election in the GDR casts serious doubt on the notion that there was a fundamental attachment to the GDR among broad circles of the populace.[72] Neubert's emphasis on popular complicity in sustaining the SED regime is perhaps understandable from the perspective of a former dissident, who no doubt felt marginalized in society and was marginalized as an unwanted disruption to the flow of daily life. But the picture he paints is simply too black-and-white, based as it is on the flawed assumption of a 'clear contrast' between opposition and conformity.[73] The principal line of conflict that he highlights – between those who actively worked for change and those who did not – was certainly not the only political cleft in East German society. Just because the vast majority of East Germans were not 'for' the dissident groups before 1989 does not mean that they were 'for' the regime. On both empirical and conceptual grounds, there are profound shortcomings with an interpretation 'that contrasts a small group of upright people with a great mass of conformists'.[74]

The thesis of widespread popular 'acceptance' of the regime suffers far more gravely from this failure to recognize the lack of political choice in the GDR. Although the survey material used by Niemann and Friedrich offers a valuable insight into patterns of popular opinion, there are serious questions about its reliability for analysing underlying political attitudes if taken at face value. The difficulties relate less to the obvious possibility of people being afraid to record their genuine opinions (the surveys were, as Niemann points out, conducted with quite rigorous anonymity) than to the very value of the questions they ask in the anti-pluralistic political context of the GDR. Given the lack of choices on offer,[75] one must not employ these sources too literally. The fact that the SED scored highly in opinion polls on some issues and poorly on others tells us very little in and of itself. It is far more helpful to ask *which* aspects were relatively popular. It seems glaringly obvious that the issues on which the GDR was rated highly (job security, peace policy, educational opportunities, cultural opportunities and various other aspects of everyday life) are rather superficial compared to the fundamental issues on which it received poor marks: economic inefficiency, the basic freedom to

---

72  See Kowalczuk's comments in the summary discussion from a 1997 conference in K.-D. Henke *et al.* (eds), *Widerstand und Opposition in der DDR*, p. 276.

73  See Neubert's comments in ibid., p. 276.

74  See Stefan Wolle's comments in ibid., p. 276.

75  Of course it might be noted that, despite the obvious differences with the one-party system in the GDR, practical choices are also somewhat circumscribed in Western democracies, where the crowding of the so-called centre ground is reflected in a long-term trend of declining electoral turnouts.

travel, the lack of democratic input into the political process and the lack of reliable information. One might indeed surmise, as does Kowalczuk, that few East Germans would have voted for the SED's peace policy and cultural opportunities over a better economy and civil rights if given the choice. The question in the title of Friedrich's article – 'did the SED govern against the will of the majority?' – itself misses this fundamental point. Just because specific measures or certain aspects of SED rule met with some degree of approval does not mean that the party was governing with consent in any meaningful sense of the word. The institutionalized rigging of the elections alone offers more than ample proof of the 'democratic illegitimacy' of SED rule that Friedrich places in question.

Of course, disliking the regime was not the same thing as resisting or opposing it. That there was mass discontent with many aspects of life in the GDR is indisputable. How much of this discontent spilled over into popular dissent towards the regime's demands? Even in the absence of open dissent, did it merge with or nourish other forms of (often unconscious) *'Resistenz'* towards the regime's penetration of society?

Apart from a smaller stream of work on Christian communities and youth subcultures, much of the research on this question has focused on industrial workers and disputes in the factories. It is clear that the bulk of dissent on the shopfloor was not explicitly regarded as such and was not directly geared towards undermining the regime. On the whole, such disruptions as occurred were primarily a form of reaction against demands imposed on individuals by the state, a self-protective response in defence of one's interests. To be sure, the internal reports are full of innumerable minor acts of protest in the factories, some of them quite explicitly political in content: defacing political posters, the daubing of 'enemy slogans' on factory walls, disrupting political presentations, refusals to sign resolutions in support of SED policies.[76] But it is symptomatic of popular protest in general in the GDR that criticism at factory assemblies and other public gatherings was generally limited to immediate material grievances, whereas most expressions of specifically political dissent were anonymous. The bulk of protest in the factories centred on narrower material issues, above all on the regime's periodic attempts to raise work norms and reassert control over wages.

The most drastic strategy for opposing such measures were periodic strikes and work stoppages. It is impossible to establish with any degree of certainty how common such occurrences were. For what it is worth, the FDGB registered 166 work stoppages or strikes in 1960, which FDGB chief Herbert Warnke conceded was 'not nearly all of them'.[77] The overwhelming

---

76 Cf. M. Fulbrook, *Anatomy of a Dictorship*, pp. 159–61; A. Port, 'The "Grumble Gesellschaft": Industrial Defiance and Worker Protest in Early East Germany', in P. Hüber and K. Tenfelde (eds), *Arbeiter in der SBZ/DDR*, pp. 787–810; and generally P. Hüber, *Konsens, Konflikt, Kompromiß*.
77 SAPMO-BA DY30/IV2/6.11/66, fo. 34. Warnke's quote from P. Hübner, *Konsens*, p. 209.

majority of such strikes were small, spontaneous and basically unorganized, and were usually quite quickly and effectively dealt with at the local level.[78] But given their politicization, strikes were the exception, not the rule. Far more common were slow-downs or threats to take one's skills to a higher bidder as a means of coming to a suitable arrangement with local management. This plethora of essentially defensive, non-political acts on the shopfloor has been interpreted as a form of 'resistance' among East German workers, not in the conscious or moral sense of the word, but rather in terms of how shopfloor milieux and the structures of industrial relations acted as blocks to the total claims of the regime. As Jeffrey Kopstein has argued, it was not intellectuals but workers who really 'resisted over the longue durée' through their countless small acts of self-defence and self-interest. More than the periodic protestations of intellectuals or the scheming of party elites, it was 'the small-scale, largely nonpolitical acts of everyday resistance that chipped away at the long-term capacity of communist regimes to meet the demands of society at large'.[79]

As prevalent as such forms of behaviour were, it is best not to make too much of them as conscious acts of opposition or dissent. It would seem that very little of the protest in the factories was intended as 'opposition' to the regime as such. Indeed, much of it could be seen as a product of the nature of factory work itself, whether the disciplining pressures of the Taylorist assembly line or the frustration with poor supply and organization that could affect workers' pay. Shopfloor protests against the introduction of the 'enterprise collective contracts' in the early 1950s, for instance, were more a response to concerns about productivity and pay than a direct challenge to the authorities. Similarly, the prevalent pattern of complaint and informal wage-bargaining that emerged over the following years can in many ways be regarded as a rational response to the lack of any independent unions or representative structures. Many instances of apparent 'dissent' in the factories thus arguably represented fairly normal forms of behaviour under 'abnormal' (by Western standards) political conditions. One runs the risk here of adopting the regime's own view of 'resistance' or 'opposition', that is, of politicizing any behaviour that was not explicitly supportive and viewing it as aimed against the regime or its goals. One also runs the risk of positing conscious oppositional intentions where there were none. While it is certainly true that the 'lack of political voice' among East German workers 'should not be confused for absence of will or powerlessness',[80] it is nonetheless difficult to discern the 'will' of most workers. To what extent

---

78  There were reportedly a total number of only 1,400 participants in the 135 strikes in 1961, or an average of around ten participants per incident. SAPMO-BA DY30/IV2/6.11/66, fo. 29. See, more generally, P. Hübner, 'Arbeitskonflikte in Industriebetrieben der DDR nach 1953. Annäherungen an eine Struktur- und Prozeßanalyse', in R. Eckart *et al.* (eds), *Zwischen Selbstbehauptung und Anpassung*, pp. 178–91.

79  J. Kopstein, 'Chipping Away at the State. Workers' Resistance and the Demise of East Germany', *World Politics*, vol. 48 (Apr. 1996), pp. 391–423, here pp. 393–4.

80  Ibid., p. 394.

was 'chipping away at the state' a deliberate intention, to what extent merely a function of their actions?[81]

The problems in evaluating these kinds of behaviour as instances of dissent recall the earlier debates over these issues for the Third Reich. As a number of scholars have pointed out with reference to the Nazi regime, the notion of widespread *'Resistenz'* can all too easily render an unrealistic image of popular refusal and disapproval that de-emphasizes the degree of consensus, or at least the degree of willingness to conform, however unenthusiastically, to the regime's demands.[82] Despite the concept's claims to deal with the effect of non-conformist actions instead of the motivations behind them, in practice one cannot neatly separate the two in evaluations of dissenting behaviour. The question of why particular individuals or groups 'resisted' the regime's demands – whether for moral and ethical reasons, out of self-interest, as a product of circumstance or a reflection of social milieu – is still important for evaluating their behaviour. It is important to know, for instance, whether the 'hijacking' of the socialist brigades by their members in 1959–60 was motivated by the simple desire for better pay and conditions or rather as a means of improving factory organization and productivity, a desire to 'work properly'.[83] In addition, although the notion of *'Resistenz'* appears at first sight to undermine 'totalitarian' and monolithic images of society by highlighting the blocks to dictatorial control, in some ways it also lets the basic conceptual framework of totalitarianism in 'through the back door'[84] by positing too rigid a picture of 'state versus populace', too stark a division between regime and society.

The emphasis needs to lie not solely on consensus, dissent, or *Resistenz*, but on the many ways in which they overlapped and coexisted. Although recent research has unearthed countless instances of 'deviant' behaviour, the bulk of evidence points to what has aptly been called the 'disaffected loyalty' *(mißmutige Loyalität)*[85] of the majority of East Germans towards the regime. Neither ideas of a 'latent civil war' nor the widespread notion of a

---

81  Although Kopstein is primarily interested in the systemic roots and effects of workers' behaviour, his findings do raise this important question. Employing the term 'resistance' for such acts recalls some of the debates about categorizing dissenting behaviour spawned by Tim Mason's path-breaking work on the Third Reich, whose conceptual approach Kopstein explicitly draws on. See especially Kopstein's 'Chipping Away at the State', pp. 422–3.

82  K. Mallmann and G. Paul, 'Resistenz oder loyale Widerwilligkeit? Anmerkungen zu einem umstrittenen Begriff', *ZfG* vol. 41 (1993), pp. 99–116; I. Kershaw, *The Nazi Dictatorship*, Chapter 8; Detlev Peukert, *Inside Nazi Germany*; M. Prinz, 'Der Nationalsozialismus – eine "braune Revolution"?', in M. Hettling (ed.), *Revolution in Deutschland? 1789–1989* (Göttingen, 1991), pp. 70–89.

83  Cf. Jörg Roesler, 'Probleme des Brigadealltags: Arbeitsverhältnisse und Arbeitsklima in volkseigenen Betrieben', *APuZG*, 47/38 (1997), pp. 3–17; J. Roesler, 'Zur Rolle der Arbeitsbrigaden in der betrieblichen Hierarchie der VEB: eine politik- und sozialgeschichtliche Betrachtung', *DA*, vol. 30 (1997), pp. 737–50.

84  Quoted from M. Prinz, 'Der Nationalsozialismus – eine "braune Revolution"?', p. 80.

85  A. Lüdtke, '"Helden der Arbeit" – Mühe beim Arbeiten. Zur mißmutigen Loyalität von Industriearbeitern in der DDR', in Kaelble *et al.* (eds), *Sozialgeschiche*, pp. 188–213. This notion is very similar to Mallmann and Paul's suggestion of *'loyale Widerwilligkeit'*, or 'loyal unwillingness', for the Third Reich. K. Mallmann and G. Paul, 'Resistenz oder loyale Widerwilligkeit?'.

'niche society' characterized by a mass retreat into private life sufficiently capture this mixture of refusal and conformity. The recently popular idea of '*Eigen-Sinn*' points towards ways of bridging the divide between the competing images of ubiquitous dissent and widespread conformity by emphasizing how the pursuit of one's interests – indeed, the very definition of one's interests in the first place – is integrally related to social and political circumstances. One might, for instance, be willing to participate in a 'socialist competition' at work out of a sense of occupational pride, yet protest against the introduction of stiffer work norms or refuse to take on the time-consuming duties of a union representative. As the post-1989 controversies surrounding many GDR intellectuals demonstrate (which we will briefly discuss in Chapter 8), one might even be highly critical of the regime yet agree to act as a *Stasi* informant as a means of maintaining space for critical artistic expression. On a more general level, admiration for the GDR's generous social benefits could easily coexist with utter rejection of other areas of policy. It is only by recognizing the coexistence of consensus and refusal that we will be able to paint a more nuanced picture of popular political behaviour that was both reactive and pro-active, that showed signs of resistance to certain measures within wider structures of strained consensus, that maintained small, semi-autonomous spheres of action within public institutions, and that changed significantly in accordance with the shifting parameters of political life over the course of the GDR's history.

There remains the difficult question of whether these relatively common acts of non-conformity had any meaningful effect on the regime. Even if acts of low-level protest were a fundamental feature of the regime in terms of their frequency, were they nonetheless a fringe phenomenon in terms of their impact? Few have thus far dared to speculate. The conventional wisdom points to the inefficacy of popular protest in the GDR compared to most other Eastern European states. The general impression has been, as Mary Fulbrook puts it, that 'popular disaffection and protest remained largely spontaneous, isolated, and politically without serious effects'.[86] As we have seen, Ehrhart Neubert takes this conclusion a step further by arguing that even instances of refusal were an element of overall conformity which ultimately served to stabilize the political system more than undermine it.[87] It would indeed appear that popular dissent had little, if any, overt and immediate impact on the regime's stability apart from the two existential crises of 1953 and 1989. Yet the *cumulative* effect of decades of small-scale acts of refusal, especially concerning the regime's demands in the work sphere, nonetheless appear highly significant over the long term. Although it is difficult to discern workers' intentions, Kopstein's contention that the *function* of these small-scale acts crucially handicapped the regime and helped pave the way for its ultimate collapse is compelling. In his view, the countless sick

86 M. Fulbrook, *Anatomy of a Dictatorship*, p. 127.
87 E. Neubert, *Geschichte der Opposition*, p. 24.

days, slow-downs, and refusals to participate in production competitions contributed to a 'long-term creeping immobilization of regime capacity to formulate and implement effective economic policies'.[88] The pattern of local wage and productivity arrangements that had emerged by the early 1950s was never successfully abolished, but was rather regarded by officials on the ground as a 'hot potato' that was better left alone. Although much more needs to be done before we know the limits of this thesis, the idea of situating popular acts of refusal within the 'politics of economic decline' certainly promises a more integrated understanding of the political dynamics of 'disaffected loyalty' than the rather static picture of a depoliticized 'niche society' or the reduction of 'opposition' to a matter of individual morality and choice.

Whatever verdict future research might reach on this approach, it clearly demonstrates how seemingly 'unpolitical' acts of non-conformity, even when expressed within a broader framework of acquiescence, could have consequences that were consummately political. Although these unheroic actions were not as visible as the various 'oppositional' activities of 1989, were they perhaps equally important insofar as they prepared the ground for the events of 1989 in the first place? Have the creeping, long-term factors that undermined the regime been somewhat obscured by the concentration of attention on the more short-term process of political mobilization? These questions bring us to the multitude of issues surrounding the events of autumn 1989, which is the focus of the next chapter.

---

88  J. Kopstein, 'Chipping Away at the State', p. 422.

# 6

# The end of the GDR: Revolution from below, implosion from within, collapse from outside?

Despite the protestations of a handful of hindsight-prophets, almost no one foresaw the collapse of the GDR.[1] The planned reception of Erich Honecker by Helmut Kohl in West Germany in 1987 was certainly not arranged with the intention of cultivating better relations with a leader whose days were numbered. Former Chancellor Helmut Schmidt's assertion in September 1989 that 'the German question will only be solved in the next century' was not, even at this late stage, particularly controversial.[2] Kohl's successor to the chancellorship, Gerhard Schröder, was equally certain in June 1989 that 'one should not lie about the chances of reunification. There is no chance.'[3] The *Bild-Zeitung*'s decision in summer 1989 to cease its long-standing tradition of placing the 'GDR' in inverted commas as a means of highlighting its illegitimacy was certainly not prompted by an assumption that it would cease to exist in little over a year.

Despite being caught by surprise, the initial speechlessness of journalists and scholars over the unexpected 'return of history' in autumn 1989 was soon swept away by a flood of explanations for the GDR's collapse.

---

1 Fortunately, this sort of literature is relatively rare. Cf. Konrad Löw, 'War der Fall der Mauer vorherse-hbar?', in Karl Eckart, Jens Hacker and Siegfried Mampel (eds), *Wiedervereinigung Deutschlands. Festschrift zum 20-jährigen Bestehen der Gesellschaft für Deutschlandforschung* (Berlin, 1998), pp. 243–57; Tilman Mayer, 'Warum es zur Wiedervereinigungschance kam', in ibid., pp. 233–41; Immanuel Geiss, *Zukunft als Geschichte. Historisch-politische Analysen und Prognosen zum Untergang des Sowjetkommunismus, 1980–1991* (Stuttgart, 1998). For a more convincing evaluation of predictions before 1989, see Randall Collins and David Waller, 'Der Zusammenbruch von Staaten und die Revolutionen im sowjetischen Block: welche Theorien machten zutreffende Voraussagen?', in H. Joas and M. Kohli (eds), *Der Zusammenbruch der DDR*, pp. 302–23.

2 Helmut Schmidt in *Die Zeit*, 22 Sept. 1989, cited in Martin Sabrow, 'Der Konkurs der Konsensdiktatur. Überlegungen zum inneren Zerfall der DDR aus kulturgeschichtlicher Perspektive', in K. Jarausch and M. Sabrow (eds), *Weg in den Untergang. Der innere Zerfall der DDR* (Göttingen, 1999), pp. 83–116, here p. 83.

3 Cited in Martin Sabrow, 'Der Konkurs der Konsensdiktatur', p. 83.

Scholarly commentators quickly lined up to explain how an event which few of them foresaw was actually an obvious and inevitable outcome of a long process of decline. Participants in the dissident movements often pointed to their own actions against the regime as crucial challenges to its authority. In the accounts of some West German politicians, one soon encountered a story of deft negotiation and visionary statesmanship.[4] The memoirs of former East German leaders have presented a range of interpretations emphasizing either the cruelty of fate, the 'sell-out' of the GDR by opportunists or even the conspiratorial machinations of shadowy figures intent upon undermining the regime.[5] Against the background of the previous dearth of predictions, the multiplicity of explanations testifies to both the unexpected and highly complex character of the events of 1989.

To be sure, no revolution is a simple matter. Highlighting individual factors, focusing on certain themes or merely describing the events that took place does not offer a sufficient explanation of why they came about. Although all revolutions are, historically speaking, unique, all appear to be characterized by a combination of factors. The existence of an internal movement for change capable of mobilizing widespread support is essential, as is the growth of uncertainty and/or divisions within the ruling elite. In addition, international constellations also frequently play a central role in the unfolding of revolutionary developments. In the case of East Germany in 1989, these three elements broadly correspond to the three main historiographic perspectives on the GDR's downfall: was this a 'revolution from below', an 'implosion from above', or a 'collapse from outside'?[6]

Of course the initial answer to this question might simply be 'yes'. Few would disagree that it was all of these things, and quite obviously the end of the GDR cannot be explained monocausally. These differing perspectives on the downfall of the regime do not, therefore, necessarily represent irreconcilable alternatives. The question is rather one of emphasis and how one pieces them together. Although the literature on the end of the GDR has expanded into literally thousands of works,[7] the bulk of debate has revolved around a number of key issues: What significance should be attributed to the external pressures, the processes of regime dissolution and the popular revolt in relation to one another? How did their relative importance vary over time? How do they fit together in terms of cause and effect? And, perhaps most controversially, how should we evaluate the entire set of events

---

4 For instance, Wolfgang Schäuble, *Der Vertrag. Wie ich über die deutsche Einheit verhandelte* (Stuttgart, 1991).

5 Cf. Egon Krenz, *Wenn Mauern fallen* (Wien, 1990); Günter Schabowski, *Das Politbüro* (Hamburg, 1990); E. Krenz, *Der Absturz* (Berlin, 1991), all of which try to portray the opening of the Wall as the intended outcome of their actions. On the conspiracy theories about the opening of the Wall as a plot by the *Stasi*, see Henryk Broder, 'Eine schöne Revolution', *Die Zeit*, no. 3, 1992.

6 Cf. the discussion in M. Fulbrook, *Anatomy of a Dictatorship*, pp. 243–6; C. Maier, *Dissolution*, pp. 108ff.

7 See Hendrik Berth and Elmar Brähler, *Zehn Jahre deutsche Einheit. Die Bibliographie* (Berlin, 2000); see also the exhaustive bibliography at http://www.wiedervereinigung.de.

within the wider historical context? Simply put, did the events of 1989 add up to a 'revolution' in any meaningful sense of the word? This last question in many ways encapsulates the issues at stake since the relative weight one assigns to domestic versus external factors or to popular pressure versus bureaucratic disintegration has a direct bearing on what kind of a 'revolution' one perceives the transformation of 1989 to be, or indeed whether one considers it a 'revolution' at all.

# Interpretations

Certainly one of the most prevalent images of the events of 1989 in the mainstream media is of a people's uprising originating in the small opposition groups and rapidly mushrooming into mass demonstrations that eventually brought the regime to its knees. In this view, the initially small stream of protest quickly converged with a deep reservoir of popular discontent to form a torrent of opposition that swept away the apparently stable dictatorial system with breathtaking speed. Inspired by the emigration crisis over the summer of 1989 and the increasingly defiant tone of the existing dissident groups, the previously small protest marches in Leipzig swelled into mass demonstrations from early October, forcing the resignation of the old guard and eventually culminating in the fall of the Wall on 9 November. From this stage onwards, as the protest movements were able to wring concession after concession out of the crumbling regime and the West became increasingly involved in negotiating a solution to the emigration crisis, the momentum of events moved inexorably towards German unification. The events of 1989 were, in this view, driven by popular demands for basic political freedoms and the desire for a better life. The wresting of political power from the ruling elite by the crowds eventually swept away not only the dictatorial political system, but the very state itself. In this version of events, the collapse of the regime and the emergence of a 'civil society'[8] that broke the strictures on public discourse imposed by the regime was undoubtedly a 'revolutionary' upheaval, whether a 'democratic revolution', 'peaceful revolution', or 'citizens' revolution'.[9]

---

8  For analyses centred on notions of 'civil society', see Patrick von zur Mühlen, *Aufbruch und Umbruch in der DDR. Bürgerbewegungen, kritische Öffentlichkeit und Niedergang der SED-Herrschaft* (Bonn, 2000); Karsten Timmer, *Vom Aufbruch zum Umbruch. Die Bürgerbewegung in der DDR 1989* (Göttingen, 2000).

9  Cf. Bernd Lindner, *Die demokratische Revolution in der DDR 1989–90* (Bonn, 1998), which is a good example of this conventional 'whiggish' account of 1989. A particularly interesting and readable account which stresses the role of the crowds is provided by Hartmut Zwahr, a historian and participant in the demonstrations, *Ende einer Selbstzerstörung. Leipzig und die Revolution in der DDR* (Göttingen, 1993). As Zwahr argues, 'From my own experience I cannot confirm that this was merely a collapse (*Zusammenbruch*)', ibid., p. 9.

Yet as early as December 1989, doubts were raised about the 'revolutionary' character of the preceding months.[10] For some observers, the bloodless weeks in autumn 1989 gave more the impression of a short-term popular revolt, after which the crowds merely confirmed the dismantling of the East German state that was, in various ways, already beginning even before the mass demonstrations. The inflationary employment of the term 'revolution' during autumn 1989 was rapidly displaced over the early months of 1990 by the decidedly tepid term '*Wende*', which has prevailed ever since in colloquial usage. Employed originally by Egon Krenz, Honecker's successor as head of the SED, as a self-serving description of events while they unfolded, this label denotes little more than a change of course or direction. As Christa Wolf pointed out on 4 November 1989, it conjures the image of a ship merely altering course – without any change of direction at the helm – in order to tack more effectively against the wind.[11] The accusatory term '*Wendehals*' (or 'wryneck') soon gained popularity as a means of pillorying Honecker's supposedly 'reformist' successors and of expressing disappointment with the limited extent of political change underway. It is perhaps because of the many difficulties associated with the subsequent process of unification that the more neutral and detached notion of a '*Wende*' has, despite its dubious origins, largely displaced 'revolution' in mainstream discourse.

The idea that the events of 1989 constituted a 'revolution' has been challenged from a number of different directions.[12] Many former dissidents shun the notion on the grounds that no domestic alternative political platform was pushed through; that is, the indigenous protest movements managed only to dismantle the regime without putting another system in its place, which was taken care of by the West German government in an act of 'annexation'. Because the reform-socialist programme of most of the dissident groups – insofar as they possessed a clear programme at all – was signally not fulfilled, many former activists view the events of 1989 as a 'deflected', 'aborted' or 'hijacked' revolution that was knocked off its supposedly 'original' course by the arrival of the masses on the political scene and the turn towards national unification which none of the alternative groups had espoused.[13] As late as 4 November one could still hear talk of a 'November Revolution', but after the fall of the Wall on 9 November and

10 Robert Darnton, 'Did East Germany Have a Revolution?', *New York Times*, 3 Dec. 1989, p. A19.
11 See Michael Richter, *Die Revolution in Deutschland 1989/90. Anmerkungen zum Charakter der 'Wende'* (Dresden, 1995); Ludger Kühnhardt, 'Umbruch – Wende – Revolution. Deutungsmuster des deutschen Herbstes 1989', *APuZG* B40/97, pp. 12–18; Winfried Steffani, 'Wende oder Umbruch?', *DA* 31 (1998), pp. 282–5.
12 It is worth noting – though we will not deal with them further – that a few die-hard Marxist–Leninist voices have not shied away from calling these events a 'counter-revolution'. Cf. Hanfried Müller, '"Zusammenbruch" und/oder "Konterrevolution"', in Weißenseer Arbeitskries, *Wider die Resignation der Linken. Stimmen gegen Antikommunismus, Konterrevolution und Annexion* (Cologne, 1994), pp. 240–53.
13 Representative works of this genre are Michael Schneider, *Die abgetriebene Revolution. Von der Staatsfirma in die DM-Kolonie* (Berlin, 1990); Heinz Kallabis, *Ade DDR!* (Berlin, 1990).

the increasingly central role played by the West German government the change in tone was remarkably swift. As Bärbel Bohley explained in February 1990, 'I always doubted that this was revolution. I perceived it rather as a revolt that arose from a great sense of helplessness.'[14] Konrad Weiß has likewise preferred to call the events an '*Umbruch*' ('radical change') or at best a 'failed revolution' (*mißglückt*).[15]

In scholarly discourse, the notion of regime collapse or 'systems failure' (*Zusammenbruch*) has gradually come to prevail in Germany, especially among West German social scientists. Strongly influenced by hindsight, this perspective sees the events of 1989 essentially as the culmination of a long process of economic and political deterioration, as if the regime finally stopped working and fell prey to its own internal malfunctioning. From this point of view, the transformation was driven less by popular will or political pressure 'from below' than by the disintegration of the regime that, for various reasons, had lost the will and/or capacity to rule. The combination of growing economic failures and the new uncertainties arising from Gorbachev's reformist programme in Moscow undermined the entire value-system that the SED had attempted to construct since the 1940s, sapping the confidence of party leaders as well as rank-and-file functionaries.[16] This 'erosion of the Marxist-Leninist claim to legitimacy'[17] is seen as crucial to the unfolding of events in autumn 1989. It was, for instance, in large part due to the internal implosion of the regime that there was so little violence. The East German authorities effectively handed over power to the Leipzig demonstrators on the crucial night of 8–9 October instead of opting for a Tiananmen Square-style solution to the demonstrations as the Chinese government had done only months earlier (to the applause of many SED leaders, it might be noted). Not only the renunciation of repression, but also the ousting of Honecker on 18 October and the confusions between Schabowski, Krenz and other party leaders that led to the opening of the Wall on 9 November can be traced back to divisions and uncertainties within the ruling elite.[18] The perception that the regime was crumbling over autumn 1989 can in fact be viewed as a primary cause, not effect, of the popular mobilization against it. The regime's apparent vulnerability crucially

---

14 Cited in Hagen Findeis (ed.), *Die Entzauberung des politischen. Was ist aus den politisch alternativen Gruppen der DDR geworden?* (Leipzig, 1994), p. 57.

15 Konrad Weiß, 'Ich haben keinen Tag in diesem Land umsonst gelebt', *Blätter für deutsche und internationale Politik* 5 (1990), p. 555.

16 For a fascinating analysis of the disintegration of the SED's cultivated value system, see Martin Sabrow, 'Der Konkurs der Konsensdiktatur'; see also Rolf Reißig, 'Das Scheitern der DDR und des realsozialistischen Systems – Einige Ursachen und Folgen', in H. Joas and M. Kohli (eds), *Der Zusammenbruch der DDR*, pp. 49–69, esp. p. 51.

17 Frank Wilhelmy, *Der Zerfall der SED-Herrschaft. Zur Erosion des marxistisch-leninistischen Legitimitätsanspruches in der DDR* (Münster, 1995).

18 For an extremely detailed account of these developments that is in fact highly critical of the structuralist '*Zusammenbruch*-thesis', see Hans-Hermann Hertle, *Der Fall der Mauer. Die unbeabsichtigte Selbstauflösung des SED-Staates* (Opladen, 1996).

lowered the threshold of fear that had previously kept people from speaking up. Of course, some degree of bureaucratic disintegration or division among elites usually precedes or accompanies 'revolutionary' upheavals. But for many observers the events of 1989 represented at the most what Timothy Garton Ash has called a 'refolution', a mixture of reform at the top and revolution on the streets.[19]

A whole other strain of scholarly analysis has approached the collapse of the GDR not in terms of internal pressures but rather of the changing external environment. Instead of interpreting 1989 as a case of 'implosion' or 'revolution', some commentators have found the notion of 'decolonization' or 'geostrategic retreat' more compelling, thus emphasizing the international perspective and the importance of the Soviet Union's renunciation of force as a means of supporting the SED regime. The roots of this process reached back to Gorbachev's ascension to power in 1985, and especially to the acceleration of his reforms from 1986 onwards. The first signs of friction between East Berlin and Moscow appeared at the SED's Eleventh Party Congress in April 1986, where Gorbachev was visibly unimpressed by the East Germans' timid economic innovations that left the basic problem of centralization untouched.[20] One year later, Kurt Hager, *Politbüro* member in charge of ideology, (in)famously made it clear that East Berlin was not interested in following the Soviet lead on *glasnost* and *perestroika*: 'just because your neighbour puts up new wallpaper, does that mean you'd feel obliged to do the same?'[21] A more serious dispute eventually arose over the appearance of the October 1988 issue of *Sputnik*, a German-language digest of Soviet news, which suggested that the German communists were partly to blame for the rise of Hitler in 1932–33 because of their stubborn refusal to join forces with the Social Democrats. This understandably struck a nerve in a regime that based its claim to legitimacy on its anti-fascist credentials. The decision to ban *Sputnik* in November 1988 plainly revealed the widening rift between Moscow and East Berlin, and became a catalyst for reformist voices within the party.

Against this background it is easier to understand why Moscow was no longer willing to support the GDR at any price.[22] Indeed, by the late 1980s the desirability of sustaining its hegemony in Eastern Europe more generally was coming into serious doubt. To be sure, Moscow had no intention at this stage of ceding 'the jewel of its East European empire';[23] the replacement of

19 T. G. Ash, *We the People: The Revolution of '89 witnessed in Warsaw, Budapest, Berlin and Prague* (Cambridge, 1990).
20 Cf. the recollections of Günter Schabowski in *Das Politüro* (Hamburg, 1990), pp. 34ff.
21 Interview with Kurt Hager in *Stern*, 9 Apr. 1987.
22 M. McCauley, 'Gorbachev, the GDR and Germany', in G. -J. Glaeßner and I. Wallace (eds), *The German Revolution of 1989: Causes and Consequences* (Oxford, 1992).
23 Charles Krauthammer, 'Bless Our Pax Americana', *Washington Post*, 22 March 1991, cited in Jeffrey Gedmin, *The Hidden Hand: Gorbachev and the Collapse of East Germany* (Washington DC, 1992), p. 117.

Honecker by a more reform-minded leadership was the desired aim. But the lack of support from Moscow is widely regarded as a crucial prerequisite to the regime's seemingly paralytic inability to respond to the crises that gripped it over the summer and autumn of 1989: namely, the haemorrhage of people through the Iron Curtain and the new reformist currents in neighbouring states such as Hungary and Poland. Once the challenge from within had finally materialized, the geostrategic retreat of the Soviet Union meant that, unlike 1953, 1956 or 1968, there were no Soviet tanks to come to the rescue. Of course this concentration on the changing international framework by no means excludes the possibility of calling these events revolutionary. Historically speaking, processes of decolonization have often been accompanied or caused by revolutionary upheavals. But in practice it nonetheless de-emphasizes the popular upsurge from below. The principal actors from this perspective were not the dissidents or the crowds of people in the streets, but the Soviet reformers, 'who, believing that East Germany could be transformed into a legitimate and viable Socialist state, took steps that led to the dissolution of an empire'.[24] Their 'grand miscalculation' about the possibility of democratizing the communist system was the primary cause of what has been called the 'inadvertent revolution' in the GDR.[25]

Again, no serious proponent of any of these views is claiming to offer 'the' answer to the causes of the transformation of 1989. Individual scholarly works focusing on the role of popular protest, the internal disintegration of the regime or the international context do not, generally speaking, deny the importance of all of these factors. Yet the question of where the emphasis should lie and how they fit together is nonetheless an important one for historians to ask if we do not wish to capitulate before the complexity of events. Any attempt to evaluate this exceedingly difficult question must grapple with a number of basic issues: internal versus external pressures, change 'from above' versus mobilization 'from below', long-term causes versus short-term catalysts. In addition, an elemental yet important question to bear in mind is how the constellation of factors changed over time, when different pressures appear to have been more important than others. On a methodological level there are also problems concerning how the questions we ask and the particular aspects on which we focus structure our understanding of the transformation of 1989 more generally. One's choice of concepts to describe events depends largely on one's particular analytical interest. Integrally related to this are a number of more normative issues: What do we mean by 'revolution'? What do the various labels for the events of 1989 illuminate or explain, what do they obscure? The following evaluation will briefly attempt to address these questions.

24 Jeffrey Gedmin, *The Hidden Hand: Gorbachev and the Collapse of East Germany* (Washington DC, 1992), p. 117.
25 Ibid.

# Evaluation

It makes sense to begin by focusing on the wider international context. Obvious though it seems, it is worth repeating once again that the GDR was a product of the Cold War that owed its existence to the bipolar division of Europe and Soviet strategic interests after the Second World War. It stands to reason, therefore, that the same international political factors that underpinned its very existence could also spell its doom. There can be no doubt that the Soviet geostrategic retreat was of paramount importance for the dissolution of the East German regime. The shift in Soviet foreign policy had a number of serious repercussions for the GDR, some of them eventually proving fatal.

In the medium term, the struggles over reform within the Soviet bloc meant that by 1989 the GDR leadership was faced with the unattractive prospect of either dangerously distancing itself from its great benefactor or embarking upon a path of reforms that could ultimately place in question the regime's very reason to exist alongside the Federal Republic. Of course *glasnost* and *perestroika* presented challenges to other East European states as well. In Hungary and Poland in particular they helped to initiate and accelerate wide-ranging reformist currents that had a direct impact on governmental policies. But because of the GDR's unique 'national' problem, the challenges for the SED were especially daunting; hence the leadership's pronounced reluctance to board Gorbachev's reformist bandwagon. The upshot of the reforms was not only the creation of new divisions within the SED itself, but also between the various East European regimes over trade issues and how to handle the GDR's emigration crisis once it started.

In the short term, the opening of the barbed wire between Hungary and Austria in May 1989 – one of the most visible consequences of liberalization measures in Budapest – was of course the immediate trigger for the emigration crisis. Although the Hungarian authorities had not initially intended to allow non-Hungarians through their border crossings (thus upholding prior agreements between communist states not to allow travellers to exit to third countries), they had not reckoned with the number of East Germans who would attempt to cross elsewhere. Clashes between East Germans and Hungarian border guards prompted the Budapest authorities in August to cease stamping the passports of East Germans who were caught in the act, which effectively meant there was no deterrent from trying.[26] By September the Hungarians had officially removed all restrictions on border crossings for East Germans. In the meantime, thousands of refugees were also piling up in West German embassies in Prague, Warsaw and Budapest, eventually to be allowed to travel to the Federal Republic either via Austria or in special sealed trains. Crucially, the Soviets were of no help whatsoever in the

26 Cf. C. Maier, *Dissolution*, pp. 125–6.

ensuing recriminations among the Warsaw Pact allies over the issue of travel restrictions. The SED leadership, incensed over its 'betrayal' by Hungary, was fatally weakened by the population haemorrhage. Because it had made control over its citizens' movements the fundamental precept of its authority since 1961, its inability to enforce its will in this sphere crucially emboldened the protest movement within the GDR as well.[27]

Events in the GDR were an integral part of the wider crisis of communism. As we have already seen, the Eastern bloc as a whole had conspicuously failed to keep pace with the West in economic terms since the 1960s, especially in the critical area of electronics and computing technology. The increasing economic lag made the costs of rearmament during the 1980s downturn in East–West relations all the more crippling. It also nourished popular disgruntlement over the glaringly lower living standard than in the West, which helped undermine popular consent to the regime. The growing sense of stagnation – economic, political, and cultural – led to a widespread loss of faith in the system and the ideology that underpinned it. Although Soviet-style socialism had already lost much of its moral authority after the suppression of the Prague Spring in 1968, by the 1980s this was compounded by its dwindling capacity to compensate for the lack of political freedoms though material subsidies.

The international context is, then, absolutely essential for understanding the collapse of the GDR. The renunciation of the Brezhnev Doctrine was the crucial precondition for the events of 1989. Had the Soviet Union made the maintenance of a separate East German state a priority, developments would almost certainly have run a very different course. But by no means did the Soviet retreat make these events inevitable. The stage may have been set by developments beyond the GDR's borders, but other actors still had a critical role to play. After all, it was not Moscow's intention to initiate the disappearance of the GDR from the map of Europe; as late as January 1990 Gorbachev was still fighting to maintain its existence. Despite the Soviet reformers' recognition that economic improvements necessitated political changes as well, they were themselves quickly overtaken by events in the GDR. The focus on the international framework and the shifts in Soviet foreign policy pays too little attention to what was happening in the GDR to serve as a general explanation of events. For one thing, it fails to capture the dissolving loyalties and loss of confidence in the socialist system that led to such a strong and widespread desire for change. More importantly, it also tends to obscure the role of the popular protest movement. Although the Soviets had effectively pulled the props from under the GDR by autumn 1989, the regime still needed to be toppled. SED leaders did not blithely or magnanimously hand over power after their patrons had departed the scene.

---

27  For a stimulating theoretical perspective on this relationship, see the seminal article by Albert Hirschman, 'Exit, Voice, and the Fate of the German Democratic Republic: An Essay in Conceptual History', *World Politics*, vol. 45 (1993), pp. 173–202.

On the contrary, they tried desperately to cling to power by attempting to control the emigration problem (even by denying access to Czechoslovakia), by police intimidation at demonstrations and through rather unconvincing displays of goodwill. The protests of the crowds forced the leaders' hand at every turn. Although the events of autumn 1989 were crucially predicated upon the Soviet retreat, they were not pre-determined by it. To argue otherwise would be to assume that mass mobilization would inevitably happen instead of explaining why it did – an argument loaded with assumptions about the nature of the GDR's stability.[28]

In reconstructing the causes for the GDR's collapse in autumn 1989, it would seem that the internal pressures for change largely followed and were made possible in the first place by changes in the external environment. Whereas exogenous factors were clearly prominent during the period from May to September 1989 – the triggering of the emigration crisis and the unwillingness of other states to abide by the old travel arrangements – domestic pressures largely eclipsed them during the crescendo of street demonstrations and regime concessions in October and early November (which were also, to an extent, inspired by the transformations underway in Hungary and Poland). In other words, although changes in the external environment were crucial, the search for internal causes is still important. The question we must ask is therefore not merely 'Why did the GDR collapse?', but rather: 'Why did it collapse so quickly once the external props were pulled out?'[29] In addition, why did it collapse in the way that it did, and why was unification with West Germany the ultimate result? These are in many ways more contentious issues. Which internal factors were most important at which specific times? Was the process of transformation decisively driven forward by a revolutionary crowd, or was this, like previous would-be revolutions in German history (1848, 1918), less the product of a coherent challenge to authority than the result of a process of bureaucratic decomposition?[30]

The signs of regime decay were clear enough over summer and autumn 1989. As we have seen, the GDR's economic position had been slipping for years, and by the end of the 1980s the balance of payments was spiralling out of control. Moreover – and this was crucial in terms of popular sentiment – the economic deterioration could no longer be hidden by Western loans, but was becoming tangible in everyday life. The effects of years of capital

---

28 This is the main problem with the idea of an 'inadvertent revolution' arising from the Kremlin's miscalculations. It is based on too narrow a view of the causes of the great transformation and the actors who made it happen. While this term may well describe the actions of communist reformers in Moscow or East Berlin, autumn 1989 was anything but an 'inadvertent' revolution to the thousands who deliberately took to the streets in active protest. Cf. J. Gedmin, *The Hidden Hand*.

29 H. Joas and M. Kohli (eds), *Der Zusammenbruch der DDR*, p. 19.

30 See the thought-provoking discussion in C. Maier, *Dissolution*, pp. 108–18; also in C. Maier, 'Die Umwälzung in der DDR und die Frage einer deutschen Revolution', in K. Jarausch and M. Middell (eds), *Nach dem Erdbeben. (Re)Konstruktion ostdeutscher Geschichte und Geschichtswissenschaft* (Leipzig, 1994), pp. 339–52.

underinvestment could be felt everywhere, from the potholed roads to the crumbling house façades to the incessant breakdowns of old, worn-out equipment to the unavailability of consumer goods. Environmental degradation in particular, which was a major public health hazard in the industrial cities, was beginning to concern large groups of people. This not only nourished popular discontent, but also added to the mounting dissatisfaction with the leadership among the party rank-and-file. Moreover, the party leadership itself was also becoming divided to an extent not seen since the 1950s.[31] There were stirrings within the second rank of the *Politbüro* over the need to change course, and if necessary to change the leadership. As early as February 1989, Gerhard Schürer suggested to Egon Krenz that they try to remove Honecker, which Krenz was not yet prepared to do. There were also divisions of loyalty in the provinces and within key ministries. Markus Wolf, the *Stasi* chief of foreign espionage, was strongly in favour of *perestroika* from as early as 1986 and supported reformers within the party. Hans Modrow, long-serving party boss in Dresden who was eventually appointed prime minister in November 1989, was well known for his reformist views and was widely considered to be Gorbachev's favourite to replace Honecker. While mid-level officials in Leipzig showed themselves willing to negotiate with dissidents in order to avoid a bloodbath on the crucial night of 9 October, local SED leaders in Dresden opened dialogue with a 'Group of 20' representing the citizens.[32]

Under the pressure of mass demonstrations from October onwards, these splits within the leadership increasingly came into the open. In a vain attempt to stabilize the situation, the *Politbüro* finally decided to replace the ageing Honecker with Egon Krenz on 18 October (with the face-saving excuse of Honecker's ill health). Many of the reform-minded party officials joined the dissident bandwagon by publicly calling for far-reaching change. The culmination of these defections to the reformist camp was reached at the officially permitted mass demonstration of some 500,000 people on 4 November in East Berlin's Alexanderplatz, with speeches by writers such as Christa Wolf and Stefan Heym, civil rights campaigners such as Jens Reich, and former pillars of the political establishment such as Markus Wolf and *Politbüro* member Günter Schabowski. Over the following days the pressures for reform led to a series of concessions from above. On 6 November a proposal was published for a new travel law permitting trips abroad for up to thirty days. The next day the Council of Ministers resigned *en bloc*, to be followed on 8 November by the nomination of a new *Politbüro* including reformers such as Hans Modrow.

But despite all of these obvious signs of decay, there was still a discernible will to rule. The palace revolution of 18 October was undoubtedly

31  Cf. H.-H. Hertle and G.-R. Stephan (eds), *Das Ende der SED. Die letzten Tage des Zentralkomitees* (Berlin, 1997).
32  Michael Richter and Erich Sobeslavsky (eds), *Die Gruppe der 20. Gesellschaftlicher Aufbruch und politische Opposition in Dresden 1989–90* (Cologne, 1999).

conceived as a holding operation, not as the advent of a series of principled reforms. All the concessions over late October and early November – up to and including the opening of the Wall on 9 November – were cynically designed for the purpose of regrouping and retaining power, to ensure as strong a position as possible in order to amend or even rescind the reforms at a later stage. At this juncture there was absolutely no intention of any genuine renunciation of the SED's claim to rule on the part of Krenz and his supporters. All appearances of willingness to introduce genuine political pluralism were just that: appearances. At his meeting with Gorbachev on 1 November, Krenz had commented about the necessity of using brute force in the event of a mass attempt to breach the Wall at the upcoming mass demonstration on 4 November. As late as 3 November the *Politbüro* was still discussing how to regain the initiative and win back the 'trust' of the people.[33] In the revealing words of a report by the Central Committee's Propaganda Department of 6 November, 'the demands for free elections can in principle be supported ... , nevertheless this must not entail opening the door to bourgeois party pluralism'. Any demands for the abolition of the leading role of the SED were still considered 'totally unacceptable'. It was even cynically recommended that party officials disingenuously deviate from the official line in order to gain the confidence of the population: 'to give the appearance of being thoughtful and realistic, in order to win back our credibility'.[34] The opening of the Wall on 9 November was itself a product of administrative confusion and individual blunders, most notably on the part of Schabowski, whose ill-prepared comments about the new travel laws at a press conference were what triggered the throngs of people demanding passage through the frontier crossings from the bewildered border guards.[35]

It was only after 9 November that the will to rule really collapsed. Earlier that same day, only hours before the Wall was breached, Central Committee delegates had been listening with shock and dismay to the revelations by Gerhard Schürer and Günter Ehrensperger about the extent of the financial crisis.[36] At the Central Committee's meeting on 10 November, as East Germans were pouring through the border crossings in Berlin, a handful of the old guard, including former *Politbüro* members who had been deposed two days earlier, were expelled from the Central Committee. The rest of the old guard followed three days later. The revelations of mismanagement and corruption at the Central Committee's meetings and the upswell of anger in the factories and on the streets were a bitter pill for many comrades. Disillusioned functionaries resigned from their positions

---

33 SAPMO-BA DY30/IV2/2.039/317, *Politbüro* memorandum of 3 Nov. 1989, cited in M. Fulbrook, *Anatomy of a Dictatorship*, p. 261.

34 Ibid., 'Erste Einschätzung der Demonstration und Kundgebung am 4. November 1989 in Berlin', cited in M. Fulbrook, *Anatomy of a Dictatorship*, p. 261.

35 See, generally, H.-H. Hertle, *Der Fall der Mauer.*

36 Cf. C. Maier, *Dissolution*, pp. 162–3.

*en masse*; people began leaving the party in droves. Within only a few weeks the party apparatus was hardly capable of functioning on the ground. As one Central Committee delegate put it, 'The party is basically kaput ... It's an avalanche.'[37] Even the *Stasi* generals, the wielders of the 'sword and shield of the party', lacked a sense of direction in the midst of party disintegration.[38]

In this context of regime decomposition it almost goes without saying that the popular will to consent had all but completely evaporated. But is it fair to call this an instance of 'systems failure'? Clearly, the regime was coming unravelled over summer and autumn 1989. The renunciation of the use of force to halt the mass demonstrations in Leipzig on 9 October was a crucial test of resolve that revealed the limits of the regime's confidence and emboldened the protests. The series of concessions after the Alexanderplatz demonstration of 4 November and the opening of the Wall five days later confirmed the *Politbüro*'s loss of political control. But was it the dilapidated system's inability to respond or the challenge to its authority itself that drove events? Why did travel regulations become an issue for debate in the first place? The same can be asked of the expulsion of the old guard and the risks of using force. Were the SED leaders not forced into pondering these unattractive alternatives by the popular mobilization against the regime? Or was the mobilization of protest as much a consequence as a cause of the transformation that was under way?

These questions defy any clear-cut answer. Bureaucratic breakdown and popular mobilization were not neatly separable. There was a strong synergy between the two in 1989, with each one driving the other forward. Every concession by the regime emboldened protesters to demand more; every new demand undermined the confidence of the authorities and prompted further concessions. But in spite of this element of interaction, I would nonetheless contend that at each critical juncture it was collective action 'from below' on the part of ordinary East Germans that pushed the process of regime erosion beyond the point of no return, most notably on the nights of 9 October and 9 November. As Charles Maier has put it: 'The fact that the regime revealed elements of "systems failure" does not diminish the role of the popular movement.'[39] The regime may have been seriously weakened by its own failures, but it did not abdicate power willingly. Any account that loses sight of the pivotal role played by the crowds in wresting power to the

---

37 SAPMO-BA DY30/IV2/1/709, Stenographische Niederschrift der 10. Tagung des Zentralkomitees der SED, 10 Nov. 1989, cited in C. Maier, *Dissolution*, p. 163.
38 See esp. Walter Süß, 'Selbstblockierung der Macht. Wachstum und Lähmung der Staatssicherheit in den siebziger und achtziger Jahren', in K. Jarausch and M. Sabrow (eds), *Weg in den Untergang*, pp. 239–57; and K. W. Fricke, *MfS intern. Macht, Strukturen, Auflösung der DDR-Staatsicherheit* (Cologne, 1991), both of which emphatically reject the notion that the *Stasi* leadership consciously chose not to commit a 'Chekist' crackdown in order to save itself. As they convincingly contend, this argument grossly overestimates the generals' clairvoyance.
39 C. Maier, *Dissolution*, p. 120.

streets and claiming public space – thus breaking the communist hegemony – is woefully incomplete.

The popular movement was, in other words, the principal driving force behind the watershed events of October and November 1989 that were made possible in the first place by the changes in the international framework and the reformist currents within Eastern Europe. But this assertion leads directly to another set of issues about the internal mobilization against the regime. If the popular movement was the engine of transformation, what fuelled the engine? Who was mobilizing whom, and to what end? Did the nature of the mass protests make this a 'revolution' in any meaningful sense of the word? Simply put, who, if anyone, were the 'revolutionaries' of 1989?

Any attempt to answer these questions must distinguish at the outset between two different currents of political opposition during summer and autumn 1989: the emigration movement facing westwards and advocating rapid (re-)unification with West Germany, and the organized dissident groups oriented towards 'dialogue' with the party over democratic reforms within the GDR. There was already a long history of tension between the two, dating back to disagreements in the 1970s and 1980s over whether one should seek to leave for the Federal Republic (a rare privilege which the regime sometimes offered its critics) or stay in East Germany in order to pressure the authorities from within.[40] This rift remained in place throughout 1989 and has continued to colour interpretations of events long afterwards. Was it 'the tiny minority of human and civil rights campaigners' who 'contributed most to Germany's peaceful October revolution'?[41] Or is it more appropriate to conclude that 'the transformation in the GDR was not a product of the opposition'?[42] Were the emigrants and the masses the 'real revolutionaries'[43] of 1989? Or does no one deserve the label of 'revolutionary'? Was it simply a case of two separate movements that together 'failed to add up to a "revolution" in any rigorous sense'?[44]

The rise of the mass protests is commonly perceived as a more or less linear process of mobilization beginning with the existing dissident groups.

---

40 The issue came to a head in 1984 as the authorities handed out some 21,000 visas to its growing reservoir of emigration applicants in an attempt to rid itself of potential troublemakers – a move which in some ways weakened the alternative groups. Although some groups welcomed the cooperation of emigration applicants, in many cases the latter were shunned for taking what was viewed as the 'easy way out'. See Bernd Eisenfeld, 'Die Ausreisebewegung – eine Erscheinungsform widerständigen Verhaltens', in R. Eckart *et al.* (eds), *Zwischen Selbstbehauptung und Anpassung*, pp. 192–223.

41 T. G. Ash, 'Germany Unbound', *New York Review of Books*, 22 Nov., 1990, p. 11.

42 T. Klein, 'Die doppelte Isolation. Zum Ausgang der oppositionellen Gruppen in der "Wende"', in K. Jarausch and M. Sabrow (eds), *Weg in den Untergang*, pp. 259–77, here p. 274.

43 Mark Thompson, 'Die "Wende" in der DDR als demokratische Revolution', *APuZG* B45/99, pp. 15–23, here pp. 20f.

44 John Torpey, 'Two Movements, Not a Revolution: Exodus and Opposition in the East German Transformation, 1989–1990', *German Politics and Society*, 26 (1992), pp. 21–42, here p. 25. Torpey expands this argument in J. Torpey (ed.), *Intellectuals, Socialism and Dissent: The East German Opposition and its Legacy* (Minneapolis, 1995).

Out of the initial handful of courageous souls opposing the system there grew a broader civil rights movement which supposedly inspired the mass demonstrations that eventually led to the liberation of the East German people from the communist dictatorship. Helmut Fehr, for instance, sees the demonstrations as the outgrowth of earlier actions by the alternative peace, environmental and civil rights initiatives. In this view, the well-orchestrated protests over the rigging of electoral results in May 1989 and the autonomous street music festival of 10 June represent nothing less than 'forerunners of the spontaneous mass demonstrations of autumn 1989'.[45] Ehrhart Neubert, too, portrays the dissident groups as both initiators and shepherds of the wider transformation. Popular discontent needed to be channelled in order to be effective, and moreover needed mouthpieces to be expressed. The downfall of the system required 'political subjects who gave a form to this process. And these could be none other than those who had long ago refused to be bound to the system, the opponents of SED rule.'[46]

From this perspective, a crucial watershed was reached in mid-September at one of the marches following the well-known Monday night prayer meetings at the Nikolaikirche in Leipzig. For the first time, the chant of 'We want out' was emphatically answered with chants of 'We're staying here', signalling a demand not only for the right to emigrate (thousands were leaving illegally at the time) but for wider civil liberties at home as well. This, according to many accounts, was when the public protests became a significant political factor, when the demonstrations – though still composed predominantly of a small dissident minority – openly challenged the regime by seeking to change the GDR from within instead of taking the exit alternative. When the first major demonstrations took place in Leipzig on 25 September, 'We're staying here' was a central rallying cry, and would remain so over the following weeks as the numbers of participants swelled into the tens of thousands and inspired parallel demonstrations in other cities. The small dissident groups not only provided the spark for the mass demonstrations, but also gave a form to dissent through organizations such as New Forum, Democracy Now (*Demokratie Jetzt*) and Democratic Awakening (*Demokratischer Aufbruch*). In Neubert's view, it was 'the historic service of the GDR-opposition to have made the societal self-emancipation politically possible through the struggle against a totalitarian regime'.[47]

As important as the Nikolaikirche services were as a crystallization point for protest, the problem with this linear account is that it obscures how the emigration crisis made much of their impact possible in the first place. It is worth noting that the earliest crowd of demonstrators emanating from the

45 Helmut Fehr, *Unabhängige Öffentlichkeit und soziale Bewegungen. Fallstudien über Bürgerbewegungen in Polen und der DDR* (Opladen, 1996), p. 242.

46 E. Neubert, *Geschichte der Opposition in der DDR*, p. 25. Mary Fulbrook likewise emphasizes the importance of the dissident groups in giving organizational form to otherwise inchoate currents of discontent, *Anatomy of a Dictatorship*, Chapters 8 and 9.

47 E. Neubert, *Geschichte der Opposition in der DDR*, p. 149.

Nikolaikirche was actually composed of would-be emigrants, not reformist dissidents.[48] 'We're staying here!' was actually a response to their incessant demands for travel visas, a reflection of the growing need among many to justify their decision to stay in the GDR through demands for reform. As late as August, the oppositional groups in the GDR were still weak and fragmented – 'as pallid as the party', in the words of one dissident.[49] But over the summer of 1989 the old relationship between emigration and dissent, between 'exit' and 'voice', reversed.[50] Whereas the 'exit' of critical voices to the West (whether voluntarily or by force, as in the case of Wolf Biermann) had long served to undermine the growth of outspoken opposition in the GDR, it now encouraged dissent towards the regime, which was visibly weakened by the emigration crisis. Exit was, in other words, 'the very *condition* of "voice"' in 1989.[51] Even in the case of the famous Leipzig marches, the emigration movement both preceded and provoked the demands for reform within the GDR.

The flood of emigrants to the West not only emboldened the dissident groups to extend their activities, it also inspired the crowd's demands for the unhindered right to travel abroad. Understandably, this was considered the clearest symbol of governmental goodwill. Although the vast majority of East Germans stayed in the GDR over summer and autumn 1989, the emigrant stream represented the tip of an iceberg of discontent. Halfway liberalization would not suffice, which placed enormous pressure on the authorities. The unhindered right to travel was what most compelled the crowds, not the dissidents' arguments about reforming socialism. As Charles Maier has suggested, there were 'two languages of revolution' in 1989: the 'discourse of flawed functionalism' shared by the regime and the reformist intellectuals ('the vocabulary of social needs, interests, roles, groups'), and a simpler 'rhetoric of primeval popular assembly', a visceral language of freedom and community that proved the more potent in the end.[52]

Did the combination of these two discourses really add up to a 'revolution'? Both participants and observers certainly thought so until the borders were opened. But as I have already remarked, it was precisely after 9 November that the vocabulary changed. Disappointed civil rights activists in particular became reluctant to use the term after seeing how the revolution had been supposedly 'hijacked' by the crowds, 'aborted', or 'deflected' from their own 'Third-wayist' goals of reforming socialism. As understandable

48 Michael Hofmann and Dieter Rink, 'Der Leipziger Aufbruch: Zur Genesis einer Heldenstadt', in Jürgen Grabner, Christiane Heinze and Detlef Pollack (eds), *Leipzig im Oktober: Kirchen und alternative Gruppen im Umbruch der DDR* (Berlin, 1990), pp. 114–22.
49 Reinhard Schult, 'Kirche von unten', cited in C. Maier, *Dissolution*, p. 113.
50 Cf. A. Hirschman, 'Exit, Voice, and the Fate of the German Democratic Republic'.
51 J. Torpey, 'Two Movements, Not a Revolution', p. 23. Cf. also C. Joppke, *East German Dissidents and the Revolution of 1989*, Chapter 5; J. Grix, *The Role of the Masses in the Collapse of the GDR* (Basingstoke, 2000).
52 C. Maier, *Dissolution*, pp. 131–5, here p. 134.

as this disappointment is, the notion of an 'aborted' or 'deflected' revolution rests on the untenable assumption that the dissidents and intellectuals in the civic movement determined the trajectory of protest beforehand, that they were the 'revolutionaries of the first hour' who were instrumental in wringing the change. On the basis of this assumption, the 'transformation within the transformation' ('*Wende in der Wende*') – the calls for German unification – represented a distorted outcome. This could no longer be a 'revolution' because there was no more revolutionary autonomy in the GDR. After 9 November the role of the East German crowds became a passive one as the process of Western takeover gathered pace. 'Revolution' had given way to 'annexation'. Instead of pushing for further change and acquiring power at home, the domestic opposition failed to translate its moral authority into a concrete political programme in the face of the West German political machine.

The masses, however, apparently did possess a programme, albeit a different one from that of the civic movement. It soon became clear that the crowds on the streets did not share the aim of reforming socialism within the GDR. Chants of 'We are one people' could already be heard at the demonstrations by late November. Like the emigrants taking advantage of the opportunity to leave, most ordinary East Germans were oriented more towards the West and what it represented than towards dialogue with the SED. And what the West represented was more than just bananas and BMWs. The arrogant suggestion that the crowds were merely 'bought off' by hedonistic dreams of consumerism does not do justice to the range of motivations that brought the crowds onto the streets. Problematic though they are, surveys conducted among demonstrators and emigrants suggest that political discontent and the desire for basic freedoms were at least as important as hopes for material abundance.[53] Moreover, even among those who were most likely to have positive associations with the GDR (the young and the educated), this relatively favourable disposition did not necessarily translate into a desire to maintain the GDR's separate existence.[54] Well before the opening of the Wall, the vast majority of emigrants – around 84 per cent according to one study – wanted East Germany to join the Federal Republic.[55] National and democratic demands stood in close alliance in

---

53  Richard Hilmer and Anne Köhler, 'Der DDR läuft die Zukunft davon: Die Übersiedler-/Flüchtlingswelle im Sommer 1989', *DA* 22 (1989), pp. 1389–93. For similar findings, see also Karl-Dieter Opp, Peter Voß and Christiane Gern, *Die volkseigene Revolution* (Stuttgart, 1993). See also Lothar Fritze, *Die Gegenwart des Vergangenen. Über das Weiterleben der DDR nach ihrem Ende* (Cologne, 1997), pp. 96–7, where the decision to protest is described as the result of a '"balance decision", or in other words according to a consideration of advantages and disadvantages that was, as a rule, not carried out on a conscious level'.

54  Kurt Mühler and Steffan Wilsdorf, 'Meinungstrends in der Leipziger Montagsdemonstration: Nachbetrachtungen zu einer basisdemokratischen Institution', in J. Grabner *et al.* (eds), *Leipzig im Oktober*, pp. 159–75.

55  D. Voigt *et al.*, 'Die innerdeutsche Wanderung und der Vereinigungsprozeß. Soziodemographische Struktur und Einstellungen von Flüchtlingen und Übersiedlern aus der DDR vor und nach der Grenzöffnung', *DA* 23:5 (1990), pp. 732–7. Again, there are similar findings by K. Opp *et al.*, *Die volkseigene Revolution*, p. 104.

autumn 1989.[56] The dissident groups never really had the support of the masses for anything more than the common goal of getting rid of the regime.

Although the civic movements, above all New Forum, were critically important as a means of uniting and voicing diverse currents of protest during October and November, they were soon overtaken by events.[57] Many of the leading figures felt ambivalent about developments after the opening of the Wall. Bärbel Bohley, one of its co-founders, considered the opening of the Wall a misfortune since it would make reform more difficult.[58] On 9 November she appealed to the populace on GDR television to 'stay with us ... Those who go away lessen our hope. We beg you, do stay in your homeland.' Fearing that East Germany might succumb to managerialist capitalism and crass materialism, New Forum leaders admonished the crowds on 12 November not to 'be silenced by ... travel and consuming'.[59] Over the following weeks their rhetoric became increasingly utopian and divorced from political realities. The 28 November appeal drafted by Christa Wolf, Stefan Heym and other intellectuals urged people not to throw away the accomplishments of socialism and to save the separate existence of the GDR. Against the backdrop of the mass demonstrations and emigration crisis these entreaties came across as little more than disparaging idealistic postures.[60]

Was there anything worth saving when the larger German republic next door promised not only material wealth but also the basic rights and freedoms that the crowds were demanding? The only way to stem the continuing exodus was to hold free elections in the GDR. As long as this did not happen, there was little sense in intellectuals appealing to people to stay. The civic leaders' disappointment that the opening of the Wall had

---

56 A point stressed by Jürgen Kocka, 'Revolution und Nation 1989. Zur historischen Einordnung der gegenwärtigen Ereignisse', in J. Kocka, *Vereinigungskrise. Zur Geschichte der Gegenwart* (Göttingen, 1995), p. 20.

57 On the civic movements, see Helmut Müller-Enbergs, Marianne Schulz and Jan Wielgohs (eds), *Von der Illegalität ins Parlament: Werdegang und Konzept der neuen Bürgerbewegungen* (Berlin, 1991); also, very generally, 'Möglichkeiten und Formen abweichenden und widerständigen Verhaltens und oppositionellen Handelns', in *Materialien der Enquete-Kommission*, vol. VII: 1, VII: 2.

58 Some intellectuals in the West had similar feelings. Günter Grass, for instance, plainly stated that 'the order in which the changes took place was wrong. The internal process of democratization should have been pushed further before the opening of the borders was announced.' G. Grass, *Two States – One Nation?* (New York, 1990), p. 16.

59 Reprinted in *taz: DDR Journal zur Novemberrevolution. August bis Dezember 1989*, 2nd edn (Berlin, 1990), p. 126, cited in Norman Naimark, '"Ich will hier raus": Emigration and the Collapse of the German Democratic Republic', in Ivo Banac (ed.), *Eastern Europe in Revolution* (Ithaca, 1992), pp. 72–95.

60 This disapproval of the consumerist wishes of the populace has come under fierce criticism. In a particularly damning critique, Wolf Lepenies has argued that 'the resentment of those well-known writers in the GDR who pilloried the consumer desires of the East German masses was downright hypocritical. Instead of storming the department stores in West Berlin and in the border regions, the populace was supposed to wait in a state of patient asceticism and let themselves be lectured on the essential features of true socialism by those intellectuals who, whether they wanted to or not, had long beforehand become beneficiaries of false socialism.' W. Lepenies, *Folgen einer unerhörten Begebenheit. Die Deutschen nach der Vereinigung* (Berlin, 1992), pp. 35–6.

happened 'too early' and that it would lead to a 'sell-out' of socialism's accomplishments starkly revealed the fact that, as Detlef Pollack has put it, 'the opposition leadership did not represent the people at all, that it possessed no contact with the masses and that it represented a fringe group of red–green intellectuals who, plainly put, felt superior to the people'.[61]

Contrary to the common view that the dissidents and intellectuals were the 'revolutionaries of the first hour', at no point did they possess the decisive initiative. Rather, they are better understood as 'reluctant revolutionaries',[62] 'outsiders who, on the basis of processes that they neither initiated nor desired, rose to be representatives of society'.[63] Their prominence was, in other words, more an effect than a cause of events during autumn 1989. Clinging to the hope of a separate social–democratic GDR, they continually lagged behind the changes that were taking place under the pressure of popular protest. It is telling that, unlike in Poland or Hungary, the Round Table meetings between the various civic movements and the regime convened first *after* the regime had already effectively collapsed (in early December). By the end of January 1990 there had emerged the 'paradoxical situation that the Round Table and the government – with different motivations – were both representatives of an independent "GDR identity" whereas the majority of the populace had long wanted the quickest possible end to the GDR'.[64]

This assessment may sound unduly harsh towards courageous people who had worked towards undermining SED domination long before the auspicious circumstances of autumn 1989 made this a realistic possibility. The network of dissident grouplets and the organized civic movements clearly made a major contribution to events, albeit less than is often supposed. Arguably their most notable contribution, which should by no means be underestimated, was in helping to ensure the peaceful character of protest and the avoidance of violence. This was crucial after the violent clashes around the Dresden train station on the night of 3–4 October, as sealed trains carrying emigrants from the West German embassy in Prague passed through on their way to the Federal Republic. Their influence was also critical during the two watershed marches in Leipzig on 2 and 9 October, as protesters assiduously avoided any provocation of the edgy security forces. This was undoubtedly a great historic service without which the outcome of events may well have looked quite different.

---

61  D. Pollack, 'Außenseiter oder Repräsentanten. Zur Rolle der politisch alternativen Gruppen in der DDR', in D. Pollack (ed.), *Die Legitimität der Freiheit. Politisch alternative Gruppen in der DDR unter dem Dach der Kirche* (Frankfurt a. M., 1990), p. 229. H. Knabe, 'Sprachrohr oder Außenseiter? Zur gesellschaftlichen Relevanz der unabhängigen Gruppen in der DDR – Aus Analysen des Staatssicherheitsdienstes', *APuZG* B20/96, pp. 23–36.

62  Mark Thompson, 'Reluctant Revolutionaries: Anti-Fascism and the East German Opposition', *German Politics* 2 (1999), pp. 40–65.

63  D. Pollack, 'Außenseiter oder Repräsentanten', p. 227. Cf. also Karl-Rudolf Korte, *Die Chance genutzt? Die Politik zur Einheit Deutschlands* (Frankfurt a. M., 1994), which portrays the dissidents as helping to speed along a process over which they had little control.

64  Gert-Joachim Glaeßner, *Der schwierige Weg zur Demokratie: Vom Ende der DDR zur deutschen Einheit* (Opladen, 1991), p. 94.

Yet the 'real revolutionaries' of 1989 were the emigrants and the masses who rejected the parameters of dialogue offered by the regime and demanded the basic rights and freedoms enjoyed by Germans in the Federal Republic. The emigration crisis was what started the revolution; the demands of the crowd for basic political freedoms were what sustained it.[65] Against this background, the turn towards German unification can hardly be seen as a distorted outcome of the events of October and November, but rather as a fitting conclusion. The notion of a 'deflected' or 'aborted' revolution is, as one observer has put it, largely 'a legend of the so-called *"Kulturschaffenden"'* (the rather awkward GDR label for creative intellectuals).[66] The shift of rallying cries from 'We are the people' to 'We are one people' did not constitute a 'transformation in the transformation', but rather reflected a fulfilment of early aims.[67]

In view of this, there seems to me no particularly convincing reason to deny these events the label 'revolution', depending of course on precisely what one means by this term. Quite obviously, the upheaval in East Germany bore little resemblance to Jacobin, Bolshevik or Maoist conceptions of revolution with their connotations of terror, of a planned putsch carried out by an organized and self-consciously 'revolutionary' group, and of a long civil war. There was remarkably little violence or bloodshed, though as Hartmut Zwahr has pointed out, the abuses by police meant that the revolution was 'peaceful, but at no point without violence'.[68] There was no storming of the Bastille, though angry crowds did storm *Stasi* headquarters in the Normannenstraße on 15 January. Events were driven less by utopian ideas than by the tried and tested tenets of basic human rights, democracy and the rule of law. This is not to say that the revolution was merely restorative, that it neither generated nor was inspired by any new ideas. Jürgen Habermas' notion of a 'catch-up revolution' ('*nachholende Revolution*'[69]) blithely overlooks the fact that the dissident groups advocated a kind of postmodern politics not widely practised in the West at the time, one envisioning a constitutional state embodying notions of direct democracy, gender equality and environmental protection. Yet it seems quite clear that events were driven less by the poetry of new social experiments, which left the masses of East Germans rather unimpressed, than by the prose of higher living standards and the acquisition of basic freedoms that had long been denied.[70]

Revolution does not, however, necessarily have to entail bloodshed, overthrowing a robust political order, or utopian ideas. Moribund regimes often

65 Cf. Norman Naimark, '"Ich will hier raus"', p. 93.
66 Wolfgang Zapf, 'Der Untergang der DDR und die soziologische Theorie der Modernisierung', in Bernd Giesen and Claus Leggewie (eds), *Experiment Vereinigung: Ein sozialer Grossversuch* (Berlin, 1991), p. 42.
67 Cf. J. Torpey, 'Two Movements, Not a Revolution', p. 31.
68 H. Zwahr, *Ende einer Selbstzerstörung*, p. 166.
69 J. Habermas, *Die nachholende Revolution* (Frankfurt a. M., 1990).
70 J. Kocka, 'Revolution und Nation 1989', p. 10.

shy away from the use of force, and processes of institutional disintegration accompany all revolutionary transformations. As Charles Maier has recently argued, popular mobilization is the principal criterion, the seizing of the public sphere.[71] Over autumn 1989, power was both wrested and handed over to the streets as East Germans acted collectively to make demands of the regime, and eventually to vote it out of existence altogether. The fact that the domestic opposition movements were weak and poorly organized poses no insurmountable obstacle to the idea that this was a 'revolution'. Indeed, in the case of the GDR the very absence of clearly organized challenging groups – a 'revolution without revolutionaries', in the words of east German essayist Friedrich Dieckmann[72]– actually contributed to the helplessness of the authorities and the swiftness of events. The *Stasi* was well prepared to deal with any revolutionary strategists seeking to occupy the centres of state power, as the subsequent revelations about the massive infiltration of the dissident groups attested. It was less prepared to deal with a diffuse mass movement that presented no head to be severed. Moreover, however poorly organized the domestic opposition network remained, in many ways the West German establishment – encouraged by the position of the Bush administration – can be regarded as a kind of counter-elite by proxy. Though unprepared at first, they quickly proved capable of exploiting the victory of the crowds, voicing many of its desires (for instance Kohl's proclamation on 10 November that 'We are indeed one people') and formulating concrete political proposals such as the ten-point plan of 28 November (the same day, it might be pointed out, as the civic leaders' appeal 'For our country') that first implicitly put the issue of unification on the table. Granted, the relative autonomy of the crowds seemed to end quite rapidly with the massive financial and organizational input from West Germany during the run-up to the March 1990 elections. But it was the crowds that made this possible in the first place. Despite their peaceful character, the people's movements were the central engine of transformation.

Within a relatively short period of time East Germany witnessed not only an exchange of its political leadership, but a fundamental transformation of its entire societal system – its political structures, economic institutions, constitution, and ideology.[73] The notion of a '*Wende*', though neatly capturing the gradual and non-violent nature of the transformation, hardly does justice to the revolutionary scope or depth of these changes. This was far more than a mere alteration of course. The ship itself had sunk, and the captains had gone down with it. The stage for this transformation was not the battle-field or the factories or the barricades, but the public squares and streets. It was in these spaces that East German subjects demanded the rights of citizens. For this reason it seems entirely appropriate to call these events a

---

71  C. Maier, *Dissolution*, p. 120.
72  F. Dieckmann, 'Die Stunde der West-Onkel', *Die Zeit*, 8 March 1990.
73  Jürgen Kocka stresses the scope of change in 'Revolution und Nation 1989', p. 11.

'citizens' revolution' or 'democratic revolution', inspired less by Lenin or Mao, more by Gandhi or Martin Luther King.[74]

Before concluding, it is worthwhile returning to the question posed at the beginning of this chapter: was the transformation of 1989 primarily the result of a collapse from outside, an implosion from above, or a revolution from below? Clearly the end of the GDR has to be understood as a combination of these factors, as an interaction between popular challenges from below and responses from above within the wider context of changing international circumstances. Yet the evaluation of events in the GDR that I have just offered suggests that – insofar as one can separate the different factors – the forces from outside and from below were most critical. The 'implosion' of the regime and the collapse of the will to rule came largely as an unintended reaction to a situation that the regime could no longer control. The 'collapse from outside' was the crucial precondition; the 'revolt from below' was the motor for change.[75]

Perhaps a further conclusion to draw from the evidence is that we cannot and should not clinically separate these various pressures from one another. Insofar as the GDR was a 'penetrated system' – that is, shot through with Soviet economic and security interests – the collapse from outside in many ways amounted to an implosion from within. We must not view the actions of the East German leadership and their effective abdication of power solely within the analytical confines of the GDR. The new signals emanating from Moscow and the changes taking place elsewhere in Eastern Europe contributed to a loss of faith and shifting loyalties within the GDR, and crucially undermined the regime's willingness and ability to preserve itself in the moment of truth. At the same time, the 'collapse from outside' also vitally emboldened the revolt from below. Liberalization in the Soviet Union and the civic movements elsewhere in Eastern Europe encouraged dissidents and reform-minded communists to formulate a more far-reaching critique of real existing socialism.[76] Most importantly, the open borders between Hungary and the West triggered the emigration crisis that started the revolutionary process of the autumn, which in turn further exacerbated the growing uncertainties of the East German authorities.

It was this combination of factors that brought down the communist dictatorship, a confluence of different developments that the regime could probably have survived one by one, but which overwhelmed it under their assembled force.[77] But when did the dictatorship really come to an end? The

---

74  Cf. the punchy article by Mark Thompson, 'Die "Wende" in der DDR'.

75  J. Kocka, 'Revolution und Nation 1989', pp. 11–13; M. Fulbrook, *Anatomy of a Dictatorship*, pp. 244–5.

76  Cf. Helmut Fehr, 'Die Macht der Symbole. Osteuropäische Einwirkungen auf den revolutionären Umbruch in der DDR', in K. Jarausch and M. Sabrow (eds), *Weg in den Untergang*, pp. 213–38; also, generally, T. G. Ash, *We the People*.

77  Cf. the wide-ranging discussion in K. Jarausch, 'Implosion oder Selbstbefreiung? Zur Krise des Kommunismus und Auflösung der DDR', in K. Jarausch and M. Sabrow (eds), *Weg in den Untergang*, pp. 15–40; also D. Pollack, 'Der Zusammenbruch der DDR als Verkettung getrennter Handlungslinien', in ibid., pp. 41–81.

GDR itself formally ceased to exist when the two Germanies were united as the enlarged Federal Republic on 3 October 1990. But the communist dictatorship had dissolved long before then. With hindsight, one might suggest that its fate was sealed as early as the refusal to use force to suppress the Leipzig demonstration on 9 October. The opening of the Wall on 9 November is another obvious candidate for the point of no return. The purge of the SED leadership (including Krenz and the entire *Politbüro*), the establishment of the Round Table, and the SED's reconstitution as a 'party of democratic socialism' in the first week of December 1989 also marked a certain watershed. From that point onwards power was effectively shared among different political organizations, though not yet on the basis of open electoral returns. In many respects, the elections of 18 March 1990 – the first meaningful elections in eastern Germany since 1932 – marked the end of the revolution and of the dictatorial system.

The elections also gave what was in effect a mandate for rapid unification with the West, thus strengthening Kohl's negotiating position at the international level. By March 1990 it was abundantly clear that the entire 'German question' had to be reconsidered. The *'Rest-DDR'*, or remnant GDR, was already on the verge of collapse by the spring of 1990. Neither it nor the Federal Republic could afford the social and political costs of a continuing flow of refugees, which could only be halted by some form of federation. The Soviets had already demonstrated a willingness to accept unification in principle, and the US administration was emphatically supportive. The stage was set for the rapid disappearance of the GDR. The currency union on 2 July, the signature of the unification treaty on 31 August, and the conclusion of the two-plus-four negotiations on 12 September essentially served to regulate the relentless process of dissolution and effective annexation by West Germany.[78]

Compared to the heroic and dramatic imagery of communism, its actual expiration in East Germany was remarkably prosaic. As Stefan Wolle has colourfully put it:

> No one had to die with a last, sacred oath on their lips. Socialism was rather drowned in Coca-Cola and stoned with Haribo gummi-bears. The 'final battle', whose coming was so often conjured up by the solemn hymn of the Internationale, was fought over hard currency accounts in foreign banks, shady real estate deals and the retirement pensions of the SED functionaries.[79]

State socialism in Germany was at an end. But as the next two chapters will show, the process of 'coming to terms' with the East German past and re-evaluating its place in the wider sweep of German history was only just beginning.

---

78  Although the notion of 'annexation' is somewhat controversial for describing the process of German unification, it had become widely used by April 1990 at the latest. Cf. Jörg Roesler, 'Der Beitritt der DDR zur Bundesrepublik. Versuch einer historischen Einordnung', *DA* 32:3 (1999), pp. 431–40.
79  S. Wolle, *Die heile Welt der Diktatur*, p. 344.

# |7|

## 'Russian satrapy', 'Red Prussia', 'Socialist state of the German nation'? The GDR in German history

The search for stable collective identities and for political structures that would give them suitable form has been a dominant theme in the modern history of German-speaking Central Europe. In the eighteenth century, long before the formation of a unified 'nation-state', German-speaking literati constructed the idea of a 'cultural nation' that transcended the political patchwork of Central Europe. The question of whether to include the German-speaking areas of the Habsburg empire into a unified nation-state was one of the most contentious issues among liberal circles in the mid-nineteenth century, before Bismarck's *kleindeutsch* solution of 1871. After defeat in the First World War, the shrinking of the German state into its supposedly 'natural' borders nourished the kinds of nationalist resentments and stridently ethnic conceptions of the nation that benefited the rise of the Nazis to power. The chauvinistic excesses and boundless brutality of the Third Reich – including systematic genocide and the displacement of millions of people – led many, both within Germany and abroad, to conclude that the Germans had, once and for all, forfeited any right to live in a contiguous nation-state. After 1945, the 'divided nation' was continually preoccupied with debates about its own history and identity. In the shadow of Auschwitz and in the midst of political division, the nature and future of German national identity were constant themes in public discourse. The dissolution of communism and the unification of the two states in 1990 have opened a new chapter in this ongoing narrative, throwing a whole bundle of previous certainties into question and posing new problems of self-definition.

History has always played a key role in debates about German national identity, and this most recent episode since 1990 has been no exception. One of the most notable developments since unification has been a renewed interest in Germany's 'national' history and in the alleged 'normality' of the nation-state after decades of political division and supposedly 'post-nationalist' historiography.[1] Although this trend towards 're-nationalization' of the German past has been exceedingly broad and multi-faceted, the explosion of research on East Germany since 1990 has meant that the re-evaluation of the GDR and of its place within the broader sweep of German history has occupied a central place in this discussion. What was the GDR's relationship to its 'national' heritage? Were the East German regime and the character of East German society in some ways a reflection of older 'German' traditions, or were they primarily a derivation of the Soviet system? How important were, for example, the legacies of the German workers' movement or older patterns of political culture in moulding the character of the regime and its policies? How powerfully was the GDR shaped by its unique circumstance as part of a 'divided nation' after the war?

These overarching questions about the GDR's place within the wider context of German and European history serve not so much as points of open debate as different lenses through which to view the GDR and its history. Not unlike the question of whether the revolution of 1989 was a collapse from outside, an implosion from above, or a revolt from below, they do not represent exclusive alternatives. The character of GDR politics and society derived from a variety of different influences and traditions, and the extent to which any individual study adopts one or another of these lenses is largely dependent on the particular subject under analysis, not necessarily on any conscious interpretive choice. Yet however implicit these issues are in the vast literature on the GDR, they are nonetheless important in shaping our understanding of East German history. The GDR's relationship to its own past, to the idea of a German nation and to its Soviet patron have, after all, long been topics of scholarly interest.

This chapter cannot and will not address these questions in all their complexity. It will, for instance, only briefly recall the SED's efforts to construct a 'socialist nation' strictly 'demarcated' from the FRG, which were discussed in Chapter 1. The 'Sovietization' of various elite and popular cultural practices in East Germany is also only cursorily mentioned (not for lack of interest, but because of the relative scarcity of literature on the topic). Rather, it will concentrate on a number of relevant issues, some overlapping with each other and others quite distinct, that have generated considerable debate since 1989. It will focus first on the hotly contested issue of whether the foundation of the GDR was primarily a matter of Soviet design or whether the German communists themselves played a decisive part. It will then widen the focus to consider the role of certain social and political continuities within Germany in moulding the character of East German society, especially the heritage of the German communist movement and the legacies associated

---

1 For discussions of the 're-nationalization' of the German past since 1990 see Stefan Berger, *The Search for Normality: National Identity and Historical Consciousness in Germany since 1800* (Oxford, 1997); Konrad Jarausch, 'Normalisierung oder Re-Nationalisierung? Zur Umdeutung der deutschen Vergangenheit', *GG* 21 (1995), pp. 571–84.

with Germany's supposedly illiberal and authoritarian traditions. Finally, it will grapple with the controversial problem of '*Diktaturenvergleich*' (the comparison of the two German dictatorships) and the degree to which the GDR represented a break with the Nazi past or rather a continuation of many of its essential characteristics. The first part of the chapter will survey the outlines of these debates, while the second part will offer an evaluation of their implications for how we view the GDR within its wider historical context.

# Interpretations
## The GDR's foundation

Where did the GDR come from? Who founded it, and what were the motivations for doing so? Was it the result of a deliberate plan to create a socialist state in a truncated territory, or was it rather a product of *ad hoc* solutions to problems that arose, a response to unforeseen developments? Although questions concerning the foundation of the GDR represent only one aspect of the broader 'Sovietization' debate (which we will discuss in more detail below), they undoubtedly number among the most controversial and widely discussed problems in the GDR's entire history. This is in part a reflection of their political explosiveness. Both the GDR authorities and the Soviets assiduously avoided careful scrutiny of these issues, shrouding them instead behind a veil of convenient half-truths and long-cherished myths. But it also reflects the fact that they number among the most difficult to answer with any degree of certainty. Although the relevant East German sources have been available to scholars since unification, access to internal Soviet documents has remained a problem. There have been, of course, vast improvements in this regard since the end of the Soviet Union, but not all of the relevant files have been declassified for scholarly research. Many important holdings are still closed. Yet regardless of whether they remain beyond scholarly reach, it is by no means certain that even the most thorough reading of all relevant Soviet documents, no matter how sensitive, will offer definitive answers to these questions.[2]

This does not mean, however, that there is a shortage of answers in circulation. Predictably, the SED was always well armed with tendentious and self-serving arguments about the foundation of the GDR. In the official East

---

2 Cf. Bernd Bonwetsch, Gennadij Bordjugow and Norman Naimark (eds), *Sowjetische Politik in der SBZ 1945–1949. Dokumente zur Tätigkeit der Propagandaverwaltung (Informationsverwaltung) der SMAD unter Tjul'panov* (Bonn, 1998); Bernd Bonwetsch and Gennadij Bordjugov, 'Stalin und die SBZ. Ein Besuch der SED-Führung in Moskau vom 30. Januar–7. Februar 1947', *VfZ*, Nr. 2 (1994), pp. 279ff; Jochen Laufer, 'Auf dem Wege zur staatlichen Verselbständigung der SBZ. Neue Quellen zur Münchener Konferenz der Ministerpräsidenten 1947', in J. Kocka (ed.), *Historische DDR-Forschung*, pp. 27ff.

German view, all four wartime allies are blamed for the division of Germany insofar as they all set the switches for conflict at their conferences in Teheran, Yalta and Potsdam. The USA and UK, however, are held largely responsible for the breakdown of the anti-Hitler coalition because of their attempts – symbolized by the 'Truman Doctrine' and Marshall Plan – to restrict as far as possible the power and influence of the Soviet Union. In contrast to the slavish 'west orientation' of Konrad Adenauer, the GDR's leaders were portrayed as the champions and defenders of German unity (with no mention of the terms they might have accepted regarding the nature of an all-German government). At each of the crucial turning points on the road to division – the conflicts over reparations transfers between the occupation zones, the creation of Bizonia, the introduction of separate currencies, the Berlin Blockade, and finally the foundation of separate states – the actions of the German communists, like the Soviets, were portrayed as defensive responses to unilateral moves by the Western powers.[3] Although the Soviets were seen as crucial to the establishment of the GDR, any notions of 'imperialism' or outright 'dependence' were emphatically rejected. The official view was of a kind of junior partnership in the spirit of 'socialist internationalism'. The creators of the GDR were German communists.[4]

For many years the widespread view in the West was, equally predictably, quite the opposite. East Germany was simply another victim of Soviet imperialism that had the Stalinist system forced on to it by its conquerors.[5] By the summer of 1947 – around the time when the Marshall Plan was announced – the 'two camp' view had come to dominate Soviet thinking. Soon thereafter, the SED was remoulded into a 'party of a new type' (that is, a Stalinist party that stamped out any democratic inklings) and the Soviet military government began to establish an incipient state apparatus in the SBZ, including the rudiments of separate East German military forces. The continuing proclamations about the desire for German unity and the famous 'Stalin notes' of 1952 that putatively offered a unified, non-communist German state in exchange for its military neutrality were deemed little more than propaganda stunts geared towards shifting the blame for German division on to the West. Indeed, Stalin arguably had intentions of introducing the Soviet system in Germany even before the end of the Second World War. As the Soviet dictator had reputedly confided to the Yugoslav communist

3  See, generally, Heinz Heitzer, *DDR – geschichtlicher Überblick*, 4th edn (Berlin, 1987); Autorenkollektiv unter Leitung von Helmut Griebenow, *Entstehung und Entwicklung der DDR* (Leipzig, 1979); Stefan Doernberg, *Kurze Geschichte der DDR* (Berlin, 1965). The views of some historians associated with the PDS have undergone precious little reform since 1989. Cf. Harald Neubert, 'Die Vorgeschichte der deutschen Zweistaatlichkeit im internationalen Bedingungsgefüge (Thesen)', in *Ansichten zur Geschichte der DDR*, vol. 5, pp. 41–8.

4  Cf. generally Rolk Stöckigt, *Geschichte der SED. Abriß* (Berlin, 1978). For a critical post-1989 analysis, see Jörg Roesler, 'Der Handlungsspielraum der DDR-Führung gegenüber der UdSSR', *ZfG* vol. 41 (1993), pp. 293–304.

5  Cf. K.C. Thalheim, 'Die sowjetische Besatzungszone Deutschlands', in Ernst Birke and Rudolf Neumann (eds) *Die Sowjetisierung Ost-Mitteleuropas* (Berlin, 1959).

Milovan Djilas: 'This war is not as in the past; whoever occupies a territory also imposes on it his own social system. Everyone imposes his own system as far as his army has power to do so. It cannot be otherwise.'[6]

These arguments were, however, never universally accepted among Western scholars. As early as 1953, Boris Meissner considered Stalin's offer of German unity to be a genuine reflection of Soviet concerns about the prospect of rearmament in West Germany.[7] Over a decade later, Hans-Peter Schwarz concluded that Soviet aims were multiple and contradictory, and that much of the confusion arose from the fact that Stalin failed to resolve the tensions between different policy directions.[8] In the 1980s, Rolf Steininger and Dietrich Staritz voiced similar doubts about Soviet intentions to erect a separate, communist German state, which in their view contradicted key Soviet interests, in particular access to coal and steel reparations from the West German Ruhr area.[9]

The release of East German documents after 1990 promised to shed some much-needed new light on these issues. But as scholars used and interpreted these sources – most notably the handwritten notes of president Wilhelm Pieck[10] – in different ways, the end result was not always very illuminating. Over the period from 1990 to 1991 there was a discernible swing back to the older 'Sovietization' thesis, propelled not least by former East German scholars shocked at the extent of Soviet influence revealed by the internal documents they were never allowed to view before. After his first perusal of these documents, Rolf Stöckigt, for instance, remarked on the 'downright consternating impression' that Stalin's role was 'far greater than previously thought and (secretly) feared'.[11] Many West German historians likewise interpreted the newly available East German sources as confirmation of the conventional view that the Soviet Union was moving towards the creation of a separate communist state by the latter 1940s and that the 'Stalin notes' of 1952 were a ruse.[12] Manfred Wilke went so far as to posit a Soviet

6 M. Djilas, *Conversations with Stalin* (Harmondsworth, 1969), p. 90.
7 B. Meissner, *Rußland, die Westmächte und Deutschland. Die Sowjetische Deutschlandpolitik 1943–1953* (Hamburg, 1953).
8 H.-P. Schwarz, *Vom Reich zur Bundesrepublik. Deutschland im Widerstreit der außenpolitischen Konzeptionen in den Jahren der Besatzungsherrschaft 1945–1949* (Berlin/Neuwied, 1966), pp. 201–69.
9 R. Steininger, 'Eine Chance zur Wiedervereinigung? Darstellung und Dokumentation auf der Grundlage unveröffentlichter britischer und amerikanischer Akten', *AfS*, Beiheft 12 (Bonn, 1985); D. Staritz, *Geschichte der DDR, 1949–1985* (Frankfurt a. M., 1985), pp. 69–73.
10 These notes have now been edited and published by Rolf Badstübner and Wilfried Loth (eds), *Wilhelm Pieck – Aufzeichnungen zur Deutschlandpolitik 1945–1952* (Berlin, 1993).
11 R. Stöckigt, 'Beratungen bei J. W. Stalin. Neue Dokumente. Dokumente aus den Jahren 1945 bis 1948,' *Utopie kreativ*, vol. 7 (1991), p. 100. Cf. also R. Stöckigt,, 'Ein Dokument von großer historischer Bedeutung vom Mai 1953', *BzG* 32:5 (1990), pp. 648–54; R. Stöckigt, 'Direktiven aus Moskau. Sowjetische Einflußnahme auf die DDR-Politik 1952/53', in J. Cerny *et al.* (eds), *Brüche, Krisen, Wendepunkte*, pp. 81f; R. Stöckigt, 'Der 17. Juni 1953: Neue Erkenntnisse aus bisher geheimgehaltenen Dokumenten. Eine historische Chance wurde vertan', *ND*, 16–17 June 1990.
12 Cf. Stefan Creuzberger, *Die sowjetische Besatzungsmacht und das politische System der SBZ* (Weimar, 1996). On the 'Stalin notes', see G. Wettig, 'Zum Stand der Forschung über Berijas Deutschland-Politik im Frühjahr 1953', *DA* 26:6 (1993), pp. 674–82; G. Wettig, 'Die Deutschland-Note vom 10. März 1952

'*Teilungsbefehl*', or 'order to divide', and concluded that 'the division of Germany was already the goal of Soviet foreign policy in 1945'.[13] Yet not all scholars were swept along with this current. Dietrich Staritz in particular warned against any black-and-white portrayals of the Soviets' multi-faceted policy towards Germany and against the assumption of a one-sided relationship of SED dependence on Moscow.[14]

This simmering debate was brought to the boil with the publication in 1994 of Wilfred Loth's argumentative account of the GDR's foundation, revealingly entitled 'Stalin's unwanted child'.[15] As Loth unambiguously contends, 'Stalin did not want a GDR. He wanted neither a separate state on the territory of the Soviet occupation zone nor a socialist state in Germany at all.' Although provocative, these theses were not, as we have just seen, entirely new. Where Loth entered new interpretive terrain was in arguing that Stalin 'strove instead for a parliamentary democracy for all of Germany that would deprive fascism of its societal basis and open up Soviet access to the resources of the Ruhr'. The logical consequence of this assertion is that the GDR was not the product of Soviet foreign policy, but was rather 'first and foremost the product of Walter Ulbricht's revolutionary zeal, which was able to blossom against the backdrop of Western separatist policies'.[16] Not Stalin, but Ulbricht and other hardline German communists (along with Colonel Sergei Tiul'panov, a key administrator in the Soviet military government) were the main protagonists behind the GDR's foundation as a separate communist state.[17]

The response to Loth's provocative thesis was swift and broadly critical. Many were unconvinced by the idea that Stalin genuinely kept the 'German question' open after 1949. The GDR may formally have remained a bargaining chip, but it was widely considered unrealistic to suggest that it might actually have been used.[18] The importance Loth attributed to Tiul'panov

---

(*Contd*)

auf der Basis diplomatischer Akten des russischen Außenministeriums: Die Hypothese des Wiedervereinigungsangebots', *DA* 26:7 (1993), pp. 786–805. For the latter 1940s, see Jochen Laufer, 'Die DDR – ein gewollter staatlicher Neuanfang?', in J. Kocka and M. Sabrow (eds), *Die DDR als Geschichte*, pp. 177–80; J. Laufer, 'Auf dem Wege zur staatlichen Verselbständigung der SBZ'.

13 M. Wilke, 'Es wird zwei Deutschlands geben', *FAZ*, 30 March 1991; M. Wilke, 'Die Teilung Deutschlands war schon 1945 das Ziel der sowjetischen Außenpolitik', *Der Spiegel*, 15 Apr. 1991.

14 D. Staritz, 'Die SED, Stalin und die Gründung der DDR. Aus den Akten des Zentralen Parteiarchivs', *APuZG* B5/91, pp. 3–16; D. Staritz, 'Die SED, Stalin und der "Aufbau des Sozialismus" in der DDR: Aus den Akten des Zentralen Parteiarchivs', *DA* 24:7 (1991), pp. 686–700. See also the comments by Lutz Niethammer and Hans Mommsen in J. Kocka and M. Sabrow (eds), *Die DDR als Geschichte*, p. 193.

15 W. Loth, *Stalins ungeliebtes Kind. Warum Moskau die DDR nicht wollte* (Berlin, 1994).

16 Ibid., p. 10.

17 A similar view on the SED's allegedly independent actions during the spring of 1952 is offered by Wilfriede Otto, 'Sowjetische Deutschlandnote 1952: Stalin und die DDR. Bisher unveröffentlichte handschriftliche Notizen Wilhelm Piecks', *BzG* vol. 33 (1991), no. 3, pp. 374–89. For a critical response, see Ernst Wurl, 'Entscheidung "gegen das Konzept Stalins"? Zu Wilfriede Ottos Dokumentation von Notizen W. Piecks', *BzG* vol. 33 (1991), no. 6, pp. 767–70. More balanced is Elke Scherstjanoi, 'Die DDR im Frühjahr 1952: Sozialismuslosung und Kollektivierungsbeschluß in sowjetischer Perspektive', *DA* 27:4 (1994), pp. 354–63.

18 Cf. the sharply critical reviews by Peter Zolling, 'Mut ist oft sehr dumm', *Der Spiegel*, 20 June 1994; and Hennig Köhler, 'Stalin ein deutscher Demokrat', *FAZ*, 2 Aug. 1994.

was also viewed with scepticism, and many rejected outright the argument that he and Ulbricht acted off their own bat – that is, without consulting Stalin – in pursuing a harder line in 1948.[19] The notion that Stalin ever strove for a 'democratic' German republic in any Western sense of the word was almost universally dismissed, even by those who agreed with Loth's fundamental postulate that Stalin did not determinedly pursue the division of Germany and that the German communists themselves played a key role.[20] Yet the debate was to wait for five years before another synthesis was attempted. Gerhard Wettig's 1999 study in many ways represents a direct response to Loth that reaffirms more conventional views about the 'persistence (with which) the Soviets strove for the goal of a socialist Germany tied closely to the USSR'.[21]

We are, then, still nowhere near a general consensus on these issues. Quite the contrary: the interpretations we have just surveyed are fundamentally incompatible. Although based on many of the same documents, they are informed by markedly different preconceptions about Soviet intentions in Germany and about the relationship between the German communists and their Soviet patrons. The differences are based to a large extent on the speculations that scholars have made in order to piece together the contradictory evidence that is available. Until we have full access to the Soviet sources linking Stalin and his ministries, a question mark will always hang over interpretations of Soviet policy towards Germany after the war. There is, it would seem, little immediate prospect of new evidence surfacing that would promise to clear up the ambiguities. But perhaps the adoption of a wait-and-see approach is both expecting too much from the sources we do not have and asking too little about the ones we do have. The main problem we will consider in the corresponding section of our evaluation is whether so much speculation is necessary to make sense of the existing evidence.

## Soviet imports and German continuities

Apart from the controversies surrounding the foundation of the GDR, there is the wider issue of Soviet influences and German legacies well after its birth. To what extent were social and political developments in East Germany a reflection of 'Sovietization'? To what extent were they derived from older patterns, experiences and traditions within Germany itself?

We have already seen in Chapter 1 how the SED's views on these issues changed considerably over time. Whereas the initial emphasis was on the

---

19 Heinrich August Winkler, for instance, called this 'an interpretation as bizarre (*abenteuerlich*) as the policies that it purports to explain'. H.A. Winkler, 'Im Zickzackkurs zum Sozialismus', *Die Zeit*, 17 June 1994.
20 Cf. the balanced review by D. Staritz, 'Die SED und Stalins Deutschlandpolitik', *DA* 27:8 (1994), pp. 854–61, on this point pp. 857–9.
21 Gerhard Wettig, *Bereitschaft zu Einheit in Freiheit? Die Sowjetische Deutschlandpolitik 1945–1955* (Munich, 1999), p. 317. For a similar view, see also K. Schroeder, *Der SED-Staat*, pp. 71–82.

GDR's supposedly clean break with the fateful legacies of the German past, by the 1980s there was a deliberate attempt to highlight certain linkages with the national heritage and to resurrect various historic symbols and personalities. The inconsistency of arguing that the GDR was firmly rooted in 'German' history while simultaneously rejecting the notion of a single 'German' nation clearly belied the legitimatory intentions behind this instrumentalization of the past. Yet East German historical scholarship did not, on the whole, challenge the official position. Although the crucial role of the Soviets was always gratefully acknowledged, it was the German communists and the lessons they took from their experiences within Germany – the failed revolution of 1918, the fascist takeover – that usually took centre stage.[22]

In the meantime, the emphasis in the West was on the apparent uniformity of Eastern Europe under the relentless pressure of 'Sovietization'.[23] In the particular case of the GDR, the centrality of Soviet influence has been strongly reaffirmed after 1989–90. As Arnulf Baring has rather stridently put it:

> The character of foreign rule that was forced on to the Germans in the GDR will become increasingly apparent in the course of time. The GDR remained at its core an occupation regime. It began when the Russians imposed it on the Germans living there. Socialism in the GDR was in essence not something that grew in the country itself, but always remained a derivative of Russian power and the presence of the Red Army.[24]

Hans-Ulrich Wehler has similarly described the GDR as little more than a 'Russian satrapy'.[25] Many former Soviet officials would agree. As Peter Abrassimov, Soviet ambassador to East Berlin during the 1960s and 1970s, famously remarked in 1992: 'One can, strictly speaking, liken the GDR to a homunculus that was reared in the Soviet test-tube.'[26]

Yet as foreign observers had long remarked on their travels in the GDR, there was nonetheless something peculiarly 'German' about the place. As Peter Bender has argued, whereas 'the West Germans became Europeans, as far as one can, the East Germans remained German'.[27] Since unification this curious mixture of Soviet and German influences has been a subject of considerable scholarly interest. The legacies of the German communist movement, for instance, have attracted more attention by Western scholars than they had for decades. Although the often rather crude East German views

22 A good example is the work of Günter Benser, the leading GDR historian of the immediate post-war period, '"Keine Wiederholung der Fehler von 1918!" Wie KPD und SPD im Kampf um die Errichtung der Arbeiter-und-Bauern-Macht die Lehren der Novemberrevolution nutzten', *BzG* vol. 20 (1978), pp. 835–43.
23 Cf. the classic study by Z. Brzezinski, *The Soviet Bloc: Unity and Conflict* (Cambridge MA, 1967), which set the tone for years to come. For a more recent account, see K. Jowitt, *New World Disorder: The Leninist Extinction* (Berkeley, CA, 1993).
24 Arnulf Baring, 'Am Ende liegen sich alle in den Armen', *Berliner Zeitung*, 4/5 April 1995, p. 35.
25 Quoted from Hans-Ulrich Wehler, 'Ein deutsches Säkulum?', *Die Zeit*, 8 Aug. 1996, p. 18.
26 P. Abrassimov in *ND*, 13 Aug. 1992.
27 Peter Bender, *Episode oder Epoche? Zur Geschichte des geteilten Deutschlands* (Munich, 1996), p. 12.

about the heroic heritage of the KPD have not been supported, a number of historians have made real attempts to link the policies and culture of the SED with the communist traditions established during the interwar period. In Eric Weitz's view, the SED's heavy emphasis on the 'class struggle' was derived in part from the KPD's previous exclusion from the workplace by the triangle of employers, the state and the Social Democrats, which forced them on to the streets, eventually to become the representatives of the unemployed.[28] In many ways, the Weimar KPD's 'two camp' theory pitting workers against the bourgeoisie prefigured the geopolitical division of Germany after 1945. In a similar vein, Peter Ruben has portrayed the GDR as a 'state arising from the leftist opposition of 1918/19 ... with the help of the Russian communists and their victorious Red Army'.[29]

The supposedly 'German' tradition of an authoritarian state and society of subjects represents another strand of continuity in the eyes of many scholars. This idea is, of course, hardly new. Images of 'Red Prussia' – orderly and well-disciplined Germans capable of making even socialism work – go back decades, and were especially prominent in some Anglo-American accounts.[30] West Germans, too, contributed to this imagery through such notions as the 'second economic miracle' in East Germany, an idea that was not without a certain tinge of national pride.[31] The collapse of the GDR has more recently led some west German historians to interpret its history as a continuation of the German '*Sonderweg*'. Unlike the successful 'Westernization' of the Federal Republic, the GDR retained many of the anti-Western and illiberal features of the old Reich.[32] Immediately after unification, some historians were even concerned that these historic hangovers – which numbered among the supposedly insurmountable modernization deficits that led to the GDR's collapse – would potentially threaten the continued Western orientation of the new Federal Republic.[33] Apart from the GDR's lack of 'Westernization', others have claimed to discern significant 'German' continuities in the oft-cited quiescence of GDR society. While

---

28  Eric Weitz, *Creating German Communism, 1890–1990: From Popular Protests to Socialist State* (Princeton, NJ, 1997), ch. 9.

29  Peter Ruben, 'Vom Platz der DDR in der deutschen Geschichte', *Berliner Debatte Initial*, vol. 9 (1998) 2/3, pp. 22–38, here p. 23.

30  For a flavour, see Jean Edward Smith, *Germany beyond the Wall: People, Politics and Prosperity* (Boston, 1969), esp. p. 80.

31  To be sure, the East German authorities played their part in conjuring up this national imagery as well. This was manifested probably most clearly at the 'Neue Wache' on East Berlin's main boulevard Unter den Linden, which, despite serving as a memorial to the 'victims of fascism and militarism', was guarded round the clock by goose-stepping soldiers in traditional German uniforms (!).

32  J. Kocka, 'Ein deutscher Sonderweg. Überlegungen zur Sozialgeschichte der DDR', *APuZG* B40/94, pp. 34–45; Bernd Faulenbach, 'Überwindung des "deutschen Sonderweges"? Zur politischen Kultur der Deutschen seit dem Zweiten Weltkrieg', in *APuZG* B51/98, pp. 11–23; Arnold Sywottek, 'Nationaler Attentismus und anachronistischer Sozialismus. Die DDR in der deutschen Geschichte', in Klaus Schönhoven and Dietrich Staritz (eds), *Sozialismus und Kommunismus im Wandel* (Cologne, 1993), pp. 467–85.

33  J. Kocka, 'Nur keinen neuen Sonderweg', *Die Zeit*, 19 Oct. 1990, p. 11; T. Schmid, 'Die Eroberung der Bundesrepublik durch die ehemalige DDR', *Die Tageszeitung*, 14 Dec. 1990.

former dissidents have emphasized how 'the "German" inclination towards calmness and orderliness, towards cleanliness and security could be instrumentalized by the SED',[34] social scientists and historians have also suggested that the German tradition of 'unpolitical culture' and 'authoritarian-state orientation' contributed to the stability of the SED regime.[35]

## Comparing the GDR and the Third Reich

By far the most hotly contested issue concerning any 'German continuities' in the history of the GDR is the extent to which it broke with the Nazi past or rather propagated some of its basic characteristics. As we have already seen in our discussion of totalitarianism, drawing this comparison is by no means novel to the period since 1990. Whereas the GDR always portrayed itself as the true anti-fascist successor state of the Third Reich, in the West the two regimes were commonly bracketed together as flip-sides of the totalitarian coin. Although such blatant associations became increasingly rare during the 1970s and 1980s, the question of similarities between the SED and Nazi regimes has returned with a vengeance after the GDR's collapse. Since then, disagreements over the validity of '*Diktaturenvergleich*' have occupied a central place in debates about 'dealing with the past' in unified Germany.

The opposing poles of opinion are easily delineated. At one end is the argument that the two regimes were in essence highly similar and that comparing them is both useful and necessary for a proper evaluation of the nature of the SED regime and its place in German history. Particular emphasis is placed here on the structures of one-party rule, the exclusive ideology and the total claims made on citizens, often accompanied by ruminations about the need for a clear moral confrontation with dictatorial regimes after the collapse of communism. The concept of totalitarianism is generally regarded by this school of opinion as an indispensable tool for comparison and analysis.[36]

---

34  E. Neubert, *Geschichte der Opposition*, p. 20

35  Cf. for instance Sigrid Meuschel, *Legitimation und Parteiherrschaft*, pp. 15–22; S. Meuschel, 'Revolution in der DDR. Versuch einer sozialwissenschaftlichen Interpretation', in W. Zapf (ed.), *Die Modernisierung moderner Gesellschaften* (Frankfurt, 1991), pp. 558–71, here pp. 564ff; W. Mommsen, 'Der Ort der DDR in der deutschen Geschichte', in J. Kocka and M. Sabrow (eds), *Die DDR als Geschichte*, pp. 26–39.

36  Cf. Michael Wolffsohn, 'Doppelte Vergangenheitsbewältigung', in Klaus Sühl (ed.), *Vergangenheitsbewältigung 1945 und 1989. Ein möglicher Vergleich?* (Berlin, 1994), pp. 39ff; Horst Möller, 'Die Geschichte des Nationalsozialismus und der DDR: ein (un)möglicher Vergleich?', in ibid., pp. 127–38; H. Möller, *Materialien der Enquete-Kommission*, vol. IX, pp. 578–9, 584; Paul-Georg Garmer, 'Die doppelte deutsche Diktaturerfahrung: Zwischenergebnisse eines Vergleichs – ein Meinungsbeitrag', in Ludger Kühnhardt et al. (eds), *Die doppelte deutsche Diktaturerfahrung. Drittes Reich und DDR – ein historisch-politikwissenschaftlicher Vergleich*, 2nd edn (Frankfurt a. M., 1996), pp. 285–300; Wolfgang Schuller, 'Deutscher Diktaturenvergleich', in H. Timmermann (ed.), *Die DDR – Analysen eines aufgegebenen Staates*, pp. 849–57.

At the other end of the spectrum is the rejection of any such comparison as tendentious, politically motivated, and in effect (if not intention) belittling Nazi crimes. As Margherita von Brentano has put it, 'the very comparison of the Third Reich with the GDR is a horrible *Verharmlosung*. The Third Reich left behind mountains of corpses. The GDR left behind mountains of catalogue cards.'[37] Eric Weitz agrees, adding that 'such efforts are comforting to those who wish to condemn every aspect of the DDR and German communism, to make of the DDR a pariah, and, at the same time, to elevate West German politics and society to saintly status'.[38] Between these opposing poles stands a somewhat less dismissive group of sceptics who do not reject the comparison of the two regimes out of hand, but nonetheless harbour serious doubts about its usefulness and implications, and in any event see the differences between them as outweighing the similarities. The emphasis here is on the racist versus essentially humanist ideology (at least in theory), the overwhelmingly higher degree of brutality under the Nazis, the leadership cult surrounding Hitler, and the obvious fact that the Nazis unleashed a war and the GDR did not.[39]

There were, quite clearly, certain commonalities and differences between the two regimes. It seems rather fruitless to debate this point. The controversy has rather revolved around both the degree and the nature of the similarities and dissimilarities, as well as the way in which they are compared. The issues we will need to consider below are the relative weighting that should be attributed to the characteristics that they shared or did not share; what, precisely, is being compared and what is being left out; and perhaps most importantly, the methods used for comparison and what they can realistically be expected to reveal.

# Evaluation

## *Stalin's accident, Ulbricht's design?*

As a product of the Cold War, the GDR's foundation and continued existence as a separate state are almost unthinkable without Moscow's support. Even the most revisionist accounts proceed from the premise that the Kremlin's approval – or at the very least lack of disapproval – was the

---

37 M. v. Brentano, *Die Zeit*, 16 May 1991. Cf. also the classic critique by Helga Grebing, *Linksradikalismus gleich Rechtsradikalismus. Eine falsche Gleichung* (Stuttgart, 1971).

38 E. Weitz, *Creating German Communism*, p. 393.

39 See, for example, Hans Mommsen, 'Nationalsozialismus und Stalinismus. Diktaturen im Vergleich', in Klaus Sühl (ed.), *Vergangenheitsbewältigung 1945 und 1989*, pp. 109–26, which focuses on the structural differences; and Eberhard Jäckel, *Die zweifache Vergangenheit. Zum Vergleich politischer Systeme* (Bonn, 1992), which emphasizes the divergent ideologies.

crucial precondition for the existence of the GDR. However, most historians would nowadays also agree that Stalin did not initially strive for the establishment of a separate communist regime within the Soviet occupation zone, but would have preferred instead a solution to the 'German question' that gave the Soviets access to desperately needed reparations from the western occupation zones and kept the Federal Republic out of the Western military alliance. Any talk of an 'order to divide' Germany as early as 1945 is clearly off the mark.[40] But what Stalin wanted in Germany, when he opted for a separate GDR, whether he drove events or was to some extent pushed along by others in the SMAD or SED, how much autonomous influence German communists possessed on the international and domestic front during these critical early years – all of this remains open to dispute.

As we have seen, the irreconcilable interpretations[41] surrounding the GDR's foundation are by and large based on the same set of evidence that is available to scholars (though it should be noted that some historians have taken more trouble to visit Soviet archives than others). Taken together, the sources do not permit definitive answers, but offer what is essentially circumstantial evidence. Thus interpretations derived from them represent attempts to piece together these circumstances as plausibly as possible.

The chief problem is that the evidence is ambivalent and often downright contradictory, even at the most basic level. One set of elemental facts strongly suggests that the Soviets intended, or at least anticipated the need, to build socialism in Germany from early on. The 'antifascist-democratic transformation' quickly produced conditions similar to those in other Eastern European states. Likewise, the building blocks of an incipient state apparatus were established relatively early on: the communist-dominated *Land* governments, a centralized administrative structure, the German Economic Commission (officially elevated to the status of a 'central ruling organ' in February 1948), and effective single party rule. Yet at the same time, another set of elemental facts supports the opposing arguments. The Soviets continually proclaimed their desire for a unified state, repeatedly reined in the more radical elements of the SED, clearly prioritized access to the resources in the Ruhr, and tried their best to hinder the integration of the fledgling Federal Republic into the Western alliance.

Wilhelm Pieck's notes of various meetings between the KPD/SED leaders and the Soviet leadership exemplify the ambivalence of the documentary evidence. Although Pieck jotted down Stalin's prognosis in June 1945 that

---

40  Indeed, not even Wilke himself, who was the first to posit a *'Teilungsbefehl'*, has maintained this untenable position later on. See the commentaries in Peter Erler, Horst Laude and Manfred Wilke (eds), *Nach Hitler kommen wir. Dokumente zur Programmatik der Moskauer KPD-Führung 1944/45 für Nachkriegsdeutschland* (Berlin, 1994).

41  To recapitulate these positions: on the one hand, that Stalin did not want the GDR and actually tried to hinder the division of Germany even at the expense of sacrificing the socialist regime in the East; and on the other, that he desired or at least anticipated division from 1948 at the latest and that he acted accordingly by instituting a sweeping social and economic transformation of the SBZ.

'there will be two Germanies – despite all the unity among the allies', he also recorded Stalin's clear opposition to the division of Germany: 'The unity of Germany is to be ensured by the unified KPD, a unified ZK, a unified workers' party, in the central focus a unified party.'[42] At a meeting in December 1948, the Soviet dictator restrained the eager SED leaders from pushing for a more rapid 'transition to socialism' as was currently taking place elsewhere in Eastern Europe, despite the fact that the SED had already become a thoroughly 'Stalinized' party over the course of the preceding summer. In Pieck's notes, Stalin's message was: 'still no unified state, not standing [on the threshold of] power'.[43] Finally, at a meeting in Moscow in early April 1952, less than a month after the controversial 10 March note to the Western allies offering a neutral, unified Germany, Stalin assented to the SED leaders' requests, recommending that they embark on the 'path to socialism' (including collectivization), treat the demarcation line with the West as a 'hostile border', and 'create a People's Army – without a big fuss – the pacifist period is over'.[44]

Creating a consistent narrative out of this inconsistent set of evidence would appear to require emphasizing some pieces of information while disregarding or downplaying others. The existing evidence does not, in other words, fit very neatly with either the 'Sovietization' thesis or with the GDR's portrayal as 'Stalin's unwanted child'. Although this may result from the incompleteness of the evidence, it is worth considering whether it might also simply derive from the shortcomings of the interpretations themselves. An important point to recognize is that both arguments posit a basic degree of consistency in Soviet policy towards Germany. Whereas the 'Sovietization' thesis tends to see Stalin's intention to build socialism in Germany as largely unchanged from early on, thus taking the end result by around 1952 and projecting it back to the beginning, the 'unwanted child' thesis portrays a similarly constant desire to avoid German division, taking what appeared to be Stalin's initial intention and projecting it forward to 1952. A third and, in my view, more convincing group of explanations makes no such assumption of a clear or consistent Soviet policy towards Germany. First mooted in the 1960s but gaining weight in the 1990s,[45] the picture of Soviet policy that emerges is one of improvisations and contradictions, especially on the part of Stalin himself, whose single most consistent desire was to keep his options open and not commit himself any earlier than absolutely necessary

42 These notes are published in Dietrich Staritz, 'Die SED, Stalin und der "Aufbau des Sozialismus"'; also Rolf Badstübner and Wilfried Loth (eds), *Wilhelm Pieck – Aufzeichnungen zur Deutschlandpolitik*.
43 D. Staritz, 'Die SED, Stalin und der "Aufbau des Sozialismus"', p. 692.
44 Ibid., pp. 694–7.
45 Cf. H.-P. Schwarz, *Vom Reich zur Bundesrepublik*, pp. 201–69, which argues that Stalin did not manage to keep all of his irons in the fire successfully. This argument has been more recently echoed and refined in the wide-ranging and exhaustively researched account by Norman Naimark, *The Russians in Germany: A History of the Soviet Zone of Occupation, 1945–1949* (Cambridge, MA, 1995), esp. chs. 5–6. Cf. also Jan Foitzik, *Sowjetische Militäradministration in Deutschland (SMAD) 1945–1949. Struktur und Funktion* (Berlin, 1999).

to either a separate socialist Germany or a unified neutral Germany. Insofar as there was any design behind this, it was to allow a variety of policy options to be pursued simultaneously regardless of the political confusion and contradictions this produced.

A useful illustration is the case of the aforementioned Colonel Tiul'panov, head of the SMAD's Information Department. Whereas Loth has portrayed Tiul'panov as a key accomplice to Ulbricht's efforts during 1946 and 1948 to push through radical changes in the SBZ against Stalin's wishes, other scholars have deemed him relatively unimportant, simply an efficient bureaucrat anticipating division and acting accordingly at Moscow's behest. Norman Naimark has recently offered a more convincing argument that possesses elements from both of these interpretations. On the basis of internal Soviet and East German sources, Naimark has confirmed beyond any reasonable doubt that Tiul'panov was, as Loth has contended, a thorn in the side of some Soviet ministries, and that he was heavily criticized in 1946 and April 1948 for 'leftist mistakes' against the middle classes and for mistakenly leading others to believe that Moscow's goal was to erect a 'socialist republic'.[46] Some of Tiul'panov's actions were, then, apparently carried out without Stalin's prior approval, and indeed ran counter to the intentions of many high-ranking Soviet officials. But at the same time, the fact that Tiul'panov remained in the SMAD despite these seemingly grievous 'mistakes' demonstrates that his actions also did not meet with outright disapproval. It would therefore appear that Stalin's views on the matter were not entirely clear or consistent. As Naimark has concluded, 'More than anything else, the fact that Tiul'panov was not removed from his post indicates that Stalin himself shared many of the Colonel's instincts. ... With Tiul'panov in the zone, Stalin kept his options open.'[47]

Not that all options were equally open. The immediate Soviet priorities of securing reparations and denazifying the zone's administration set in train a transformation of the SBZ that neither the Soviet Military Government nor the SED were wholeheartedly prepared to sacrifice in order to achieve more congenial relations with the West, especially after the onset of the Cold War. As the occupation progressed, the alternative of a Sovietized SBZ looked increasingly likely just as the prospect of a 'neutral' demilitarized Germany looked increasingly unlikely.[48] Developments in the SBZ had, in other words, acquired a certain momentum by 1947. Perhaps more importantly, the possible radius of Soviet actions in the SBZ was crucially constrained by the parameters of ideology and mentality. The decisions of Soviet officials were powerfully conditioned by their own experience

---

46 N. Naimark, *The Russians in Germany*, pp. 336, 342–4.
47 Ibid., p. 352.
48 Cf. generally the discussion in N. Naimark, *The Russians in Germany*. See also J. Laufer, 'From Dismantling to Currency Reform: External Origins of the Dictatorship, 1943–1948', in K. Jarausch (ed.), *Dictatorship as Experience*, pp. 73–89.

of building socialism in the Soviet Union. Lacking any kind of overall plan for the political development of the zone (such as the US policy statement JCS 1067 offered for its zone), the Soviets drew their models from their own first Five-Year Plan, from the New Economic Policy of the 1920s and from agricultural collectivization in the 1930s. As Naimark has argued, 'Soviet officers bolshevized the zone not because there was a plan to do so, but because that was the only way they knew to organize society'.[49] The erection of a socialist order in East Germany was, in other words, as much a matter of mentality and social instincts as of articulated policies. If one applies this notion to Stalin himself, it seems extremely doubtful that the Soviet dictator ever endorsed the creation of a 'democratic' Germany in the Western parliamentary sense of the word (an idea which, it has to be said, Loth is alone in advancing so strongly). Although this may well have been in the Soviets' 'objective' interests – indeed, the US CIA and State Department thought that Moscow would be prepared to make 'radical concessions' in order to avoid the creation of a separate West German state[50] – to suggest that it was a central political aim greatly underappreciates the importance of Leninist ideology in moulding the outer parameters of Soviet policy, in circumscribing what could be deemed politically possible. Even if introducing a 'democratic' republic had been a specific policy goal, it is highly doubtful that it could ever have been achieved by an apparatus whose very structure and instincts ran counter to notions of Western 'bourgeois' democracy.[51]

The bolshevizing predilections of the Soviet governing system eventually played into the hands of the German communists, who, after the discouraging electoral results of 1946, knew that their only chance of maintaining power would be in a separate socialist German state. Although Stalin somewhat grudgingly accepted the foundation of the GDR in 1949, a question mark, however faint, still hung over the permanance of the SED regime until spring 1952. The SED leadership had good reason to be worried about the faithfulness of their Soviet patrons, who continually tried to hinder the Federal Republic's integration into the Western alliance and remained adamant that the SED not jeopardize the prospects of German unity through pursuing further societal changes. Despite the public pronouncements about the goal of a unified socialist Germany, it seems clear that Ulbricht and his associates were pushing Moscow towards accepting more thorough-going

---

49 N. Naimark, *The Russians in Germany*, p. 467.
50 William Stivers, 'Amerikanische Sichten auf die Sowjetisierung Ostdeutschlands 1945–1949', in Michael Lemke (ed.), *Sowjetisierung und Eigenständigkeit in der SBZ/DDR (1945–1953)* (Cologne, 1999), pp. 275–304, here p. 303.
51 As Loth himself has argued, there was a 'fundamental tension between programme and system'. The 'increasing contradictions of their policy' resulted not least from 'the systemic incapability of German and Soviet communists, including Stalin, to think and act in a consistently democratic manner in the practical administration of the occupation zone'. Wilfried Loth, 'Stalin, die deutsche Frage und die DDR. Eine Antwort an meine Kritiker', *DA* 28:3 (1995), pp. 290–8, here pp. 294, 298.

changes in the GDR that would in effect deepen the divide with the FRG and thereby cement the SED's position. Stalin's March note to the Western allies sent shock waves through the SED leadership, who did not put it past the Soviet dictator to sacrifice the SED regime in exchange for neutrality. The fact that the Soviets abruptly reversed their previously cautious stance in early April 1952 by assenting to the build-up of military forces and the introduction of agricultural collectivization does not disprove the sincerity of the 10 March note.[52] Although one can interpret this about-face as evidence that the note was a publicity stunt, it seems more likely that it was a response to the rejection of the note on 20 March by the Western powers, whose scepticism was, it should be noted, all too understandable in the light of their previous dealings with Stalin.[53] After this last-ditch effort to hinder the FRG's integration into the Western alliance had failed, there was little left to divide Soviet and SED interests in Germany. Although Stalin was probably only using the German question as a strategic bargaining chip, that is not to say he was unwilling to cash in on it, depending on the Western allies' response.[54]

The evidence suggests that the German communists around Ulbricht played a far more active role in the foundation of the GDR than has often been assumed. Though it sounds paradoxical at first, in many ways they drove forward the process of 'Sovietization' more forcefully than the Soviets themselves. To be sure, they found many allies within the SMAD and the Soviet ruling elite who shared their basic view. The difference between the Soviets and the SED was arguably more one of tactics than of overall strategy. As Staritz has suggested, both parties pushed for far-reaching changes in the SBZ, only the SED was simply not as adept as the Soviets at doing this 'without making a fuss' and 'in the zig-zag to socialism', as the great dictator himself famously put it.[55] Yet the divisions over whether to pursue a separate socialist state were complex and ran through both the German and the Soviet parties. Not all German communists agreed with Ulbricht, and there were numerous tensions within and between the Soviet ministries over what their aims should be. Clearly, it is too simplistic to argue that 'the Soviet political system and the communist ideology were implants of a foreign power, in spite of the willing helpers on the German side'.[56] The SED regime

---

52  It is in any event impossible to determine whether the 10 March note was a sincere offer or a publicity stunt. It arguably could have been both: in the event of a rejection by the West it would make for good publicity, and in the unlikely event of it leading to new negotiations over the future of Germany it would serve key Soviet interests. Either way, Stalin had nothing to lose and everything to gain.

53  As Loth points out, taking the meetings of early April as indicative of previous Soviet intentions for East Germany is methodologically flawed. Cf. Gerhard Wettig, 'Die Deutschland-Note vom 10. März 1952 auf der Basis diplomatischer Akten des russischen Außenministeriums. Die Hypothese des Wiedervereinigungsangebots', *DA* 26:7 (1993), pp. 786–805; Hermann Graml, 'Die Legende von der verpaßten Gelegenheit', *VfZ* vol. 29 (1981), pp. 307–41; also Hennig Köhler, 'Stalin ein deutscher Demokrat', *FAZ* (2 Aug. 1994).

54  Dietrich Staritz, 'Die SED und Stalins Deutschlandpolitik', p. 859.

55  Ibid.

56  Wolfgang Schuller in *Berliner Zeitung*, 28/29 Mar. 1998.

was not merely a Soviet implant. The Soviet Union obviously made the GDR possible and in many ways encouraged its formation in practice, but as regards the foundation of the separate socialist state, the German communists were much more than mere executors of Stalin's will (enigmatic as it was). The notion of 'Sovietization', though nicely capturing the fact that the GDR was largely dependent and modelled on the Soviet Union, tends to ignore the degree of autonomy that existed.

## Made in Germany?

Can the same be said for Soviet influence on the GDR during subsequent periods and beyond the narrow political realm? There is simply no escaping the fact that Soviet support was the fundamental precondition for the GDR's existence. As Brezhnev none too subtly reminded Honecker at a meeting in July 1970: 'Erich ... never forget it: without us there is no GDR.'[57] This has long been clear to everyone in both East and West. But recent research suggests that over the 40 years of the GDR's existence, the SED leadership acted with more independence and was more willing to risk tensions with Moscow than has often been assumed.

The SED's limited degree of political autonomy that we have already seen during the early years seems gradually to have increased later on. It is now clear, for instance, that the 'second Berlin crisis' that preceded the construction of the Berlin Wall in August 1961 – first triggered by Kruschev's 1958 ultimatum to the Western powers regarding the incorporation of West Berlin into the territory of the GDR – was in large part the product of Ulbricht's constant pressure on Kruschev for more decisive action.[58] During the latter stages of the economic reforms of the 1960s, Ulbricht stubbornly clung to his pet project and even continued his smug ideological pretensions about their correctness well after Brezhnev's dismantling of the reforms in the Soviet Union had set reformers on the defensive throughout Eastern Europe. And as we have seen in the preceding chapter, Honecker, who initially got his job because of Ulbricht's onerous rigidity, himself waged a relentless stonewalling campaign against Soviet *glasnost* during the latter 1980s. As one commentator has remarked, 'the dynamic of an intransigent, even provocative, SED seeking to force the hand of a relatively cautious Soviet Union would become a fixed element of postwar international relations'.[59]

57  Quoted in Peter Przybylski, *Tatort Politbüro. Band 1: Die Akte Honecker* (Berlin, 1991), p. 281.
58  See esp. Michael Lemke, *Die Berlinkrise 1958 bis 1963. Interessen und Handlungsspielräume der SED im Ost-West Konflikt* (Berlin, 1995); André Steiner, 'Politische Vorstellungen und ökonomische Probleme im Vorfeld der Errichtung der Berliner Mauer. Briefe Walter Ulbrichts an Nikita Chruschtschow', in Hartmut Mehringer (ed.), *Von der SBZ zur DDR* (Munich, 1995), pp. 233–68; Hope Harrison, 'Ulbricht and the Concrete "Rose": New Archival Evidence on the Dynamics of Soviet–East German Relations and the Berlin Crisis 1958–1961', in *Cold War International History Project Working Paper*, no. 5 (May 1993).
59  E. Weitz, *Creating German Communism*, p. 349.

Yet one must not lose sight of the fact that all of these actions occurred within an overall relationship of dependence – or better: assymetrical mutual dependence. It is unhelpful to approach GDR–Soviet relations as if they were 'closed systems' in relation to one another. The GDR was, as I remarked in the last chapter, shot through with Soviet security and economic interests. For this reason, it is more fruitfully approached as a 'penetrated system'. Whether one considers the strategic importance of the GDR to Moscow or the critical lifeline of trade between their economies, the web of power and interests that bound the two states together is impossible to disentangle neatly.[60] That the GDR needed the Soviet Union is obvious. But the fact that the Soviets also needed the GDR helps to explain the limited autonomy that the SED leadership apparently exercised in relations with its patron state.

Crucial though it was, the continual focus on Soviet predominance has long tended to obscure other influences and traditions that made the GDR what it was, often under the motto 'The Russians were to blame'.[61] The legacies of the German communist movement played an important and largely underappreciated role in shaping East German politics and society. This is certainly true regarding developments within the SED itself. As Hurwitz and Malycha have shown, the party's so-called 'Stalinization' in 1948 was not primarily the result of 'Sovietization' coming 'from outside', but was driven first and foremost by hard-line German communists, and indeed began as early as 1946.[62] After the war, the older divisions within the German Left between reformism and revolution were not so much reconciled as forcefully resolved in favour of the latter. As Weitz has argued, this triumph of the 'politics of intransigence' over the 'politics of gradualism' also marked a reversion to the ideological traditions of the Weimar period after the intervening years of communist collaboration with the socialists and liberals in the Resistance and in exile.[63] The prior experiences of the SED's 'founder generation' also informed their political choices in a variety of other areas. The zeal with which they pushed through socio-economic

---

60 Cf. the stimulating introduction by Michael Lemke (ed.), *Sowjetisierung und Eigenständigkeit*, esp. pp. 12–13.

61 Cf. the criticisms of this view in Felix Philipp Lutz, 'Verantwortungsbewußtsein und Wohlstandschauvinismus', in Werner Weidenfeld (ed.), *Deutschland, eine Nation – doppelte Geschichte* (Cologne, 1993), p. 161. For an unsparing criticism of attempts to remove the GDR from German history, see Erhard Crome, 'DDR-Perzeptionen. Kontext und Zugangsmuster', in *Berliner Debatte Initial* 9 (1998) 2/3, pp. 45–58; see also E. Crome, 'Die DDR in der deutschen Geschichte', in Heiner Timmermann (ed.), *Die DDR – Analysen eines aufgegebenen Staates* (Berlin, 2001), pp. 101–18.

62 Harold Hurwitz, *Die Stalinisierung der SED. Zum Verlust von Freiräumen und sozialdemokratischer Identität in den Vorständen 1946–1949* (Opladen, 1997); Andreas Malycha, *Partei von Stalins Gnaden? Die Entwicklung der SED zur Partei neuen Typs in den Jahren 1946 bis 1950* (Berlin, 1996). Both authors convincingly argue against not only the 'legend of the voluntary foundation' of the SED in 1946 (which entailed considerable coercion towards the SPD), but also the 'legend of the missed opportunity' to build a progressive and democratic Germany that ended only with the Stalinization of politics and society from 1948 onwards. In their view, the supposed goodwill that existed between the parties until 1948 is little more than a cherished left-wing myth.

63 E. Weitz, *Creating German Communism*, p. 312.

transformations was no doubt a reflection of their disappointment with the limited degree of social change after the 1918–19 revolution. The deprivation they had witnessed during the initial years after the First World War and especially during the Depression also moulded their social and welfare policies.[64] Their experience of the rising tide of fascism and the widespread popularity of Hitler among their 'own' constituency, the working class, also helps explain the particularly stark divide between party intellectuals and workers in the GDR in comparison to other East European states.[65]

If German communist traditions played a role in the GDR, so too did non-communist ones. The SED quite deliberately tapped into older 'German' values of diligence, order and discipline in order to appeal to the masses and to stabilize its authority. No longer a disruptive revolutionary movement, the communists consciously employed older patriotic concepts such as 'German quality work' and traditional notions of 'honourable labour' in an attempt to raise productivity in the factories and minimize discontent.[66] Instead of promoting '*Proletkult*' – the deliberate flouting of bourgeois norms and rules for behaviour – SED cultural policy deliberately espoused the 'embourgeoisement' of workers' tastes and morality. Self-discipline and good manners better befitted the present level of civilization under socialism than proletarian 'non-culture'.[67] Ulbricht in particular strove to wed together the traditionally belligerent rhetoric of the KPD with this older language of cleanliness into a new strategy for order and discipline (virtues that were, it might parenthetically be noted, undermined by the 'Sovietization' of various cultural practices in East Germany such as the culture of clientelism, bartering and work under-performance).[68]

It is precisely this emphasis on state authority and political subservience that has led some scholars to suggest certain continuities with the old German '*Sonderweg*'. Despite the communists' proclaimed intention to overcome this historical legacy,[69] surely Kocka and others are correct to see

64 Cf. D. Hoffmann, *Sozialpolitische Neuordnung in der SBZ/DDR. Der Umbau der Sozialversicherung 1945–1956* (Munich, 1996); H.-G. Hockerts, 'Grundlinien und soziale Folgen der Sozialpolitik in der DDR', in H. Kaelble *et al.* (eds), *Sozialgeschichte der DDR*, pp. 519–44.

65 See, generally, S. Meuschel, *Legitimation und Parteiherrschaft*; W. Mommsen, 'Der Ort der DDR in der deutschen Geschichte', pp. 36–7; E. Weitz, *Creating German Communism*, p. 383.

66 Cf. generally, A. Lüdtke, 'Helden der Arbeit'.

67 Cf. generally, Anna-Sabine Ernst, 'The Politics of Culture'.

68 Cf. the discussion in E. Weitz, *Creating German Communism*, pp. 371–6. On everyday Soviet cultural practices and their impact in the GDR, see A. Ledeneva, *Russia's Economy of Favours*; also Konrad Jarausch and Hannes Siegrist (eds), *Amerikanisierung und Sowjetisierung in Deutschland 1945–1970* (Frankfurt a. M., 1997), esp. S. Merl, 'Sowjetisierung in der Welt des Konsums', pp. 167–94. On the Soviet influence on elite culture, see David Pike, *The Politics of Culture in Soviet-occupied Germany, 1945–1949* (Stanford, CA, 1992); David Bathrick, *The Powers of Speech: The Politics of Culture in the GDR* (Lincoln, 1995).

69 Immediately after the war, the KPD portrayed its aim as overcoming precisely the supposed 'failures' of German history that underlie notions of a *Sonderweg*, in particular the failure of a 'bourgeois revolution' against Germany's pre-modern elites in 1848, which the KPD appeal in June 1945 explicitly vowed to complete. Likewise, the 'People's Congress Movement' – launched not coincidentally in March 1948, one hundred years after the opening of the Paulskirche convention in 1848 – was also presented as an important stride away from Germany's fateful political legacies.

more of the characteristics of this illiberal, anti-Western tradition preserved in the GDR than in the FRG.[70] The problem is that it is impossible to discern whether these characteristics derived primarily from endogenous or exogenous sources – in other words, whether they represented a case of 'German continuities' or what one might call 'communist commonalities'.[71] After all, authoritarian leaders and anti-Western sentiments were also very much a part of Russia's political traditions. One could certainly argue that the GDR derived these features more from its adoption of the Soviet system and ideology – which was strongly coloured by these older Russian traditions – than from any supposed indigenous patterns of political culture. If employed too exclusively, neither '*Sonderweg*' nor 'Sovietization' notions are very compelling in themselves. It seems more helpful to view their relationship as interactive, or as East German historians might say, a 'dialectical process'. It was arguably, in other words, precisely because the authoritarian features of the Soviet system found fertile soil in East Germany – whether due to a lack of strong democratic traditions or a widespread desire to 'keep one's head down' after the disaster of Nazism – that they could take root and reproduce themselves over four decades of state socialism.

Insofar as the GDR had something distinctly 'German' about it that set it apart from other communist states, this is better sought in two other dimensions: its unique relationship with its West German rival state and its attempts to deal with the Nazi past. The Federal Republic played an absolutely crucial role throughout the GDR's history.[72] The refugee problem before 1961, the constant (and largely unfavourable) comparisons drawn by ordinary East Germans between the two states, the SED's policy of political and cultural *Abgrenzung* and attempts to create a specific GDR 'national identity' (see Chapter 1), and of course the ubiquity of West German radio and television

---

70  Though it should be pointed out that this interpretation clearly works better for the period after the cultural upheavals of the latter 1960s which helped create a more tolerant and open political culture in the Federal Republic.

71  The militaristic atmosphere in the GDR, for example, has often been attributed to 'Prussian' hangovers; the fact that the National People's Army consciously tailored its uniforms and rituals on older Prussian models is often regarded as significant. Yet the uniforms were the exception. In most other regards – officers' training, education, weaponry and tactics – the East German army was modelled after the Red Army. Cf. C. Ross, 'Protecting the Accomplishments of Socialism?: The (Re)militarization of the GDR', in Patrick Major and Jonathan Osmond (eds), *The 'Workers' and Peasants' State': Communism and Society under Ulbricht, 1945–1971* (Manchester, 2002).

72  Cf. esp. Arnd Bauerkämper, Martin Sabrow and Bernd Stöver (eds), *Doppelte Zeitgeschichte. Deutsch-deutsche Beziehungen 1945–1990* (Bonn, 1998), which persuasively recommends approaching post-war German history as a 'double contemporary history' that enquires into the patterns of 'assymetric interweaving in the context of demarcation' between the two German states instead of approaching them in terms of 'parallel history' or 'national history'. Cf. also C. Kleßmann, 'Verflechtung und Abgrenzung. Aspekte der geteilten und zusammengehörigen deutschen Nachkriegsgeschichte', *APuZG* B29-30/93, pp. 30–41; Jürgen Kocka's Introduction in J. Kocka (ed.), *Historische DDR-Forschung*; Hans-Günter Hockerts, 'Zeitgeschichte in Deutschland. Begriffe, Methoden, Themenfelder', *APuZG* B29-30/93, pp. 3–19. On SED policy towards the Federal Republic, see Heike Amos, *Die Westpolitik der SED 1948/49–1961* (Berlin, 1999); Jochen Staadt, *Die geheime Westpolitik der SED 1960–1970. Von der gesamtdeutschen Orientierung zur sozialistischen Nation* (Berlin, 1993).

are among the most obvious examples of Western influence.[73] Less obvious, but no less important, were the effects which national division had on the SED leadership's particularly rigid and uncomprising stance towards basic reforms and on the nature of organized dissidence in the GDR, which, as we have seen, remained semi-loyal to the regime because of its rejection of capitalism. The development of a fundamental opposition platform was also undoubtedly undermined by the Nazi past. East German intellectuals commonly felt a certain reverance towards the old guard in the SED, many of whom had risked their lives fighting against the Nazis. As Christa Wolf explained in 1989: 'We felt a strong inhibition about engaging in resistance against people who spent the Nazi period in concentration camps.'[74] On a more general level, German socialists and communists were perhaps particularly willing to tolerate the shortcomings of the socialist system in view of the Nazi debacle. As Rolf Badstübner has argued, the supporters of socialism

> saw the Federal Republic with its huge burdens from the past. That strengthened their self-confidence and their conviction that they stood in the right camp. At the same time it also legitimated the GDR in spite of its obvious deformations, which were regarded as the 'teething troubles' of a 'century-long project'.[75]

## The 'Second German Dictatorship'?

To what extent did these 'deformations' represent continuities or similarities with the Third Reich? It is this question that underlies the controversial comparison of the SED and National Socialist regimes. Is the very act of drawing such a comparison a polemical statement? If so, what can it possibly be expected to reveal? Are the perceived motivations behind this comparison the only objection, or is it tendentious by its very nature? An evaluation of the arguments and approaches concerning these questions has to consider both methodological as well as empirical issues, which, to be sure, are not completely separable.

The most basic issue concerns the validity of such a comparison in the first place. It would seem that most scholars consider this a legitimate exercise that should not be taboo for political reasons.[76] In response to the objection

---

73  See, generally, S. Wolle, 'Der Traum vom Westen. Wahrnehmungen der bundesdeutschen Gesellschaft in der DDR', in K. Jarausch and M. Sabrow (eds), *Weg in den Untergang*, pp. 195–211; Peter Förster, 'Die deutsche Frage im Bewußtsein der Bevölkerung in beiden Teilen Deutschlands', in *Materialien der Enquete-Kommission*, vol. V: 2, pp. 1212–380. On the uptake and impact of West German media, see Axel Schildt, 'Zwei Staaten – eine Hörfunk- und Fernsehnation. Überlegungen zur Bedeutung der elektronischen Massenmedien in der Geschichte der Kommunikation zwischen der Bundesrepublik und der DDR', in A. Bauerkämper *et al.* (eds), *Doppelte Zeitgeschichte*, pp. 58–71.

74  Christa Wolf, *Reden im Herbst* (Berlin, 1990), p. 135.

75  Rolf Badstübner, *Von 'Reich' zum doppelten Deutschland. Gesellschaft und Politik im Umbruch* (Berlin, 1999), p. 550.

76  J. Kocka, 'Nationalsozialismus und SED-Diktatur im Vergleich', in J. Kocka, *Vereinigungskrise*, p. 100; Klaus Schönhoven, 'Drittes Reich und DDR: Probleme einer vergleichenden Analyse von deutschen

that comparing the two regimes unacceptably downplays Nazi crimes, it has frequently been argued that comparison does not mean equation. Quite obviously, comparison can also highlight contrasts, not just similarities; indeed, neither contrast nor similarity can be established without it. In any event, comparison is an accepted and highly useful tool of historical analysis, so it makes no sense to deny its intrinsic validity in this particular case.

Why, then, do some scholars – and many who lived in the GDR – reject it? Is it simply because of the connotations of equivalence inherent in the very term 'comparison'? Is such a comparison merely an affront to their 'anti-fascist' political sensibilities?[77] Or are there sounder reasons for doubting the validity of *'Diktaturenvergleich'*? Stating the obvious fact that comparison is not equation does not really address these objections. The problem is, as Ludger Kühnhardt has put it, that 'comparison is both a method as well as a statement of content'.[78] It is, in other words, both a 'value-free' and a 'normative' exercise at the same time. It is value-free insofar as it pursues the justifiable objective of discerning both similarities and dissimilarities between historical developments, events or entities. Consistent analysis on the basis of common criteria and an unbiased appraisal of the results are the essence of the comparative method. But it is also normative in that the choice of subjects for comparison depends on preliminary decisions about what is worth comparing and under what conceptual framework they should be compared. These preliminary decisions are strongly conditioned by contemporary concerns and by the particular analytical interests of scholars. In order to compare two things it is necessary to bring them under a common heading, to discern common criteria according to which they can be compared. It is this act of 'bracketing together', even if the aim is to distinguish both similarities and differences, that frequently prompts objection.

(Contd)
Diktaturerfahrungen', *JHK* (1995), pp. 189–200; Hans-Ulrich Wehler, 'Diktaturenvergleich, Totalitarismustheorie und DDR-Geschichte', in Arnd Bauerkämper *et al.* (eds), *Doppelte Zeitgeschichte*, pp. 346–52.

77  This would appear to be the case within certain circles of the PDS. Their 'minority vote' on the Enquete commission's report about comparing the GDR and Third Reich concedes that all historical comparisons are legitimate, but nonetheless rejects this particular case of comparison as invalid because it is supposedly motivated by a political desire to discredit the GDR along with the Nazi regime. Cf. Dietmar Keller, 'Minderheitenvotum zum Bericht der Enquete-Kommission des Deutschen Bundestages "Aufarbeitung von Geschichte und Folgen der SED-Diktatur in Deutschland"', in *Ansichten zur Geschichte der DDR*, vol. 4, pp. 46–50. By contrast, Gerhard Lozek has reversed his previous stance against this comparison: Gerhard Lozek, 'Zum Diktaturenvergleich von NS-Regime und SED-Staat. Zum Wesen der DDR im Spannungsfeld von autoritären, aber auch demokratischen Strukturen und Praktiken', in *Ansichten zur Geschichte der DDR*, vol. 4, pp. 109–21. For a sharper critique of the PDS's position, see Wolfgang-Uwe Friedrich, 'Denkblockaden: Das Totalitarismusmodell aus der Sicht der PDS', in Rainer Eckert and Bernd Faulenbach (eds), *Halbherziger Revisionismus: Zum postkommunistischen Geschichtsbild* (Munich, 1996), pp. 111–39.

78  Ludger Kühnhardt *et al.* (eds), *Die doppelte deutsche Diktaturerfahrung. Drittes Reich und DDR – ein historisch-politikwissenschaftlicher Vergleich*, 2nd edn (Frankfurt a. M., 1996), p. 11. See also Klaus Sühl (ed.), *Vergangenheitsbewältigung 1945 und 1989*, Introduction, pp. 7–8.

The GDR in German history

In the case of the GDR and Third Reich, the common criterion is that both regimes contrasted with the values and institutions of liberal democracy, in other words that both are considered 'dictatorships'. While this postulate itself arouses little controversy, any analysis based upon it tends to focus solely on the GDR's dictatorial features, which undoubtedly show some parallels to those of the Third Reich. Because the focus of attention is on these dictatorial features, other characteristics that contrast sharply with the Third Reich can easily be obscured from view. Critics contend that the result is both a one-sided picture of the GDR as a 'state of injustice' and a somewhat 'sanitized' image of the Third Reich, which is unfairly grouped together with the incomparably less violent East German regime. The criticism is, in my view, partially justified. Comparing the two regimes does require boiling the GDR down to its institutions and mechanisms of repression to such an extent that the remaining residue is often unrecognizable to many people who lived there. In addition, the obsessive focus on the 'two German dictatorships' since 1990[79] has drawn attention away from other, arguably more fruitful axes of comparison, for instance between ways of dealing with the Nazi past in the GDR and FRG,[80] and above all between the GDR and other communist states in Eastern Europe.[81] But the idea that such a comparison inevitably sanitizes the Nazi regime or de-emphasizes its brutality is not very compelling. Clearly it can function in this way if the basic criminality and unparalleled brutality of the Third Reich are not at the forefront of evaluation. But there is little evidence that this is happening in scholarly debate. If anything, perhaps the GDR's persecution of its own 'enemies' has been somewhat de-emphasized by the frequent references to the Third Reich's 'mountain of corpses'.[82] It is important to remember that

79  This has been aided in large part by the powerful Volkswagen Foundation, which throughout the 1990s financed research on comparing Nazi Germany and the GDR. See Edgar Wolfrum, 'Diktaturen im Europa des 20. Jahrhunderts. Ein neuer zeitgeschichtlicher Förderschwerpunkt der Stiftung Volkswagenwerk', *VfZ* 40 (1992), pp. 155–8.
80  Although this has clearly been a subject of considerable interest throughout the 1990s. See Jürgen Danyel (ed.), *Die geteilte Vergangenheit. Zum Umgang mit Nationalsozialismus und Widerstand in beiden deutschen Staaten* (Berlin, 1995); U. Herbert and O. Groehler (eds), *Zweierlei Bewältigung. Vier Beiträge über den Umgang mit NS-Vergangenheit in den beiden deutschen Staaten* (Hamburg, 1992); C. Kleßmann (ed.), *Deutsche Vergangenheiten – eine gemeinsame Herausforderung. Der schwierige Umgang mit der doppelten Nachkriegsgeschichte* (Berlin, 1999); Norbert Frei, 'NS-Vergangenheit unter Ulbricht und Adenauer. Gesichtspunkte einer "vergleichenden Bewältigungsforschung"', in J. Danyel (ed.), *Die geteilte Vergangenheit*, pp. 125–32; J. Herf, *Divided Memory: The Nazi Past in the Two Germanies* (Cambridge, MA, 1997); M. Fulbrook, *German National Identity after the Holocaust* (London, 1999).
81  This remains a markedly under-researched area with a small but slowly growing literature. See esp. John Connelly, *Captive University: The Sovietization of East German, Czech and Polish Higher Education, 1945–1956* (Chapel Hill, 2000); J. Connelly, 'Stalinismus und Hochschulpolitik in Ostmitteleuropa nach 1945', in *GG* 24 (1998), pp. 5–23; Michael Brie, 'Staatssozialistische Länder Europas im Vergleich. Alternative Herrschaftstrategien und divergente Typen', in Helmut Wiesenthal (ed.), *Einheit als Privileg: vergleichende Perspektiven auf die Transformation Ostdeutschlands* (Frankfurt a. M., 1996), pp. 39–104; Leonid Gibianskij, 'Sowjetisierung Osteuropas – Charakter und Typologie', in M. Lemke (ed.), *Sowjetisierung und Eigenständigkeit*, pp. 31–79; Klaus von Beyme, 'Stalinismus und Post-Stalinismus im osteuropäischen Vergleich', *Potsdamer Bulletin*, no. 13 (July 1998), pp. 8–22.
82  M. v. Brentano, *Die Zeit*, 16 May 1991.

real people – real victims – are behind the 'mountain of files' that the East German regime left in its wake.[83]

Comparing the two regimes is a legitimate exercise, and probably an unavoidable one given its moral and political implications in Germany. It is not only appropriate, but arguably imperative for scholars to participate in this debate since the issue is widely discussed in politics and public discourse anyway. This debate has not, it should be pointed out, been driven primarily by scholarly but rather by political interests. It is a prime example of the way in which scholarship on the GDR continues to be shaped by political concerns. But insofar as historians conceive of themselves as contributors to public debates, they are obliged to address the issue. In any event, the comparison is implicit in many accounts – indeed, Brentano herself makes a tacit comparison between the two regimes when she rejects the validity of comparing them, so it would clearly be better to be explicit (and thereby systematic and consistent) about it.

If we accept that it is a legitimate exercise despite the political concerns behind it, this still leaves open the question of how best to do it and which concepts should be employed. 'Totalitarianism' has clearly been the dominant concept, despite the fact that it severely narrows the focus to the dictatorial features of the GDR and results in a rather superficial comparison of the formal techniques and mechanisms of rule. The efforts at comparison on the basis of 'totalitarianism' have, for the most part, remained curiously abstract, the application of a concept without much empirical research. A notable exception has been the work of Günter Heydemann, Christoph Beckmann and a group of scholars undertaking research on 'Saxony under totalitarian authority' who have tried to link together the 'theory and practice' of comparing the two dictatorships.[84] They draw a useful distinction between 'integral' and 'sectoral' comparison, that is, comparing the two regimes *in toto* and comparing certain aspects of their rule or its manifestation in particular segments of society. The sectoral analyses they have carried out on policy towards the churches, exerting authority in the factories and at the communal level, allow for concrete comparison on the basis of empirical evidence.[85] As one might expect, they have revealed a number of

---

83 A point made by Günther Heydemann and Christopher Beckmann, 'Zwei Diktaturen in Deutschland. Möglichkeiten und Grenzen des historischen Diktaturenvergleichs', *DA* 30:1 (1997), pp. 12–40, here p. 14; also Bernd Faulenbach, 'Problem des Umgangs mit der Vergangenheit im vereinten Deutschland: Zur Gegenwartsbedeutung der jüngsten Geschichte', in Werner Weidenfeld (ed.), *Deutschland. Eine Nation – doppelte Geschichte* (Cologne, 1993), pp. 175–90, here p. 190.

84 So the subtitle of a collection of essays: Günther Heydemann and Eckhard Jesse (eds), *Diktaturvergleich als Herausforderung. Theorie und Praxis* (Berlin, 1998). The same approach is also followed in G. Heydemann and C. Beckmann, 'Zwei Diktaturen in Deutschland', and further explicated in G. Heydemann, 'Integraler und sektoraler Vergleich. Zur Methodologie der empirischen Diktaturforschung', in H. Timmermann (ed.), *Die DDR – Analysen eines aufgegebenen Staates*, pp. 841–8.

85 Cf. Thomas Schaarschmidt, 'Vom völkischen Mythos zum "sozialistischen Patriotismus" – Sächsische Regionalkultur im Dritten Reich und in der SBZ/DDR', in G. Heydemann and E. Jesse (eds), *Diktaturvergleich als Herausforderung*, pp. 235–58; Christopher Beckmann, 'Zweierlei Gleichschaltung. Die Durchsetzung des Machanspruchs von NSDAP und SED auf kommunaler Ebene', pp. 259–82; Georg

similarities and differences. All have indicated analogous strategies on the part of the Nazi and SED regimes to push through and establish their authority at the local level, with some similarities in terms of effects: pastors rebuffing attempts to create a single state-run youth organization; similar tendencies towards local 'wage bargaining' in the factories because of the lack of independent unions; and more generally, the inability of both regimes to push through their policies at the local level. Yet there were just as many differences, such as pastors' greater instinctive aversion towards communism than Nazism as well as the relative ease with which the Nazis could exert their influence within and through local *Heimat* groups. It is very difficult to squeeze these empirical findings – especially the fact that the attempt at total penetration of society failed in both cases – into a broader integral comparison of the two regimes at large, especially one based on totalitarianism theory. Although there were many similarities in terms of immediate aims, intentions and strategies of rule, the effects and the long-term goals of the regimes were markedly different. Thus the overall impression of the sectoral comparisons is that empirical '*Diktaturenvergleich*' actually places the concept of 'totalitarianism' in question more than affirms it.

The GDR and Third Reich were clearly similar in their suspension of the liberal state and the rule of law. They also showed unmistakable parallels in their efforts to mobilize the masses that set them apart from older forms of authoritarian rule. In addition, they fostered many of the same values in the populace: 'narrow participation in public life, the tendency to shun responsibility for the shadow side of politics, ducking one's head, conformity and a lack of civic courage'.[86] The parallels in their respective systems and techniques of authority were certainly striking; their form does say something about their content, and it would be wrong to dismiss these similarities as merely formal or secondary.[87]

Yet in the final analysis it seems that the differences between the regimes significantly outweigh the similarities in terms of their overall importance. Apart from their very different socio-economic bases, what divides the two

---

(*Contd*)

Wilhelm, 'Zweierlei Obrigkeit – Die Haltung der Leipziger Pfarrerschaft nach 1933 und 1945', pp. 283–302; Oliver Werner, 'Ein Betrieb in zwei Diktaturen: Die Bleichert Transportanlagen GmbH/ VEB VTA Leipzig im Dritten Reich und in der SBZ/DDR', pp. 303–320.

86 J. Kocka, 'Nationalsozialismus und SED-Diktatur im Vergleich', pp. 94–5.

87 For balanced and relatively detailed discussions, see Bernd Faulenbach, 'Die Verfolgungssysteme des Nationalsozialismus und des Stalinismus. Zur Frage ihrer Vergleichbarkeit', in A. Bauerkämper *et al.* (eds), *Doppelte Zeitgeschichte*, pp. 268–81; Clemens Vollnhals, 'Geheimpolizei und politische Justiz im Nationalsozialismus und im SED-Staat', in Klaus-Dietmar Henke (ed.), *Totalitarismus* (Dresden, 1999), pp. 39–59. For a comparative discussion of the repressive apparatus from the perspective of opposition, see Werner Bramke, 'Widerstand und Dissens. Gedanken über die Vergleichbarkeit von Widersetzlichkeit im Faschismus und im "realen Sozialismus"', in K. Jarausch and M. Middell (eds), *Nach dem Erdbeben*, pp. 219–43; Bernd Stöver, 'Leben in Deutschen Diktaturen. Historiographische und methodologische Aspekte der Erforschung von Widerstand und Opposition im Dritten Reich und in der DDR', in D. Pollack and D. Rink (eds), *Zwischen Verweigerung und Opposition*, pp. 30–53.

most starkly is the GDR's essentially humanistic goals – however unrealized and distorted these became under state socialism – and the unparalleled violence and bestiality of the Third Reich. This elemental disparity was not a product of circumstance or coincidence, but was based on the fundamentally different internal characteristics of the two regimes. The murderous, expansive dynamism of the Third Reich which culminated in unprecedented destruction in Europe could hardly be more different from the creeping sclerosis of state socialism, which disappeared from the stage of history with hardly a shot being fired. These violent and self-destructive energies were not a side-effect of Nazism, they were its very essence. This essential distinction renders any comparison between the Third Reich and the GDR a highly superficial one.[88] In evaluating this emotive issue, one must distinguish between the legitimacy and the utility of such comparisons. While it is, in my view, inappropriate to deny the validity of '*Diktaturenvergleich*' as a scholarly exercise, I would nonetheless contend that it has precious little to add to our understanding of either regime. That it is legitimate does not, in other words, necessarily mean that it is particularly useful. Though public and political debate demands that historians address the issue, the comparison of the GDR and Third Reich has already claimed more attention and resources than it deserves.

88  A point convincingly made by Ian Kershaw, 'Totalitarianism Revisited', p. 40.

# 8

# The GDR as contemporary history

Insofar as 'contemporary history' (*Zeitgeschichte*) is concerned quite explicitly with the present as well as the past, the history of the GDR has been the epitome of it. Many of the debates we have encountered in the preceding chapters have not been confined solely to the academic arena, but have overlapped with broader public controversies. From the rationale behind the questions we ask to the political implications of new research findings, public debate and academic controversy are always related. But as this book has sought to argue, there has always been a particularly close relationship between scholarly and political concerns in the case of the GDR.

Since unification, the stakes in the debate about the East German past have been remarkably high. During the first years after the GDR's collapse, before the completion of the academic restructuring of eastern Germany, arguments over how to evaluate the defunct regime often involved the very tangible distribution of jobs and resources. Although the end of this process has allowed for a somewhat more dispassionate exchange of views, the controversies are still intense since they continue to touch upon emotive issues – different memories of the GDR, different life experiences, personal biographies. Moreover, the debate is constantly stimulated by its implications for the political orientation and political culture of unified Germany. An important part of the consolidation of democracy in all post-communist societies is developing public trust in political leaders and institutions – not easy in societies where the previous regime had cultivated a culture of concealment and suppression – and finding a consensus on the fundamental political principles that the new system will espouse. All of this involves a complex renegotiation of society's values, which in the case of post-unification Germany has been further complicated by the concurrent attempt to marry together two very different societies. While this process of 'working through' the GDR's past (*Aufarbeitung*) and its implications for the future has been wide and varied, it is useful to conceive of it as taking place on three primary levels: the individual or moral level, the political level and the judicial level.[1] In this chapter we will discuss each of these in turn, focusing first on the debates about the GDR's political legacies before proceeding to address the controversies surrounding individuals' complicity with the regime. We will then consider the attempts to redress some of the injustices of the East German past through both the courts and the special parliamentary investigative commission, the *Enquete-Kommission*.


# What's left?

One of the primary questions since the dissolution of state socialism has been whether socialism and communism *per se*, as well as the parties that espouse them, have been irretrievably discredited by the repressive history of state socialism in Europe or whether there are noble aspects to salvage. Many of the answers offered so far have been singularly unhelpful. There has certainly been no shortage of triumphalist conservative proclamations that 'socialism is dead'. Equally, the exonerating idea that 'true socialism' has lost nothing of its credibility with the dissolution of 'Stalinist' communism is still cherished among die-hards in the East and the old Left in the West.[2] For Marxist successor parties and intellectuals in particular, it has been hard to come to terms with the collapse of state socialism. Although voices from within the SED had long criticized particular aspects of the regime, the final demise and disappearance of the GDR's socialist experiment nonetheless came as a shock. The question of 'what's left' from 40 years of socialism on German soil and the issue of what should be celebrated, preserved or built upon in the future has been wrestled with, in quite different ways, by all of the major political parties as well as within the scholarly community. It is here, probably more than with the other issues covered in this chapter, that we can see the broadest overlap between scholarly debate and immediate political interests.[3]

---

1  This categorization follows the suggestion of east German theologian and philosopher Richard Schröder, *Deutschland schwiering Vaterland. Für eine neue politische Kultur* (Freiburg, 1993), pp. 105f. See also, generally, Bernd Faulenbach *et al.* (eds), *Die Partei hatte immer recht – Aufarbeitung von Geschichte und Folgen der SED-Diktatur* (Essen, 1994).

2  Cf. the quite extraordinary contributions to Weißenseer Arbeitskreis, *Wider die Resignation der Linken. Stimmen gegen Antikommunismus, Konterrevolution und Annexion* (Cologne, 1994), esp. Kurt Gossweiler, 'Hatte der Sozialismus nach 1945 je eine Chance?', pp. 204–19, who argues that the main reason for the collapse of socialism was the insufficient attention paid to Marxist–Leninist theory, which served as a kind of compass for the successful navigation of state socialism. When this compass was thrown overboard, the socialist project was doomed to run aground eventually. From this viewpoint, as Gossweiler contends, 'Marxism–Leninism has not been disproven, but rather – albeit negatively – fully confirmed' (pp. 218–19).

3  How immediate these interests could be was demonstrated in late 1994 when the SPD faction in Mecklenburg-Vorpommern called upon the PDS to admit that the SED's founding involved coercion and to excuse itself for this and other acts of persecution against Social Democrats in the SBZ/DDR. The PDS responded that the SPD should excuse itself for its own past sins (voting for war credits in 1914, suppression of the Spartacist Uprising in 1919, the 'Bloody May' of 1929), which the SPD has, in fact, very painfully dealt

Although these questions have confronted all of the post-communist states in Europe, in each country the debate has taken on its own particular colouration. In Germany, with its uniquely problematic past, the GDR's much-vaunted 'anti-fascist' traditions have been a particular point of contention, and have certainly presented some of the most sensitive problems for the SED's successor party, the PDS, in its attempts to come to terms with its own past.

The GDR presented itself from beginning to end as a state based on 'anti-fascist' foundations and traditions. Lacking both open elections and clear 'national' borders, this was its single most important pillar of legitimacy, its central 'founding myth', its official 'state doctrine', or what some have even called its 'civil religion'.[4] In the SED's official mythology, the construction of a new social order in East Germany was the direct consequence of a reckoning with the Nazi past. The 'anti-fascist-democratic transformation' of the SBZ/GDR was understood as nothing less than the realization of the goals of the anti-fascist resistance during the war: society was to be 'cleansed' of Nazism root and branch, its societal foundations had to be 'liquidated'. Because of the communists' economistic understanding of the basis of fascism, policies such as the land reform, the confiscation of large-scale enterprises and the construction of a new social order more generally were all justified on anti-fascist grounds. This was constantly contrasted with the supposedly 'compromised' Federal Republic, which was accused of not only failing to root out fascism, but of positively perpetuating it in its socio-economic order.

The 'leading role' of the communists in East Germany was, from this perspective, a reflection of their leading role in resisting the Nazi regime. The communists lost far more than any other political group in their fight against fascism within Germany, just as the Soviet Union had lost far more than any other state fighting Hitler's armies abroad. Communist propaganda understandably made the most of this moral capital, and the fact that many communists had genuinely struggled against and suffered under the Nazi system motivated many people, especially young people, to help them build a new social order in Germany. The GDR's anti-fascist legacy was memorialized in a pantheon of heroic resistance fighters, in the names of streets and public squares, and at former concentration camps, some of

---

(*Contd*)

with over the past decades. Cf. 'SPD erwartet von der PDS eine Entschuldigung', *Süddeutsche Zeitung*, 28 Oct. 1994. The spat lingered for well over a year: W. Thierse, 'Eine schlimme Beschönigung'; L. Bisky, 'Wir reden vergeblich miteinander', both in *Berliner Zeitung*, 24–25 Feb. 1996, pp. 36–7. On the SED and PDS interpretations of the Weimar period, see H. A. Winkler, 'Kein Bruch mit Lenin: Die Weimarer Republik aus der Sicht von SED und PDS', in Rainer Eckert and Bernd Faulenbach (eds), *Halbherziger Revisionismus: Zum postkommunistischen Geschichtsbild* (Munich, 1996), pp. 11–23.

4   Cf. the lucid overview in B. Faulenbach, 'Die DDR als antifaschistischer Staat', in R. Eckert and B. Faulenbach (eds), *Halbherziger Revisionismus*, pp. 47–68, on which this section draws extensively. See also, generally, Antonia Grunenberg, *Antifaschismus – ein deutscher Mythos* (Reinbek, 1993). For an overview of the anti-fascist mythology and its centrality to East German political culture, see A. Nothnagle, *Building the East German Myth*.

which (Buchenwald, Sachsenhausen, Ravensbrück) were transformed into sites of pilgrimage.[5] There the communist inmates were frequently portrayed in superhuman, almost saintly form, displaying all of the virtues the SED wanted to propagate – discipline, sacrifice and loyalty. The message was unequivocal and ubiquitous: the enemies were the imperialist capitalist fascists, and the heroes were the fighters in the political resistance, above all the communists. This ceaseless rhetoric of GDR anti-fascism echoed to the bitter end. Even as late as 10 September 1989, the rallies for the 'International Memorial Day for the Victims of Fascist Terror' still took place under the motto: 'Forty Years of the GDR – in the struggle for socialism and peace, against fascism and war, we are fulfilling the anti-fascist legacy!'[6]

It is more than obvious that the SED instrumentalized the anti-fascist myth for its own purposes. Although this had long been recognized in the West, after 1989 the legitimatory and exculpatory functions of this myth were subjected to a new and withering attack. What the SED had long propagated as the legitimatory basis of its regime was soon denigrated as little more than a 'prescribed' or 'ritualized' anti-fascism.[7] As scholars stripped away the layers of varnish and distortion that had covered so many previously taboo areas of East German history, the anti-fascist myth soon appeared as a thin veneer of ideological piety that largely functioned to cover up communist oppression. It was, in this view, nothing other than a propaganda coup that prevented internal criticism, encouraged a selective view of history, created and sustained a culture of enemy-hatred, prevented any genuine confrontation with the Nazi past, and that belittled or obscured 'communist crimes' such as the party purges or the incarceration of alleged 'political enemies' in the Soviet 'special camps' after the war.[8] The central emphasis on the communist resistance meant that other forms of resistance – Christian, Social Democratic, conservative – were either completely obscured or, as with the plot to assassinate Hitler on 20 July 1944, greatly devalued. The 'Association for those persecuted by the Nazi regime' (VVN, *Vereinigung für die Verfolgten des Naziregimes*) made a legal distinction between resistance that was 'worthy of recognition' and that which was not, and indeed purged many of its members who were politically out of line before it was disbanded in 1952.[9] Moreover, the very fact that persecution by the

---

5  For an overview, see M. Fulbrook, *German National Identity after the Holocaust* (London, 1999), pp. 28–35.

6  See Olaf Groehler, 'Vom öffentlichen Umgang mit der Erfahrung des Nationalsozialsmus in der DDR und BRD', *Geschichtsrundbrief*, vol. 5 (1994), p. 24.

7  W. Schubarth *et al.*, 'Verordneter Antifaschismus und die Folgen. Das Dilemma antifaschistischer Erziehung am Ende der DDR', *APuZG* B9/91, pp. 3–16.

8  On the 'special camps', see Michael Klonovsky and Jan von Flocken, *Stalins Lager in Deutschland 1945–1950* (Berlin, 1991); Bodo Ritscher (ed.), *Die sowjetischen Speziallager in Deutschland 1945–1950. Eine Bibliographie* (Göttingen, 1996); Peter Reif-Spirek, *Speziallager in der SBZ* (Berlin, 1999).

9  O. Groehler, 'Integration und Ausgrenzung von NS-Opfern. Zur Anerkennungs- und Entschädigungsdebatte in der SBZ Deutschlands 1945 bis 1949', in J. Kocka (ed.), *Historische DDR-Forschung*, pp. 105–27, here p. 126.

Nazi system of terror was portrayed as persecution of political enemies meant that the racial background to Nazi crimes was largely obliterated, the murder of millions of Jews, 'asocials', Sinti and Roma barely touched upon.[10] Besides distorting history, anti-fascism has also been seen as a crucial element in the construction of a dichotomous worldview that encouraged the criminalization or exclusion of anyone who did not wholeheartedly support the party line. If the communists were the principal anti-fascists, anyone working against them from whatever angle was in effect promoting fascism. There are numerous tragic stories of genuine anti-fascists who ended up being persecuted by the communist authorities for their political beliefs.[11] This criminalization of dissent was extended to the East German populace at large. The uprising of 17 June was officially denigrated as a 'fascist putsch attempt'.[12] Anti-fascism also served to legitimize a range of repressive measures. Indeed, the Berlin Wall itself was pitifully justified as an 'anti-fascist protective wall' against Western revanchism.[13]

Insofar as anti-fascism was the fundamental legitimatory prop of the GDR, debunking it as nothing more than a cynical ploy to justify communist repression essentially amounts to denying the GDR any historical legitimacy or any chance of contributing a positive legacy to unified Germany. It is therefore hardly surprising that the response from the PDS has been to defend the anti-fascist legacy of the GDR and to claim for it a contemporary purpose and relevance. The 1993 party programme of the PDS was remarkably forthright in its defence of the 'anti-fascist-democratic transformation

---

10  On the sensitive issue of restitution payments, see Angelika Timm, *Jewish Claims against East Germany: Moral Obligations and Pragmatic Policy* (Budapest, 1998); also Jutta Illichmann, *Die DDR und die Juden. Die deutschlandpolitische Instrumentalisierung von Juden und Judentum durch die Partei- und Staatsführung der SBZ/DDR von 1945 bis 1990* (Frankfurt a. M., 1997). On the remaining Jewish communities in the GDR, see Ulrike Offenberg, *Seid vorsichtig gegen die Machthaber. Die jüdischen Gemeinden in der SBZ und der DDR 1945 bis 1990* (Berlin, 1998); Robin Ostow, *Jews in Contemporary East Germany* (Basingstoke, 1989).

11  Cf. generally K. W. Fricke, *Warten auf Gerechtigkeit. Kommunistische Säuberungen und Rehabilitierungen*; B. Bouvier, *Ausgeschaltet! Sozialdemokraten in der Sowjetischen Besatzungszone und in der DDR*. This logic also worked in reverse, namely that anyone willing to work for the GDR could potentially be considered a good 'anti-fascist' regardless of their past. Arno von Lenski, for instance, was an honourary judge for the Nazi *Volksgerichtshof* until 1942, and was involved in passing a number of death sentences. As commander of a tank division he was taken prisoner at Stalingrad in 1943, was released to the GDR in 1949, and helped develop the KVP's tank units from 1952 onwards, for which he eventually received the medal: 'Outstanding anti-fascist fighter, 1933–1945'. Cf. F. Werkentin, *Politische Strafjustiz in der Ära Ulbricht*, p. 195.

12  Ilko-Sascha Kowalczuk, '"Faschistischer Putsch" – "Konterrevolution" – "Arbeitererhebung": Der 17. Juni 1953 im Urteil von SED und PDS', in R. Eckart and B. Faulenbach (eds), *Halbherziger Revisionismus*, pp. 69–82.

13  This was clearly a low point in the use of the term 'anti-fascist' which has proven difficult to deal with afterwards. It has taken until 2 July 2001, in the run-up to the 40th anniversary commemorations of the erection of the Berlin Wall and in the midst of an election campaign, for the PDS executive committee to issue a declaration clearly condemning the 'inhumane border regime' and the 'deaths at the Wall' as the GDR's 'mark of Cain'. A motion that the PDS ask the victims of the Wall for forgiveness was voted down. The declaration is reprinted in *DA* 34:4 (2001), pp. 723–6. For the PDS position on the Wall prior to this declaration, see Manfred Rexin, 'Mauer-Schatten: Die PDS zum 13. August 1961', in R. Eckart and B. Faulenbach (eds), *Halbherziger Revisionismus*, pp. 83–92.

in eastern Germany and the subsequent efforts to build a new society', which stood in 'justified contrast to the preservation of capitalism in West Germany, which had been weakened by the unparalleled crimes of German fascism'.[14] The retention of the economistic interpretation of fascism and the defence of the GDR's social order on the basis of its anti-fascist qualities is particularly striking here.[15] Indeed, the leadership of the PDS has explicitly presented the party as the inheritors of this legacy, which did not exclude distancing itself from individual 'anti-fascists' such as Honecker. As Gregor Gysi asserted in 1990, there were two groups of anti-fascists: those who had considerable power in the GDR (among them the top party functionaries who had spent the Nazi period in the Soviet Union) and the vast majority who did not. It was this latter group that the PDS claimed to represent.[16]

As this suggests, many post-communists distinguish between what they see as the negative and positive sides of the anti-fascist tradition, or between the principles it embodies and its admittedly imperfect practice in the GDR. This is especially common among intellectual circles close to the PDS. The historian Günter Benser, for instance, has sharply criticized the instrumentalization of anti-fascism and the poor treatment of many anti-fascists by the communists, but nonetheless considers the particular means of dealing with fascism chosen by the GDR as legitimate, and indeed as more consistent than in the West, where the social structure changed relatively little (again revealing an economistic understanding of fascism).[17] Ludwig Elm and Manfred Weißbecker have similarly criticized the deformations of the anti-fascist myth, but nonetheless insist on a healthy core, at least in the beginning, that progressively degenerated over the years.[18]

Anti-fascism was, as these observers justifiedly point out, more than merely a functional tool of the communist regime. It is certainly not reducible to a legitimatory instrument for left-wing extremism and it is clearly more than a last refuge of an embattled and embittered Left.[19] Many of the sharpest criticisms of GDR anti-fascism tend to divorce it from its historical context and obscure the fact that anti-fascist sentiments were very

---

14  *Programm der Partei des demokratischen Sozialismus*, cited in B. Faulenbach, 'Die DDR als antifaschistischer Staat', p. 62.

15  For a more explicit defence of the Comintern definition of fascism, see K. Pätzold, 'Vom lautlosen Tausch der Begriffe. Der Faschismus und die "Komintern-Formel" – ein Widerruf ist nicht nötig, Defizite aber haben Folgen', *ND*, 22–23 July 1995.

16  Gregor Gysi, 'Referat auf der Klausurtagung des Parteivorstandes der PDS am 12./13. Mai 1990', *ND*, 16 May 1990; cited in B. Faulenbach, 'Die DDR als antifaschistischer Staat', pp. 60–1.

17  G. Benser, 'Möglichkeiten und Grenzen einer antifaschistisch-demokratischen Erneuerung in Deutschland nach dem Zweiten Weltkrieg', in *Ansichten zur Geschichte der DDR*, vol. 4, pp. 137ff.

18  L. Elm, *Nach Hitler. Nach Honecker. Zum Streit der Deutschen um die eigene Vergangenheit* (Berlin, 1991); M. Weißbecker, 'Gedanken zum Antifaschismus – Verlust in der Geschichte der DDR', *BzG* 33 (1991), pp. 194ff.

19  All too one-sided is Klaus Schroeder's argument that 'the crimes of the Nazi regime ... prompted many people in post-war Germany to follow the SED's anti-fascist slogans. Their idealism was to be disappointed. The SED leadership was concerned with the introduction of a totalitarian order, for which their anti-fascist-democratic rhetoric would merely supply the necessary legitimation.' K. Schroeder, *Der SED-Staat*, p. 82.

important to many East Germans, especially during the immediate post-war years.[20] But equally, many of the arguments mounted in defence of the anti-fascist legacy are informed by rather rosy views of these critical early years of the GDR's history.[21] Although anti-fascism may well have meant to many East Germans 'certain political and moral values; speaking out against intolerance and inhumanity…; social and solidaristic behaviour; opposition against cultural barbarity, nationalism and chauvinism…; the chance for common interest and joint action',[22] any sober look at its political role in the construction and maintenance of the regime cannot escape the conclusion that the communist leadership instrumentalized this idea in order to silence opposition and erect a dictatorship without consulting the populace. As the poor treatment of many anti-fascists after the war attests, anti-fascism was less an inspiration than a legitimation for the communist transformation of East Germany. Even the process of denazification – the eradication of fascist influences and the removal of compromised persons from positions of power – was geared primarily towards 'the erection of (communist) authority, changes in societal structure and the repression of oppositional political efforts', not punishing past crimes.[23] As Bernd Faulenbach has put it, 'for the creation of a socialist society the anti-fascist reasoning was not actually causal, but rather accidental'.[24]

Anti-fascism served as a fig-leaf that protected other legends from criticism as well: for instance, the legend of the alleged 'voluntary union' of the KPD and SPD in 1946, of the 'democratic start' that got perverted 'from outside' by the introduction of Stalinism, and of the supposedly ruthless reckoning with the Nazi past.[25] As far as the latter is concerned, it seems quite clear that the anti-fascist myth actually hindered a genuine reckoning with the past more than promoted it. As members of the 'better Germany',

---

20 For a reflective and revealing personal account, see Fritz Klein, 'Ein schlimmes gemeinsames Erbe kritisch und selbstkritisch auf beiden Seiten aufarbeiten', in J. Danyel (ed.), *Die geteilte Vergangenheit*, pp. 139–41. See also the balanced judgement in W. Mommsen, 'Der Ort der DDR in der deutschen Geschichte', p. 33.

21 For instance, K. Pätzold, 'Die Legende vom "verordneten Antifaschismus"', in *Ansichten zur Geschichte der DDR*, vol. 3, pp. 111–30.

22 H. Kühnrich, '"Verordnet" – und nichts weiter? Nachdenken über Antifaschismus in der DDR', *ZfG* 40 (1992), p. 820.

23 Damian van Melis, *Entnazifizierung in Mecklenburg-Vorpommern: Herrschaft und Verwaltung 1945–1948* (Munich, 1999), p. 330. Timothy Vogt, *Denazification in Soviet-Occupied Germany: Brandenburg, 1945–1948* (Cambridge, MA, 2000); Olaf Kappelt, *Die Entnazifizierung in der SBZ sowie die Rolle und der Einfluß ehemaliger Nationalsozialisten in der DDR als ein soziologisches Phänomen* (Hamburg, 1997), esp. pp. 564–9; Clemens Vollnhals (ed.), *Entnazifizierung. Politische Säuberung und Rehabilitierung in den vier Besatzungszonen 1945–1949* (Munich, 1991), pp. 218f; Christian Meyer-Seitz, *Die Verfolgung von NS-Straftaten in der Sowjetischen Besatzungszone* (Berlin, 1998); Ruth-Kristin Rößler (ed.), *Die Entnazifizierungspolitik der KPD/SED 1945–1948: Dokumente und Materialien* (Goldbach, 1994).

24 B. Faulenbach, 'Die DDR als antifaschistischer Staat', p. 52.

25 Cf. H. Hurwitz, *Die Stalinisierung der SED*; A. Malycha, *Partei von Stalins Gnaden?*; A. Malycha, *Die SED. Geschichte ihrer Stalinisierung 1946–1953* (Paderborn, 2000); H. Weber, 'Hauptfeind Sozialdemokratie: Zur Politik der deutschen Kommunisten gegenüber den Sozialdemokraten zwischen 1930 und 1950', in R. Eckart and B. Faulenbach (eds), *Halbherziger Revisionismus*, pp. 25–46.

socialist citizens were almost by definition considered 'anti-fascists'. This myth allowed anyone who showed a willingness to work for the good of socialism to disavow their own past and become good 'anti-fascists', even 'victors of history'.[26] The SED itself offered a home to thousands of former Nazis, many of whom served as functionaries at the local, regional and central levels, their careers benefiting from the internal party purges of the early 1950s.[27]

Given the political and moral implications of this debate, it is understandable that many east Germans find it difficult to concede how compromised the entire anti-fascist mythology really was. What the GDR's anti-fascist legacy needs is, to borrow a phrase from Lutz Niethammer, 'salvaging criticism'. That is, in order to maintain its credibility for the future one must be prepared to approach it and discuss it critically and without taboos. This has not proven easy amidst the media-hype surrounding many of these controversies since 1990. A willingness among post-communists to engage in sober reflection about the positive and negative sides of the anti-fascist coin has hardly been promoted by sensationalist attempts to denigrate the communist resistance as a quasi-mafia and to present the communist inmates at Buchenwald – the 'red *Kapos*' who managed much of the everyday running of the camp and faced difficult moral choices in doing so – as little different than the SS guards who ran it.[28] Indeed, such defamatory efforts to make the most of new archival discoveries in order to discredit the PDS and the communist past (and sell newspapers) have provoked anything but a balanced and reflective response.[29] As we will now see, this emotionalization of debates is all the more pronounced when what is at stake is not the collective history of the communist party or state, but the reputation of individual persons.

# Fellow travellers?

The efforts of individuals in and close to the PDS to salvage the worthwhile elements of the GDR's political legacy have by and large involved people

---

26  See esp. U. Herbert and O. Groehlert (eds), *Zweierlei Bewältigung*, pp. 21ff, 35ff.

27  Olaf Kappelt, *Die Entnazifizierung in der SBZ*, pp. 564–9.

28  Cf. the inflammatory article in *Bild Zeitung*, 'So halfen Kommunisten den Nazis beim Morden', 20 Feb. 1994. The controversy was sparked by Lutz Niethammer (ed.), *Der 'gesäuberte' Antifaschismus. Die SED und die roten Kapos von Buchenwald. Dokumente* (Berlin, 1994), which presents a differentiated reconstruction of the communists' role in Buchenwald. However, some of his findings were picked up and misused by the boulevard press and the extreme right in order to discredit the communist resistance. For a sound judgement of the ensuing controversy, see Jürgen Danyel, 'Wandlitz auf dem Ettersberg? Zur Debatte um die roten Kapos von Buchenwald', *ZfG* 43 (1995), pp. 159–66; also Manfred Overesch, *Buchenwald und die DDR, oder: Die Suche nach Selbstlegitimation* (Göttingen, 1995).

29  Cf. the highly polemical declaration of the former camp inmates association, 'Kalter Krieg gegen Buchenwald: Schamlosigkeiten als "Wissenschaft". Die Bild-Zeitung und ihr Prof. Niethammer', *ND*, 12 Dec. 1994.

who supported the regime, who fairly unambiguously worked for or at least 'within' it. The question of how far this support and complicity extended touches many more people, and has been a source of intense public debate in Germany since 1989. Who was a 'fellow traveller' of the regime and what should be done about them? How far should 'de-Stasification' draw upon the lessons of the rather half-hearted denazification after the Second World War? Who should be punished and who compensated for injustices committed against them? What are the risks of sweeping past injustices under the carpet, and what are the dangers of appearing to pursue them too vigorously, especially in comparison to the punishments previously meted out for the far more serious crimes of the Third Reich?

The difficult decisions about purging or at least reprimanding those seen to have been complicit in human rights abuses confronted all of the post-communist successor states throughout Eastern Europe. In Hungary it was decided that the country's interests were best served by a general amnesty; in Poland and Czechoslovakia similar arrangements were reached. But in some respects East Germany presented a unique case. Accession into the larger and much wealthier Federal Republic, which offered both pre-existing political and judicial institutions as well as a sizeable budget to resource them, has meant that the process of seeking 'corrective justice' has been particularly rapid and thorough in Germany.

It has also been particularly contentious. One of the main reasons for this was the decision to open the archives of the secret police in order to overcome public distrust and promote the process of healing. The primary instrument in this process has been the Federal Commissioner for the Records of the State Security Services of the Former German Democratic Republic – commonly shortened to the 'Gauck Authority' after Joachim Gauck, the east German pastor and civic activist who first headed it. Formally established in December 1991, the authority's task has been to regulate the use of *Stasi* files for the 'political, historical, and juridical reappraisal of *Stasi* activities'.[30] Much of its activity has been to screen personnel for prospective employers or public agencies, which can enquire whether a given name appeared in *Stasi* records as an informant. Private citizens are also guaranteed access to their own secret police files, unlike citizens in most post-communist countries.[31] The millions of requests have necessitated a huge expansion of the Authority's resources. By the latter 1990s it employed over 3,000 people and managed a budget of around a quarter billion DM.

---

30 *Brochure of the Federal Commissioner for the Records of the State Security Service of the GDR*, quoted in Jennifer Yoder, 'Truth without Reconciliation: An Appraisal of the Enquete Commission on the SED Dictatorship in Germany', *German Politics* 8 (1999), pp. 59–80, p. 65. The 'Gauck Authority' evolved out of the citizens' committees of 1989–90 that initially safeguarded the *Stasi* files after foiling attempts by officials to destroy incriminating evidence.
31 J. Yoder, 'Truth Without Reconciliation', p. 65.

The revelations from the *Stasi* files and the regulation of information by the Gauck Authority have been controversial, to say the least.[32] As a series of east German public figures were revealed as alleged 'unofficial collaborators', the suspicion grew that the *Stasi* itself had drawn up lists of names of people whom it wished to discredit. In some cases it was not clear that the supposed collaborator was aware that s/he had been enlisted. There have even been instances of apparent forgery of signatures by *Stasi* officers keen to claim new recruits.[33] Moreover, the records released by the Gauck Authority frequently did not specify the degree of collaboration. Whereas in some cases collaborators unambiguously placed others in danger of persecution through their denunciations, in other instances the supposed agent might merely have fed the *Stasi* useless information to keep it at bay, perhaps even in order to protect colleagues or acquaintances. The truthfulness of the *Stasi* material in general has been questioned since the authors of these documents were paid according to the length and content of their reports, just as the *Stasi* officers were promoted according to the number and rank of the informants they handled.[34] For its part, the Gauck Authority has continually insisted on the veracity of the material in its care. But even when the probity of the information is not in question, the piecemeal and potentially misleading manner in which the information was sometimes released has often been criticized. The way in which some figures have been 'outed' by the release of incriminating material to the media has made the Gauck Authority often seem 'more like a prosecutor than an archivist'.[35]

The stream of *Stasi* revelations has been a crucial backdrop behind the controversies about the moral complicity of individuals with the regime. It has certainly played a central role in debates about the role of East German writers and artists. The 'literature dispute' (*Literaturstreit*), as it has often been called, was sparked by the publication in 1990 of Christa Wolf's novel *Was bleibt?*, a kind of personal memoir of *Stasi* surveillance, which was savaged by a number of west German critics as an embarrassingly belated attempt to distance herself from the regime that she had criticized but never fundamentally rejected before its collapse.[36] In response, her defenders

---

32 See the criticisms (of greatly varying quality and persuasiveness) in Jochen Zimmer (ed.), *Das Gauck-Lesebuch. Eine Behörde abseits der Verfassung?* (Frankfurt a. M., 1998).

33 Stefan Heym, 'Die Wahrheit, und nichts als die Wahrheit', in ibid., p. 236.

34 Ibid., pp. 235–6.

35 Konrad Jarausch, 'The German Democratic Republic as History in Unified Germany: Reflections on Public Debate and Academic Controversy', *German Politics and Society*, 15:2 (1997), pp. 33–48, here p. 36.

36 Frank Schirrmacher, 'Dem Druck des härteren, strengeren Lebens standhalten', *FAZ*, 2 June 1990; Ulrich Greiner, 'Mangel an Feingefühl', *Die Zeit*, 1 June 1990. Had the book been published before autumn 1989 it would have been a sensation. The controversy quickly mushroomed into a wider debate about cowardice and courage among the GDR's intellectuals, and about the role of writers in society more generally. As Wolf Biermann ironically put it: 'It's about Christa Wolf, or more precisely: it's not about Christa Wolf.' For an overview and documentation, see Thomas Anz (ed.), *'Es geht nicht nur um Christa Wolf'. Der Literaturstreit im vereinten Deutschland* (Munich, 1991). For a balanced overview of the 'literature dispute' more generally, see Guenter Erbe, *Die verfemte Moderne. Die Auseinandersetzung mit dem 'Modernismus' in*

attacked the critics' self-righteousness by arguing that west Germans who never faced the kinds of pressures confronting their counterparts in the East could hardly sit in moralistic judgement.[37] Many intellectuals from both East and West saw the attacks on Wolf as little more than an attempt to discredit all GDR authors who were not incarcerated or deported to the West. The controversy reached a new pitch in autumn 1991 with the relevation that the well-known writer Sascha Anderson had worked for the *Stasi* from as early as 1975, and indeed even after his emigration in 1986 to West Berlin, where he continued to spy on other emigrant artists.[38] Since Anderson was one of the main figures of the Prenzlauer Berg arts 'scene', the entire milieu fell into discredit as having been thoroughly infiltrated and indeed partially created by the *Stasi*. Thereafter a string of authors was 'exposed' for leaving *Stasi* tracks: Hermann Kant (President of the League of Writers), Helga Novak, Gabriele Eckart. By far the most high-profile case was that of Christa Wolf, who in January 1993 admitted having worked as an 'unofficial collaborator' from 1959–62. To her credit, Wolf was an exceedingly poor informant. She only ever reported – very reservedly – on one person, and the *Stasi* found her useless enough to drop her when she moved from Halle to Kleinmachnow in 1962. As her defenders pointed out, these three years of relatively innocuous 'collaboration' paled in comparison to her 20-odd years of being an 'enemy' of the *Stasi*, which in the meantime had compiled a 41-volume file on her. But Wolf had known of her 'collaborator' file since April 1992, and had also rather unconvincingly claimed to have forgotten about these activities in the meantime. After the Wolf controversy, the revelations of *Stasi* collaboration within the GDR writers' guild continued, eventually to include even Monika Maron, a fierce critic of the regime.[39] But the disputes generated more heat than light. While the conservative dailies gleefully reported the moral failings of the GDR's intellectuals, left-leaning commentators accused them of attempting to undermine all leftist criticism of the Federal Republic.[40]

A similar *cause célèbre*, but one of more direct political consequence, was that of Manfred Stolpe, a former church administrator in Brandenburg who

---

(Contd)
> *Kulturpolitik, Literaturwissenschaft und Literatur der DDR* (Opladen, 1993). For a similarly balanced judgement of the visual arts in the GDR, see Ulrike Goeschen, *Vom sozialistischen Realismus zur Kunst im Sozialismus. Die Rezeption der Moderne in Kunst und Kunstwissenschaft der DDR* (Berlin, 2001).

37 For instance, Lew Kopelew, Günter Grass, and Walter Jens. Cf. Wolfgang Emmerich, *Kleine Literaturgeschichte der DDR* (Leipzig, 1997), pp. 462–76; also T. Anz (ed.), *'Es geht nicht nur um Christa Wolf'*.

38 In his acceptance speech for the Büchner Prize on 20 October 1991, Wolf Biermann surprised his listeners by attacking the 'untalented wind-bag Sascha *Arschloch*' as a 'Stasi-spy still coolly playing the role of poet and hoping that his file never surfaces'. The writer Jürgen Fuchs had come across Anderson's file and informed Biermann shortly before the speech. See H. J. Schädlich (ed.), *Aktenkundig* (Berlin, 1992).

39 In 1995 it emerged that Maron, who had emigrated to Hamburg in 1988, had compiled reports on others for around a year during the 1970s before becoming an object of extensive surveillance herself.

40 For a brief but informative commentary, see T. Anz, 'Christa Wolf', *Das Parlament* 12/19 Aug. 1994, p. 10.

became minister-president at the head of an SPD-led coalition in Brandenburg after the October 1990 elections. As with many other east Germans seeking public office, allegations of working for the *Stasi* soon surfaced after the Gauck Authority confirmed that his name appeared in *Stasi* records as an informant. When his file was released in January 1992, Stolpe admitted that, as a powerful administrator of the Brandenburg and East German Federation of Lutheran Churches, he had regular contact with the *Stasi*. He contended that he always negotiated on behalf of the church, helping to further its interests and to keep colleagues who were under suspicion from being arrested. But as it transpired, Stolpe also consciously and promptly reported to the *Stasi* on a remarkably wide range of issues, in the process doing considerable harm to other individuals as well as the opposition groups close to the church. Unlike most other churchmen who kept each other informed of their meetings with the authorities, thus precluding any oppor-tunity to recruit them as informants, Stolpe did not observe this practice.[41]

By any standard, Stolpe's actions were dubious. The question of how far he had swum with the tides, and what the consequences for his political career after 1989 should be, was the subject of a two-year parliamentary investigation in Brandenburg from 1992 to 1994.[42] The media fury accom-panying the investigation – whipped up by the pre-publication of excerpts from his memoirs and from selective revelations of incriminating material – soured the atmosphere and laid bare the competing political motivations behind the enquiry. The debate was characterized by bitter personal attacks, including one from Rainer Eppelmann, the radical East Berlin pastor who was appointed chairman of the *Enquete-Kommission*. But again, the debate was not solely about Stolpe. It raised the more general question of whether it was right to compromise with the state at all, and if so, to what extent. This ultimately touched on the fundamental question of the degree of evil and injustice represented by the regime. Whereas conservatives by and large condemned the GDR as an '*Unrechtsstaat*', or state of injustice, others accepted Stolpe's arguments that there were opportunities to improve the state from within despite its dictatorial character.[43]

As widely expected, the official report split along party lines, and con-cluded that Stolpe was to be exonerated. Although Stolpe was eventually forced to admit that he should have proceeded more openly about his meet-ings with the *Stasi*, he was not removed from his position. Neither the inves-tigation nor the media controversy surrounding it could show that Stolpe

41 Cf. Ralf Geort Ruth, *IM 'Sekretär'. Die 'Gauck-Recherche' und die Dokumente zum Fall 'Stolpe'* (Frankfurt a. M., 1992). See also the brief overviews in M. Fulbrook, *Anatomy*, pp. 119–23, C. Maier, *Dissolution*, pp. 317–19.

42 Cf. E. Neubert (ed.), *Abschlußbericht des Stolpe-Untersuchungsausschüsses des Landtags Brandenburg* (Cologne, 1994).

43 Cf. C. Maier, *Dissolution*, p. 319, drawn from M. Stolpe, 'Wer hierblieb, wollte das Land verbessern', in idem, *Den Menschen Hoffnung geben: Reden, Aufsätze, Interviews aus zwölf Jahren* (Berlin, 1991), pp. 249–55; also 'Spiegel-Gespräch mit Ministerpräsident Manfred Stolpe, *Der Spiegel*, 18 May 1992, pp. 32–6.

had crossed the boundary from working in the long-term interests of the church to working essentially for the regime. In the end Stolpe argued that condemning his actions effectively repudiated the Lutheran Church's general policy of maintaining good relations with the state in order to safeguard the church's essential interests. Yet whatever one thinks of Stolpe's actions before 1989 – whether they were self-serving or well intentioned – it is clear that his frequently evasive responses to the allegations against him set 'new standards in the suppression of an unpleasant past'.[44] To be fair, however, such stonewalling and selective forgetting has only been encouraged by the witchhunt atmosphere and obvious political motivations surrounding some of these controversies. The pattern of repressed memories and 'economical' revelations of past misdeeds that has characterized the responses of many political figures and intellectuals is not solely a reflection of individual moral shortcomings, but is also a product of the nature and tone of the allegations against them.

Personalized attacks and blanket denunciations have not been confined solely to the spotlight of cultural celebrity and the combative world of politics. They have also surfaced in the debates about 'fellow travellers' in the relatively low-profile academic arena. Nowhere has this been more pronounced than in the disputes surrounding GDR historiography and who should be allowed to write it – or more crudely, to whom it 'belongs' – after 1990. Despite increasingly positive assessments by many Western colleagues during the 1980s, the East German historical profession was almost completely dismantled after 1990 in a drawn-out process of what might be interpreted as academic renewal, colonization, or destruction, depending on one's point of view.[45] As the unified Germany took control over the east German university landscape, dozens of audit committees, composed largely but not solely of west German scholars, decided what should be salvaged and reorganized, and what should simply be '*abgewickelt*' ('wound up'). Dismissal of individuals could occur for a variety of reasons: the closure of an institute, *Stasi* collaboration, scholarly improprieties (like dismissing students with dissenting views), or inadequate qualifications or research potential. Party hacks and conspicuous time-servers presented fairly clear-cut cases, but it was more difficult with respect to the better scholars who accommodated themselves to the regime but maintained contacts with the West and sought to widen the parameters for scholarly debate

44  Clemens Vollnhals, 'Zugleich Helfer der Opfer und Helfer der Täter? Gegenwärtige und historische Sperren für die evangelische Kirche bei der Aufarbeitung ihrer DDR-Vergangenheit', in C. Vollnhals (ed.), *Die Kirchenpolitik von SED und Staatssicherheit. Eine Zwischenbilanz* (Berlin, 1996), pp. 434–46, here p. 438.
45  In English, see C. Maier, *Dissolution*, pp. 303–11; S. Berger, *The Search for Normality*, pp. 158–67; K. Pätzold, 'What New Start? The End of Historical Study in the GDR', *GH* 10 (1992), pp. 392–404; G. A. Ritter, 'The Reconstruction of History at the Humboldt University: A Reply', *GH* 11 (1993), pp. 339ff. Cf. also R. Eckart, W. Küttler and G. Seeber, *Krise-Umbruch-Neubeginn. Eine kritische und selbstkritische Dokumentation der DDR-Geschichtswissenschaft* (Stuttgart, 1992); A. Fischer, *Das Bildungssystem der DDR. Entwicklung, Umbruch und Neugestaltung seit 1989* (Darmstadt, 1992); J. Reich, 'Wissenschaft und Politik im deutschen Einigungsprozeß', *APuZG* B9/92, pp. 34f.

within the GDR. In this atmosphere of institutional 'downsizing' and dismissal of East German historiography as nothing more than a 'legitimatory science', there ensued a pitched battle over history positions which has come to be known as the 'East German *Historikerstreit*' (with obvious reference to the West German 'historians dispute' of the latter 1980s).[46]

The dispute started in early 1990 when members of the newly-formed Independent Historians Association (*Unabhängiger Historikerverband*, or UHV), composed of dissident historians who had fallen out with the East German academic establishment, demanded a sweeping purge of the profession, aimed in particular at researchers formerly affiliated with the official Institutes of History. This early conflict, primarily a confrontation between east German historians, ended with the dissolution of the GDR Academy of Sciences and the 'winding up' of the historical faculty at Berlin's Humboldt University in December 1990. The simmering controversy boiled over again in autumn 1993, when a handful of UHV members denounced the new 'Research Centre for Contemporary Historical Studies' (now the *Zentrum für zeithistorische Forschung* in Potsdam, whose purpose was to act as a forum for exchange between scholars of the former East and West) for offering positions to a number of east Germans who had supposedly collaborated with the regime but nonetheless been given positive evaluations by the review committees. In a series of rather shrill articles they castigated the 'entanglement' (*Verstrickung*) of these historians in the 'SED system', and questioned both the morality of using public monies to employ such compromised scholars as well as their capacity to produce intellectually creative work.[47] The criticism continued unabated despite Jürgen Kocka's defence of his colleagues and the decision of the Centre to employ them. At the same time, the UHV combined their attacks on the Research Centre with demands for the establishment of an alternative research institute more in tune with the concerns of the civic movements of 1989, an institute in which many of the critics would find a natural home.

From the very beginning it was clear that this conflict over research positions was also a battle over differing historical interpretations of the GDR. Indeed, the east German critics who fired the first salvos speak themselves of 'a historians dispute over positions, structures, finances and interpretive authority'.[48] In their view, the history of the GDR must be approached in terms of dictatorial repression; these themes must be at the forefront of research and interpretation. It also rapidly became apparent that the attack on the Research Centre in Potsdam also amounted to an attack on the key

---

46 A thorough documentation of the controversy can be found in R. Eckart *et al.* (eds), *Hure oder Muse? Klio in der DDR. Dokumente und Materialien des Unabhängigen Historikerverbandes* (Berlin, 1994).

47 See esp. A. Mitter and S. Wolle, 'Der Bielefelder Weg', *FAZ*, 10 Aug. 1993; also in R. Eckart *et al.* (eds), *Hure oder Muse?*, pp. 277–9

48 R. Eckart *et al.* (eds), *Wer schreibt die DDR-Geschichte? Ein Historikerstreit um Stellen, Strukturen, Finanzen und Deutungskompetenz* (Berlin, 1995). See also J. Danyel, 'Die Historiker und die Moral. Anmerkungen zur Debatte über die Autorenrechte an der DDR-Geschichte', *GG* 21 (1995), pp. 290–303.

representatives of the west German 'left-liberal' historical establishment who conceived and ran the institute. It was, therefore, not just a confrontation between former East German historians, but involved older West German disputes as well. This was plainly revealed in the title of the *FAZ* article that sparked the dispute. The *'Bielefelder Weg'* (or Bielefeld Path) was not only a direct reference to the academic affiliation of Jürgen Kocka, whom the article accused of forming self-serving networks among his east German friends, but also a none-too-subtle association of this left-leaning historical school with the so-called *'Bitterfelder Weg'*, a dogmatic literature campaign instigated by the SED in 1959.[49] In a strange marriage of political opinion, the main west German conservative daily thus joined a group of scholars close to the former East German civic movement in attacking the institute and portraying its aim as one of shoring up the threatened left-liberal historiographic hegemony after 1990.

The many shortcomings of pre-1989 GDR research presented a kind of Achilles heel for these attacks. Time and again it was lambasted for its 'system-immanent' and 'value-free' approach, which, in line with the allegedly dominant left-liberal academic *Zeitgeist* before 1989, had led it to abandon the goal of unified Germany and in effect to serve as an 'accomplice of the SED-dictatorship in the West'.[50] Claiming for themselves the moral highground, Klaus Schroeder and Jochen Staadt from the *Forschungsverbund SED-Staat* have viciously attacked what they call 'the "unprejudicial" GDR research' for its alleged 'conformity to the policy of reducing tensions', its 'limitless value liberties', its 'dreamland analyses', and for its overall *'Verharmlosung* of the SED state'.[51] Although one can hardly refute the basic argument that mainstream research on the GDR before 1989 tended to downplay the dictatorial nature of the system and over-estimate the capabilities of its social and economic system, the vehemence of such criticism has often been far out of proportion. Schroeder and Staadt's portrayal of the pre-1989 GDR-research establishment as essentially an organized cartel of mediocre SPD hacks rests on a series of false allegations and misrepresentations.[52] The same can be said of their attacks on 'left-liberal' scholars after 1989. Defamatory attempts to discredit Jürgen Kocka for alleged dealings with 'other social-democratic Grand Moguls in the historical guild' to dole out funding and chairs in his interests, or to malign Lutz Niethammer by misrepresenting his conciliatory requests for Honecker's permission to carry

---

49  A. Mitter and S. Wolle, 'Der Bielefelder Weg'. It should be pointed out, however, that the title of this article was not chosen by the authors themselves, but by the *FAZ* editors, who obviously were interested in using this article to perpetuate a much older historiographic feud.

50  Thus the misleadingly inflammatory subtitle of the book by Jens Hacker, *Deutsche Irrtümer. Schönfärber und Helfershelfer der SED-Diktatur im Westen.*

51  K. Schroeder and J. Staadt, 'Der diskrete Charme des Status-quo', pp. 312, 323, 328, 342.

52  For a largely persuasive counter-critique, albeit without much discussion of the real shortcomings to which Schroeder and Staadt justifiedly draw attention, cf. Gert-Joachim Glaeßner, 'Das Ende des Kommunismus und die Sozialwissenschaften. Anmerkungen zum Totalitarismusproblem', *DA* 28:9 (1995), pp. 920–36.

out interviews in the GDR during the latter 1980s, simply has no place in scholarly debate.[53] A better understanding of the GDR is certainly not fur- thered by creating a climate in which, as Christoph Kleßmann has put it, anyone who had not been 'governed by the preamble of the Basic Law, which apparently, like the ten commandments, came direct from heaven, is given a hammering and denied the legitimacy of his research method- ology'.[54] Moreover, the complaints of Schroeder and Staadt about 'social- democratic attitude inspectors (*Gesinnungsprüfer*), now in the guise of "historical GDR-research", who presume to decide what counts as serious scholarship and what does not'[55] ring hollow in view of their own pontifica- tions – reminiscent of the worst Marxist–Leninist traditions – about what the correct 'line' on GDR history must be. It seems difficult to escape the ironic conclusion that these critics have been doing exactly what they have accused others of doing: being led by current political breezes.

This is, of course, a perennial problem for historians, and is by no means unique to writing on East Germany or other dictatorial regimes. Jürgen Danyel is undoubtedly right to argue that these debates are not the sole con- cern of east German scholars. One cannot approach these disputes as a com- pletely detached outsider, 'as if issues about conformity and resistance, about compromises and different life-strategies, about the tension between political engagement and scholarly ethics were not of this world and as if their transference to the West represented an imposition'.[56] Clearly some retrospective self-criticism has been necessary, and many – though not all – scholars have openly admitted the shortcomings of their previous work. But it is worth pointing out that the bulk of research on the GDR before 1989 was quality scholarship. As Hermann Weber has commented: 'In difficult circumstances, this subject has made a great contribution to scholarship, and – all due self-criticism apart – its representatives have no reason to appear in penitential robes now.'[57] If there is any lesson to be learned from the shortcomings of pre-1989 research, then surely it is that the last thing to

---

53  These slurs appear to have been prompted by Kocka's accusation that they published archival finds 'with political intentions'. J. Kocka, 'Von der Verantwortung der Zeithistoriker. Das Interesse an der Geschichte der DDR ist – auch – Munition in der Tagespolitik', *Frankfurter Rundschau*, 3 May 1994, p. 10. See also Hermann Weber, 'Was beweisen die Akten? Anmerkungen zu Veröffentlichungen von Archivalien aus der DDR', *Internationale wissenschaftliche Korrespondenz zur Geschichte der deutschen Arbeiterbewegung* 2 (1997), pp. 232–43. Weber's measured criticism of the personalized, vehement and polemical tone of the debate was met not with sensible counter-arguments, but defamatory attacks. See K. Schroeder, 'Zu Hermann Webers polemischer Aktenkunde. Replik auf Hermann Weber: Was beweisen die Akten?', *Internationale wissenschaftliche Korrespondenz zur Geschichte der deutschen Arbeiterbewegung* 4 (1997), pp. 523–5.

54  From J. Kocka and M. Sabrow (eds), *Die DDR als Geschichte*, p. 225, as translated in S. Berger, *The Search for Normality*, p. 167.

55  K. Schroeder and J. Staadt, 'Der diskrete Charme des Status-quo', p. 351.

56  J. Danyel, 'Die Historiker und die Moral', p. 301.

57  H. Weber, 'Das Büßergewand bleibt im Schrank', *FAZ*, 10 Sept. 1994, p. 30, as translated in S. Berger, *The Search for Normality*, p. 167. For a similar defence of pre-1989 GDR research and its results, see also Gisela Helwig (ed.), *Rückblicke auf die DDR* (Cologne, 1995).

benefit historical research – unavoidably conditioned as it is by current political concerns – is for it to be straitjacketed by a moralizing political orthodoxy.

## 'Transitional justice'

The desire to 'right the wrongs' of the GDR past has not just involved personnel purges, journalistic enquiries and moral debates. There have been real trials as well, ranging from cases of doping, electoral fraud and economic criminality to the policy of shooting illegal border crossers.[58] Since 1990 the government of unified Germany has spent considerable time, money and effort on a wide-ranging programme of transitional justice whose purpose, its supporters have continually argued, is not mere retribution. If the legacies of the dictatorial past are swept under the rug, how can a democratic political culture develop? How can a society generate trust, consensus and unity behind the new political institutions if the bases of the pervasive culture of distrust under the old regime – authoritarian leadership, secret police, misinformation and human rights violations – are not explicitly addressed?

The rationale for Germany's 'official' reckoning with the GDR past has been to demonstrate a clean break with the SED regime, which it is hoped will help generate public trust in the rule of law and help heal the social divisions that could hinder the consolidation of democracy. The risk of this strategy is that it might have just the opposite effect by re-opening older wounds or, more seriously, undermining trust in the rule of law by appearing to dispense a 'victor's justice', twisting the law to fit political ends in a way reminiscent of the old communist regime.[59] Could the Federal German authorities really criminalize the policies of a state to which it had granted official recognition? Could actions that accorded with the policies of the GDR be retroactively declared crimes by another judicial system? Even if one attempted to convict former GDR leaders on the basis of East German law, was it valid for West German judges to interpret these laws in ways that were never intended and certainly never practised in the GDR, in effect judging East German realities by West German norms?

On all of these issues, the early high-profile cases were not particularly encouraging. The trial of Erich Honecker was perhaps the most anti-climactic

---

58 For an overview, see Volkmar Schöneburg, 'Strafrecht und Vergangenheit. Eine Zwischenbilanz', *Berliner Debatte Initial* 9 (1998) 2/3, pp. 79–88.

59 For probing analyses of this balancing act, see Anne Sa'adah, *Germany's Second Chance: Trust, Justice and Democratization* (Cambridge, MA, 1998); A. James McAdams, *Judging the Past in Unified Germany* (Cambridge, 2001); also J. Yoder, 'Truth Without Reconciliation', on which this section draws extensively.

of all.[60] As early as December 1989, shortly after the East German prosecuting attorney's office launched an investigation against him for high treason, doctors declared the former SED leader unfit for detention or questioning. After undergoing an operation for a tumour in January 1990, Honecker convalesced for part of the year in a Red Army hospital before moving on to Moscow. An awkward and largely unwanted guest in Russia, Honecker took refuge in the Chilean embassy before being finally handed over to German authorities in July 1992. At this stage doctors declared him capable of undergoing hearings of limited frequency and duration. Despite the widespread impression that this was a representative trial for the old regime, in the event it hardly touched on the burning questions of what Honecker could and could not do according to East German and international law, and where the limits of state authority should lie. Rather, it quickly became bogged down in procedural issues concerning what kind of a conviction could justifiedly be pursued against the ageing defendant. Honecker spoke meaningfully only once. Reading from a prepared statement, he stubbornly stuck to SED dogma to the bitter end, placing himself in a long line of persecuted communists and accusing the Berlin court of attempting to discredit socialism through misuse of the judicial system. He did not use the opportunity to admit any political mistakes whatsoever. Soon thereafter the whole trial was called off because of his poor health.[61]

The trial of *Stasi* chief Erich Mielke over 1992–93 also skirted the crucial issues concerning the relationship between state authority and human rights. This was, to be sure, hardly a high point in the judicial reckoning with the East German regime since Mielke was not put on trial for his actions as head of the *Stasi*, but for the murder of two policemen in 1931. Many people were understandably cynical about the motivations behind the pursuit of this crime. It was apparent that the Federal authorities were concerned that his organizational work alone would not be punishable, and that it would in any event carry a far lighter sentence than the charge of murder. By any standard this was an odd trial. The most obvious criticism was that the 60-year-old case came under Germany's 20-year statute of limitations. However, the courts decided that the limitation period did not count between May and November 1945 (during which all Berlin courts were closed by the Allies) or, more importantly, between February 1947 (when a military commander in the Soviet sector of Berlin demanded the file, never

---

60  See Uwe Wesel, *Ein Staat vor Gericht: Der Honecker-Prozeß* (Eichborn, 1994); Christoph Schaefgen, 'Der Honecker-Prozeß', in Jürgen Weber and Michael Piazolo (eds), *Eine Diktatur vor Gericht. Aufarbeitung von SED-Unrecht durch die Justiz* (Munich, 1995), pp. 89–100.

61  Reactions to the trial were mixed. Whereas some saw it as confirmation that political crimes cannot be effectively tried by normal judicial procedures (for instance, B. Rüthers, *Das Ungerechte an der Gerechtigkeit: Defizite eines Begriffs* (Zurich, 1993), esp. p. 99), others contended that the procedures were never given a chance to work since the trial was stopped before the presentation of evidence. Defenders of the trial generally argued that it sent an important message that bigwigs were not necessarily immune, and that the anonymous system alone was not responsible for crimes, but also the people who committed them.

to return it to the German authorities) and February 1990, when the file was miraculously found in Mielke's safe at *Stasi* headquarters in the Normannenstraße(!). Because the file had been inappropriately withheld from the judicial system, the limitation statutes were interrupted for this entire period, which left the courts several more years to seek a conviction. Like Honecker, Mielke also chose to forgo the opportunity for self-reflection. In spite of overwhelming evidence against him, his only words to the court were to protest his innocence and to discredit the prosecution for using evidence gathered under the Nazis (which, to be fair, some of it was). The trial ended with a conviction and six-year sentence, whereafter a series of other accusations (manslaughter at the border, kidnapping, unlawful imprisonment) were submitted to Berlin's district court.[62]

Probably the most dubious trial of all was that of Markus Wolf, chief of foreign espionage for the *Stasi* and a kind of legendary figure in the intelligence community, who was sentenced to six years' imprisonment in September 1993. To many Germans in both East and West, this seemed little more than a vindictive response to his astounding successes in recruiting spies against the Federal Republic. In 1995 the Federal Constitutional Court ruled 5 to 3 that East German spies could not be found guilty of treason against West Germany, since these acts accorded with the laws of what was, at the time, their country. Although this decision meant the reversal of Wolf's six-year sentence, the amnesty did not necessarily apply to all of the spies under his command, in particular West Germans whom he had recruited. As critics at the time remarked, many former *Stasi* operatives – whether passing on highly sensitive or fairly innocuous information, whether acting for money, love or political convictions – were, unlike the mastermind behind it all, subject to prosecution. This decision raised the vexed question of how far amnesty for former GDR leaders acting under East German laws should extend, and also of the relative accountability of those making the decisions and those carrying them out.

Both of these questions played a pivotal role in the decisive legal trials arising from the shootings at the inner German border.[63] Around two hundred East Germans had been killed trying to reach the West since 1961, the last death occurring in Berlin in February 1989. Illegal border crossing had been outlawed since the closure of the demarcation line between the GDR and FRG in 1952 and subject to stiffer penalties after the 'Passport Law' of 1957. Border guards were told to fire on would-be escapists since 1958; NVA troops, who assumed control of the borders shortly after the construction of the Berlin Wall in 1961, were likewise ordered to shoot. Responsibility for the border controls ultimately lay with the National Defence Council

---

62 Peter Jochen Winters, 'Der Mielke-Prozeß', in J. Weber and M. Piazolo (eds), *Eine Diktatur vor Gericht*, pp. 101–13; idem, 'Erich Mielke – der falsche Prozeß?', *DA* 26:12 (1993), pp. 1347f.

63 Hans-Jürgen Grasemann, '"Grenzverletzer sind zu vernichten!" Tötungsdelikte an der innerdeutschen Grenze', in J. Weber and M. Piazolo (eds), *Eine Diktatur vor Gericht*, pp. 67–87.

(*Nationale Verteidigungsrat*), chaired by the general secretary of the party (Ulbricht or Honecker) and composed largely of *Politbüro* members and army generals, which periodically reviewed and upgraded them. The East German parliament passed a new Border Law in March 1982 that formally authorized firing on fugitives in order to stop illegal border crossing. Were these shootings in themselves punishable crimes? Was the criminalization of efforts to leave the country itself a prosecutable human rights violation? If so, who should be held responsible?

The first trials involved the guards who carried out the shootings, not their superiors who ordered them. On 20 January 1992 a Berlin court convicted two defendants for shooting and killing Chris Gueffroy on 6 February 1989, issuing a three-and-a-half-year prison sentence to the guard who fired the lethal shots. Turning to previous rulings on Nazi crimes, the judges employed Gustav Radbruch's 1946 formula that written law must prevail *unless* it is considered to be 'intolerably' unjust – that is, in effect placing 'justice' above 'law' in cases where the law does not even strive for justice.[64] In this case, the judges ruled that the disproportionality between the offence of illegal border crossing and the sanction of shooting was indeed 'intolerable', thereby nullifying the legality of the shots. One month later the Berlin court convicted two guards for shooting and killing Michael Schmidt in December 1984 after he had disregarded their commands to cease traversing no-man's-land. The guards had fired over 50 shots and left Schmidt lying injured for two hours; he died later in hospital. The initial conviction was for employing what, even according to GDR law, was clearly more than minimal force, and for unnecessarily endangering his life by shooting. But the Federal Constitutional Court ruled on appeal that the conviction should be upheld on different grounds, namely that the intolerable injustice of the shooting warranted the application of Radbruch's formula.[65]

These rulings garnered widespread criticism. The prosecutors' focus on the trigger-men dismayed many east Germans who felt that the 'small fry' were being punished for past deeds while their superiors went free, some even testifying at the trials and receiving a day's pay for their time. Equally disappointing was the fact that the trials shed little light on the nature of complicity and authority under communist rule. The guards were punished for using excessive force or for contravening GDR norms – aiming at the torso instead of the legs, leaving the injured to bleed to death. These rulings stopped well short of examining whether the policy of securing the border by lethal force was itself criminal.[66]

This issue was central to the next round of trials, which shifted to second-tier government officials. The challenge lay in connecting the lethal shots by

64 Cf. Jörg Arnold, 'Gustav Radbruch und die "Mauerschützenfälle": Ein Kontinuitätsproblem', in J. Arnold (ed.), *Strafrechtliche Auseinandersetzung mit Systemvergangenheit am Beispiel der DDR* (Baden-Baden, 2000), pp. 147–73.

65 See C. Maier, *Dissolution*, pp. 320–2.

66 Cf. C. Maier, *Dissolution*, p. 322; J. Yoder, 'Truth Without Reconciliation', pp. 67–8.

the border guards with the actions of their superiors, in particular with what became known as 'Order 101', the shoot-to-kill policy. In 1993, three prominent figures – former defence minister Heinz Keßler, former Army chief of staff Fritz Streletz, and former member of the National Defence Council Hans Albrecht – were convicted on charges of manslaughter for their roles in the lethal border regime and were sentenced to between five and seven years. In August 1995 the focus shifted to the army with the so-called 'generals' trial', which eventually led to the conviction of six generals as accessories to manslaughter in implementing 'Order 101'. Although the accused generals strenuously contended that the infamous directive 'border violators are to be destroyed' was not tantamount to a 'shoot to kill' policy, the context of the border regime and the incentive structures for soldiers – when in doubt, shoot – unambiguously show that such a policy did exist in practice, and was implemented from on high.[67] The question of how high was not unimportant to these trials, for the generals in particular sought to exonerate themselves by passing the blame up the chain of command, claiming that they merely carried out the directives of the *Politbüro*, which ultimately took its orders from Moscow.[68]

In 1996 these claims were put to the test as the *Politbüro* itself finally came under judicial scrutiny.[69] Six of its members – Kurt Hager, Erich Mückenberger, Egon Krenz, Horst Dohlus, Günter Kleiber and Günther Schabowski – were charged with 66 cases of manslaughter and attempted manslaughter for the killings at the border over the period from 1962 to 1989. The prosecution's rationale was that the *Politbüro* was the sovereign body within the GDR, and that it made all fundamental decisions concerning this issue as all others. Predictably, this basic postulate was disputed from the outset. In his opening statement, Mückenberger insisted that Moscow was to blame and that the *Politbüro* was merely doing the Soviet Union's bidding. Krenz similarly blamed the border regime on the broader East–West confrontation, which the *Politbüro* could do nothing about. After echoing Krenz's objection, Hager also dismissed the charges as a political act, claiming the court had no right to try them. Dohlus, for his part, still pathetically clung to the notion that the border regime was not an injustice, but rather protected GDR citizens. Of the six, Schabowski was the only one to acknowledge the competence of the court to deal with this issue or to admit personal blame and responsibility, albeit in a moral, not legal sense. Although the cases against Hager, Mückenberger and Dohlus soon ceased for health reasons (Dohlus was the last of the three to die, in 1997),

---

67 Cf. Ingolf Bossenz, 'Der Schießbefehl war kein Phantom. Licence to kill – für Frieden und Sozialismus. Im Zweifelsfall war für den DDR-Grenzer ein toter Flüchtling besser als eine geglückte Flucht', *DA* 26:6 (1993), pp. 736f; also Hans-Jürgen Grasemann, '"Grenzverletzer sind zu vernichten!"'.
68 Cf. P. J. Winters, 'Wie souverän war die DDR?', *DA* 2/1996, pp. 170–2.
69 For a useful compilation of articles on the trial, see Dietmar Jochum (ed.), *'Das Politbüro auf der Anklagebank'. Eine Dokumentation mit 8 Interviews und Nachworten* (Berlin, 1996).

the other three were convicted and sentenced in summer 1997, Krenz to six-and-a-half years, Kleiber and Schabowski to three years each. In its ruling, the Berlin court explained that, despite the Soviet Union's powerful influence, the *Politbüro* was still responsible for the specific way in which the border was secured, and that it in any event condoned the lost lives at the border, which was in contravention of international human rights accords to which the GDR was a signatory.[70]

This ruling echoed an earlier 1996 decision by the Federal Constitutional Court that, with hindsight, can be seen as a watershed in the trial of the GDR leadership. By upholding the Berlin court's 1993 ruling against Heinz Keßler, Fritz Streletz and Hans Albrecht, the court effectively denied East German leaders the possibility of hiding behind GDR laws for their actions relating to the lethal border controls. The decision was also important in at least two other respects. First, it unambiguously affirmed that the regime violated basic human rights in order to stay in power. And, second, it made individuals accountable for these violations – whether in the halls of power or in the watch-towers – on the basis of international codes of human rights and not merely West German law, thus weakening (though for some observers not entirely negating) the impression of a spectacle of 'victor's justice'. Finally, a 1999 Constitutional Court ruling similarly upheld the Berlin court's 1997 decision against the *Politbüro* members with the same reasoning.[71] The essence of this verdict was characterized by the *Tagesspiegel* in strikingly plain language: '[the *Politbüro* members] are being punished for the simple reason that no politician has the right to kill citizens. And indeed not a single one. ... The GDR leadership did not want the GDR to "bleed to death" (Schabowski). Therefore they let blood flow themselves.'[72]

# Truth and reconciliation?

In many ways the 1999 decision by the Federal Constitutional Court marked the climax of the judicial reckoning with the old regime. By the end of 1999, the other *Politbüro* members were either dead (ten), unable to stand trial (five), or accused on other charges (namely, Hans-Joachim Böhme and Siegfried Lorenz, who were acquitted in July 2000). But the nature of the judicial procedures, geared as they necessarily were towards establishing individual culpability against the background of collective regime structures and practices, also meant that it was individual representatives of the regime rather than the regime as such that was on trial. Was there any way to have

---

70 P. J. Winters, 'Das Urteil gegen Krenz und andere', *DA* 5/1997, pp. 693–6.
71 Roman Grafe, '"Die Politbüro-Beschlüsse waren Bedingungen der tödlichen Schüsse". Der Prozess gegen sechs Mitglieder des SED-Politbüros', *DA* 33:1 (2000), pp. 19–25.
72 Hans Toeppen, *Der Tagesspiegel*, 9 Nov. 1999.

some kind of reckoning with the collective abuses of the system *per se*, a kind of middle path between the extremes of blanket retribution, which would not be possible under the rule of law in any event, and general amnesty? In addition to political, individual and judicial *Aufarbeitung*, could there also be a kind of officially sanctioned 'historical' *Aufarbeitung* that, without the ability to impose punishment, might focus instead on the political and bureaucratic structures themselves which allowed such individual acts in the first place?

The concept of a kind of 'truth commission' allowing an open confrontation with the past was broadly advocated by east German civic activists as a means of overcoming disillusion and suspicion and thereby contributing to the political health of unified Germany more generally. Although a number of suggestions were tabled about the precise nature of such a tribunal, it soon became clear that a cross-party parliamentary committee was the most widely preferred alternative. Not only did it promise to avoid the appearance of a self-selected group of moralists passing judgement on others, it would also minimize the danger of an emotionalization or political instrumentalization of the debate potentially arising from a people's tribunal-type of commission. In early 1992 each of the five main political parties, including the PDS, approved the concept. In May the *Bundestag* agreed the committee's composition (16 members of parliament and 11 outside experts) and terms of reference, thus establishing the 'Investigatory Commission on the Appraisal of the History and Consequences of the SED Dictatorship in Germany', more conveniently known as the *Enquete-Kommission*.

As numerous observers have commented, the purpose of the commission was explicitly didactic, very much in the Federal Republic's tradition of 'political education'.[73] Its primary aim was to uncover the inner workings of the SED regime in order to offer victims some sense of historical justice, to promote the 'inner unity' of Germany and to cement its democratic consensus by demonstrating the unjust nature of the defunct state – its power structure, the role of ideology, the justice and police institutions (including of course the *Stasi*), as well as the possibility and types of dissent and opposition.[74] To its credit, the commission was intended to be a nonpartisan evaluation body and was in fact organized on cross-party lines. But the testimony at hearings often amounted to 'contending narratives that had been organized along party lines',[75] and by 1994 this nonpartisan spirit was

73 A. Sa'adah, *Germany's Second Chance*, p. 185; C. Maier, *Dissolution*, p. 326.
74 For a brief overview in English, see H. Weber, 'Rewriting the History of the German Democratic Republic: The Work of the Commission of Inquiry', in Reinhard Alter and Peter Monteath (eds), *Rewriting the German Past: History and Identity in the New Germany* (New York, 1997), pp. 197–221; also J. Yoder, 'Truth Without Reconciliation'.
75 C. Maier, *Dissolution*, p. 326. The CDU's '*rote Socken*' campaign, which misleadingly suggested a socialist alliance between the SPD and PDS, triggered a public mud-slinging match between the CDU and SPD about which party in the West had done the most to support the 'Stasi regime' before 1989. In the meantime, the PDS 'Historical Commission' had itself set about to review the GDR's history, eventually publishing its conclusions in a multi-volume series entitled '*Ansichten zur Geschichte der DDR*' as an alternative report to that of the *Enquete-Kommission*.

clearly evaporating in the heat of the imminent election. Moreover, although the commission went out of its way to include east German members of parliament, most of these, including the chairman of the commission Rainer Eppelmann, were from the dissident milieu and were particularly concerned with civic rights and the repressive machinery of the SED regime. The east Germans on the commission thus represented a small subculture hardly representative of the broader populace in the new *Bundesländer*, and moreover tended to be strongly critical of those who had compromised with the state (as Eppelmann himself had made abundantly clear in his earlier attacks on Manfred Stolpe).

This touches on arguably the greatest weakness of the commission: that it stood little chance of success as a tool for didactic public history because it failed to engage ordinary east Germans.[76] Its audience was not the wider public but the Federal parliament, which heard expert academic reports instead of personal accounts by victims and perpetrators. Although the hearings were open to the public and were held all across eastern Germany, they resembled a professional conference more than a people's tribunal. The presentations were pitched at an academic or journalistic audience instead of a layperson. Nowhere was this more clearly expressed than in the official findings of the two-and-a-half-year investigation, which sprawl across 18 volumes and over 1500 pages. Few citizens – indeed, few academics – could find the time to read the volumes, which in the end contained no surprises and left a sense of dissatisfaction. Many of these criticisms could equally be levelled at the second *Enquete-Kommission* on 'Overcoming the Consequences of the SED-Dictatorship in the Process of German Unity' established in May 1995 and completed in 1998. Although it tried to address the issues of experience and everyday life omitted from the agenda of the first commission, it too placed no emphasis on public involvement in the process of 'overcoming the past'. Moreover, the second commission was plagued to an even greater degree by party-political wrangling over who was 'fit' to sit on the commission in the light of their past, and indeed who was in a position to make such judgements in the first place.[77]

After attending the final meeting of the first *Enquete-Kommission* in May 1994, the dissident writer Jürgen Fuchs made some interesting remarks on his impressions:

> As I heard the many intelligent thoughts that have already been discussed at length in the academic world and which will certainly continue with progressive, critical, inquisitive, provocative and explanatory new diploma theses, dissertations, *Habilitationen* and momentous publications in prestigious journals and publishing houses, I suddenly realized that we are lost. ... Naturally, every discipline

---

76 See esp. J. Yoder, 'Truth without Reconciliation', pp. 71–5, on which this discussion is based; also A. Sa'adah, *Germany's Second Chance*, pp. 184–6.

77 In 1998, Hartmut Koschyk, one of the CDU members of the commission, publicly argued that PDS member Rolf Kutzmutz was not fit to sit on the commission because it was revealed that he had been an 'unofficial collaborator' of the *Stasi*. J. Yoder, 'Truth Without Reconciliation', p. 74.

has its own vocabulary. I can respect this; it is not possible otherwise. Perhaps it is in any event unavoidable that historians have the last word. But we are still here, we contemporaries. A bit of patience must still be summoned before the last dissection and classification, before the final evaluation and ultimate deprivation of power (*Entmachten*).[78]

This feeling that east Germans are 'lost' from the picture, that their views have been overlooked or deemed unimportant for interpreting the East German past has been widespread in the new *Bundesländer* since the early 1990s. Against the backdrop of the *Enquete-Kommission*'s work, the feeling of being somewhat robbed of one's own identity, the sense that the west Germans 'have even colonized our memory', are regrettably understandable.

This failure to make sufficient room for the stories and perspectives of ordinary east Germans in the GDR's history is by no means confined to the work of the parliamentary commissions. As we have seen in the preceding chapters, it characterizes the distinctly politics- and regime-centred histor-iography on the GDR more generally since 1990. Although the focus on the repressive elements of the system and on the experiences of victims may indeed be morally justifiable, and although contemporary historical schol-arship must of course be based on more than the nebulous foundations of 'experience' and 'memory', the conspicuous inattention shown towards these avenues of enquiry by the parliamentary commissions and by recent historical scholarship[79] seems questionable both in scholarly as well as political-pedagogical terms. It is simply unrealistic to ask the bulk of east Germans to abandon their own viewpoints and adopt the perspective of a small dissident subculture or a conventional west German understanding of the recent past. Such an approach jeopardizes the search for any 'unifying' historical consciousness in eastern Germany. If the experience of 'dealing with' the Nazi past has any relevant lessons for confronting the legacy of the GDR, surely one crucial insight must be that authoritative declarations and officially-sanctioned positions – 'prescribed anti-fascism', 'totalitarian dictatorship' – have a very limited influence on the memories of 'ordinary' people. Just as the 'positive' memories of the National Socialist period – experiences in the Hitler Youth or League of German Girls – did not so much disappear after 1945 as become 'banished to *Stammtische* or coffee circles',[80] so the same phenomenon appears to have happened to positive

---

78 *Materialien der Enquete-Kommission*, vol. IX, p. 695.
79 Notable exceptions include: L. Niethammer, A. v. Plato and D. Wierling, *Die Volkseigene Erfahrung*; also L. Niethammer, 'Erfahrungen und Strukturen. Prolegomena zu einer Geschichte der Gesellschaft der DDR'; D. Wierling, 'The Hitler Youth Generation in the GDR: Insecurities, Ambitions and Dilemmas', in K. Jarausch (ed.), *Dictatorship as Experience*, pp. 307–24; A. v. Plato, 'The Hitler Youth Generation and its Role in the two Postwar German States', in Mark Roseman (ed.), *Generations in Conflict* (Cambridge, 1995), pp. 210–26.
80 A. v. Plato, 'Eine zweite "Entnazifizierung"? Zur Verarbeitung politischer Umwälzungen in Deutschland 1945 und 1989' in R. Eckert *et al.* (eds), *Wendezeiten – Zeitenwende. Zur 'Entnazifizierung' und 'Entstalinisierung'* (Hamburg, 1992), pp. 7–32. See also Ulrich Herbert, 'Die guten und die schlechten Zeiten', in L. Niethammer (ed.), *'Die Jahre weiß man nicht, wo man die heute hinsetzen soll.'*

memories of the GDR. Whether the fun of FDJ activities or the feelings of
solidarity within one's work brigade, such memories have by and large been
consigned to the margins of political and academic debate, and often sum-
marily dismissed in the mainstream media as an outgrowth of unenlightened
'*Ostalgie*'.[81] This disparagement seems more like a recipe for stirring up
animosity than for achieving 'democratic consensus' and 'inner unity'. As
one commentator has astutely put it:

> As praiseworthy as the project of dealing with the Nazi- and SED-regime is, a
> central pedagogical principle is often lost from view in driving this process for-
> ward – the necessity of meeting the 'pupils', especially the adults, on the ground
> of their own experiences if the desired result is to be achieved.[82]

Perhaps the 'loss' of ordinary east Germans from their own history also has
to do with the unexpected and exhilaratingly swift 'rush to German unity'[83]
itself. In some ways the speed of events has engendered a corresponding
'rush to overcome' the East German past, an almost irresistible sense of
urgency to engage with it and explain it while the impressions are still fresh.
Certainly the opening of the intoxicatingly rich archives has unleashed a
veritable stampede of contemporary historians unaccustomed to the near-
unlimited access to official sources. In this great rush to study the East
German past, one of the central tasks of 'contemporary history' as a sub-
discipline has arguably not been fulfilled. In many ways contemporary history
is akin to a society's 'collective memory'. Unlike other fields of historical
enquiry, it is about the lived experience of people who are still around.

(*Contd*)

    *Faschismuserfahrungen im Ruhrgebiet* (Bonn, 1986), pp. 67–96. An abridged version of Herbert's arti-
    cle was subsequently published in English as 'Good Times, Bad Times: Memories of the Third Reich',
    in R. Bessel (ed.), *Life in the Third Reich* (Oxford, 1987), pp. 97–110.

81  For a fascinating discussion of the social and cultural bases of nostalgia for the GDR, see Lothar Fritze,
    *Die Gegenwart des Vergangenen. Über das Weiterleben der DDR nach ihrem Ende* (Cologne, 1997);
    also L. Fritze, 'Irritationen im deutsch-deutschen Einigungsprozess', *APuZG* B27/95. See also the inno-
    vative article by Paul Betts, 'The Twilight of the Idols: East German Memory and Material Culture',
    *JMH* 72 (2000) 3, pp. 731–65; also E. Ten Dyke, 'Tulips in December'. After surveying the reactions of
    6,000 visitors to an exhibition at the German Historical Museum, Rosmarie Beier has concluded that it
    had no noticeable effect in terms of 'civic education'. R. Beier, 'Deutsch-deutsche Befindlichkeiten. Die
    Besucherbücher der Ausstellung "Lebensstationen in Deutschland" als Spiegel der mentalen Lage der
    Nation', *GWU* 46 (1995), pp. 206–22.

82  Mitchell Ash, 'Geschichtswissenschaft, Geschichtskultur und der ostdeutsche Historikerstreit', *GG* 24
    (1998), pp. 283–304, here p. 303. Wolfgang Thierse, president of the Bundestag and former East
    German civil rights activist, has voiced similar concerns: 'Forty years of the GDR – nothing more than
    mistakes, failures and crimes? That many east Germans are finding it difficult to find their feet in unified
    Germany also has to do with the fact that their own memories and lived experience are fundamentally
    different from this. There was not the black-and-white image of the good, democratic and promising new
    beginning in the Federal Republic and the shabby, dictatorial and gloomy copy of Soviet patterns in the
    GDR. Reality was more complex, more differentiated, more diverse.' W. Thierse, '"Nie zuvor hatten wir
    eine solche Chance, das Wagnis der Freiheit anzunehmen." Rede vom Bundestagspräsident Wolfgang
    Thierse auf dem Geschichtsforum "Getrennte Vergangenheit – gemeinsame Geschichte?" in Berlin am
    28. Mai 1999', *Das Parlament*, 4 June 1999, p. 23.

83  Thus the title of Konrad Jarausch's account of the events of 1989–90, *The Rush to German Unity*
    (Oxford, 1994).

Compared to the study of earlier eras, it is often relatively impressionistic. Both the shortness of hindsight as well as the usual source problems normally force one to study it 'from the outside inwards', constantly chipping away at the source barriers and questioning the meaning of events as their impact on subsequent developments unfolds. With the collapse of the GDR, this situation has partially reversed. We have been seduced and overwhelmed by the governmental sources which historians do not normally have this early on, and have tended to write GDR history 'from the inside outwards', without focusing on the experiences of contemporaries, and in the process painting a picture of the past that the East Germans themselves do not recognize. As Lutz Niethammer has remarked: 'Who should be surprised that those under observation – and even more understandably those who have not been noticed – turn their backs on us and insist that no one can understand life in the GDR who did not experience it?'[84]

It is in some ways tempting to say that we should not be so concerned about these historiographic shortcomings. For one thing, one might object to the entire notion of didactic history or history in the service of identity as both politically dubious and theoretically flawed. Quite obviously, there are myriad *Aufarbeitungen* of the past, a multitude of histories and historical identities. This plurality of voices about the past is both desirable in principle and unavoidable in practice. From this point of view, it is both invidious and ultimately counter-productive to attempt to cultivate or impose a uniform historical consciousness or perspective on the past. Moreover, the importance of what historians say is perhaps exaggerated. Identity formation and the development of a sense of collective belonging are not just a matter of subscribing to some idea or set of ideas about the past, present or future. National and other political identities are also closely related to shared political and social institutions. They are products not just of conformity to some view of the collective, but also of the habits of working through certain institutions and relationships that are held in common. Over time, these shared experiences arguably contribute far more to a sense of collective belonging than any amount of political didacticism. The significance that scholars often attach to shared views about the past is perhaps overestimated.

Nonetheless, the past does shape the present, and historians do contribute, however modestly, to a society's understanding of itself. Undoubtedly the stakes in the controversy surrounding the GDR's history will remain high since it concerns not only the past, but also the present and future political culture of unified Germany. The political–ideological framework that has so powerfully moulded interpretations of the GDR over the years – as this book has sought to argue at length – will certainly continue to shape

---

84 L. Niethammer, 'Methodische Überlegungen zur deutschen Nachkriegsgeschichte', in Christoph Kleßmann *et al.* (eds), *Deutsche Vergangenheiten – eine gemeinsame Herausforderung*, pp. 307–27, here p. 316.

discussion in the future. That the GDR no longer exists is, on balance, a good thing. Although not everyone would agree with this judgement, there is a broad consensus in Germany that liberal democracy is preferable to dictatorship (even one with purportedly humanistic intentions) both in principle and in practice, and that the GDR's history offers ample evidence to support this view. But beyond this basic agreement, the East German past is not reducible to a single clear-cut reality with a single, unambiguous political message for the future. Historians should not seek to impose a 'correct' unifying narrative or create a vapid synthesis that negates the contentious nature of different views of the GDR's history and what it means. This would merely continue the pattern of ideological determinism that has so strongly influenced the debate since the founding of the regime. Rather, the abiding challenge is to adopt strategies that move beyond the ideological confrontations of the past, that disentangle and draw new connections between contending narratives instead of advancing one or the other, and that penetrate beneath the monolithic surface of dictatorship to render a better understanding of how the GDR worked, its place in the broader sweep of European history, and its legacies for the future.

# Select bibliography

The following bibliography is highly selective, and includes works cited in the main body of the text as well as many English-language works that are not. Most of the studies referred to in this book are in German, and full bibliographic references are provided in the relevant footnotes. Although the list that follows is weighted towards English-language material, it nonetheless includes a substantial proportion of important or useful works in German. Since the coverage in English is rather patchy, the suggested readings for some themes are indeed predominantly in German. Some works that transcend the thematic categories organizing this bibliography are listed more than once.

## General surveys, syntheses and collections

David Childs, *The GDR: Moscow's German Ally*, 2nd edn (London, 1988).
Mike Dennis, *German Democratic Republic: Politics, Economics and Society* (London, 1988).
Mike Dennis, *The Rise and Fall of the German Democratic Republic 1945–1990* (London, 2000).
Mary Fulbrook, *Anatomy of a Dictatorship: Inside the GDR* (Oxford, 1995).
Mary Fulbrook, *Interpretations of the Two Germanies, 1945–1990*, 2nd edn (Basingstoke, 2000).
Konrad Jarausch (ed.), *Dictatorship as Experience: Towards a Socio-Cultural History of the GDR* (New York, 1999).
Jürgen Kocka (ed.), *Historische DDR-Forschung: Aufsätze und Studien* (Berlin, 1993).
Patrick Major and Jonathan Osmond (eds), *The 'Workers' and Peasants' State': Communism and Society under Ulbricht, 1945–1971* (Manchester, 2002).

A. James McAdams, *East Germany and Detente: Building Authority after the Wall* (Cambridge, 1985).

A. James McAdams, *Germany Divided: From the Wall to Reunification* (Princeton, NJ, 1993).

Martin McCauley, *The German Democratic Republic since 1945* (London, 1983).

*Materialien der Enquete-Kommission 'Aufarbeitung von Geschichte und Folgen der SED-Diktatur in Deutschland' des Deustchen Bundestags*, 18 vols (Bonn, 1994).

Klaus Schroeder (ed.), *Geschichte und Transformation des SED-Staates* (Berlin, 1994).

Klaus Schroeder, *Der SED-Staat. Partei, Staat und Gesellschaft 1949–1990* (Munich, 1998).

Dietrich Staritz, *Geschichte der DDR. Erweiterte Neuausgabe* (Frankfurt a. M., 1996).

J. K. A. Thomaneck and J. Mellis (eds), *Politics, Society and Government in the German Democratic Republic: Basic Documents* (Oxford, 1989).

Hermann Weber, *Geschichte der DDR* (Munich, 1985).

Hermann Weber, *Die DDR 1945 bis 1990* (Munich, 2000).

# Reference works

Bernd-Rainer Barth (ed.), *Wer war wer in der DDR. Ein biographisches Handbuch*, 3rd edn (Frankfurt a. M., 1996).

Martin Broszat and Hermann Weber (eds), *SBZ-Handbuch. Staatliche Verwaltungen, Parteien, gesellschaftliche Organisationen und ihre Führungskräfte in der Sowjetischen Besatzungszone Deutschlands 1945–1949* (Munich, 1993).

Rainer Eppelmann et al. (eds), *Lexikon des DDR-Sozialismus* (Paderborn, 1996).

Andreas Herbst et al. (eds), *So funktionierte die DDR*, 3 vols (Reinbek bei Hamburg, 1994).

Andreas Herbst et al. (eds), *Die SED. Geschichte, Organisation, Politik. Ein Handbuch* (Berlin, 1997).

Hartmut Zimmermann et al. (eds), *DDR-Handbuch*, 2 vols, 3rd edn (Cologne, 1985).

# 1 The changing picture of the GDR

Thomas Baylis, *The Technical Intelligentsia and the East German Elite: Legitimacy and Social Change in Mature Communism* (Berkeley, CA, 1974).

Peter Bender, *Unsere Erbschaft. Was war die DDR – was bleibt von ihr?* (Hamburg, 1992).
Klaus v. Beyme, *Ökonomie und Politik im Sozialismus* (Munich 1975).
Bernd Faulenbach *et al.* (eds), *Die Partei hatte immer recht – Aufarbeitung von Geschichte und Folgen der SED-Diktatur* (Essen, 1994).
Mary Fulbrook, *Interpretations of the Two Germanies, 1945–1990* (Basingstoke, 2000).
Jens Hacker, *Deutsche Irrtümer. Schönfärber und Helfershelfer der SED-Diktatur im Westen* (Berlin, 1992).
Georg Iggers *et al.* (eds), *Die DDR-Geschichtswissenschaft als Forschungsproblem* (special issue no. 27 of *Historische Zeitschrift*) (Munich, 1998).
Konrad Jarausch (ed.), *Zwischen Parteilichkeit und Professionalität. Bilanz der Geschichtswissenschaft in der DDR* (Berlin, 1991).
Ken Jowitt, 'Soviet Neotraditionalism: The Political Corruption of a Leninist Regime', *Soviet Studies* 35 (1983), pp. 275–97.
Jürgen Kocka, *Vereinigungskrise. Zur Geschichte der Gegenwart* (Göttingen, 1995).
Jürgen Kocka and Martin Sabrow (eds), *Die DDR als Geschichte. Fragen, Hypothesen, Perspektiven* (Berlin, 1994).
Ilko-Sascha Kowalczuk (ed.), *Paradigmen deutscher Geschichtswissenschaft* (Berlin, 1994).
P. C. Ludz, *Parteielite im Wandel. Funktionsaufbau, Sozialstruktur und Ideologie der SED-Führung. Eine empirisch-systematische Untersuchung* (Opladen, 1968).
Norman Naimark, 'Is it True What They're Saying about East Germany?', *Orbis* 23 (1979), pp. 549–77.
Martin Sabrow (ed.), *Geschichte als Herrschaftsdiskurs. Der Umgang mit der Vergangenheit in der DDR* (Cologne, 1999).
'The GDR at Forty', special issue of *German Politics and Society*, vol. 17 (1989).

## 2 The GDR as dictatorship

Hannah Arendt, *The Origins of Totalitarianism* (London, 1951).
Stéphane Courtois (ed.), *Le livre noir du communisme: crimes, terreur, répression* (Paris, 1997).
Sheila Fitzpatrick, *Everyday Stalinism: Ordinary Life in Extraordinary Times* (Oxford, 1999).
Sheila Fitzpatrick (ed.), *Stalinism: New Directions* (London, 2000).
Carl Friedrich and Zbigniew Brzezinski, *Totalitarian Dictatorship and Autocracy* (Cambridge, MA, 1956).
Mary Fulbrook, 'The Limits of Totalitarianism: God, State and Society in the GDR', *Transactions of the Royal Historical Society* (1997) series 6:7, pp. 25–52.

Abbott Gleason, *Totalitarianism: The Inner History of the Cold War* (Oxford, 1995).

Rolf Henrich, *Der vormundschaftliche Staat. Vom Versagen des real existierenden Sozialismus* (Frankfurt, 1989).

Konrad Jarausch, 'Care and Coercion: The GDR as Welfare Dictatorship', in K. Jarausch (ed.), *Dictatorship as Experience* (New York, 1999), pp. 47–69.

Eckard Jesse (ed.), *Totalitarismus im 20. Jahrhundert: eine Bilanz der internationalen Forschung* (Baden-Baden, 1998).

Ian Kershaw, 'Totalitarianism Revisited: Nazism and Stalinism in Comparative Perspective', *Tel Aviver Jahrbuch für deutsche Geschichte*, vol. 23 (1994), pp. 23–40.

Ian Kershaw and Moshe Lewin (eds), *Stalinism and Nazism: Dictatorships in Comparison* (Cambridge, 1997).

Mario Keßler and Thomas Klein, 'Repression and Tolerance as Methods of Rule in Communist Societies', in K. Jarausch (ed.), *Dictatorship as Experience* (New York, 1999), pp. 109–21.

Thomas Klein, *'Für die Einheit und Reinheit der Partei'. Die innerparteilichen Kontrollorgane der SED in der Ära Ulbricht* (Cologne, 2002).

Jürgen Kocka, 'The GDR: A Special Kind of Modern Dictatorship', in K. Jarausch (ed.), *Dictatorship as Experience* (New York, 1999), pp. 17–26.

Gerd Koenen, *Utopie der Säuberung. Was war der Kommunismus?* (Berlin, 1998).

Juan Linz and Alfred Stepan, *Problems of Democratic Transition and Consolidation: Southern Europe, South-America and Post-Communist Europe* (Baltimore, 1996).

Andreas Malycha, *Die SED. Geschichte ihrer Stalinisierung 1946–1953* (Paderborn, 2000).

Siegfried Mampel, *Totalitäres Herrschaftssystem. Normativer Charakter – Definition – Konstante und variable Essenzialien – Instrumentarium* (Berlin, 2001).

Alfons Söllner (ed.), *Totalitarismus: eine Ideengeschichte des 20. Jahrhunderts* (Berlin, 1997).

Hermann Weber and Ulrich Mählert (eds), *Terror. Stalinistische Parteisäuberungen 1936–1953* (Paderborn, 1998).

Wolfgang Wippermann, *Totalitarismustheorien: die Entwicklung der Diskussion von den Anfängen bis heute* (Darmstadt, 1997).

# 3  State and society in East Germany

Mark Allinson, *Politics and Popular Opinion in East Germany 1945–68* (Manchester, 2000).

Leonore Ansorg and Renate Hürtgen, 'The Myth of Female Emancipation: Contradictions in Women's Lives', in K. Jarausch (ed.), *Dictatorship as Experience* (New York, 1999), pp. 163–76.

Arnd Bauerkämper (ed.), *'Junkerland in Bauernhand'? Durchführung, Auswirkungen und Stellenwert der Bodenreform in der Sowjetischen Besatzungszone* (Stuttgart, 1996).

Arnd Bauerkämper, *Ländliche Gesellschaft in der kommunistischen Diktatur. Zwangsmodernisierung und Traditionen in Brandenburg von 1945 bis zu den frühen sechziger Jahren* (Cologne, 2002).

Richard Bessel and Ralph Jessen (eds), *Die Grenzen der Diktatur: Staat und Gesellschaft in der SBZ/DDR* (Göttingen, 1996).

Grit Bühler, *Mythos der Gleichberechtigung in der DDR* (Frankfurt a. M., 1997).

Peter Hübner, *Konsens, Konflikt, Kompromiß. Soziale Arbeiterinteressen und Sozialpolitik in der SBZ/DDR 1945–1970* (Berlin, 1995).

Peter Hübner (ed.), *Eliten im Sozialismus. Beiträge zur Sozialgeschichte der DDR* (Cologne, 1999).

Peter Hübner and Klaus Tenfelde (eds), *Arbeiter in der SBZ-DDR* (Essen, 1999).

Ralph Jessen, 'Die Gesellschaft im Sozialismus. Probleme einer Sozialgeschichte der DDR', *GG*, vol. 21 (1995), pp. 96–110.

Ralph Jessen 'Mobility and Blockage during the 1970s', in K. Jarausch (ed.), *Dictatorship as Experience* (New York, 1999), pp. 341–60.

Hartmut Kaelble *et al.* (eds), *Sozialgeschichte der DDR* (Stuttgart, 1994).

Dagmar Langenhahn and Sabine Roß, 'The Socialist Glass Ceiling: Limits to Female Careers', in K. Jarausch (ed.), *Dictatorship as Experience* (New York, 1999), pp. 177–91.

Alena Ledeneva, *Russia's Economy of Favours: Blat, Networking and Informal Exchange* (Cambridge, 1998).

Thomas Lindenberger (ed.), *Herrschaft und Eigen-Sinn in der Diktatur. Studien zur Gesellschaftsgeschichte der DDR* (Cologne, 1999).

Alf Lüdtke (ed.), *Herrschaft als sozialer Praxis. Historische und sozio-anthropologische Studien* (Göttingen, 1991).

Alf Lüdtke, *Eigen-Sinn. Fabrikalltag, Arbeitererfahrungen und Politik vom Kaiserreich bis in den Faschismus. Ergebnisse* (Hamburg, 1993).

Alf Lüdtke and Peter Becker (eds), *Akten. Eingaben. Schaufenster. Die DDR und ihre Texte* (Berlin, 1997).

Sigrid Meuschel, *Legitimation und Parteiherrschaft. Zum Paradox von Stabilität und Revolution in der DDR* (Frankfurt a. M., 1992).

Lutz Niethammer, Dorothee Wierling and Alexander von Plato, *Die Volkseigene Erfahrung. Eine Ärchaeologie des Lebens in der Industrieprovinz der DDR* (Berlin, 1991).

Uta Poiger, *Jazz, Rock, and Rebels: Cold War Politics and American Culture in a Divided Germany* (Berkeley, CA, 2000).

Detlef Pollack, 'Modernization and Modernization Blockages in GDR Society', in K. Jarausch (ed.), *Dictatorship as Experience* (New York, 1999), pp. 27–45.

John Rodden, *Repainting the Little Red Schoolhouse: A History of Eastern German Education, 1945–1995* (Oxford, 2001).

Corey Ross, *Constructing Socialism at the Grass-Roots: The Transformation of East Germany 1945–65* (Basingstoke, 2000).

Corey Ross, 'Before the Wall: East Germans, Communist Authority and the Mass Exodus to the West, *Historical Journal* vol. 45 (2002), no. 4.

Gregory Sandford, *From Hitler to Ulbricht: the Communist Reconstruction of East Germany 1945–1949* (Princeton, NJ, 1983).

Heike Solga, *Auf dem Weg in eine klassenlose Gesellschaft? Klassenlagen und Mobilität zwischen Generationen in der DDR* (Berlin, 1995).

Heike Trappe, *Emanzipation oder Zwang? Frauen in der DDR zwischen Beruf, Familie und Sozialpolitik* (Berlin, 1995).

Timothy Vogt, *Denazification in Soviet-Occupied Germany: Brandenburg, 1945–1948* (Cambridge, MA, 2000).

Dorothee Wierling, 'The Hitler Youth Generation in the GDR: Insecurities, Ambitions and Dilemmas', in K. Jarausch (ed.), *Dictatorship as Experience* (New York, 1999), pp. 307–24.

Stefan Wolle, *Die heile Welt der Diktatur. Alltag und Herrschaft in der DDR 1971–1989* (Berlin, 1998).

# 4 The East German economy

B. van Ark, 'The Manufacturing Sector in East Germany: A Reassessment of Comparative Productivity Performance, 1950–1988', *Jahrbuch für Wirtschaftsgeschichte* (1995) no. 2, pp. 75–100.

Horst Barthel, *Die wirtschaftlichen Ausgangsbedingungen der DDR* (Berlin, 1979).

Phillip Bryson, *The End of the East German Economy: From Honecker to Reunification* (Basingstoke, 1991).

Christoph Buchheim (ed.), *Wirtschaftliche Folgelasten des Krieges in der SBZ/DDR* (Baden-Baden, 1995).

Burghard Ciesla and Patrice Poutrus, 'Food Supply in a Planned Economy: SED Nutrition Policy between Crisis Response and Popular Needs', in K. Jarausch (ed.), *Dictatorship as Experience* (New York, 1999), pp. 143–62.

Ian Jeffries and Manfred Melzer (eds), *The East German Economy* (London, 1987).

Rainer Karlsch, *Allein bezahlt? Die Reparationsleistungen der SBZ/DDR 1945–53* (Berlin, 1993).

Michael Keren, 'The New Economic System in the GDR: An Obituary', *Soviet Studies* 24 (1973), pp. 554–87.

Jeffrey Kopstein, *The Politics of Economic Decline in East Germany, 1945–1989* (Chapel Hill, NC, 1997).

János Kornai, *The Socialist System. The Political Economy of Communism* (Oxford, 1992).

Günter Kusch *et al.*, *Schlußbilanz – DDR. Fazit einer verfehlten Wirtschafts- und Sozialpolitik* (Berlin, 1991).

Mark Landsmann, 'Dictatorship and Demand: East Germany Between Productivism and Consumerism, 1948–1961', PhD dissertation, Columbia University, 2000.

Gert Leptin and Manfred Melzer, *Economic Reform in East German Industry* (Oxford, 1978).

C. Maier, *Dissolution: The Crisis of Communism and the End of East Germany* (Princeton, NJ, 1997).

Ina Merkel, *Utopie und Bedürfnis. Die Geschichte der Konsumkultur in der DDR* (Cologne, 1999).

Wilma Merkel and Stefanie Wahl, *Das geplünderte Deutschland. Die wirtschaftliche Entwicklung im östlichen Teil Deutschlands von 1949 bis 1989* (Bonn, 1991).

Katherine Pence, 'From Rations to Fashions: The Gendered Politics of East and West German Consumption, 1945–1961', PhD dissertation, University of Michigan, 1999.

Theo Pirker *et al.*, *Der Plan als Befehl und Fiktion. Wirtschaftsführung in der DDR* (Opladen, 1995).

Albrecht Ritschl, 'An Exercise in Futility: East German Economic Growth and Decline, 1945–89', in Nicholas Crafts and Gianni Toniolo (eds), *Economic Growth in Europe since 1945* (Cambridge, 1996), pp. 498–540.

Jörg Roesler, *Zwischen Plan und Markt. Die Wirtschaftsreform 1963–1970 in der DDR* (Berlin, 1991).

Jörg Roesler, 'The Rise and Fall of the Planned Economy in the GDR, 1945–1989', *GH*, vol. 9 (1991), pp. 46–61.

Jörg Roesler, V. Siedt and M. Elle, *Wirtschaftswachstum in der Industrie der DDR 1945–1970* (Berlin, 1986).

Peter Rutland, *The Myth of the Plan* (London, 1985).

Oskar Schwarzer, *Sozialistische Zentralplanwirtschaft in der SBZ/DDR. Ergebnisse eines ordnungspolitischen Experiments (1945–1989)* (Stuttgart, 1999).

A. Steiner, 'Dissolution of the Dictatorship over Needs? Consumer Behavior and Economic Reform in East Germany in the 1960s', in Susan Strasser *et al.* (eds), *Getting and Spending* (Cambridge, 1998), pp. 167–85.

A. Steiner, *Die DDR-Wirtschaftsreform der sechziger Jahre. Konflikt zwischen Effizienz- und Machtkalkül* (Berlin, 1999), pp. 557ff.

A. Steiner, 'Zwischen Konsumversprechen und Innovationszwang. Zum wirtschaftlichen Niedergang der DDR', in Konrad Jarausch and Martin Sabrow (eds), *Weg in den Untergang. Der innere Zerfall der DDR* (Göttingen, 1999), pp. 153–92.

Judd Stitziel, 'Fashioning Socialism: Clothing, Politics, and Consumer Culture in East Germany, 1948–1971', PhD dissertation, Johns Hopkins University, 2001.

Raymond Stokes, *Constructing Socialism: Technology and Change in East Germany 1945–1990* (Baltimore, 2000).

Wolfgang Stolper, *The Structure of the East German Economy* (Cambridge, MA, 1960).

Jan Winiecki, *The Distorted World of Soviet-Type Economies* (Pittsburgh, 1988).

J. Zatlin, 'Consuming Ideology. Socialist Consumerism and the Intershops', in P. Hübner and K. Tenfelde (eds), *Arbeiter in der SBZ-DDR* (Essen, 1999).

J. Zatlin, 'The Currency of Socialism. Money in the GDR and German Unification, 1971–1989', PhD dissertation, University of California, Berkeley, 2000.

# 5 Opposition and dissent

Beatrix Bouvier, *Ausgeschaltet! Sozialdemokraten in der Sowjetischen Besatzungszone und in der DDR 1945–1953* (Bonn, 1996).

David Childs and Richard Popplewell, *The Stasi: The East German Intelligence and Security Service* (Basingstoke, 1996).

Horst Dähn, *Konfrontation oder Kooperation? Das Verhältnis von Staat und Kirche in der SBZ/DDR 1945–1980* (Opladen, 1982).

Rainer Eckart et al. (eds), *Zwischen Selbstbehauptung und Anpassung. Formen des Widerstandes und der Opposition in der DDR* (Berlin, 1995).

Karl Wilhelm Fricke, *Selbstbehauptung und Widerstand in der Sowjetischen Besatzungszone Deutschlands*, 2nd edn (Bonn/Berlin, 1966)

Karl Wilhelm Fricke, *Warten auf Gerechtigkeit. Kommunistische Säuberungen und Rehabilitierungen. Bericht und Dokumentation* (Cologne, 1971)

Karl Wilhelm Fricke, *Politik und Justiz in der DDR. Zur Geschichte der politischen Verfolgung 1945–1968* (Cologne, 1979).

Karl Wilhelm Fricke, *Opposition und Widerstand in der DDR* (Cologne, 1984).

Karl Wilhelm Fricke, *MfS intern. Macht, Strukturen, Auflösung der DDR-Staatsicherheit* (Cologne, 1991).

Joachim Gauck, *Die Stasi-Akten. Das unheimliche Erbe der DDR* (Hamburg, 1991).

Robert Goeckel, *The Lutheran Church and the East German State* (Ithaca, 1995).

Peter Grieder, *The East German Leadership 1946–73* (Manchester, 1999).

Klaus-Dietmar Henke *et al.* (eds), *Widerstand und Opposition in der DDR* (Cologne, 1999).

Klaus-Dietmar Henke *et al.* (eds), *Anatomie der Staatssicherheit. Geschichte, Struktur und Methoden. MfS Handbuch* (Berlin, 1995).

Christian Joppke, *East German Dissidents and the Revolution of 1989. Social Movement in a Leninist Regime* (Basingstoke, 1995).

Christoph Kleßmann, 'Opposition und Resistenz in zwei Diktaturen in Deutschland', *HZ*, vol. 262 (1996), pp. 453–479.

Hubertus Knabe, 'Was war die "DDR-Opposition"? Zur Typologie des politischen Widerspruchs in Ostdeutschland', *DA* 29:2 (1996), pp. 184–98.

Jeffrey Kopstein, 'Chipping Away at the State. Workers' Resistance and the Demise of East Germany', *World Politics*, vol. 48 (1996), pp. 391–423.

Ilko-Sascha Kowalczuk, 'Von der Freiheit, Ich zu sagen. Widerständiges Verhalten in der DDR', in R. Eckart *et al.* (eds), *Zwischen Selbstbehauptung und Anpassung* (Berlin, 1995), pp. 85–115.

Eberhard Kuhrt *et al.* (eds), *Opposition in der DDR von den 70er Jahren bis zum Zusammenbruch der SED-Herrschaft* (Opladen, 1999).

Markus Meckel and Martin Gutzeit, *Opposition in der DDR. Zehn Jahre kirchliche Friedensarbeit – kommentierte Quellentexte* (Cologne, 1994).

Armin Mitter and Stefan Wolle, *Untergang auf Raten. Unbekannte Kapitel der DDR-Geschichte* (Munich, 1993).

Ehrhard Neubert, *Geschichte der Opposition in der DDR 1949–1989* (Berlin, 1997).

Heinz Niemann, *Meinungsforschung in der DDR. Die geheimen Berichte des Instituts für Meinungsforschung an das Politbüro der SED* (Cologne, 1993).

Heinz Niemann, *Hinterm Zaun. Politische Kultur und Meinungsforschung in der DDR – die geheimen Berichte an das Politbüro der SED* (Berlin, 1995).

Detlef Pollack (ed.), *Die Legitimität der Freiheit. Politisch alternative Gruppen in der DDR unter dem Dach der Kirche* (Frankfurt a. M., 1990).

Detlef Pollack and Dieter Rink, *Kirche in der Organisationsgesellschaft. Zum Wandel der gesellschaftlichen Lage der evangelischen Kirchen in der DDR* (Stuttgart, 1994).

Detlef Pollack and Dieter Rink (eds), *Zwischen Verweigerung und Opposition. Politischer Protest in der DDR 1970–1989* (Frankfurt a. M., 1997).

Andrew Port, 'The "Grumble Gesellschaft": Industrial Defiance and Worker Protest in Early East Germany', in P. Hübner and K. Tenfelde (eds), *Arbeiter in der SBZ/DDR* (Essen, 1999), pp. 787–810.

Corey Ross, 'Protecting the Accomplishments of Socialism'? The (Re)Militarization of Life in the GDR', in P. Major and J. Osmond (eds), *The 'Workers' and Peasants' State'* (Manchester, 2002).

John Torpey, *Intellectuals, Socialism and Dissent: The East German Opposition and its Legacy* (Minneapolis, 1995).

Falco Werkentin, *Politische Strafjustiz in der Ära Ulbricht* (Berlin, 1995).

Roger Woods, *Opposition in the GDR under Honecker* (Basingstoke, 1986).

# 6 The end of the GDR

Timothy Garton Ash, *We the People: The Revolution of '89 Witnessed in Warsaw, Budapest, Berlin and Prague* (Cambridge, 1990).

John Burgess, *The East German Church and the End of Communism* (Oxford, 1997).

David Childs, *The Fall of the GDR* (London, 2001).

Robert Darnton, *Berlin Journal, 1989–1990* (New York, 1991).

Helmut Fehr, *Unabhängige Öffentlichkeit und soziale Bewegungen: Fallstudien über Bürgerbewegungen in Polen und der DDR* (Opladen, 1996).

Jeffrey Gedmin, *The Hidden Hand: Gorbachev and the Collapse of East Germany* (Washington, DC, 1992).

Gert-Joachim Glaessner and Ian Wallace (eds), *The German Revolution of 1989: Causes and Consequences* (Oxford, 1992).

Jonathan Grix, *The Role of the Masses in the Collapse of the GDR* (Basingstoke, 2000).

Jürgen Habermas, *Die nachholende Revolution* (Frankfurt a. M., 1990).

Hans-Hermann Hertle, *Der Fall der Mauer. Die unbeabsichtigte Selbstauflösung des SED-Staates* (Opladen, 1996).

Hans-Hermann Hertle and Gerd-Rüdiger Stephan (eds), *Das Ende der SED. Die letzten Tage des Zentralkomitees* (Berlin, 1997).

Albert Hirschman, 'Exit, Voice, and the Fate of the German Democratic Republic: An Essay in Conceptual History', *World Politics*, vol. 45 (1993), pp. 173–202.

Harold James and Marla Stone (eds), *When the Wall Came Down: Reactions to German Unification* (London, 1992).

Konrad Jarausch, *The Rush to German Unity* (Oxford, 1994).

Konrad Jarausch and Volker Gransow (eds), *Uniting Germany: Documents and Debates 1944–1993* (Providence, 1994).

Konrad Jarausch and Martin Sabrow (eds), *Weg in den Untergang. Der innere Zerfall der DDR* (Göttingen, 1999).

Hans Joas and Martin Kohli (eds), *Der Zusammenbruch der DDR* (Frankfurt a. M., 1993).

Christian Joppke, *East German Dissidents and the Revolution of 1989: Social Movement in a Leninist Regime* (Basingstoke, 1995).

Karl-Rudolf Korte, *Die Chance genutzt? Die Politik zur Einheit Deutschlands* (Frankfurt a. M., 1994).

Karl-Dieter Opp *et al.*, *Die volkseigene Revolution* (Stuttgart, 1993).

Charles Maier, *Dissolution: The Crisis of Communism and the End of East Germany* (Princeton, NJ, 1997).

Patrick von zur Mühlen, *Aufbruch und Umbruch in der DDR. Bürgerbewegungen, kritische Öffentlichkeit und Niedergang der SED-Herrschaft* (Bonn, 2000).

Norman Naimark, ' "Ich will hier raus": Emigration and the Collapse of the German Democratic Republic', in Ivo Banac (ed.), *Eastern Europe in Revolution* (Ithaca, New York, 1992), pp. 72–95.

Dirk Philipsen (ed.), *We Were the People: Voices from East Germany's Revolutionary Autumn of 1989* (Durham, NC, 1993).

Mark Thompson, 'Reluctant Revolutionaries: Anti-Fascism and the East German Opposition', *German Politics* 2 (1999), pp. 40–65.

Karsten Timmer, *Vom Aufbruch zum Umbruch. Die Bürgerbewegung in der DDR 1989* (Göttingen, 2000).

Frank Wilhelmy, *Der Zerfall der SED-Herrschaft. Zur Erosion des marxistisch-leninistischen Legitimitätsanspruches in der DDR* (Münster, 1995).

Jonathan Zatlin, 'The Vehicle of Desire: The Trabant, the Wartburg, and the End of the GDR', *GH*, vol. 15 (1997), pp. 358–80.

Hartmut Zwahr, *Ende einer Selbstzerstörung. Leipzig und die Revolution in der DDR* (Göttingen, 1993).

# 7 The GDR in German history

Rolf Badstübner and Wilfried Loth (eds), *Wilhelm Pieck – Aufzeichnungen zur Deutschlandpolitik 1945–1952* (Berlin, 1993).

David Bathrick, *The Powers of Speech: The Politics of Culture in the GDR* (Lincoln, 1995).

Arnd Bauerkämper, Martin Sabrow and Bernd Stöver (eds), *Doppelte Zeitgeschichte. Deutsch-deutsche Beziehungen 1945–1990* (Bonn, 1998).

Peter Bender, *Episode oder Epoche? Zur Geschichte des geteilten Deutschlands* (Munich, 1996).

Ivan Berend, *Central and Eastern Europe 1944–1993: Detour from the Periphery to the Periphery* (Cambridge, 1996).

Stefan Berger, *The Search for Normality: National Identity and Historical Consciousness in Germany since 1800* (Oxford, 1997).

Zbigniew Brzezinski, *The Soviet Bloc: Unity and Conflict* (Cambridge, MA, 1967).

John Connelly, *Captive University: The Sovietization of East German, Czech and Polish Higher Education, 1945–1956* (Chapel Hill, 2000).

Stefan Creuzberger, *Die sowjetische Besatzungsmacht und das politische System der SBZ* (Weimar, 1996).

Erhard Crome, 'Die DDR in der deutschen Geschichte,' in Heiner Timmermann (ed.), *Die DDR – Analysen eines aufgegebenen Staates* (Berlin, 2001), pp. 101–18.

Jürgen Danyel (ed.), *Die geteilte Vergangenheit. Zum Umgang mit Nationalsozialismus und Widerstand in beiden deutschen Staaten* (Berlin, 1995).

Jan Foitzik, *Sowjetische Militäradministration in Deutschland (SMAD) 1945–1949. Struktur und Funktion* (Berlin, 1999).

Mary Fulbrook, *German National Identity after the Holocaust* (London, 1999).

Ulrich Herbert and Olaf Groehler (eds), *Zweierlei Bewältigung. Vier Beiträge über den Umgang mit NS-Vergangenheit in den beiden deutschen Staaten* (Hamburg, 1992).

Jeffrey Herf, *Divided Memory: The Nazi Past in the Two Germanies* (Cambridge, MA, 1997).

Günther Heydemann and Eckhard Jesse (eds), *Diktaturvergleich als Herausforderung. Theorie und Praxis* (Berlin, 1998).

Konrad Jarausch and Hannes Siegrist (eds), *Amerikanisierung und Sowjetisierung in Deutschland 1945–1970* (Frankfurt a. M., 1997).

Kenneth Jowitt, *New World Disorder: The Leninist Extinction* (Berkeley, CA, 1993).

Christoph Kleßmann (ed.), *Deutsche Vergangenheiten – eine gemeinsame Herausforderung. Der schwierige Umgang mit der doppelten Nachkriegsgeschichte* (Berlin, 1999).

Jürgen Kocka, 'Ein deutscher Sonderweg. Überlegungen zur Sozialgeschichte der DDR', *APuZG* B40/94, pp. 34–45.

Ludger Kühnhardt et al. (eds), *Die doppelte deutsche Diktaturerfahrung. Drittes Reich und DDR – ein historisch-politikwissenschaftlicher Vergleich*, 2nd edn (Frankfurt a. M., 1996).

Jochen Laufer, 'From Dismantling to Currency Reform: External Origins of the Dictatorship, 1943–1948', in K. Jarausch (ed.), *Dictatorship as Experience* (New York, 1999), pp. 73–89.

Michael Lemke (ed.), *Sowjetisierung und Eigenständigkeit in der SBZ/DDR (1945–1953)* (Cologne, 1999).

Wilfried Loth, *Stalins ungeliebtes Kind. Warum Moskau die DDR nicht wollte* (Berlin, 1994).

Wolfgang Mommsen, 'Der Ort der DDR in der deutschen Geschichte', in J. Kocka and M. Sabrow (eds), *Die DDR als Geschichte* (Berlin, 1994), pp. 26–39.

Norman Naimark, *The Russians in Germany: A History of the Soviet Zone of Occupation, 1945–1949* (Cambridge, MA, 1995).

Edward Petersen, *Russian Commands and German Resistance: The Soviet Occupation, 1945–1949* (New York, 1998).

David Pike, *The Politics of Culture in Soviet-Occupied Germany, 1945–1949* (Stanford, CA, 1992).

J. Rothschild, *Return to Diversity. A Political History of East Central Europe Since World War II* (New York, 1989).

G. Schöpflin, *Politics in Eastern Europe 1945–1992* (Oxford, 1993).

Dietrich Staritz, 'Die SED und Stalins Deutschlandpolitik', *DA* 27:8 (1994), pp. 854–61.

Klaus Sühl (ed.), *Vergangenheitsbewältigung 1945 und 1989. Ein möglicher Vergleich?* (Berlin, 1994).

Werner Weidenfeld (ed.), *Deutschland, eine Nation – doppelte Geschichte* (Cologne, 1993).

Eric Weitz, *Creating German Communism, 1890–1990: From Popular Protests to Socialist State* (Princeton, NJ, 1997).

Gerhard Wettig, *Bereitschaft zu Einheit in Freiheit? Die Sowjetische Deutschlandpolitik 1945–1955* (Munich, 1999).

# 8 The GDR as contemporary history

Reinhard Alter and Peter Monteath (eds), *Rewriting the German Past: History and Identity in the New Germany* (New York, 1997).

Thomas Anz (ed.), *'Es geht nicht nur um Christa Wolf'. Der Literaturstreit im vereinten Deutschland* (Munich, 1991).

Paul Betts, 'The Twilight of the Idols: East German Memory and Material Culture', *JMH* 72 (2000), pp. 731–65.

John Borneman, *After the Wall: East Meets West in the New Berlin* (New York, 1991).

Jürgen Danyel, 'Wandlitz auf dem Ettersberg? Zur Debatte um die roten Kapos von Buchenwald', *ZfG* 43 (1995), pp. 159–66.

Rainer Eckert and Bernd Faulenbach (eds), *Halbherziger Revisionismus: Zum postkommunistischen Geschichtsbild* (Munich, 1996).

Rainer Eckert *et al.* (eds), *Hure oder Muse? Klio in der DDR. Dokumente und Materialien des Unabhängigen Historikerverbandes* (Berlin, 1994).

Rainer Eckert *et al.* (eds), *Wer schreibt die DDR-Geschichte? Ein Historikerstreit um Stellen, Strukturen, Finanzen und Deutungskompetenz* (Berlin, 1995).

Guenter Erbe, *Die verfemte Moderne. Die Auseinandersetzung mit dem "Modernismus" in Kulturpolitik, Literaturwissenschaft und Literatur der DDR* (Opladen, 1993).

Anna-Sabine Ernst, 'Between "Investigative History" and Solid Research: The Reorganization of Historical Studies about the Former German Democratic Republic', *CEH* 28 (1995), pp. 373–95.

Bernd Faulenbach *et al.* (eds), *Die Partei hatte immer recht – Aufarbeitung von Geschichte und Folgen der SED-Diktatur* (Essen, 1994).

Lothar Fritze, *Die Gegenwart des Vergangenen. Über das Weiterleben der DDR nach ihrem Ende* (Cologne, 1997).

Antonia Grunenberg, *Antifaschismus – ein deutscher Mythos* (Reinbek, 1993).

Konrad Jarausch, 'The German Democratic Republic as History in Unified Germany: Reflections on Public Debate and Academic Controversy', *German Politics and Society*, 15:2 (1997), pp. 33–48.

Konrad Jarausch and Matthias Middell (eds), *Nach dem Erdbeben. (Re-) Konstruktion ostdeutscher Geschichte und Geschichtswissenschaft* (Leipzig, 1994).

Jürgen Kocka, *Vereinigungskrise. Zur Geschichte der Gegenwart* (Göttingen, 1995).

Charles Maier, *Dissolution: The Crisis of Communism and the End of East Germany* (Princeton, NJ, 1997).

A. James McAdams, *Judging the Past in Unified Germany* (Cambridge, 2001).

Damian van Melis, *Entnazifizierung in Mecklenburg-Vorpommern: Herrschaft und Verwaltung 1945–1948* (Munich, 1999).

Christian Meyer-Seitz, *Die Verfolgung von NS-Straftaten in der Sowjetischen Besatzungszone* (Berlin, 1998).

Lutz Niethammer (ed.), *Der 'gesäuberte' Antifaschismus. Die SED und die roten Kapos von Buchenwald. Dokumente* (Berlin, 1994).

Alan Nothnagle, *Building the East German Myth: Historical Mythology and Youth Propaganda in the German Democratic Republic, 1945–1989* (Ann Arbor, MI, 1999).

Manfred Overesch, *Buchenwald und die DDR, oder: Die Suche nach Selbstlegitimation* (Göttingen, 1995).

K. Pätzold, 'What New Start? The End of Historical Study in the GDR', *GH* 10 (1992), pp. 392–404.

Gareth Pritchard, *The Making of the GDR, 1945–53: From Antifascism to Stalinism* (Manchester, 2000).

Peter Reif-Spirek, *Speziallager in der SBZ* (Berlin, 1999).

G.A. Ritter, 'The Reconstruction of History at the Humboldt University: A Reply', *GH* 11 (1993), pp. 339ff.

Anne Sa'adah, *Germany's Second Chance: Trust, Justice and Democratization* (Cambridge, MA, 1998).

Richard Schröder, *Deutschland schwiering Vaterland. Für eine neue politische Kultur* (Freiburg, 1993).

Timothy Vogt, *Denazification in Soviet-Occupied Germany: Brandenburg, 1945–1948* (Cambridge, MA, 2000).

Clemens Vollnhals (ed.), *Die Kirchenpolitik von SED und Staatssicherheit. Eine Zwischenbilanz* (Berlin, 1996).

Jürgen Weber and Michael Piazolo (eds), *Eine Diktatur vor Gericht. Aufarbeitung von SED-Unrecht durch die Justiz* (Munich, 1995).

Jennifer Yoder, 'Truth without Reconciliation: An Appraisal of the Enquete Commission on the SED Dictatorship in Germany', *German Politics* 8 (1999), pp. 59–80.

Raina Zimmering, *Mythen in der Politik der DDR. Ein Beitrag zur Erforschung politischer Mythen* (Opladen, 2000).

# Index